Town and Country Planning Act 1971

GREAT BRITAIN

CHAPTER 78

ARRANGEMENT OF SECTIONS

A

PART III

GENERAL PLANNING CONTROL

Meaning of development and requirement of planning permission

Part IV

Additional Control in Special Cases

Buildings of special architectural or historic interest

Trees

Advertisements

Waste land

A 2

PART V

ENFORCEMENT OF CONTROL UNDER PARTS III AND IV

Development requiring planning permission

Listed buildings

Trees

Waste land

Other controls

Supplementary provisions

PART VI

ACQUISITION AND APPROPRIATION OF LAND AND RELATED PROVISIONS

Acquisition and appropriation of land

Part VII

Compensation for Planning Decisions
Restricting New Development

PART VIII

COMPENSATION FOR OTHER PLANNING RESTRICTIONS

Revocation or modification of planning permission

PART IX

PROVISIONS ENABLING OWNER TO REQUIRE PURCHASE OF HIS INTEREST

PART XIV

APPLICATION OF ACT TO SPECIAL CASES

Minerals

Crown land

Isles of Scilly

Local planning authorities

Other special cases

PART XV

MISCELLANEOUS AND SUPPLEMENTARY PROVISIONS

SCHEDULES:

540

ELIZABETH II

1971 CHAPTER 78

An Act to consolidate certain enactments relating to town and country planning in England and Wales with amendments to give effect to recommendations of the Law Commission.   [28th October 1971]

B E IT ENACTED by the Queen's most Excellent Majesty, by and with the advice and consent of the Lords Spiritual and Temporal, and Commons, in this present Parliament assembled, and by the authority of the same, as follows:—

PART I

ADMINISTRATION

1.—(1) Subject to the provisions of this section, the council Local planning of a county is the local planning authority for the county, and authorities. the council of a county borough is the local planning authority for the county borough.

(2) If it appears to the Secretary of State that it is expedient that a joint board should be established as the local planning authority for the areas of any two or more such councils as are mentioned in subsection (1) of this section, or for any parts of those areas, he may by order constitute those areas or parts as a united district for the purposes of this Act, and constitute a joint board (in this Act referred to as a " joint planning board ") as the local planning authority for that district:
Provided that the Secretary of State shall not make such an order except after holding a local inquiry unless all the councils concerned have consented to the making of the order.

(3) The provisions of Schedule 1 to this Act shall have effect with respect to the constitution of joint planning boards.

(4) Where a joint planning board is constituted for a united district, references in this Act to the area of a local planning authority—

  (*a*) in relation to the board, shall be construed as references to that district ; and

  (*b*) in relation to any local planning authority being the council of a county or county borough of which part (but not the whole) is included in that district, shall be construed as references to so much of the county or county borough as is not so included.

(5) Regulations under this Act may make such provision consequential upon or supplementary to the provisions of this section as appears to the Secretary of State to be necessary or expedient.

(6) The preceding provisions of this section, and the provisions of Schedule 1 to this Act, shall have effect subject to the provisions of section 8 of the National Parks and Access to the Countryside Act 1949 (administration of functions of local planning authorities in respect of National Parks).

2.—(1) The provisions of Schedule 2 to this Act shall have effect with respect to the establishment and functions of planning committees and joint advisory committees of local planning authorities.

(2) The provisions of the said Schedule shall have effect subject to the provisions of section 8 of the National Parks and Access to the Countryside Act 1949.

3.—(1) The Secretary of State may, after consultation with such local authorities or associations of local authorities as he considers appropriate, make regulations for authorising or requiring local planning authorities to delegate to the councils of county districts in their areas, with or without restrictions, any of their functions under the provisions of this Act specified in subsection (2) of this section ; and such regulations may be made so as to apply either generally to all local planning authorities (other than the councils of county boroughs) or to such of those authorities as may be specified in the regulations.

(2) The provisions referred to in subsection (1) of this section are Part III, Part IV, Part V, sections 171 to 173, 175, 177 and 246 and Schedules 11 and 14.

(3) In relation to a local planning authority being a joint planning board, subsection (1) of this section shall have effect as if the reference therein to the councils of county districts in their area included a reference to the councils of counties and county boroughs therein.

(4) Any regulations made for the purposes of this section may make provision—

    (*a*) for requiring any council to whom functions are delegated in accordance with the regulations to perform those functions on behalf of the local planning authority ;

    (*b*) for transferring to any such council any liability of the local planning authority to pay compensation under Part VIII or under section 187 or 237(1)(*b*) of this Act in respect of anything done by that council in the exercise of functions delegated to them in accordance with the regulations ;

    (*c*) for the transfer and compensation of any officers of a local planning authority or of any such council.

(5) The preceding provisions of this section shall have effect without prejudice to the provisions of section 8(3) of the National Parks and Access to the Countryside Act 1949 (delegation of functions to planning committees and sub-committees for National Parks). 1949 c 97.

(6) In relation to any functions under this Act delegated to a council by a local planning authority, any reference in the provisions specified in subsection (2) of this section, or in section 290(4) of this Act, to the local planning authority shall (subject to the regulations and the terms of the delegation, and so far as the context does not otherwise require) be construed as including a reference to that council ; and in relation to any compensation payable by a council, by virtue of the transfer under this section to that council of any liability of the local planning authority, any reference in this Act to the local planning authority shall be construed as a reference to that council.

4.—(1) A local planning authority may delegate to any officer of the authority the function of determining all or any, or a specified class, of the following applications, that is to say— *Delegation of functions to officers of local authorities.*

    (*a*) an application for planning permission under Part III of this Act;

    (*b*) an application for an approval required by a development order or by a condition imposed on the grant of planning permission ;

    (*c*) an application for a determination under section 53 of this Act of the questions whether the carrying out of operations on land or the making of any change in the use of land constitutes or involves development of the land and, if so, whether an application for planning permission in respect thereof is required having regard to the provisions of the development order :

(d) an application for consent under an order under section 60 of this Act to the cutting down, topping, lopping or destruction of trees ;

(e) an application for consent under regulations under section 63 of this Act to the display of advertisements ;

(f) an application for an established use certificate under section 94 of this Act.

(2) A local authority to whom the function of determining any such application as is referred to in subsection (1) of this section is delegated under section 3 of this Act may delegate either—

(a) to an officer of theirs ; or

(b) with the consent of the local planning authority, to an officer of that authority,

the function of determining all or any, or a specified class, of those applications.

(3) A delegation made by a local authority under this section to an officer of theirs or of another local authority—

(a) shall be made to the officer by name ;

(b) may be made with or without restrictions or conditions ;

(c) may be withdrawn at any time by the delegating authority (either generally or in respect of a particular application), without prejudice to anything previously done by the officer thereunder ; and

(d) shall, in the case of a delegation under paragraph (b) of subsection (2) of this section, be treated as withdrawn if the consent of the local planning authority under that paragraph is withdrawn.

(4) Where a local authority have under this section delegated to an officer of theirs or of another local authority the function of determining applications, and the officer so requests in the case of any application specified by him, the delegating authority shall themselves, instead of him, determine the application.

(5) Where any functions have under this section been delegated to an officer of a local authority, any determination by him of such an application as is referred to in subsection (1) of this section shall, if it is notified in writing to the applicant, be treated for all purposes as a determination of the delegating authority.

(6) Where an action has been brought against an officer of a local authority in respect of an act done by him in the discharge or purported discharge of functions delegated to him under this section and the circumstances are such that he is not legally entitled to require the delegating authority to indemnify him, that authority may nevertheless indemnify him against the

whole or part of any damages and costs which he may have been ordered to pay or may have incurred, if they are satisfied that he honestly believed that the act complained of was done in the discharge of those functions and that his duty required or entitled him to do it.

(7) In relation to any functions delegated under this section by a local authority to an officer of theirs or of another local authority, any reference to the local planning authority in any enactment relating to those functions shall (subject to the terms of the delegation and so far as the context does not otherwise require) be construed as including a reference to that officer.

5. Schedule 3 to this Act shall have effect as respects local planning authorities in Greater London.

PART II

DEVELOPMENT PLANS

Survey and structure plan

6.—(1) It shall be the duty of the local planning authority to institute a survey of their area, in so far as they have not already done so, examining the matters which may be expected to affect the development of that area or the planning of its development and in any event to keep all such matters under review.

(2) Notwithstanding that the local planning authority have carried out their duty under subsection (1) of this section, the authority may, if they think fit, and shall, if directed to do so by the Secretary of State, institute a fresh survey of their area examining the matters mentioned in that subsection.

(3) Without prejudice to the generality of the preceding provisions of this section, the matters to be examined and kept under review thereunder shall include the following, that is to say—

(a) the principal physical and economic characteristics of the area of the authority (including the principal purposes for which land is used) and, so far as they may be expected to affect that area, of any neighbouring areas;

(b) the size, composition and distribution of the population of that area (whether resident or otherwise);

(c) without prejudice to paragraph (a) of this subsection, the communications, transport system and traffic of that area and, so far as they may be expected to affect that area, of any neighbouring areas;

(d) any considerations not mentioned in any of the preceding paragraphs which may be expected to affect any matters so mentioned;

(e) such other matters as may be prescribed or as the Secretary of State may in a particular case direct;

(f) any changes already projected in any of the matters mentioned in any of the preceding paragraphs and the effect which those changes are likely to have on the development of that area or the planning of such development.

(4) A local planning authority shall, for the purpose of discharging their functions under this section of examining and keeping under review any matters relating to the area of another such authority, consult with that other authority about those matters.

(5) Subsection (1) of this section shall, as respects any period during which this section is in operation in part only of the area of a local planning authority, be construed as requiring a local planning authority to institute a survey of that part of that area and to keep under review matters affecting only that part of that area ; and subsection (2) of this section shall, whether or not this section is in operation in the whole of such an area, have effect as if the power thereby conferred included power for a local planning authority to institute, and for the Secretary of State to direct them to institute, a fresh survey of part only of their area ; and references in subsection (3) of this section to the area of a local planning authority or any neighbouring areas shall be construed accordingly.

Preparation of structure plans.

7.—(1) The local planning authority shall, within such period from the commencement of this section within their area as the Secretary of State may direct, prepare and send the Secretary of State a report of their survey under section 6 of this Act and at the same time prepare and submit to him for his approval a structure plan for their area complying with the provisions of subsection (3) of this section.

(2) The said report shall include an estimate of any changes likely to occur during such period as the Secretary of State may direct in the matters mentioned in section 6(3) of this Act ; and different periods may be specified by any such direction in relation to different matters.

(3) The structure plan for any area shall be a written statement—

(a) formulating the local planning authority's policy and general proposals in respect of the development and other use of land in that area (including measures for the improvement of the physical environment and the management of traffic) ;

(b) stating the relationship of those proposals to general proposals for the development and other use of land in neighbouring areas which may be expected to affect that area ; and

(c) containing such other matters as may be prescribed or as the Secretary of State may in any particular case direct.

(4) In formulating their policy and general proposals under subsection (3)(a) of this section, the local planning authority shall secure that the policy and proposals are justified by the results of their survey under section 6 of this Act and by any other information which they may obtain and shall have regard—

(a) to current policies with respect to the economic planning and development of the region as a whole ;

(b) to the resources likely to be available for the carrying out of the proposals of the structure plan ; and

(c) to such other matters as the Secretary of State may direct them to take into account.

(5) A local planning authority's general proposals under this section with respect to land in their area shall indicate any part of that area (in this Act referred to as an " action area ") which they have selected for the commencement during a prescribed period of comprehensive treatment, in accordance with a local plan prepared for the selected area as a whole, by development, redevelopment or improvement of the whole or part of the area selected, or partly by one and partly by another method, and the nature of the treatment selected.

(6) A structure plan for any area shall contain or be accompanied by such diagrams, illustrations and descriptive matter as the local planning authority think appropriate for the purpose of explaining or illustrating the proposals in the plan, or as may be prescribed, or as may in any particular case be specified in directions given by the Secretary of State ; and any such diagrams, illustrations and descriptive matter shall be treated as forming part of the plan.

(7) At any time before the Secretary of State has under section 9 of this Act approved a structure plan with respect to the whole of the area of a local planning authority, the authority may with his consent, and shall, if so directed by him, prepare and submit to him for his approval a structure plan relating to part of that area ; and where the Secretary of State has given a consent or direction for the preparation of a structure plan for part of such an area, references in this Part of this Act to such an area shall, in relation to a structure plan, be construed as including references to part of that area.

PART II
Publicity in
connection
with
preparation
of structure
plans.

8.—(1) When preparing a structure plan for their area and before finally determining its content for submission to the Secretary of State, the local planning authority shall take such steps as will in their opinion secure—

> (a) that adequate publicity is given in their area to the report of the survey under section 6 of this Act and to the matters which they propose to include in the plan ;
>
> (b) that persons who may be expected to desire an opportunity of making representations to the authority with respect to those matters are made aware that they are entitled to an opportunity of doing so ; and
>
> (c) that such persons are given an adequate opportunity of making such representations ;

and the authority shall consider any representations made to them within the prescribed period.

(2) Not later than the submission of a structure plan to the Secretary of State, the local planning authority shall make copies of the plan as submitted to the Secretary of State available for inspection at their office and at such other places as may be prescribed ; and each copy shall be accompanied by a statement of the time within which objections to the plan may be made to the Secretary of State.

(3) A structure plan submitted by the local planning authority to the Secretary of State for his approval shall be accompanied by a statement containing such particulars, if any, as may be prescribed—

> (a) of the steps which the authority have taken to comply with subsection (1) of this section ; and
>
> (b) of the authority's consultations with, and consideration of the views of, other persons with respect to those matters.

(4) If after considering the statement submitted with, and the matters included in, the structure plan and any other information provided by the local planning authority, the Secretary of State is satisfied that the purposes of paragraphs (a) to (c) of subsection (1) of this section have been adequately achieved by the steps taken by the authority in compliance with that subsection, he shall proceed to consider whether to approve the structure plan ; and if he is not so satisfied, he shall return the plan to the authority and direct them—

> (a) to take such further action as he may specify in order better to achieve those purposes ; and
>
> (b) after doing so, to resubmit the plan with such modifications, if any, as they then consider appropriate and, if so required by the direction, to do so within a specified period.

(5) Where the Secretary of State returns the structure plan to the local planning authority under subsection (4) of this section, he shall inform the authority of his reasons for doing so and, if any person has made to him an objection to the plan, shall also inform that person that he has returned the plan.

(6) A local planning authority who are given directions by the Secretary of State under subsection (4) of this section shall forthwith withdraw the copies of the plan made available for inspection as required by subsection (2) of this section.

(7) Subsections (2) to (6) of this section shall apply, with the necessary modifications, in relation to a structure plan resubmitted to the Secretary of State in accordance with directions given by him under subsection (4) as they apply in relation to the plan as originally submitted.

9.—(1) The Secretary of State may, after considering a structure plan submitted (or resubmitted) to him, either approve it (in whole or in part and with or without modifications or reservations) or reject it.

Approval or rejection of structure plan by Secretary of State.

(2) In considering any such plan the Secretary of State may take into account any matters which he thinks are relevant, whether or not they were taken into account in the plan as submitted to him.

(3) Where on taking any such plan into consideration the Secretary of State does not determine then to reject it, he shall, before determining whether or not to approve it—

(a) consider any objections to the plan, so far as they are made in accordance with regulations under this Part of this Act;

(b) afford to any persons whose objections so made are not withdrawn an opportunity of appearing before, and being heard by, a person appointed by him for the purpose; and

(c) if a local inquiry or other hearing is held, also afford the like opportunity to the local planning authority and such other persons as he thinks fit.

(4) Without prejudice to subsection (3) of this section, on considering a structure plan the Secretary of State may consult with, or consider the views of, any local planning authority or other persons, but shall not be under an obligation to consult with, or consider the views of, any other authority or persons or, except as provided by that subsection, to afford an opportunity for the making of any objections or other representations, or to cause any local inquiry or other hearing to be held.

PART II
Alteration of
structure
plans.

10.—(1) At any time after the approval of a structure plan for their area a local planning authority may submit to the Secretary of State and shall, if so directed by the Secretary of State, submit to him within a period specified in the direction, proposals for such alterations to that plan as appear to them to be expedient or as the Secretary of State may direct, as the case may be, and any such proposals may relate to the whole or to part of that area.

(2) The local planning authority shall send with the proposals submitted by them under this section a report of the results of their review of the relevant matters under section 6 of this Act together with any other information on which the proposals are based, and sections 8 and 9 of this Act shall apply, with any necessary modifications, in relation to the proposals as they apply in relation to a structure plan.

Local plans

Preparation
of local plans.

11.—(1) A local planning authority who are in course of preparing a structure plan for their area, or have prepared for their area a structure plan which has not been approved or rejected by the Secretary of State, may, if they think it desirable, prepare a local plan for any part of that area.

(2) Where a structure plan for their area has been approved by the Secretary of State, the local planning authority shall as soon as practicable consider, and thereafter keep under review, the desirability of preparing and, if they consider it desirable and they have not already done so, shall prepare a local plan for any part of the area.

(3) A local plan shall consist of a map and a written statement and shall—

    (a) formulate in such detail as the authority think appropriate the authority's proposals for the development and other use of land in that part of their area or for any description of development or other use of such land (including in either case such measures as the authority think fit for the improvement of the physical environment and the management of traffic) ; and

    (b) contain such matters as may be prescribed or as the Secretary of State may in any particular case direct.

(4) Different local plans may be prepared for different purposes for the same part of any area.

(5) A local plan for any area shall contain, or be accompanied by, such diagrams, illustrations and descriptive matter as the local planning authority think appropriate for the purpose of explaining or illustrating the proposals in the plan, or as may

be prescribed, or as may in any particular case be specified in directions given by the Secretary of State; and any such diagrams, illustrations and descriptive matter shall be treated as forming part of the plan.

(6) Where an area is indicated as an action area in a structure plan which has been approved by the Secretary of State, the local planning authority shall (if they have not already done so), as soon as practicable after the approval of the plan, prepare a local plan for that area.

(7) Without prejudice to the preceding provisions of this section, the local planning authority shall, if the Secretary of State gives them a direction in that behalf with respect to a part of an area for which a structure plan has been, or is in course of being, prepared, as soon as practicable prepare for that part a local plan of such nature as may be specified in the direction.

(8) Directions under subsection (7) of this section may be given by the Secretary of State either before or after he approves the structure plan; but no such directions shall require a local planning authority to take any steps to comply therewith until the structure plan has been approved by him.

(9) In formulating their proposals in a local plan the local planning authority shall secure that the proposals conform generally to the structure plan as it stands for the time being (whether or not it has been approved by the Secretary of State) and shall have regard to any information and any other considerations which appear to them to be relevant, or which may be prescribed, or which the Secretary of State may in any particular case direct them to take into account.

(10) Before giving a direction under the preceding provisions of this section to a local planning authority, the Secretary of State shall consult the authority with respect to the proposed direction.

(11) Where a local planning authority are required by this section to prepare a local plan, they shall take steps for the adoption of the plan.

12.—(1) A local planning authority who propose to prepare a local plan shall take such steps as will in their opinion secure— *Publicity in connection with preparation of local plans.*

    (a) that adequate publicity is given in their area to any relevant matter arising out of a survey of the area carried out by them under section 6 of this Act and to the matters proposed to be included in the plan;

(b) that persons who may be expected to desire an opportunity of making representations to the authority with respect to those matters are made aware that they are entitled to an opportunity of doing so ; and

(c) that such persons are given an adequate opportunity of making such representations ;

and the authority shall consider any representations made to them within the prescribed period.

(2) When the local planning authority have prepared a local plan, they shall, before adopting it or submitting it for approval under section 14(4) of this Act (but not before the Secretary of State has approved the structure plan so far as it applies to the area of that local plan), make copies of the local plan available for inspection at their office and at such other places as may be prescribed and send a copy to the Secretary of State ; and each copy made available for inspection shall be accompanied by a statement of the time within which objections to the local plan may be made to the authority.

(3) A copy of a local plan sent to the Secretary of State under subsection (2) of this section shall be accompanied by a statement containing such particulars, if any, as may be prescribed—

(a) of the steps which the authority have taken to comply with subsection (1) of this section ; and

(b) of the authority's consultations with, and their consideration of the views of, other persons.

(4) If, on considering the statement submitted with, and the matters included in, the local plan and any other information provided by the local planning authority, the Secretary of State is not satisfied that the purposes of paragraphs (a) to (c) of subsection (1) of this section have been adequately achieved by the steps taken by the authority in compliance with that subsection, he may, within twenty-one days of the receipt of the statement, direct the authority not to take any further steps for the adoption of the plan without taking such further action as he may specify in order better to achieve those purposes and satisfying him that they have done so.

(5) A local planning authority who are given directions by the Secretary of State under subsection (4) of this section shall—

(a) forthwith withdraw the copies of the local plan made available for inspection as required by subsection (2) of this section ; and

(b) notify any person by whom objections to the local plan have been made to the authority that the Secretary of State has given such directions as aforesaid.

13.—(1) For the purpose of considering objections made to a
local plan the local planning authority may, and shall in the case of objections so made in accordance with regulations under this Part of this Act, cause a local inquiry or other hearing to be held by a person appointed by the Secretary of State or, in such cases as may be prescribed by regulations under this Part of this Act, by the authority themselves, and—

    (*a*) subsections (2) and (3) of section 290 of the Local Government Act 1933 (power to summon and examine witnesses) shall apply to an inquiry held under this section as they apply to an inquiry held under that section ;

    (*b*) the Tribunals and Inquiries Act 1971 shall apply to a local inquiry or other hearing held under this section as it applies to a statutory inquiry held by the Secretary of State, but as if in section 12(1) of that Act (statement of reasons for decisions) the reference to any decision taken by the Secretary of State were a reference to a decision taken by a local authority.

(2) Regulations made for the purposes of subsection (1) of this section may—

    (*a*) make provision with respect to the appointment and qualifications for appointment of persons to hold a local inquiry or other hearing under that subsection, including provision enabling the Secretary of State to direct a local planning authority to appoint a particular person, or one of a specified list or class of persons ;

    (*b*) make provision with respect to the remuneration and allowances of a person appointed for the said purpose.

14.—(1) After the expiry of the period afforded for making objections to a local plan or, if such objections have been duly made during that period, after considering the objections so made, the local planning authority may, subject to section 12 of this Act and subsections (2) and (3) of this section, by resolution adopt the plan either as originally prepared or as modified so as to take account of any such objections or of any matters arising out of such objections.

(2) The local planning authority shall not adopt a local plan unless it conforms generally to the structure plan as approved by the Secretary of State.

(3) After copies of a local plan have been sent to the Secretary of State and before the plan has been adopted by the local planning authority, the Secretary of State may direct that the plan shall not have effect unless approved by him.

(4) Where the Secretary of State gives a direction under subsection (3) of this section, the local planning authority shall submit the plan accordingly to him for his approval, and—

(a) section 9 of this Act shall, subject to paragraph (b) of this subsection, apply in relation to the plan as it applies in relation to a structure plan ;

(b) before deciding whether or not to approve the plan the Secretary of State shall not be obliged to consider any objections thereto if objections thereto have been considered by the authority, or to cause an inquiry or other hearing to be held into the plan if any such inquiry or hearing has already been held at the instance of the authority ; and

(c) after the giving of the direction the authority shall have no further power or duty to hold a local inquiry or other hearing under section 13 of this Act in connection with the plan.

Alteration of local plans.

15.—(1) A local planning authority may at any time make proposals for the alteration, repeal or replacement of a local plan adopted by them and may at any time, with the consent of the Secretary of State, make proposals for the alteration, repeal or replacement of a local plan approved by him.

(2) Without prejudice to subsection (1) of this section, a local planning authority shall, if the Secretary of State gives them a direction in that behalf with respect to a local plan adopted by them or approved by him, as soon as practicable prepare proposals of a kind specified in the direction, being proposals for the alteration, repeal or replacement of the plan.

(3) The provisions of sections 11(9) to (11), 12, 13 and 14 of this Act shall apply in relation to the making of proposals for the alteration, repeal or replacement of a local plan under this section, and to alterations to a local plan so proposed, as they apply in relation to the preparation of a local plan under section 11 of this Act and to a local plan prepared thereunder, but as if the reference in section 14(4)(a) to section 9 of this Act were a reference to section 10 of this Act.

Supplementary provisions

Disregarding of representations with respect to development authorised by or under other enactments.

16. Notwithstanding anything in the preceding provisions of this Act, neither the Secretary of State nor a local planning authority shall be required to consider representations or objections with respect to a structure plan, a local plan or any proposal to alter, repeal or replace any such plan if it appears to the Secretary of State or the authority, as the case may be, that

those representations or objections are in substance representations or objections with respect to things done or proposed to be
done in pursuance of—

(a) an order or scheme under section 7, 9, 11, 13 or 20 of
the Highways Act 1959 (trunk road orders, special 1959 c. 25.
road schemes and ancillary orders) ;

(b) a scheme under section 3 of the Highways (Miscel- 1961 c. 63.
laneous Provisions) Act 1961 (scheme for construction
of bridge or tunnel as part of maintainable highway) ;

(c) an order under section 1 of the Highways Act 1971 1971 c. 41.
(classified road order) or section 10 thereof (order
authorising diversion of navigable watercourse) ;

(d) an order under section 1 of the New Towns Act 1965 1965 c. 59.
(designation of sites of new towns).

17.—(1) Where, by virtue of any of the preceding provisions Default
of this Part of this Act, any survey is required to be carried powers of
out, or any structure or local plan or proposals for the alteration, Secretary of
repeal or replacement thereof are required to be prepared or State.
submitted to the Secretary of State, or steps are required to
be taken for the adoption of any such plan or proposals, then—

(a) if at any time the Secretary of State is satisfied, after
holding a local inquiry or other hearing, that the local
planning authority are not carrying out the survey or
are not taking the steps necessary to enable them to
submit or adopt such a plan or proposals within a
reasonable period ; or

(b) in a case where a period is specified for the submission
or adoption of any such plan or proposals, if no such
plan or proposals have been submitted or adopted
within that period,

the Secretary of State may carry out the survey or prepare and
make a structure plan or local plan or, as the case may be, alter,
repeal or replace it, as he thinks fit.

(2) Where under subsection (1) of this section the Secretary of
State has power to do anything which should have been done by
a local planning authority, he may, if he thinks fit, authorise any
other local planning authority who appear to the Secretary of
State to have an interest in the proper planning of the area of
the first-mentioned authority to do that thing.

(3) Where under this section anything which ought to have
been done by a local planning authority is done by the Secretary
of State or another such authority, the preceding provisions of this
Part of this Act shall, so far as applicable, apply with any necessary modifications in relation to the doing of that thing by the
Secretary of State and the latter authority and the thing so done.

(4) Where the Secretary of State incurs expenses under this section in connection with the doing of anything which should have been done by a local planning authority, so much of those expenses as may be certified by the Secretary of State to have been incurred in the performance of functions of that authority shall on demand be repaid by that authority to the Secretary of State.

(5) Where under this section anything which should have been done by one local planning authority is done by another such authority, any expenses reasonably incurred in connection with the doing of that thing by the latter authority, as certified by the Secretary of State, shall be repaid to the latter authority by the former authority.

18.—(1) Without prejudice to the preceding provisions of this Part of this Act, the Secretary of State may make regulations with respect to the form and content of structure and local plans and with respect to the procedure to be followed in connection with their preparation, submission, withdrawal, approval, adoption, making, alteration, repeal and replacement; and in particular any such regulations may—

(a) provide for the publicity to be given to the report of any survey carried out by a local planning authority under section 6 of this Act;

(b) provide for the notice to be given of, or the publicity to be given to, matters included or proposed to be included in any such plan, and the approval, adoption or making of any such plan or any alteration, repeal or replacement thereof or to any other prescribed procedural step, and for publicity to be given to the procedure to be followed as aforesaid;

(c) make provision with respect to the making and consideration of representations with respect to matters to be included in, or objections to, any such plan or proposals for its alteration, repeal or replacement;

(d) without prejudice to paragraph (b) of this subsection, provide for notice to be given to particular persons of the approval, adoption or alteration of any plan, if they have objected to the plan and have notified the local planning authority of their wish to receive notice, subject (if the regulations so provide) to the payment of a reasonable charge for receiving it;

(e) require or authorise a local planning authority to consult with, or consider the views of, other persons before taking any prescribed procedural step;

(f) require a local planning authority, in such cases as may be prescribed or in such particular cases as the Secretary of State may direct, to provide persons making a request in that behalf with copies of any plan or document which has been made public for the purpose mentioned in section 8(1)(*a*) or 12(1)(*a*) of this Act or has been made available for inspection under section 8(2) or 12(2) of this Act, subject (if the regulations so provide) to the payment of a reasonable charge therefor :

(*g*) provide for the publication and inspection of any structure plan or local plan which has been approved, adopted or made, or any document approved, adopted or made altering, repealing or replacing any such plan, and for copies of any such plan or document to be made available on sale.

(2) Regulations under this section may extend throughout England and Wales or to specified areas only and may make different provisions for different cases.

(3) Subject to the preceding provisions of this Part of this Act and to any regulations under this section, the Secretary of State may give directions to any local planning authority, or to local planning authorities generally,—

(*a*) for formulating the procedure for the carrying out of their functions under this Part of this Act ;

(*b*) for requiring them to give him such information as he may require for carrying out any of his functions under this Part of this Act.

(4) Subject to the provisions of section 242 of this Act, a structure plan or local plan or any alteration, repeal or replacement thereof shall become operative on a date appointed for the purpose in the relevant notice of approval, resolution of adoption or notice of the making, alteration, repeal or replacement of the plan.

19. In their application to Greater London the preceding provisions of this Part of this Act shall have effect subject to the provisions of Schedule 4 to this Act.

Application of Part II to Greater London.

20.—(1) For the purposes of this Act, any other enactment relating to town and country planning, the Land Compensation Act 1961 and the Highways Act 1959, the development plan for any district outside Greater London (whether the whole or part of the area of a local planning authority) shall be taken as consisting of—

Meaning of " development plan."
1961 c. 33.
1959 c. 25.

(*a*) the provisions of the structure plan for the time being in force for that area or the relevant part of that area, together with the Secretary of State's notice of approval of the plan ;

(b) any alterations to that plan, together with the Secretary of State's notices of approval thereof ;

(c) any provisions of a local plan for the time being applicable to the district, together with a copy of the authority's resolution of adoption or, as the case may be, the Secretary of State's notice of approval of the local plan ; and

(d) any alterations to that local plan, together with a copy of the authority's resolutions of adoption or, as the case may be, the Secretary of State's notices of approval thereof.

(2) For the said purposes the development plan for any district in Greater London (whether the whole or part of the area of a London borough) shall be taken as consisting of—

(a) the provisions of the Greater London development plan and of the structure plan prepared by the council of that borough and for the time being in force in that area or the relevant part of that area together with the Secretary of State's notices of approval of the plans ;

(b) any alterations to those plans, together with the Secretary of State's notices of approval thereof ;

(c) any provisions of a local plan for the time being applicable to the district, together with a copy of the resolution of adoption of the relevant council or, as the case may be, the Secretary of State's notice of approval of the local plan ; and

(d) any alterations to that local plan, together with a copy of the resolutions of adoption of the relevant council or, as the case may be, the Secretary of State's notices of approval thereof.

(3) References in subsections (1) and (2) of this section to the provisions of any plan, notices of approval, alterations and resolutions of adoption shall, in relation to a district forming part of the area to which they are applicable, be respectively construed as references to so much of those provisions, notices, alterations and resolutions as is applicable to the district.

(4) References in subsections (1) to (3) of this section to notices of approval shall in relation to any plan or alteration made by the Secretary of State under section 17 of this Act be construed as references to notices of the making of the plan or alteration.

(5) This section has effect subject to Schedule 7 and Part I of Schedule 23 to this Act.

21.—(1) The preceding provisions of this Part of this Act (other than section 18 and except so far as they enable any matter or thing to be prescribed) and Part I of Schedule 23 to this Act shall come into operation on a day appointed by an order made by the Secretary of State.

PART II
Commence-
ment of
Part II and
interim
provisions.

(2) The provisions of Schedules 5 and 6 to this Act shall have effect until they are repealed by an order made by the Secretary of State.

(3) Schedule 7 to this Act shall have effect as respects the transition from the said Schedules 5 and 6 to the preceding provisions of this Part of this Act.

(4) Different days may be appointed under this section for different purposes and, in particular, different days may be so appointed for the coming into operation or repeal of the same provisions in different areas.

(5) Any reference in this Part of this Act to the commencement of any provision thereof shall be construed as a reference to the day appointed for the coming into operation of that provision or, in the case of a provision which comes into operation on different days in different areas, shall, in relation to any area, be construed as a reference to the day appointed for the coming into operation of that provision in that area.

(6) An order under this section may make such transitional provision as appears to the Secretary of State to be necessary or expedient in connection with the provisions thereby brought into operation or repealed, including such adaptation of those provisions or of any other provision of this Act then in force as appears to him to be necessary or expedient in consequence of the partial operation of this Act (whether before or after the day appointed by the order).

(7) The Secretary of State for the time being having general responsibility in planning matters in relation to England shall, for England, and the Secretary of State for the time being having such responsibility in relation to Wales shall, for Wales, each maintain and keep up to date a register showing the effect of orders made under this section in such a way as enables members of the public to inform themselves—

    (*a*) as to the provisions which have come, or are to be brought, into operation or have been, or are to be, repealed, and on which dates and in relation to which areas ; and

    (*b*) as to whether, in the case of a particular area, any transitional provision has been made by such an order.

(8) The register maintained under this section by the Secretary of State for the time being having general responsibility in

planning matters in relation to England shall be kept at his principal offices in London, and the register so maintained by the Secretary of State for the time being having general responsibility in planning matters in relation to Wales shall be kept at his principal offices in Cardiff ; and both registers shall be available for inspection by the public at reasonable hours.

Part III

General Planning Control

Meaning of development and requirement of planning permission

Meaning of
" develop-
ment " and
" new develop-
ment ".
    22.—(1) In this Act, except where the context otherwise requires, " development ", subject to the following provisions of this section, means the carrying out of building, engineering, mining or other operations in, on, over or under land, or the making of any material change in the use of any buildings or other land.

(2) The following operations or uses of land shall not be taken for the purposes of this Act to involve development of the land, that is to say—

    (*a*) the carrying out of works for the maintenance, improvement or other alteration of any building, being works which affect only the interior of the building or which do not materially affect the external appearance of the building and (in either case) are not works for making good war damage or works begun after 5th December 1968 for the alteration of a building by providing additional space therein below ground ;

    (*b*) the carrying out by a local highway authority of any works required for the maintenance or improvement of a road, being works carried out on land within the boundaries of the road ;

    (*c*) the carrying out by a local authority or statutory undertakers of any works for the purpose of inspecting, repairing or renewing any sewers, mains, pipes, cables or other apparatus, including the breaking open of any street or other land for that purpose ;

    (*d*) the use of any buildings or other land within the curtilage of a dwellinghouse for any purpose incidental to the enjoyment of the dwellinghouse as such ;

    (*e*) the use of any land for the purposes of agriculture or forestry (including afforestation) and the use for any of those purposes of any building occupied together with land so used ;

(f) in the case of buildings or other land which are used for a purpose of any class specified in an order made by the Secretary of State under this section, the use thereof for any other purpose of the same class.

(3) For the avoidance of doubt it is hereby declared that for the purposes of this section—

(a) the use as two or more separate dwellinghouses of any building previously used as a single dwellinghouse involves a material change in the use of the building and of each part thereof which is so used ;

(b) the deposit of refuse or waste materials on land involves a material change in the use thereof, notwithstanding that the land is comprised in a site already used for that purpose, if either the superficial area of the deposit is thereby extended, or the height of the deposit is thereby extended and exceeds the level of the land adjoining the site.

(4) Without prejudice to any regulations made under the provisions of this Act relating to the control of advertisements, the use for the display of advertisements of any external part of a building which is not normally used for that purpose shall be treated for the purposes of this section as involving a material change in the use of that part of the building.

(5) In this Act " new development " means any development other than development of a class specified in Part I or Part II of Schedule 8 to this Act ; and the provisions of Part III of that Schedule shall have effect for the purposes of Parts I and II thereof.

23.—(1) Subject to the provisions of this section, planning permission is required for the carrying out of any development of land.

(2) Where on 1st July 1948 (in this Act referred to as " the appointed day ") land was being temporarily used for a purpose other than the purpose for which it was normally used, planning permission is not required for the resumption of the use of the land for the last-mentioned purpose before 6th December 1968.

(3) Where on the appointed day land was normally used for one purpose and was also used on occasions, whether at regular intervals or not, for another purpose, planning permission is not required—

(a) in respect of the use of the land for that other purpose on similar occasions before 6th December 1968 ; or (*b*) in respect of the use of the land for that other purpose on similar occasions on or after that date if the land has been used for that other purpose on at least one similar occasion since the appointed day and before the beginning of 1968.

(4) Where land was unoccupied on the appointed day, but had before that day been occupied at some time on or after 7th January 1937, planning permission is not required in respect of any use of the land begun before 6th December 1968 for the purpose for which the land was last used before the appointed day.

(5) Where planning permission to develop land has been granted for a limited period, planning permission is not required for the resumption, at the end of that period, of the use of the land for the purpose for which it was normally used before the permission was granted.

(6) In determining, for the purposes of subsection (5) of this section, what were the purposes for which land was normally used before the grant of planning permission, no account shall be taken of any use of the land begun in contravention of the provisions of this Part of this Act or in contravention of previous planning control.

(7) Notwithstanding anything in subsections (2) to (4) of this section, the use of land as a caravan site shall not, by virtue of any of those subsections, be treated as a use for which planning permission is not required, unless the land was so used on one occasion at least during the period of two years ending with 9th March 1960.

(8) Where by a development order planning permission to develop land has been granted subject to limitations, planning permission is not required for the use of that land which (apart from its use in accordance with that permission) is the normal use of that land, unless the last-mentioned use was begun in contravention of the provisions of this Part of this Act or in contravention of previous planning control.

(9) Where an enforcement notice has been served in respect of any development of land, planning permission is not required for the use of that land for the purpose for which (in accordance with the provisions of this Part of this Act) it could lawfully have been used if that development had not been carried out.

(10) For the purposes of this section a use of land shall be taken to have been begun in contravention of previous planning control if it was begun in contravention of the provisions of Part III of the Act of 1947 or of Part III of the Act of 1962.

Development orders

24.—(1) The Secretary of State shall by order (in this Act referred to as a " development order ") provide for the granting of planning permission.

(2) A development order may either—

(a) itself grant planning permission for development specified in the order, or for development of any class so specified ; or

(b) in respect of development for which planning permission is not granted by the order itself, provide for the granting of planning permission by the local planning authority (or, in the cases hereinafter provided, by the Secretary of State) on an application in that behalf made to the local planning authority in accordance with the provisions of the order.

(3) A development order may be made either as a general order applicable (subject to such exceptions as may be specified therein) to all land, or as a special order applicable only to such land as may be so specified.

(4) Planning permission granted by a development order may be granted either unconditionally or subject to such conditions or limitations as may be specified in the order.

(5) Without prejudice to the generality of subsection (4) of this section—

(a) where planning permission is granted by a development order for the erection, extension or alteration of any buildings, the order may require the approval of the local planning authority to be obtained with respect to the design or external appearance of the buildings ;

(b) where planning permission is granted by a development order for development of a specified class, the order may enable the Secretary of State or the local planning authority to direct that the permission shall not apply either in relation to development in a particular area or in relation to any particular development.

(6) Any provision of a development order whereby permission is granted for the use of land for any purpose on a limited number of days in a period specified in that provision shall (without prejudice to the generality of references in this Act to limitations) be taken to be a provision granting permission for the use of land for any purpose subject to the limitation that the land shall not be used for any one purpose in pursuance of that provision on more than that number of days in that period.

B 3

(7) For the purpose of enabling development to be carried out in accordance with planning permission, or otherwise for the purpose of promoting proper development in accordance with the development plan, a development order may direct that any enactment to which this subsection applies, or any regulations, orders or byelaws made at any time under any such enactment, shall not apply to any development specified in the order, or shall apply thereto subject to such modifications as may be so specified.

(8) Subsection (7) of this section applies—

(*a*) to any enactment passed before 6th August 1947 (being the date of the passing of the Act of 1947) ; and

1959 c. 25.

(*b*) to any enactment contained in the Highways Act 1959 being an enactment which re-enacts (with or without modifications) any such enactment as is mentioned in paragraph (*a*) of this subsection.

Applications for planning permission

Form and content of applications.

25. Any application to a local planning authority for planning permission shall be made in such manner as may be prescribed by regulations under this Act, and shall include such particulars, and be verified by such evidence, as may be required by the regulations or by directions given by the local planning authority thereunder.

Publication of notices of applications.

26.—(1) Provision may be made by a development order for designating the classes of development to which this section applies, and this section shall apply accordingly to any class of development which is for the time being so designated.

(2) An application for planning permission for development of any class to which this section applies shall not be entertained by the local planning authority unless it is accompanied—

(*a*) by a copy of a notice of the application, in such form as may be prescribed by a development order, and by such evidence as may be so prescribed that the notice has been published in a local newspaper circulating in the locality in which the land to which the application relates is situated ; and

(*b*) by one or other of the following certificates, signed by or on behalf of the applicant, that is to say—

(i) a certificate stating that he has complied with subsection (3) of this section and when he did so ; or

(ii) a certificate stating that he has been unable to comply with it because he has not such rights of access or other rights in respect of the land as would enable him to do so, but that he has taken such reasonable steps as are open to him (specifying them) to acquire those rights and has been unable to acquire them.

(3) In order to comply with this subsection a person must—

(a) post on the land a notice, in such form as may be prescribed by a development order, stating that the application for planning permission is to be made ; and

(b) leave the notice in position for not less than seven days in a period of not more than one month immediately preceding the making of the application to the local planning authority.

(4) The said notice must be posted by affixing it firmly to some object on the land, and must be sited and displayed in such a way as to be easily visible and legible by members of the public without going on the land.

(5) The applicant shall not be treated as unable to comply with subsection (3) of this section if the notice is, without any fault or intention of his, removed, obscured or defaced before the seven days referred to in subsection (3)(b) of this section have elapsed, so long as he has taken reasonable steps for its protection and, if need be, replacement ; and, if he has cause to rely on this subsection, his certificate under subsection (2)(b) of this section shall state the relevant circumstances.

(6) The notice mentioned in subsection (2)(a) or required by subsection (3) of this section shall (in addition to any other matters required to be contained therein) name a place within the locality where a copy of the application for planning permission, and of all plans and other documents submitted with it, will be open to inspection by the public at all reasonable hours during such period as may be specified in the notice, not being a period of less than twenty-one days beginning with the date on which the notice is published or first posted, as the case may be.

(7) An application for planning permission for development of any class to which this section applies shall not be determined by the local planning authority before the end of the period of twenty-one days beginning with the date of the application.

(8) If any person issues a certificate which purports to comply with the requirements of subsection (2)(b) of this section and which contains a statement which he knows to be false or misleading in a material particular, or recklessly issues a certificate which purports to comply with those requirements and which

contains a statement which is false or misleading in a material particular, he shall be guilty of an offence and liable on summary conviction to a fine not exceeding £100.

(9) Any certificate issued for the purpose of this section shall be in such form as may be prescribed by a development order.

27.—(1) Without prejudice to section 26 of this Act, a local planning authority shall not entertain any application for planning permission unless it is accompanied by one or other of the following certificates signed by or on behalf of the applicant, that is to say—

> (a) a certificate stating that, in respect of every part of the land to which the application relates, the applicant is either the estate owner in respect of the fee simple or is entitled to a tenancy thereof;

> (b) a certificate stating that the applicant has given the requisite notice of the application to all the persons (other than the applicant) who, at the beginning of the period of twenty-one days ending with the date of the application, were owners of any of the land to which the application relates, and setting out the names of those persons, the addresses at which notice of the application was given to them respectively, and the date of service of each such notice;

> (c) a certificate stating that the applicant is unable to issue a certificate in accordance with either of the preceding paragraphs, that he has given the requisite notice of the application to such one or more of the persons mentioned in the last preceding paragraph as are specified in the certificate (setting out their names, the addresses at which notice of the application was given to them respectively, and the date of the service of each such notice), that he has taken such steps as are reasonably open to him (specifying them) to ascertain the names and addresses of the remainder of those persons and that he has been unable to do so;

> (d) a certificate stating that the applicant is unable to issue a certificate in accordance with paragraph (a) of this subsection, that he has taken such steps as are reasonably open to him (specifying them) to ascertain the names and addresses of the persons mentioned in paragraph (b) of this subsection and that he has been unable to do so.

(2) Any such certificate as is mentioned in paragraph (c) or paragraph (d) of subsection (1) of this section shall also contain a statement that the requisite notice of the application, as set out in the certificate, has on a date specified in the certificate

(being a date not earlier than the beginning of the period mentioned in paragraph (*b*) of that subsection) been published in a local newspaper circulating in the locality in which the land in question is situated.

(3) In addition to any other matters required to be contained in a certificate issued for the purposes of this section, every such certificate shall contain one or other of the following statements, that is to say—

(*a*) a statement that none of the land to which the application relates constitutes or forms part of an agricultural holding ;

(*b*) a statement that the applicant has given the requisite notice of the application to every person (other than the applicant) who, at the beginning of the period of twenty-one days ending with the date of the application, was a tenant of any agricultural holding any part of which was comprised in the land to which the application relates, and setting out the name of each such person, the address at which notice of the application was given to him, and the date of service of that notice.

(4) Where an application for planning permission is accompanied by such a certificate as is mentioned in subsection (1)(*b*), (*c*) or (*d*) of this section, or by a certificate containing a statement in accordance with subsection (3)(*b*) of this section, the local planning authority shall not determine the application before the end of the period of twenty-one days beginning with the date appearing from the certificate to be the latest of the dates of service of notices as mentioned in the certificate, or the date of publication of a notice as therein mentioned, whichever is the later.

(5) If any person issues any certificate which purports to comply with the requirements of this section and which contains a statement which he knows to be false or misleading in a material particular, or recklessly issues a certificate which purports to comply with those requirements and which contains a statement which is false or misleading in a material particular, he shall be guilty of an offence and liable on summary conviction to a fine not exceeding £100.

(6) Any certificate issued for the purposes of this section shall be in such form as may be prescribed by a development order ; and any reference in any provision of this section to the requisite notice, where a form of notice is prescribed by a development order for the purposes of that provision, is a reference to a notice in that form.

PART III

1948 c. 63.

Publicity for
applications
affecting
conservation
areas.

(7) In this section " owner ", in relation to any land, means
a person who is for the time being the estate owner in respect of
the fee simple thereof or is entitled to a tenancy thereof granted
or extended for a term of years certain of which not less than
ten years remain unexpired, and " agricultural holding " has the
same meaning as in the Agricultural Holdings Act 1948.

28.—(1) This section applies where an application for planning permission for any development of land is made to a
local planning authority and either—

   (a) the development would, in the opinion of the authority,
      affect the character or appearance of a conservation
      area ; or

   (b) the development is of a kind specified by the Secretary
      of State for the purposes of this section and in respect
      of land in or adjacent to a conservation area.

(2) The local planning authority shall—

   (a) publish in a local newspaper circulating in the locality
      in which the land is situated ; and

   (b) for not less than seven days display on or near the land,

a notice indicating the nature of the development in question
and naming a place within the locality where a copy of the
application, and of all plans and other documents submitted
with it, will be open to inspection by the public at all reasonable
hours during the period of twenty-one days beginning with the
date of publication of the notice under paragraph (a) of this
subsection.

(3) The application shall not be determined by the local
planning authority before both the following periods have
elapsed, namely—

   (a) the period of twenty-one days referred to in subsection
      (2) of this section ; and

   (b) the period of twenty-one days beginning with the date
      on which the notice required by that subsection to be
      displayed was first displayed.

*Determination by local planning authorities of applications
for planning permission*

Determination
of applications.

29.—(1) Subject to the provisions of sections 26 to 28 of
this Act, and to the following provisions of this Act, where
an application is made to a local planning authority for planning
permission, that authority, in dealing with the application, shall

have regard to the provisions of the development plan, so far as material to the application, and to any other material considerations, and—

    (a) subject to sections 41, 42, 70 and 77 to 80 of this Act, may grant planning permission, either unconditionally or subject to such conditions as they think fit ; or

    (b) may refuse planning permission.

(2) In determining any application for planning permission for development of a class to which section 26 of this Act applies, the local planning authority shall take into account any representations relating to that application which are received by them before the end of the period of twenty-one days beginning with the date of the application.

(3) Where an application for planning permission is accompanied by such a certificate as is mentioned in subsection (1)(b), (c) or (d) of section 27 of this Act, or by a certificate containing a statement in accordance with subsection (3)(b) of that section, the local planning authority—

    (a) in determining the application, shall take into account any representations relating thereto which are made to them, before the end of the period mentioned in subsection (4) of that section, by any person who satisfies them that he is an owner of any land to which the application relates or that he is the tenant of an agricultural holding any part of which is comprised in that land ; and

    (b) shall give notice of their decision to every person who has made representations which they were required to take into account in accordance with the preceding paragraph.

(4) In determining any application for planning permission to which section 28 of this Act applies, the local planning authority shall take into account any representations relating to the application which are received by them before the periods mentioned in subsection (3) of that section have elapsed.

(5) Before a local planning authority grant planning permission for the use of land as a caravan site, they shall, unless they are also the authority having power to issue a site licence for that land, consult the local authority having that power.

(6) In this section " site licence " means a licence under Part I of the Caravan Sites and Control of Development Act 1960 authorising the use of land as a caravan site and " owner " and " agricultural holding " have the same meanings as in section 27 of this Act.

1960 c. 62.

PART III
Conditional
grant of
planning
permission.

30.—(1) Without prejudice to the generality of section 29(1) of this Act, conditions may be imposed on the grant of planning permission thereunder—

(a) for regulating the development or use of any land under the control of the applicant (whether or not it is land in respect of which the application was made) or requiring the carrying out of works on any such land, so far as appears to the local planning authority to be expedient for the purposes of or in connection with the development authorised by the permission ;

(b) for requiring the removal of any buildings or works authorised by the permission, or the discontinuance of any use of land so authorised, at the end of a specified period, and the carrying out of any works required for the reinstatement of land at the end of that period.

(2) Any planning permission granted subject to such a condition as is mentioned in subsection (1)(b) of this section is in this Act referred to as " planning permission granted for a limited period ".

(3) Where—

(a) planning permission is granted for development consisting of or including the carrying out of building or other operations subject to a condition that the operations shall be commenced not later than a time specified in the condition (not being a condition attached to the planning permission by or under section 41 or 42 of this Act) ; and

(b) any building or other operations are commenced after the time so specified,

the commencement and carrying out of those operations do not constitute development for which that permission was granted.

Directions
etc. as to
method of
dealing with
applications.

31.—(1) Subject to the provisions of section 29(2) to (5) of this Act, provision may be made by a development order for regulating the manner in which applications for planning permission to develop land are to be dealt with by local planning authorities, and in particular—

(a) for enabling the Secretary of State to give directions restricting the grant of planning permission by the local planning authority, either indefinitely or during such period as may be specified in the directions, in respect of any such development, or in respect of development of any such class, as may be so specified ;

(b) for authorising the local planning authority, in such cases and subject to such conditions as may be prescribed by the order, or by directions given by the

Secretary of State thereunder, to grant planning permission for development which does not accord with the provisions of the development plan ;

(c) for requiring the local planning authority, before granting or refusing planning permission for any development, to consult with such authorities or persons as may be prescribed by the order or by directions given by the Secretary of State thereunder ;

(d) for requiring the local planning authority to give to any applicant for planning permission, within such time as may be prescribed by the order, such notice as may be so prescribed as to the manner in which his application has been dealt with ;

(e) for requiring the local planning authority to give to the Secretary of State, and to such other persons as may be prescribed by or under the order, such information as may be so prescribed with respect to applications for planning permission made to the authority, including information as to the manner in which any such application has been dealt with.

(2) The Secretary of State may give directions to local planning authorities with respect to the matters which they are to take into consideration in determining an application to which section 28 of this Act applies and with respect to the consultations which such authorities are to undertake before determining any such application.

(3) Different directions may under subsection (2) of this section be given to different local planning authorities ; and any such directions may require an authority—

(a) before determining an application to consult such persons or bodies of persons as the Secretary of State may specify, being persons or bodies appearing to him to be competent to give advice in relation to the development or description of development to which the directions have reference ;

(b) to supply to any person or body, whom they are required by the directions to consult, specified documents or information enabling the body to form an opinion on which to base their advice ;

(c) to establish committees, consisting either of members of the authority or of other persons, or of both, to advise the authority in relation to the determination of any application referred to in subsection (2) of this section.

PART III
Permission to
retain
buildings
or works or
continue use
of land.

32.—(1) An application for planning permission may relate to buildings or works constructed or carried out, or a use of land instituted, before the date of the application, whether—

(a) the buildings or works were constructed or carried out, or the use instituted, without planning permission or in accordance with planning permission granted for a limited period ; or

(b) the application is for permission to retain the buildings or works, or continue the use of the land, without complying with some condition subject to which a previous planning permission was granted.

(2) Any power to grant planning permission to develop land under this Act shall include power to grant planning permission for the retention on land of buildings or works constructed or carried out, or for the continuance of a use of land instituted, as mentioned in subsection (1) of this section ; and references in this Act to planning permission to develop land or to carry out any development of land, and to applications for such permission, shall be construed accordingly:

Provided that this subsection shall not affect the construction of section 26, 28, 29(2) or (4) or 59, of sections 66 to 86 or of Part VII of this Act.

(3) Any planning permission granted in accordance with subsection (2) of this section may be granted so as to take effect from the date on which the buildings or works were constructed or carried out, or the use was instituted, or (in the case of buildings or works constructed or a use instituted in accordance with planning permission granted for a limited period) so as to take effect from the end of that period, as the case may be.

33.—(1) Without prejudice to the provisions of this Part of this Act as to the duration, revocation or modification of planning permission, any grant of planning permission to develop land shall (except in so far as the permission otherwise provides) enure for the benefit of the land and of all persons for the time being interested therein.

(2) Where planning permission is granted for the erection of a building, the grant of permission may specify the purposes for which the building may be used ; and if no purpose is so specified, the permission shall be construed as including permission to use the building for the purpose for which it is designed.

34.—(1) Every local planning authority shall keep, in such manner as may be prescribed by a development order, a register containing such information as may be so prescribed with

respect to applications for planning permission made to that
authority, including information as to the manner in which
such applications have been dealt with.

(2) A development order may make provision for the register
to be kept in two or more parts, each part containing such
information relating to applications for planning permission
made to the authority as may be prescribed by the order, and
may also make provision—

    (*a*) for a specified part of the register to contain copies
        of applications and of any plans or drawings submitted
        therewith ; and

    (*b*) for the entry relating to any application, and every
        thing relating thereto, to be removed from that part of
        the register when the application (including any appeal
        arising out of it) has been finally disposed of, without
        prejudice to the inclusion of any different entry relating
        thereto in another part of the register.

(3) Every register kept under this section shall be available
for inspection by the public at all reasonable hours.

Secretary of State's powers in relation to planning applications and decisions

35.—(1) The Secretary of State may give directions requiring
applications for planning permission, or for the approval of any
local planning authority required under a development order, to
be referred to him instead of being dealt with by local planning
authorities.   Reference of applications to Secretary of State.

(2) A direction under this section—

    (*a*) may be given either to a particular local planning
        authority or to local planning authorities generally ;
        and

    (*b*) may relate either to a particular application or to
        applications of a class specified in the direction.

(3) Any application in respect of which a direction under
this section has effect shall be referred to the Secretary of State
accordingly.

(4) Subject to subsection (5) of this section, where an application for planning permission is referred to the Secretary of State
under this section, the following provisions of this Act, that is
to say, sections 26(2) and (7), 27, 29(1) to (3) and 30(1), shall
apply, with any necessary modifications, as they apply to an
application for planning permission which falls to be determined
by the local planning authority.

(5) Before determining an application referred to him under this section, other than an application for planning permission referred to a Planning Inquiry Commission under section 48 of this Act, the Secretary of State shall, if either the applicant or the local planning authority so desire, afford to each of them an opportunity of appearing before, and being heard by, a person appointed by the Secretary of State for the purpose.

(6) The decision of the Secretary of State on any application referred to him under this section shall be final.

Appeals
against
planning
decisions.

36.—(1) Where an application is made to a local planning authority for planning permission to develop land, or for any approval of that authority required under a development order, and that permission or approval is refused by that authority or is granted by them subject to conditions, the applicant, if he is aggrieved by their decision, may by notice under this section appeal to the Secretary of State.

(2) Any notice under this section shall be served within such time (not being less than twenty-eight days from the date of notification of the decision to which it relates) and in such manner as may be prescribed by a development order.

(3) Where an appeal is brought under this section from a decision of a local planning authority, the Secretary of State, subject to the following provisions of this section, may allow or dismiss the appeal, or may reverse or vary any part of the decision of the local planning authority, whether the appeal relates to that part thereof or not, and may deal with the application as if it had been made to him in the first instance.

(4) Before determining an appeal under this section, other than an appeal referred to a Planning Inquiry Commission under section 48 of this Act, the Secretary of State shall, if either the applicant or the local planning authority so desire, afford to each of them an opportunity of appearing before, and being heard by, a person appointed by the Secretary of State for the purpose.

(5) Subject to subsection (4) of this section, the following provisions of this Act, that is to say, sections 27, 29(1) and (3) and 30(1) shall apply, with any necessary modifications, in relation to an appeal to the Secretary of State under this section as they apply in relation to an application for planning permission which falls to be determined by the local planning authority.

(6) The decision of the Secretary of State on any appeal under this section shall be final.

(7) If before or during the determination of an appeal under this section in respect of an application for planning permission to develop land, the Secretary of State forms the opinion that, having regard to the provisions of sections 29(1), 30(1), 67 and 74 of this Act and of the development order and to any directions given under that order, planning permission for that development—

> (a) could not have been granted by the local planning authority ; or
>
> (b) could not have been granted by them otherwise than subject to the conditions imposed by them,

he may decline to determine the appeal or to proceed with the determination.

(8) Schedule 9 to this Act applies to appeals under this section, including appeals under this section as applied by or under any other provision of this Act.

37. Where an application is made to a local planning authority Appeal in for planning permission, or for any approval of that authority default of required under a development order, then unless within such planning period as may be prescribed by the development order, or within decision. such extended period as may at any time be agreed upon in writing between the applicant and the local planning authority, the local planning authority either—

> (a) give notice to the applicant of their decision on the application ; or
>
> (b) give notice to him that the application has been referred to the Secretary of State in accordance with directions given under section 35 of this Act,

the provisions of section 36 of this Act shall apply in relation to the application as if the permission or approval to which it relates had been refused by the local planning authority, and as if notification of their decision had been received by the applicant at the end of the period prescribed by the development order, or at the end of the said extended period, as the case may be.

38.—(1) The provisions of this section and of section 39 of this Review of Act shall have effect where, in accordance with the provisions of planning Part VII of this Act, one or more claims for compensation in decisions respect of a planning decision have been transmitted to the where Secretary of State, and the claim, or (if there is more than one) compensation one or more of the claims, has not been withdrawn. claimed.

(2) If, in the case of a planning decision of the local planning authority, it appears to the Secretary of State that, if the application for permission to develop the land in question had

been referred to him for determination, he would have made a decision more favourable to the applicant, the Secretary of State may give a direction substituting that decision for the decision of the local planning authority.

(3) If, in any case, it appears to the Secretary of State that planning permission could properly be granted (either unconditionally or subject to certain conditions) for some development of the land in question other than the development to which the application for planning permission related, the Secretary of State may give a direction that the provisions of this Act shall have effect in relation to that application and to the planning decision—

    (a) as if the application had included an application for permission for that other development, and the decision had included the grant of planning permission (unconditionally or subject to the said conditions, as the case may be) for that development ; or

    (b) as if the decision had been a decision of the Secretary of State and had included an undertaking to grant planning permission (unconditionally or subject to the said conditions, as the case may be) for that development,

as may be specified in the direction.

(4) The reference in subsection (2) of this section to a decision more favourable to the applicant shall be construed—

    (a) in relation to a refusal of permission, as a reference to a decision granting the permission, either unconditionally or subject to conditions, and either in respect of the whole of the land to which the application for permission related or in respect of part of that land ; and

    (b) in relation to a grant of permission subject to conditions, as a reference to a decision granting the permission applied for unconditionally or subject to less stringent conditions.

Provisions
supplementary
to s. 38.
    39.—(1) Before giving a direction under section 38 of this Act the Secretary of State shall give notice in writing of his proposed direction to the local planning authority to whose decision that direction relates, and to any person who made, and has not since withdrawn, a claim for compensation in respect of that decision ; and, if so required by the local planning authority or by any such person, shall afford to each of them an opportunity to appear before, and be heard by, a person appointed by the Secretary of State for the purpose.

(2) In giving any direction under section 38 of this Act, the Secretary of State shall have regard to the provisions of the

development plan for the area in which the land in question is situated, in so far as those provisions are material to the development of that land, and shall also have regard to the local circumstances affecting the proposed development, including the use which prevails generally in the case of contiguous or adjacent land, and to any other material considerations.

(3) Where the Secretary of State gives a direction under section 38 of this Act, he shall give notice of the direction to the local planning authority to whose decision the direction relates, and to every person (if any) who made, and has not since withdrawn, a claim for compensation in respect of that decision.

Deemed planning permission

40.—(1) Where the authorisation of a government department is required by virtue of an enactment in respect of development to be carried out by a local authority, or by statutory undertakers not being a local authority, that department may, on granting that authorisation, direct that planning permission for that development shall be deemed to be granted, subject to such conditions (if any) as may be specified in the directions.

(2) The provisions of this Act (except Parts VII and XII thereof) shall apply in relation to any planning permission deemed to be granted by virtue of directions under this section as if it had been granted by the Secretary of State on an application referred to him under section 35 of this Act.

(3) For the purposes of this section development shall be taken to be authorised by a government department if—

(a) any consent, authority or approval to or for the development is granted by the department in pursuance of an enactment ;

(b) a compulsory purchase order is confirmed by the department authorising the purchase of land for the purpose of the development ;

(c) consent is granted by the department to the appropriation of land for the purpose of the development or the acquisition of land by agreement for that purpose ;

(d) authority is given by the department for the borrowing of money for the purpose of the development, or for the application for that purpose of any money not otherwise so applicable ; or

(e) any undertaking is given by the department to pay a grant in respect of the development in accordance with an enactment authorising the payment of such grants,

and references in this section to the authorisation of a government department shall be construed accordingly.

Duration of planning permission

Limit of
duration of
planning
permission.

41.—(1) Subject to the provisions of this section, every planning permission granted or deemed to be granted shall be granted or, as the case may be, be deemed to be granted, subject to the condition that the development to which it relates must be begun not later than the expiration of—

(a) five years beginning with the date on which the permission is granted or, as the case may be, deemed to be granted; or

(b) such other period (whether longer or shorter) beginning with the said date as the authority concerned with the terms of the planning permission may direct, being a period which the authority considers appropriate having regard to the provisions of the development plan and to any other material considerations.

(2) If planning permission is granted without the condition required by subsection (1) of this section, it shall be deemed to have been granted subject to the condition that the development to which it relates must be begun not later than the expiration of five years beginning with the date of the grant.

(3) Nothing in this section applies—

(a) to any planning permission granted by a development order ;

(b) to any planning permission granted for a limited period ;

(c) to any planning permission granted under section 32 of this Act on an application relating to buildings or works completed, or a use of land instituted, before the date of the application ; or

(d) to any outline planning permission, as defined by section 42 of this Act.

Outline
planning
permission.

42.—(1) In this section and section 41 of this Act " outline planning permission " means planning permission granted, in accordance with the provisions of a development order, with the reservation for subsequent approval by the local planning authority or the Secretary of State of matters (referred to in this section as " reserved matters ") not particularised in the application.

(2) Subject to the provisions of this section, where outline planning permission is granted for development consisting in or including the carrying out of building or other operations, it shall be granted subject to conditions to the following effect—

(a) that, in the case of any reserved matter, application for approval must be made not later than the expiration of three years beginning with the date of the grant of outline planning permission ; and (*b*) that the development to which the permission relates must be begun not later than whichever is the later of the following dates—

    (i) the expiration of five years from the date of the grant of outline planning permission; or

    (ii) the expiration of two years from the final approval of the reserved matters or, in the case of approval on different dates, the final approval of the last such matter to be approved.

(3) If outline planning permission is granted without the conditions required by subsection (2) of this section, it shall be deemed to have been granted subject to those conditions.

(4) The authority concerned with the terms of an outline planning permission may, in applying subsection (2) of this section, substitute, or direct that there be substituted, for the periods of three years, five years or two years referred to in that subsection such other periods respectively (whether longer or shorter) as they consider appropriate.

(5) The said authority may, in applying the said subsection, specify, or direct that there be specified, separate periods under paragraph (*a*) of the subsection in relation to separate parts of the development to which the planning permission relates; and, if they do so, the condition required by paragraph (*b*) of the subsection shall then be framed correspondingly by reference to those parts, instead of by reference to the development as a whole.

(6) In considering whether to exercise their powers under subsections (4) and (5) of this section, the said authority shall have regard to the provisions of the development plan and to any other material considerations.

43.—(1) For the purposes of sections 41 and 42 of this Act, development shall be taken to be begun on the earliest date on which any specified operation comprised in the development begins to be carried out. Provisions supplementary to ss. 41 and 42.

(2) In subsection (1) of this section "specified operation" means any of the following, that is to say—

(*a*) any work of construction in the course of the erection of a building;

(*b*) the digging of a trench which is to contain the foundations, or part of the foundations, of a building;

(*c*) the laying of any underground main or pipe to the foundations, or part of the foundations, of a building or to any such trench as is mentioned in the last preceding paragraph;

(*d*) any operation in the course of laying out or constructing a road or part of a road ;

(*e*) any change in the use of any land, where that change constitutes material development.

(3) In subsection (2)(*e*) of this section " material development " means any development other than—

(*a*) development for which planning permission is granted by a general development order for the time being in force and which is carried out so as to comply with any condition or limitation subject to which planning permission is so granted ;

(*b*) development falling within any of paragraphs 1, 2, 3 and 5 to 8 of Schedule 8 to this Act, as read with Part III of that Schedule ; and

(*c*) development of any class prescribed for the purposes of this subsection ;

and in this subsection " general development order " means a development order made as a general order applicable (subject to such exceptions as may be specified therein) to all land in England and Wales.

(4) The authority referred to in sections 41(1)(*b*) and 42(4) of this Act is the local planning authority or the Secretary of State, in the case of planning permission granted by them, and in the case of planning permission under section 40 of this Act is the department on whose direction planning permission is deemed to be granted.

(5) For the purposes of section 42 of this Act, a reserved matter shall be treated as finally approved when an application for approval is granted or, in a case where the application is made to the local planning authority and there is an appeal to the Secretary of State against the authority's decision on the application and the Secretary of State grants the approval, on the date of the determination of the appeal.

(6) Where a local planning authority grant planning permission, the fact that any of the conditions of the permission are required by the provisions of sections 41 or 42 of this Act to be imposed, or are deemed by those provisions to be imposed, shall not prevent the conditions being the subject of an appeal under section 36 of this Act against the decision of the authority.

(7) In the case of planning permission (whether outline or other) having conditions attached to it by or under section 41 or 42 of this Act—

(*a*) development carried out after the date by which the conditions of the permission require it to be carried out shall be treated as not authorised by the permission ; and

(b) an application for approval of a reserved matter, if it is made after the date by which the conditions require it to be made, shall be treated as not made in accordance with the terms of the permission.

44.—(1) The following provisions of this section shall have effect where, by virtue of section 41 or 42 of this Act, a planning permission is subject to a condition that the development to which the permission relates must be begun before the expiration of a particular period and that development has been begun within that period but the period has elapsed without the development having been completed.

Termination of planning permission by reference to time limit.

(2) If the local planning authority are of opinion that the development will not be completed within a reasonable period, they may serve a notice (in this section referred to as a " completion notice ") stating that the planning permission will cease to have effect at the expiration of a further period specified in the notice, being a period of not less than twelve months after the notice takes effect.

(3) A completion notice—

(a) shall be served on the owner and on the occupier of the land and on any other person who in the opinion of the local planning authority will be affected by the notice ; and

(b) shall take effect only if and when it is confirmed by the Secretary of State, who may in confirming it substitute some longer period for that specified in the notice as the period at the expiration of which the planning permission is to cease to have effect.

(4) If, within such period as may be specified in a completion notice (not being less than twenty-eight days from the service thereof) any person on whom the notice is served so requires, the Secretary of State, before confirming the notice, shall afford to that person and to the local planning authority an opportunity of appearing before, and being heard by, a person appointed by the Secretary of State for the purpose.

(5) If a completion notice takes effect, the planning permission therein referred to shall at the expiration of the period specified in the notice, whether the original period specified under subsection (2) of this section or a longer period substituted by the Secretary of State under subsection (3) of this section, be invalid except so far as it authorises any development carried out thereunder up to the end of that period.

(6) The local planning authority may withdraw a completion notice at any time before the expiration of the period specified

therein as the period at the expiration of which the planning permission is to cease to have effect ; and if they do so they shall forthwith give notice of the withdrawal to every person who was served with the completion notice.

Revocation or modification of planning permission

45.—(1) If it appears to the local planning authority, having regard to the development plan and to any other material considerations, that it is expedient to revoke or modify any permission to develop land granted on an application made under this Part of this Act, the authority, subject to the following provisions of this section, may by order revoke or modify the permission to such extent as (having regard to those matters) they consider expedient.

(2) Except as provided in section 46 of this Act, an order under this section shall not take effect unless it is confirmed by the Secretary of State ; and the Secretary of State may confirm any such order submitted to him either without modification or subject to such modifications as he considers expedient.

(3) Where a local planning authority submit an order to the Secretary of State for his confirmation under this section, the authority shall serve notice on the owner and on the occupier of the land affected and on any other person who in their opinion will be affected by the order ; and if within such period as may be specified in that notice (not being less than twenty-eight days from the service thereof) any person on whom the notice is served so requires, the Secretary of State, before confirming the order, shall afford to that person and to the local planning authority an opportunity of appearing before, and being heard by, a person appointed by the Secretary of State for the purpose.

(4) The power conferred by this section to revoke or modify permission to develop land may be exercised—

(a) where the permission relates to the carrying out of building or other operations, at any time before those operations have been completed ;

(b) where the permission relates to a change of the use of any land, at any time before the change has taken place :

Provided that the revocation or modification of permission for the carrying out of building or other operations shall not affect so much of those operations as has been previously carried out.

46.—(1) The following provisions shall have effect where the local planning authority have made an order under section 45 of this Act but have not submitted the order to the Secretary of State for confirmation by him, and—

(a) the owner and the occupier of the land and all persons who in the authority's opinion will be affected by the order have notified the authority in writing that they do not object to the order ; and

(b) it appears to the authority that no claim for compensation is likely to arise under section 164 of this Act on account of the order.

(2) The authority shall advertise in the prescribed manner the fact that the order has been made, and the advertisement shall specify—

(a) the period (not being less than twenty-eight days from the date on which the advertisement first appears) within which persons affected by the order may give notice to the Secretary of State that they wish for an opportunity of appearing before, and being heard by, a person appointed by the Secretary of State for the purpose ; and

(b) the period (not being less than fourteen days from the expiration of the period referred to in paragraph (a) of this subsection) at the expiration of which, if no such notice is given to the Secretary of State, the order may take effect by virtue of this section and without being confirmed by the Secretary of State.

(3) The authority shall also serve notice to the same effect on the persons mentioned in subsection (1)(a) of this section, and the notice shall include a statement to the effect that no compensation is payable under section 164 of this Act in respect of an order under section 45 of this Act which takes effect by virtue of this section and without being confirmed by the Secretary of State.

(4) The authority shall send a copy of any advertisement published under subsection (2) of this section to the Secretary of State, not more than three days after the publication.

(5) If within the period referred to in subsection (2)(a) of this section no person claiming to be affected by the order has given notice to the Secretary of State as aforesaid, and the Secretary of State has not directed that the order be submitted to him for confirmation, the order shall, at the expiration of the period referred to in subsection (2)(b) of this section, take effect by virtue of this section and without being confirmed by the Secretary of State as required by section 45(2) of this Act.

(6) This section does not apply to an order revoking or modifying a planning permission granted or deemed to have been granted by the Secretary of State under this Part of this Act or under Part IV or V thereof ; nor does it apply to an order modifying any conditions to which a planning permission is subject by virtue of section 41 or 42 of this Act.

Reference of certain matters to Planning Inquiry
Commission or independent tribunal

Constitution
of Planning
Inquiry
Commission.

47.—(1) The Secretary of State may constitute a Planning Inquiry Commission to inquire into and report on any matter referred to them under section 48 of this Act.

(2) Any such commission shall consist of a chairman and not less than two nor more than four other members appointed by the Secretary of State.

(3) The Secretary of State may pay to the members of any such commission such remuneration and allowances as he may with the consent of the Minister for the Civil Service determine, and may provide for each such commission such officers or servants, and such accommodation, as appears to him expedient to provide for the purpose of assisting the commission in the discharge of their functions.

(4) The validity of any proceedings of any such commission shall not be affected by any vacancy among the members of the commission or by any defect in the appointment of any member.

1957 c. 20.

(5) In Part II of Schedule 1 to the House of Commons Disqualification Act 1957 (commissions, tribunals and other bodies all members of which are disqualified under that Act), in its application to the House of Commons of the Parliament of the United Kingdom, the following entry shall be inserted at the appropriate place in alphabetical order:—

"A Planning Inquiry Commission constituted under Part III of the Town and Country Planning Act 1971 ".

(6) The " Secretary of State ", in relation to any matter affecting both England and Wales, means in subsections (1) and (2) of this section the Secretaries of State for the time being having general responsibility in planning matters in relation to England and in relation to Wales acting jointly, and in subsection (3) of this section one of those Secretaries of State authorised by the other to act on behalf of both of them for the purposes of that subsection.

References to
a Planning
Inquiry
Commission.

48.—(1) The following matters may, in the circumstances mentioned in subsection (2) of this section, be referred to a Planning Inquiry Commission, that is to say—

    (*a*) an application for planning permission which the Secretary of State has under section 35 of this Act

directed to be referred to him instead of being dealt
with by a local planning authority ;

(*b*) an appeal under section 36 of this Act (including that
section as applied by or under any other provision of
this Act) ;

(*c*) a proposal that a government department should give
a direction under section 40 of this Act that planning
permission shall be deemed to be granted for development by a local authority or by statutory undertakers
which is required by any enactment to be authorised
by that department ;

(*d*) a proposal that development should be carried out by
or on behalf of a government department.

(2) Any of the matters mentioned in subsection (1) of this
section may be referred to any such commission under this
section if it appears expedient to the responsible Minister or
Ministers that the question whether the proposed development
should be permitted to be carried out should be the subject of
a special inquiry on either or both of the following grounds—

(*a*) there are considerations of national or regional importance which are relevant to the determination of that
question and require evaluation, but a proper evaluation thereof cannot be made unless there is a special
inquiry for the purpose ;

(*b*) the technical or scientific aspects of the proposed
development are of so unfamiliar a character as to
jeopardise a proper determination of that question
unless there is a special inquiry for the purpose.

(3) Two or more of the matters mentioned in subsection (1)
of this section may be referred to the same commission under
this section if it appears to the responsible Minister or Ministers
that they relate to proposals to carry out development for
similar purposes on different sites.

(4) Where a matter referred to a commission under this
section relates to a proposal to carry out development for any
purpose at a particular site, the responsible Minister or Ministers
may also refer to the commission the question whether development for that purpose should instead be carried out at an
alternative site.

(5) The responsible Minister or Ministers shall, on referring
a matter to a commission under this section, state in the reference the reasons therefor and may draw the attention of the
commission to any points which seem to him or them to be
relevant to their inquiry.

(6) A commission inquiring into a matter referred to them under this section shall—

(a) identify and investigate the considerations relevant to, or the technical or scientific aspects of, that matter which in their opinion are relevant to the question whether the proposed development should be permitted to be carried out and assess the importance to be attached to those considerations or aspects;

(b) thereafter, if the applicant, in the case of a matter mentioned in subsection (1)(a), (b) or (c) of this section, or the local planning authority in any case so desire, afford to each of them, and, in the case of an application or appeal mentioned in the said subsection (1)(a) or (b), to any person who has made representations relating to the subject matter of the application or appeal which the authority are required to take into account under section 29 (2) or (3) of this Act, an opportunity of appearing before and being heard by one or more members of the commission;

(c) report to the responsible Minister or Ministers on the matter referred to them.

(7) Any such commission may, with the approval of the Secretary of State and at his expense, arrange for the carrying out (whether by the commission themselves or by others) of research of any kind appearing to them to be relevant to a matter referred to them for inquiry and report.

In this subsection "the Secretary of State", in relation to any matter affecting both England and Wales, means the Secretary of State for the time being having general responsibility in planning matters in relation to England or the Secretary of State for the time being having such responsibility in relation to Wales acting, by arrangements between the two of them, on behalf of both.

(8) Schedule 10 to this Act shall have effect for the construction of references in this section and in section 49 of this Act to "the responsible Minister or Ministers".

Procedure on
reference to
a Planning
Inquiry
Commission.

49.—(1) A reference to a Planning Inquiry Commission of a proposal that development should be carried out by or on behalf of a government department may be made at any time and a reference of any other matter mentioned in section 48 of this Act may be made at any time before, but not after, the determination of the relevant application referred under section 35 of this Act or the relevant appeal under section 36 of this Act or, as the case may be, the giving of the relevant direction under section 40 of this Act, notwithstanding that an inquiry or other hearing has been held into the proposal by a person appointed by any Minister for the purpose.

(2) Notice of the making of a reference to any such commission shall be published in the prescribed manner, and a copy of the notice shall be served on the local planning authority for the area in which it is proposed that the relevant development shall be carried out, and—

(*a*) in the case of an application for planning permission referred under section 35 of this Act or an appeal under section 36 of this Act, on the applicant and any person who has made representations relating to the subject matter of the application or appeal which the authority are required to take into account under section 29 (2) or (3) of this Act ;

(*b*) in the case of a proposal that a direction should be given under section 40 of this Act with respect to any development, on the local authority or statutory undertakers applying for authorisation to carry out that development.

(3) A Planning Inquiry Commission shall, for the purpose of complying with section 48(6)(*b*) of this Act, hold a local inquiry ; and they may hold such an inquiry, if they think it necessary for the proper discharge of their functions, notwithstanding that neither the applicant nor the local planning authority desire an opportunity of appearing and being heard.

(4) Where a Planning Inquiry Commission are to hold a local inquiry under subsection (3) of this section in connection with a matter referred to them, and it appears to the responsible Minister or Ministers, in the case of some other matter falling to be determined by a Minister of the Crown and required or authorised by an enactment other than this section to be the subject of a local inquiry, that the two matters are so far cognate that they should be considered together, he or, as the case may be, they may direct that the two inquiries be held concurrently or combined as one inquiry.

(5) An inquiry held by such a commission under this section shall be treated for the purposes of the Tribunals and Inquiries Act 1971 as one held by a Minister in pursuance of a duty imposed by a statutory provision. 1971 c. 62.

(6) Subsections (2) to (5) of section 290 of the Local Government Act 1933 (evidence and costs at local inquiries) shall apply in relation to an inquiry held under subsection (3) of this section as they apply in relation to an inquiry caused to be held by a department under subsection (1) of that section, with the substitution for references to a department (other than the first reference in subsection (4)) of references to the responsible Minister or Ministers. 1933 c. 51.

PART III

(7) Subject to the provisions of this section and to any directions given to them by the responsible Minister or Ministers, a Planning Inquiry Commission shall have power to regulate their own procedure.

Appeal to
independent
tribunal.

50.—(1) Provision may be made by a development order for securing that, in the case of decisions of a local planning authority of such classes as may be prescribed by the order, being decisions relating to the design or external appearance of buildings or other similar matters, any appeal under section 36 of this Act shall lie to an independent tribunal constituted in accordance with the provisions of that order, instead of being an appeal to the Secretary of State ; and in relation to any such appeal the provisions of that section (except subsections (7) and (8) and, in subsection (5) thereof, the references to sections 27 and 29(3) of this Act) and the provisions of section 37 of this Act shall apply, subject to such adaptations and modifications as may be specified in the order, as they apply in relation to appeals to the Secretary of State under the said section 36.

(2) If any tribunal is constituted in accordance with subsection (1) of this section, the Secretary of State may pay to the chairman and members of the tribunal such remuneration, whether by way of salaries or by way of fees, and such reasonable allowances in respect of expenses properly incurred in the performance of their duties, as the Minister for the Civil Service may determine.

Additional powers of control

Orders
requiring
discontinuance
of use or
alteration or
removal of
buildings or
works.

51.—(1) If it appears to a local planning authority that it is expedient in the interests of the proper planning of their area (including the interests of amenity), regard being had to the development plan and to any other material considerations—

(a) that any use of land should be discontinued, or that any conditions should be imposed on the continuance of a use of land ; or

(b) that any buildings or works should be altered or removed,

the local planning authority may by order require the discontinuance of that use, or impose such conditions as may be specified in the order on the continuance thereof, or require such steps as may be so specified to be taken for the alteration or removal of the buildings or works, as the case may be.

(2) An order under this section may grant planning permission for any development of the land to which the order relates, subject to such conditions as may be specified in the order ; and the provisions of section 45 of this Act shall apply in relation to any planning permission granted by an order under this

section as they apply in relation to planning permission granted by the local planning authority on an application made under this Part of this Act.

(3) The power conferred by subsection (2) of this section shall include power, by an order under this section, to grant planning permission, subject to such conditions as may be specified in the order—

(a) for the retention, on the land to which the order relates, of buildings or works constructed or carried out before the date on which the order was submitted to the Secretary of State ; or

(b) for the continuance of a use of that land instituted before that date ;

and subsection (3) of section 32 of this Act shall apply to planning permission granted by virtue of this subsection as it applies to planning permission granted in accordance with subsection (2) of that section.

(4) An order under this section shall not take effect unless it is confirmed by the Secretary of State, either without modification or subject to such modifications as he considers expedient.

(5) The power of the Secretary of State under this section to confirm an order subject to modifications shall include power—

(a) to modify any provision of the order granting planning permission, as mentioned in subsection (2) or subsection (3) of this section ;

(b) to include in the order any grant of planning permission which might have been included in the order as submitted to the Secretary of State.

(6) Where a local planning authority submit an order to the Secretary of State for his confirmation under this section, that authority shall serve notice on the owner and on the occupier of the land affected, and on any other person who in their opinion will be affected by the order ; and if within the period specified in that behalf in the notice (not being less than twenty-eight days from the service thereof) any person on whom the notice is served so requires, the Secretary of State, before confirming the order, shall afford to that person and to the local planning authority an opportunity of appearing before, and being heard by, a person appointed by the Secretary of State for the purpose.

(7) Where an order under this section has been confirmed by the Secretary of State, the local planning authority shall serve a copy of the order on the owner and occupier of the land to which the order relates.

(8) Where the requirements of an order under this section will involve the displacement of persons residing in any premises, it shall be the duty of the local planning authority, in so far as there is no other residential accommodation suitable to the reasonable requirements of those persons available on reasonable terms, to secure the provision of such accommodation in advance of the displacement.

(9) In the case of planning permission granted by an order under this section, the authority referred to in sections 41(1)(*b*) and 42(4) of this Act is the local planning authority making the order or, where the Secretary of State in confirming the order exercises his powers under subsection (5) of this section, the Secretary of State.

Agreements
regulating
development
or use of land.

52.—(1) A local planning authority may enter into an agreement with any person interested in land in their area for the purpose of restricting or regulating the development or use of the land, either permanently or during such period as may be prescribed by the agreement; and any such agreement may contain such incidental and consequential provisions (including provisions of a financial character) as appear to the local planning authority to be necessary or expedient for the purposes of the agreement.

(2) An agreement made under this section with any person interested in land may be enforced by the local planning authority against persons deriving title under that person in respect of that land, as if the local planning authority were possessed of adjacent land and as if the agreement had been expressed to be made for the benefit of such land

(3) Nothing in this section or in any agreement made thereunder shall be construed—

(*a*) as restricting the exercise, in relation to land which is the subject of any such agreement, of any powers exercisable by any Minister or authority under this Act so long as those powers are exercised in accordance with the provisions of the development plan, or in accordance with any directions which may have been given by the Secretary of State as to the provisions to be included in such a plan; or

(*b*) as requiring the exercise of any such powers otherwise than as mentioned in paragraph (*a*) of this subsection.

(4) The power of a local planning authority to make agreements under this section may be exercised also—

(*a*) in relation to land in a county district, by the council of that district;

(b) in relation to land in the area of a joint planning board, by the council of the county or county borough in which the land is situated,

and references in this section to a local planning authority shall be construed accordingly.

Determination whether planning permission required

53.—(1) If any person who proposes to carry out any operations on land, or to make any change in the use of land, wishes to have it determined whether the carrying out of those operations, or the making of that change, would constitute or involve development of the land, and, if so, whether an application for planning permission in respect thereof is required under this Part of this Act, having regard to the provisions of the development order, he may, either as part of an application for planning permission, or without any such application, apply to the local planning authority to determine that question.

Applications to determine whether planning permission required.

(2) The provisions of sections 24, 29(1), 31(1), 34(1) and (3) and 35 to 37 of this Act shall, subject to any necessary modifications, apply in relation to any application under this section, and to the determination thereof, as they apply in relation to applications for planning permission and to the determination of such applications.

PART IV

ADDITIONAL CONTROL IN SPECIAL CASES

Buildings of special architectural or historic interest

54.—(1) For the purposes of this Act and with a view to the guidance of local planning authorities in the performance of their functions under this Act in relation to buildings of special architectural or historic interest, the Secretary of State shall compile lists of such buildings, or approve, with or without modifications, such lists compiled by other persons or bodies of persons, and may amend any list so compiled or approved.

Lists of buildings of special architectural or historic interest.

(2) In considering whether to include a building in a list compiled or approved under this section, the Secretary of State may take into account not only the building itself but also—

(a) any respect in which its exterior contributes to the architectural or historic interest of any group of buildings of which it forms part ; and

(b) the desirability of preserving, on the ground of its architectural or historic interest, any feature of the

C

building consisting of a man-made object or structure fixed to the building or forming part of the land and comprised within the curtilage of the building.

(3) Before compiling or approving, with or without modifications, any list under this section, or amending any list thereunder the Secretary of State shall consult with such persons or bodies of persons as appear to him appropriate as having special knowledge of, or interest in, buildings of architectural or historic interest.

(4) As soon as may be after any list has been compiled or approved under this section, or any amendments of such a list have been made, a copy of so much of the list as relates to any county borough, London borough or county district, or of so much of the amendments as relates thereto, as the case may be, certified by or on behalf of the Secretary of State to be a true copy thereof, shall be deposited with the clerk of the council of that borough or district, and also, where that council is not the local planning authority, with the clerk of the local planning authority.

(5) A copy of anything required by subsection (4) of this section to be deposited with the clerk of a London borough shall be deposited also with the clerk of the Greater London Council.

(6) Any copy deposited under subsection (4) of this section shall be registered in the register of local land charges in such manner as may be prescribed by rules made for the purposes 1925 c. 22. of this section under section 15(6) of the Land Charges Act 1925 by the proper officer of the council of the county borough, London borough or county district.

(7) As soon as may be after the inclusion of any building in a list under this section, whether on the compilation or approval of the list or by the amendment thereof, or as soon as may be after any such list has been amended by the exclusion of any building therefrom, the council of the county borough, London borough or county district in whose area the building is situated, on being informed of the fact by the Secretary of State, shall serve a notice in the prescribed form on every owner and occupier of the building, stating that the building has been included in, or excluded from, the list, as the case may be.

(8) The Secretary of State shall keep available for public inspection, free of charge at reasonable hours and at a convenient place, copies of all lists and amendments of lists compiled, approved or made by him under this section ; and every authority with whose clerk copies of any list or amendments are deposited

under this section shall similarly keep available copies of so much of any such list or amendment as relates to buildings within their area.

(9) In this Act " listed building " means a building which is for the time being included in a list compiled or approved by the Secretary of State under this section ; and, for the purposes of the provisions of this Act relating to listed buildings and building preservation notices, any object or structure fixed to a building, or forming part of the land and comprised within the curtilage of a building, shall be treated as part of the building.

(10) Every building which immediately before 1st January 1969 was subject to a building preservation order under Part III of the Act of 1962 but was not then included in a list compiled or approved under section 32 of that Act, shall be deemed to be a listed building ; but the Secretary of State may at any time direct, in the case of any building, that this subsection shall no longer apply to it and the council of the county borough, London borough or county district in whose area the building is situated, on being notified of the Secretary of State's direction, shall give notice of it to the owner and occupier of the building.

(11) Before giving a direction under subsection (10) of this section in relation to a building, the Secretary of State shall consult with the local planning authority and with the owner and the occupier of the building.

55.—(1) Subject to this Part of this Act, if a person executes or causes to be executed any works for the demolition of a listed building or for its alteration or extension in any manner which would affect its character as a building of special architectural or historic interest, and the works are not authorised under this Part of this Act, he shall be guilty of an offence.

Control of works for demolition, alteration or extension of listed buildings.

(2) Works for the demolition of a listed building, or for its alteration or extension, are authorised under this Part of this Act only if—

    (*a*) the local planning authority or the Secretary of State have granted written consent (in this Act referred to as " listed building consent ") for the execution of the works and the works are executed in accordance with the terms of the consent and of any conditions attached to the consent under section 56 of this Act ; and

    (*b*) in the case of demolition, notice of the proposal to execute the works has been given to the Royal Commission and thereafter either—

        (i) for a period of at least one month following the grant of listed building consent, and before the commencement of the works, reasonable access to the building has been made available to members or officers of the Commission for the purpose of recording it ; or

(ii) the Commission have, by their Secretary or other officer of theirs with authority to act on the Commission's behalf for the purposes of this section, stated in writing that they have completed their recording of the building or that they do not wish to record it.

(3) In subsection (2) of this section " the Royal Commission " means, in relation to England, the Royal Commission on Historical Monuments (England) and, in relation to Wales, the Royal Commission on Ancient and Historical Monuments (Wales and Monmouthshire) ; but the Secretary of State may, in relation to either England or Wales, or both, by order provide that the said subsection shall, in the case of works executed or to be executed òn or after such date as may be specified in the order, have effect with the substitution for the reference to the Royal Commission of a reference to such other body as may be so specified.

(4) Without prejudice to subsection (1) of this section, if a person executing or causing to be executed any works in relation to a listed building under a listed building consent fails to comply with any condition attached to the consent under section 56 of this Act, he shall be guilty of an offence.

(5) A person guilty of an offence under this section shall be liable—

    (a) on summary conviction to imprisonment for a term not exceeding three months or a fine not exceeding £250, or both ; or

    (b) on conviction on indictment to imprisonment for a term not exceeding twelve months or a fine, or both ;

and, in determining the amount of any fine to be imposed on a person convicted on indictment, the court shall in particular have regard to any financial benefit which has accrued or appears likely to accrue to him in consequence of the offence.

(6) In proceedings for an offence under this section it shall be a defence to prove that the works were urgently necessary in the interests of safety or health, or for the preservation of the building, and that notice in writing of the need for the works was given to the local planning authority as soon as reasonably practicable.

Provisions supplementary to s. 55.   **56.**—(1) Section 55 of this Act shall not apply to works for the demolition, alteration or extension of—

    (a) an ecclesiastical building which is for the time being used for ecclesiastical purposes or would be so used but for the works ; or

(b) a building which is the subject of a scheme or order under the enactments for the time being in force with respect to ancient monuments ; or

(c) a building for the time being included in a list of monuments published by the Secretary of State under any such enactment.

For the purposes of this subsection, a building used or available for use by a minister of religion wholly or mainly as a residence from which to perform the duties of his office shall be treated as not being an ecclesiastical building.

(2) Where, on an application in that behalf, planning permission is granted, or has been granted since the end of 1968, and—

(a) the development for which the permission is or was granted includes the carrying out of any works for the alteration or extension of a listed building ; and

(b) the planning permission or any condition subject to which it is or was granted is or was so framed as expressly to authorise the execution of the works (describing them),

the planning permission shall operate as listed building consent in respect of those works but, except as provided by this subsection, the grant of planning permission for any development shall not make it unnecessary for such consent to be obtained in respect of any works to which section 55 of this Act applies.

(3) In considering whether to grant planning permission for development which consists in or includes works for the alteration or extension of a listed building, and in considering whether to grant listed building consent for any works, the local planning authority or the Secretary of State, as the case may be, shall have special regard to the desirability of preserving the building or any features of special architectural or historic interest which it possesses.

(4) Without prejudice to subsection (1) of section 29 of this Act, the conditions which may under that subsection be attached to a grant of planning permission shall, in the case of such development as is referred to in subsection (2) of this section, include conditions with respect to—

(a) the preservation of particular features of the building, either as part of it or after severance therefrom ;

(b) the making good, after the works are completed, of any damage caused to the building by the works ;

(c) the reconstruction of the building or any part of it following the execution of any works, with the use of original materials so far as practicable and with

C 3

PART IV

such alterations of the interior of the building as may be specified in the conditions.

(5) Listed building consent may be granted either unconditionally or subject to conditions, which may include such conditions as are mentioned in subsection (4) of this section.

(6) Part I of Schedule 11 to this Act shall have effect with respect to applications to local planning authorities for listed building consent, the reference of such applications to the Secretary of State and appeals against decisions on such applications ; and Part II of that Schedule shall have effect with respect to the revocation of listed building consent by a local planning authority or the Secretary of State.

Acts causing or likely to result in damage to listed buildings.

57.—(1) Where a building, not being a building excluded by section 56(1) of this Act from the operation of section 55, is included in a list compiled or approved under section 54 of this Act, then, if any person who, but for this section, would be entitled to do so, does or permits the doing of any act which causes or is likely to result in damage to the building (other than an act for the execution of excepted works) and he does or permits it with the intention of causing such damage, he shall be guilty of an offence and liable on summary conviction to a fine not exceeding £100.

(2) In subsection (1) of this section " excepted works " means works authorised by planning permission granted or deemed to be granted in pursuance of an application under this Act and works for which listed building consent has been given under this Act.

(3) Where a person convicted of an offence under this section fails to take such reasonable steps as may be necessary to prevent any damage or further damage resulting from the offence, he shall be guilty of a further offence and liable on summary conviction to a fine not exceeding £20 for each day on which the failure continues.

Building preservation notice in respect of building not listed.

58.—(1) If it appears to the local planning authority, in the case of a building in their area which is not a listed building, that it is of special architectural or historic interest and is in danger of demolition or of alteration in such a way as to affect its character as such, they may (subject to subsection (2) of this section) serve on the owner and occupier of the building a notice (in this section referred to as a " building preservation notice ")—

(a) stating that the building appears to them to be of special architectural or historic interest and that they have requested the Secretary of State to consider including it in a list compiled or approved under section 54 of this Act ; and

(*b*) explaining the effect of subsections (3) and (4) of this
section.

(2) A building preservation notice shall not be served in respect of an excepted building, that is to say—

(*a*) an ecclesiastical building which is for the time being used for ecclesiastical purposes ; or

(*b*) a building which is the subject of a scheme or order under the enactments for the time being in force with respect to ancient monuments ; or

(*c*) a building for the time being included in a list of monuments published by the Secretary of State under any such enactment.

For the purposes of this subsection, a building used or available for use by a minister of religion wholly or mainly as a residence from which to perform the duties of his office shall be treated as not being an ecclesiastical building.

(3) A building preservation notice shall come into force as soon as it has been served on both the owner and occupier of the building to which it relates and shall remain in force for six months from the date when it is served or, as the case may be, last served ; but it shall cease to be in force if, before the expiration of that period, the Secretary of State either includes the building in a list compiled or approved under section 54 of this Act or notifies the local planning authority in writing that he does not intend to do so.

(4) While a building preservation notice is in force with respect to a building, the provisions of this Act (other than section 57) shall have effect in relation to it as if the building were a listed building ; and if the notice ceases to be in force (otherwise than by reason of the building being included in a list compiled or approved under the said section 54) the provisions of Part III of Schedule 11 to this Act shall have effect with respect to things done or occurring under the notice or with reference to the building being treated as listed.

(5) If, following the service of a building preservation notice, the Secretary of State notifies the local planning authority that he does not propose to include the building in a list compiled or approved under section 54 of this Act, the authority—

(*a*) shall forthwith give notice of the Secretary of State's decision to the owner and occupier of the building ; and

(*b*) shall not, within the period of twelve months beginning with the date of the Secretary of State's notification, serve another such notice in respect of the said building.

C 4

Planning
permission
to include
appropriate
provision for
preservation
and planting
of trees.

Trees

59. It shall be the duty of the local planning authority—

    (a) to ensure, whenever it is appropriate, that in granting planning permission for any development adequate provision is made, by the imposition of conditions, for the preservation or planting of trees ; and

    (b) to make such orders under section 60 of this Act as appear to the authority to be necessary in connection with the grant of such permission, whether for giving effect to such conditions or otherwise.

Tree
preservation
orders.

60.—(1) If it appears to a local planning authority that it is expedient in the interests of amenity to make provision for the preservation of trees or woodlands in their area, they may for that purpose make an order (in this Act referred to as a " tree preservation order ") with respect to such trees, groups of trees or woodlands as may be specified in the order ; and, in particular, provision may be made by any such order—

    (a) for prohibiting (subject to any exemptions for which provision may be made by the order) the cutting down, topping, lopping or wilful destruction of trees except with the consent of the local planning authority, and for enabling that authority to give their consent subject to conditions ;

    (b) for securing the replanting, in such manner as may be prescribed by or under the order, of any part of a woodland area which is felled in the course of forestry operations permitted by or under the order ;

    (c) for applying, in relation to any consent under the order, and to applications for such consent, any of the provisions of this Act falling within subsection (2) of this section, subject to such adaptations and modifications as may be specified in the order.

(2) References in this Act to provisions thereof falling within this subsection are references to—

    (a) the provisions of Part III of this Act relating to planning permission and to applications for planning permission, except sections 25, 26, 27, 28, 29(2) to (6), 34(2), 38, 39, 41 to 44 and 47 to 49 of this Act ; and

    (b) such of the provisions of Part IX of this Act as are therein stated to be provisions falling within this subsection ;

    (c) section 270 of this Act.

(3) A tree preservation order may be made so as to apply, in relation to trees to be planted pursuant to any such conditions as are mentioned in section 59(a) of this Act, as from the time when those trees are planted.

(4) Except as provided under subsection (5)(*c*) of this section and in section 61 of this Act, a tree preservation order shall not take effect until it is confirmed by the Secretary of State, and the Secretary of State may confirm any such order either without modification or subject to such modifications as he considers expedient.

(5) Provision may be made by regulations under this Act with respect to the form of tree preservation orders, and the procedure to be followed in connection with the submission and confirmation of such orders ; and the regulations may (without prejudice to the generality of this subsection) make provision as follows—

(*a*) that, before a tree preservation order is submitted to the Secretary of State for confirmation, notice of the making of the order shall be given to the owners and occupiers of land affected by the order and to such other persons, if any, as may be specified in the regulations ;

(*b*) that objections and representations with respect to the order, if duly made in accordance with the regulations, shall be considered before the order is confirmed by the Secretary of State ;

(*c*) that, if no objections or representations are so made, or if any so made are withdrawn, the order, instead of requiring the confirmation of the Secretary of State in accordance with subsection (4) of this section, may be confirmed (but without any modification), as an unopposed order, by the authority who made it ; and

(*d*) that copies of the order, when confirmed by the Secretary of State or the authority, shall be served on such persons as may be specified in the regulations.

(6) Without prejudice to any other exemptions for which provision may be made by a tree preservation order, no such order shall apply to the cutting down, topping or lopping of trees which are dying or dead or have become dangerous, or the cutting down, topping or lopping of any trees in compliance with any obligations imposed by or under an Act of Parliament or so far as may be necessary for the prevention or abatement of a nuisance.

(7) In relation to land in respect of which the Forestry Commissioners have made advances under section 4 of the Forestry Act 1967 or in respect of which there is in force a forestry 1967 c. 10. dedication covenant entered into with the Commissioners under section 5 of that Act, a tree preservation order may be made only if—

(*a*) there is not in force in respect of the land a plan of operations or other working plan approved by the Commissioners under such a covenant ; and (*b*) the Commissioners consent to the making of the order.

(8) Where a tree preservation order is made in respect of land to which subsection (7) of this section applies, the order shall not have effect so as to prohibit, or to require any consent for, the cutting down of a tree in accordance with a plan of operations or other working plan approved by the Forestry Commissioners, and for the time being in force, under such a covenant as is mentioned in that subsection or under a woodlands scheme made under the powers contained in the said Act of 1967.

1967 c. 10.   (9) In the preceding provisions of this section references to provisions of the Forestry Act 1967 include references to the corresponding provisions (replaced by that Act) in the Forestry Acts 1919 to 1951.

(10) The preceding provisions of this section shall have effect subject to the provisions—

1958 c. 69.   (*a*) of section 2(4) of the Opencast Coal Act 1958 (land comprised in an authorisation under that Act which is affected by a tree preservation order) ; and

      (*b*) of section 15 of the Forestry Act 1967 (licences under that Act to fell trees comprised in a tree preservation order).

Provisional tree preservation orders.   **61.**—(1) If it appears to a local planning authority that a tree preservation order proposed to be made by that authority should take effect immediately without previous confirmation, they may include in the order as made by them a direction that this section shall apply to the order.

(2) Notwithstanding section 60(4) of this Act, an order which contains such a direction shall take effect provisionally on such date as may be specified therein and shall continue in force by virtue of this section until—

      (*a*) the expiration of a period of six months beginning with the date on which the order was made ; or

      (*b*) the date on which the order is confirmed or, in the case of an order which can be confirmed only by the Secretary of State, on which he notifies the authority who made the order that he does not propose to confirm it,

whichever first occurs.

(3) Provision shall be made by regulations under this Act for securing—

      (*a*) that the notices to be given of the making of a tree preservation order containing a direction under this section shall include a statement of the effect of the direction ; and

(b) that where the Secretary of State, in the case of an order which can be confirmed only by him, within the period of six months referred to in subsection (2) of this section, notifies the authority that he does not propose to confirm the order, copies of that notice shall be served on the owners and occupiers of the land to which the order related.

62.—(1) If any tree in respect of which a tree preservation order is for the time being in force, other than a tree to which the order applies as part of a woodland, is removed or destroyed in contravention of the order or is removed or destroyed or dies at a time when its cutting down is authorised only by virtue of the provisions of section 60(6) of this Act relating to trees which are dying or dead or have become dangerous, it shall be the duty of the owner of the land, unless on his application the local planning authority dispense with this requirement, to plant another tree of an appropriate size and species at the same place as soon as he reasonably can. Replacement of trees.

(2) In relation to any tree planted pursuant to this section, the relevant tree preservation order shall apply as it applied to the original tree.

(3) The duty imposed by subsection (1) of this section on the owner of any land shall attach to the person who is from time to time the owner of the land and may be enforced as provided by section 103 of this Act and not otherwise.

Advertisements

63.—(1) Subject to the provisions of this section, provision shall be made by regulations under this Act for restricting or regulating the display of advertisements so far as appears to the Secretary of State to be expedient in the interests of amenity or public safety. Control of advertisements.

(2) Without prejudice to the generality of subsection (1) of this section, any such regulations may provide—

(a) for regulating the dimensions, appearance and position of advertisements which may be displayed, the sites on which advertisements may be displayed, and the manner in which they are to be affixed to the land;

(b) for requiring the consent of the local planning authority to be obtained for the display of advertisements, or of advertisements of any class specified in the regulations;

(c) for applying, in relation to any such consent and to applications for such consent, any of the provisions of this Act falling within section 60(2) thereof, subject to such adaptations and modifications as may be specified in the regulations;

(*d*) for the constitution, for the purposes of the regulations, of such advisory committees as may be prescribed by the regulations, and for determining the manner in which the expenses of any such committee are to be defrayed.

(3) Regulations made for the purposes of this section may make different provision with respect to different areas, and in particular may make special provision with respect to areas defined for the purposes of the regulations as areas of special control, being either rural areas or areas other than rural areas which appear to the Secretary of State to require special protection on grounds of amenity; and, without prejudice to the generality of the preceding provisions of this subsection, the regulations may prohibit the display in any such area of all advertisements except advertisements of such classes (if any) as may be specified in the regulations.

(4) Areas of special control for the purposes of regulations under this section may be defined by means of orders made or approved by the Secretary of State in accordance with the provisions of the regulations.

(5) Where the Secretary of State is authorised by the regulations to make or approve any such order as is mentioned in subsection (4) of this section, the regulations shall provide for the publication of notice of the proposed order in such manner as may be prescribed by the regulations, for the consideration of objections duly made thereto, and for the holding of such inquiries or other hearings as may be so prescribed, before the order is made or approved.

(6) Regulations made under this section may be made so as to apply to advertisements which are being displayed on the date on which the regulations come into force, or to the use for the display of the advertisements of any site which was being used for that purpose on that date; but any regulations made in accordance with this subsection shall provide for exempting therefrom—

(*a*) the continued display of any such advertisement; and

(*b*) the continued use for the display of advertisements of any such site,

during such period as may be prescribed in that behalf by the regulations, and different periods may be so prescribed for the purposes of different provisions of the regulations.

(7) Without prejudice to the generality of the powers conferred by the preceding provisions of this section, regulations made for the purposes of this section may provide that any appeal from the decision of the local planning authority, on an application for their consent under the regulations, shall be to an independent tribunal constituted in accordance with the regu-

lations, instead of being an appeal to the Secretary of State; and subsection (2) of section 50 of this Act shall apply to any tribunal so constituted as it applies to any tribunal constituted in accordance with subsection (1) of that section.

64. Where the display of advertisements in accordance with regulations made under section 63 of this Act involves development of land, planning permission for that development shall be deemed to be granted by virtue of this section, and no application shall be necessary in that behalf under Part III of this Act.

Application for planning permission not needed for advertisements complying with regulations.

Waste land

65.—(1) If it appears to a local planning authority that the amenity of any part of their area, or of any adjoining area, is seriously injured by the condition of any garden, vacant site or other open land in their area, then, subject to any directions given by the Secretary of State, the authority may serve on the owner and occupier of the land a notice requiring such steps for abating the injury as may be specified in the notice to be taken within such period as may be so specified.

Proper maintenance of waste land.

(2) Subject to the provisions of Part V of this Act, a notice under this section shall take effect at the end of such period (not being less than twenty-eight days after the service thereof) as may be specified in the notice.

Industrial development

66.—(1) In this Part of this Act " industrial building " means a building used or designed for use—

Meaning of " industrial building "

(a) for the carrying on of any process for or incidental to any of the following purposes, that is to say—

(i) the making of any article or of part of any article ; or

(ii) the altering, repairing, ornamenting, finishing, cleaning, washing, freezing, packing or canning, or adapting for sale, or breaking up or demolition, of any article ; or

(iii) without prejudice to the preceding sub-paragraphs, the getting, dressing or preparation for sale of minerals or the extraction or preparation for sale of oil or brine ;

(b) for the carrying on of scientific research,

being a process or research carried on in the course of a trade or business.

(2) For the purposes of subsection (1) of this section, premises which—

(a) are used or designed for use for providing services or facilities ancillary to the use of other premises for the carrying on of any such process or research as is mentioned in that subsection ; and

(b) are or are to be comprised in the same building or the same curtilage as those other premises,

shall themselves be treated as used or designed for use for the carrying on of such a process or, as the case may be, of such research.

(3) In this section—

"article" means an article of any description, including a ship or vessel ;

"building" includes a part of a building ;

"scientific research" means any activity in the fields of natural or applied science for the extension of knowledge.

Industrial development certificates.
67.—(1) Subject to the provisions of this section and of section 68 of this Act, an application to the local planning authority for permission to develop land by—

(a) the erection thereon of an industrial building of one of the prescribed classes ; or

(b) a change of use whereby premises, not being an industrial building of one of the prescribed classes, will become such an industrial building,

shall be of no effect unless a certificate (in this Act referred to as an "industrial development certificate") is issued under this section by the Secretary of State, certifying that the development in question can be carried out consistently with the proper distribution of industry, and a copy of the certificate is furnished to the local planning authority together with the application.

(2) Subject to subsection (5) of this section, an industrial development certificate shall be required for the purposes of an application for planning permission made as mentioned in section 32(1) of this Act if the circumstances are such that, in accordance with subsection (1) of this section, such a certificate would have been required if the application had been for planning permission to construct the building, or to institute the use of land, which the application seeks permission to retain or continue or (as the case may be) seeks permission to retain or continue without complying with a condition previously imposed, and the provisions of this section shall have effect in relation to that application accordingly.

(3) In considering whether any development for which an industrial development certificate is applied for can be carried out consistently with the proper distribution of industry, the Secretary of State shall have particular regard to the need for providing appropriate employment in development areas.

(4) An industrial development certificate shall not be required for the extension of an industrial building if the extension, taken by itself, would not be an industrial building of one of the prescribed classes, but (subject to the provisions of section 68 of this Act) an industrial development certificate shall be required for the extension of any building if the extension, taken by itself, would be such an industrial building.

(5) An industrial development certificate shall not be required for the purposes of an application for planning permission to retain a building or continue a use of land after the end of any period specified in, or otherwise without complying with, a condition subject to which a previous planning permission was granted if the condition in question is not one subject to which the previous planning permission was granted in accordance with the provisions of section 70 of this Act or subject to which that planning permission is by virtue of that section deemed to have been granted.

(6) The preceding provisions of this section shall have effect without prejudice to any provisions for restricting the granting of planning permission by local planning authorities which are included in a development order by virtue of section 31(1) of this Act.

(7) In this section—

"the prescribed classes" means such classes or descriptions of industrial buildings as may be prescribed by regulations made for the purposes of this section by the Secretary of State ;

"development area" means any area for the time being specified as such under section 15 of the Industrial 1966 c. 34. Development Act 1966, and subsection (6) of that section (which provides for references to a development area in certain provisions to have effect as if certain localities outside that area were included therein) shall apply to any such reference in this section ;

and any reference to an application made as mentioned in section 32(1) of this Act includes a reference to an application which by virtue of section 88(7) or 95(6) of this Act is deemed to have been made for such planning permission as is mentioned in the said section 88(7) or, as the case may be, the said section 95(6).

68.—(1) Notwithstanding anything in section 67 of this Act, Exemption of but subject to section 69 of this Act, an industrial development certain certificate shall not be required if the industrial floor space to classes of be created by the development in question (in this section development. referred to as "the proposed development"), together with any

PART IV   other industrial floor space created or to be created by any
related development, does not exceed 5,000 square feet, excluding, where an industrial development certificate has been issued
in respect of any related development, any floor space created
or to be created by that development or by development carried
out, or for which planning permission has been granted, before
the issue of that certificate.

(2) Regulations made for the purposes of section 67 of this
Act by the Secretary of State may direct that no industrial
development certificate shall be required in respect of the
erection, in any area prescribed by or under the regulations, of
industrial buildings of any such class or description as may be
so prescribed, or in respect of a change of use whereby premises
in any such area, not being an industrial building of a class or
description so prescribed, will become an industrial building
of such a class or description.

(3) In this section " industrial floor space " means floor space
comprised in an industrial building or industrial buildings of any
of the prescribed classes.

(4) For the purposes of subsection (1) of this section development shall, in relation to an application for planning permission
(in this section referred to as " the relevant application "), be
taken to be " related development " if—

(a) it related, or is to relate, to the same building as that
to which the proposed development is to relate (in this
subsection referred to as the " relevant building ");
or

(b) it related, or is to relate, to a building which is, or is
to be, contiguous or adjacent to the relevant building,
and it was, or is to be, development comprised in, or
for the purposes of, the same scheme or project or
for the purposes of the same undertaking as the
proposed development,

and (in either case) it fulfils one or other of the conditions
mentioned in subsection (5) of this section.

(5) The said conditions are—

(a) that it is development for which, before the date of
the relevant application, planning permission has been
granted by a planning decision made on or after 1st
April 1960;

(b) that it is development which has been initiated on or
after 1st April 1960 but before the date of the relevant
application and is not development for which planning
permission has been granted by a planning decision
made on or after 1st April 1960;

(c) that it is development in respect of which an application
to the local planning authority for planning permission
either is pending on the date of the relevant application
or is made on that date.

(6) For the purposes of subsection (5)(c) of this section, an
application is pending on a particular date if—

(a) it is made before that date and not withdrawn ; and

(b) no planning decision on that application has been made
before that date.

(7) In subsection (4) of this section and in this subsection
" building " does not include a part of a building ; and any
reference in subsection (4) of this section to development relating
to a building is a reference to the erection, extension, alteration
or re-erection of the building or a change of use of the whole
or part of the building.

(8) In this section " the prescribed classes " has the same
meaning as in section 67 of this Act.

69.—(1) The Secretary of State may by order direct that
subsection (1) of section 68 of this Act shall be amended by
substituting, for the number of square feet specified in the
subsection as originally enacted or as previously amended under
this subsection, such number of square feet as may be specified
in the order being not less than 1,000 square feet.

*Power to
vary exemption
limit as to
industrial
floor space.*

(2) Any amendment made by an order under this section
may be made so as to have effect either in relation to the whole
of England and Wales or in relation only to a part of England
and Wales specified in the order.

(3) Any amendment made by such an order shall have
effect—

(a) in relation to applications for planning permission relating to land in any area to which the order applies
which are made on or after the date on which the
order comes into operation ; and

(b) in relation to applications relating to land in such an
area which have been made before that date, other than
any application on which a planning decision has been
made before that date.

(4) Where in accordance with subsection (3) of this section
an amendment made by such an order has effect in relation
to an application for planning permission made before the date
on which the order comes into operation, so much of section 67(1)
of this Act as requires a copy of an industrial development
certificate to be furnished to the local planning authority together
with the application shall have effect in relation to that applica-

PART IV

tion with the substitution, for the words "together with the application", of the words "as soon as practicable after the certificate is issued"

(5) In this section any reference to land in any area to which an order under this section applies shall be construed as a reference to land of which any part is in that area.

Restrictions or conditions attached to certificates.

70.—(1) An industrial development certificate in respect of any development may be issued subject to such restrictions on the making of an application for planning permission for that development (whether as to the period within which, or the persons by whom, such an application may be made, or otherwise) as the Secretary of State considers appropriate having regard to the proper distribution of industry ; and where an industrial development certificate in respect of any development is issued subject to any such restrictions, and an application for planning permission for that development is made which does not comply with those restrictions, the provisions of section 67 of this Act shall apply in relation to that application as if no such certificate had been issued.

(2) Without prejudice to subsection (1) of this section, an industrial development certificate may be issued either unconditionally or subject to such conditions as the Secretary of State considers appropriate having regard to the proper distribution of industry ; and any reference in this section to conditions attached to an industrial development certificate is a reference to conditions subject to which such a certificate is issued.

(3) Without prejudice to the generality of subsection (2) of this section, conditions may be attached to an industrial development certificate—

(a) for requiring the removal of any building or the discontinuance of any use of land to which the certificate relates at the end of a specified period and the carrying out of any works required for the reinstatement of land at the end of that period ;

(b) restricting the amount of office floor space (as defined in section 85 of this Act) to be contained in any building to which the certificate relates, or precluding it from containing any office floor space (as so defined) ;

and conditions of the kind mentioned in paragraph (b) of this subsection may be framed so as to apply (either or both) to the building as originally erected or as subsequently extended or altered.

(4) In so far as any of the conditions attached to an industrial development certificate are of such a description that (apart from this section) they could not have been imposed under this Act.

this Act shall apply in relation to any application for planning permission for the purposes of which that certificate is required, and to any planning permission granted on such an application, as if the powers conferred by this Act included power to impose conditions of that description.

(5) Where conditions are attached to an industrial development certificate, and, on an application for planning permission for the purposes of which that certificate is required, planning permission is granted, the authority granting the permission shall grant it subject to those conditions, with or without other conditions.

(6) Planning permission to which subsection (5) of this section applies shall not be invalid by reason only that the requirements of that subsection are not complied with; but where any such planning permission is granted without complying with the requirements of that subsection the planning permission shall be deemed to have been granted subject to the conditions attached to the industrial development certificate, or (if any other conditions were imposed by the authority granting the permission) to have been granted subject to the conditions attached to the certificate in addition to the other conditions.

71.—(1) This section applies to any condition subject to which planning permission is granted in accordance with the provisions of section 70 of this Act, or subject to which planning permission is by virtue of that section deemed to have been granted, whether it is a condition which could have been imposed apart from that section or not.

(2) If the planning permission is or was granted by the local planning authority, the Secretary of State shall not be required to entertain an appeal under section 36 of this Act from the decision of the local planning authority, in so far as that decision relates or related to any condition to which this section applies.

(3) If any condition imposed by an authority granting planning permission is inconsistent with any condition to which this section applies, the last-mentioned condition shall prevail so far as it is inconsistent with the condition so imposed.

(4) Where on an application made as mentioned in section 32(1) of this Act (as modified by section 67 of this Act) planning permission is granted (either unconditionally or subject to conditions) for a building to be retained, or a use of a building to be continued, without complying with a condition to which this section applies (that condition being one subject to which a previous planning permission was granted or is deemed to have

PART IV

been granted), nothing in section 70 of this Act or in the foregoing provisions of this section shall be construed as preventing the subsequent planning permission from operating so as to extinguish or modify that condition, as the case may be.

Provision for cases where certificate withheld.

72.—(1) Where such an application as is mentioned in subsection (1) or (2) of section 67 of this Act is, by virtue of those subsections, of no effect by reason that the requirements of those subsections are not fulfilled, the local planning authority shall consider whether, if those requirements had been fulfilled, they would nevertheless have refused the permission sought by the application, either in respect of the whole or in respect of part of the land to which the application relates ; and if they are of the opinion that they would so have refused that permission, they shall serve on the applicant a notice in writing to that effect.

(2) Where a notice is served under subsection (1) of this section in respect of the whole or part of any land, it shall operate, for the purposes of sections 38 and 39 of this Act, as if the application for planning permission had been an effective application and the notice had been a planning decision of the local planning authority refusing that permission in respect of that land or that part thereof, as the case may be ; and the provisions of those sections (if in those circumstances they would have been applicable) shall have effect accordingly.

Office development

Meaning of " office premises "

73.—(1) Subject to the provisions of this section, in these provisions " office premises " means premises falling within either of the following descriptions, that is to say—

(*a*) premises whose sole or principal use is to be use as an office or for office purposes ;

(*b*) premises to be occupied together with premises falling within the preceding paragraph and to be so occupied wholly or mainly for the purposes of the activities to be carried on in the last-mentioned premises.

(2) Where, in relation to an application for planning permission for the erection of a building, or in relation to a grant of such planning permission, it falls to be determined, for the purposes of subsection (1) of this section, what is to be the sole or principal use of any premises to be contained in the building, regard shall be had—

(*a*) in the case of an application for planning permission, to the proposed use (as indicated in the application) of the building or of different parts of the building ; and

(*b*) in the case of a grant of planning permission, to the
purposes specified in the planning permission as those
for which the building, or different parts of the
building, may be used.

(3) Where, in relation to an application for planning permission for the extension or alteration of a building, or in relation
to a grant of such planning permission, it falls to be determined,
for the purposes of subsection (1) of this section, what is to be
the sole or principal use of any premises which are to be added
to the building or altered within it (in this subsection referred
to as " the new premises "), regard shall be had—

(*a*) in the case of an application for planning permission,
to the proposed use (as indicated in the application) of
the new premises ; and

(*b*) in the case of a grant of planning permission, to the
purposes specified in the planning permission as those
for which the new premises may be used.

(4) For the purposes of the application of these provisions
in relation to development in so far as it consists of a change
in the use of land " office premises " (subject to the following
provisions of this section) means premises falling within either
of the following descriptions, that is to say—

(*a*) premises whose sole or principal use is as an office or
for office purposes ;

(*b*) premises occupied together with premises falling within
the preceding paragraph and so occupied wholly or
mainly for the purposes of the activities carried on in
the last-mentioned premises ;

and for the purposes of paragraph (*a*) of this subsection any
question as to sole or principal use, in relation to premises
contained in a building, shall be determined by reference to those
premises alone and not by reference to the building taken as a
whole.

(5) In this section " office purposes " includes the purposes
of administration, clerical work, handling money, telephone
and telegraph operating and the operation of computers, and
" clerical work " includes writing, book-keeping, sorting
papers, filing, typing, duplicating, punching cards or tapes,
machine calculating, drawing and the editorial preparation of
matter for publication.

(6) The Secretary of State may by order provide that premises
of any description specified in the order, or premises used or
to be used for any purposes so specified, shall not be office
premises for the purposes of these provisions.

(7) In this section, in sections 74 to 86 of this Act and in Schedule 12 to this Act " these provisions " means the provisions of this section, of those sections, of that Schedule and of Schedule 13 to this Act.

Office development permits.

74.—(1) Subject to these provisions, an application to the local planning authority for planning permission to carry out, on land within an area to which these provisions apply, any development to which these provisions apply, that is to say, any development of land which consists of or includes—

(a) the erection of a building containing office premises ; or

(b) the extension or alteration of a building by the addition of, or the conversion of premises into, office premises ; or

(c) a change of use whereby premises which are not office premises become office premises,

shall be of no effect unless a permit (in these provisions referred to as an " office development permit ") in respect of that development is issued under these provisions by the Secretary of State, and a copy of the permit is furnished to the local planning authority together with the application.

(2) An office development permit shall be required for the purposes of an application for planning permission made as mentioned in section 32(1) of this Act if the circumstances are such that, in accordance with subsection (1) of this section, such a permit would have been required if the application had been for planning permission to construct or carry out the building or works, or to institute the use of land, which the application seeks permission to retain or continue or (as the case may be) seeks permission to retain or continue without complying with a condition previously imposed, and subsections (1) and (3) of this section shall have effect in relation to that application accordingly.

(3) In exercising his discretion to issue or withhold office development permits, the Secretary of State shall have particular regard to the need for promoting the better distribution of employment in Great Britain.

(4) The areas to which these provisions apply are—

(a) the metropolitan region ;

(b) any area in Great Britain outside the metropolitan region which is for the time being designated for the purposes of this paragraph by an order made by the Secretary of State:

Provided that the Secretary of State may at any time by order direct that the metropolitan region, or a part of that region specified in the order, shall cease to be, or to be included in, an area to which these provisions apply.

75.—(1) Notwithstanding anything in section 74 of this Act,
an office development permit shall not be required for the
purposes of an application for planning permission to carry
out any development (in this section referred to as " the proposed
development ") if the office floor space to be created by the
proposed development, together with any office floor space
created or to be created by any related development, does not
exceed the prescribed exemption limit.

(2) For the purposes of subsection (1) of this section development shall, in relation to an application for planning permission
(in this section referred to as " the relevant application "), be
taken to be " related development " if—

(a) it related, or is to relate, to the same building as that to
which the proposed development is to relate (in this
subsection referred to as the " relevant building ") ; or

(b) it related, or is to relate, to a building which is, or is to
be, contiguous or adjacent to the relevant building,
and it was, or is to be, development comprised in, or for
the purposes of, the same scheme or project or for
the purposes of the same undertaking as the proposed
development,

and (in either case) it fulfils one or other of the conditions
mentioned in subsection (3) or (4) of this section, as the case
may be, and is not excluded by subsection (5) or (6) of this
section.

(3) The said conditions, in relation to land within the metropolitan region, are—

(a) that it is development for which, before the date of the
relevant application, planning permission has been
granted by a planning decision made on or after 5th
November 1964 (whether before or after the passing
of this Act) ;

(b) that it is development (not falling within the preceding
paragraph) which has (whether before or after the
passing of this Act) been initiated on or after 5th
November 1964 but before the date of the relevant
application and is not development for which planning
permission was granted by a planning decision made
before 5th November 1964 ;

(c) that it is development in respect of which an application
to the local planning authority for planning permission
either is pending on the date of the relevant application
or is made on that date.

PART IV   (4) The said conditions, in relation to land within an area to which these provisions apply outside the metropolitan region, are—

   (a) that it is development for which, before the date of the relevant application, planning permission has been granted by a planning decision made on or after the specified date ;

   (b) that it is development (not falling within the preceding paragraph) which has been initiated on or after the specified date but before the date of the relevant application and is not development for which planning permission was (whether before or after the passing of this Act) granted by a planning decision made before the specified date ;

   (c) that it is development in respect of which an application to the local planning authority for planning permission either is pending on the date of the relevant application or is made on that date,

and in this subsection " the specified date " in relation to an area, means such date (not being earlier than the date on which the order comes into operation) as may be specified in the order designating that area as an area to which these provisions apply.

(5) Where, before the date of the relevant application, an office development permit has been issued in respect of development which, apart from this subsection, would be related development for the purposes of subsection (1) of this section—

   (a) the development in respect of which the permit was issued ; and

   (b) any other development which was carried out before the issue of that permit, or for which planning permission was granted by a planning decision made before the issue of that permit,

shall not be taken to be related development for those purposes.

(6) Development in respect of which there has been issued by the Secretary of State an industrial development certificate with conditions attached to it by virtue of section 70(3)(b) of this Act shall not be taken to be related development for the purposes of subsection (1) of this section.

(7) In this section " the prescribed exemption limit ", subject to subsection (8) of this section, means 3,000 square feet ; any reference to development relating to a building is a reference to development consisting of or including the erection, extension or alteration of the building or a change of use of the whole or part of the building ; and any reference to an application pending on a particular date is a reference to an application

made before that date and not withdrawn, where no planning
decision on that application has been made before that date.

(8) The Secretary of State may by order direct that such
number of square feet (whether greater or less than 3,000 but
not less than 1,000) as may be specified in the order shall be the
prescribed exemption limit for the purposes of this section, either
generally or in relation to any particular area to which these
provisions apply in accordance with section 74(4) of this Act or
in relation to any particular part of such an area.

76.—(1) Subject to subsection (2) of this section and to paragraph 3 of Schedule 12 to this Act, these provisions shall have
effect without prejudice to the operation of sections 67 and 68
of this Act; and, where these provisions and those sections are
applicable to the same application for planning permission, the
requirements of both must be complied with.

Mixed
industrial
and office
development.

(2) Compliance with section 74(1) of this Act shall not be
required in respect of an application for planning permission for
the development of land in any manner specified in section 67(1)
of this Act if—

(a) no office premises will result from the development
except such as are comprised within the curtilage of an
industrial building and are used or designed for use
for providing services or facilities ancillary to the use
of other premises in the same building or curtilage; and

(b) there has been issued by the Secretary of State and
furnished to the local planning authority with the application a copy of an industrial development certificate
with conditions attached to it by virtue of section
70(3)(b) of this Act.

77.—(1) An office development permit in respect of any
development may be issued subject to such restrictions on the
making of an application for planning permission for that
development (whether as to the period within which, or the
persons by whom, such an application may be made, or otherwise) as the Secretary of State considers appropriate in the
exercise of his discretion as mentioned in section 74(3) of this
Act; and, where an office development permit in respect of any
development is issued subject to any such restrictions, and an
application for planning permission for that development is made
which does not comply with those restrictions, these provisions
shall apply in relation to that application as if no such permit
had been issued.

Restrictions or
conditions
attached
to office
development
permits.

(2) Without prejudice to subsection (1) of this section, an office
development permit may be issued either unconditionally or

subject to such conditions as the Secretary of State considers appropriate in the exercise of his discretion as mentioned in section 74(3) of this Act ; and any reference in these provisions to conditions attached to an office development permit is a reference to conditions subject to which such a permit is issued.

(3) In so far as any of the conditions attached to an office development permit are of such a description that (apart from this section) they could not have been imposed under this Act, this Act shall apply in relation to any application for planning permission for the purposes of which that permit is required, and to any planning permission granted on such an application, as if the powers conferred by this Act included power to impose conditions of that description.

(4) Where conditions are attached to an office development permit, and, on an application for planning permission for the purposes of which that permit is required, planning permission is granted, the authority granting the permission shall grant it subject to those conditions, with or without other conditions.

(5) Planning permission to which subsection (4) of this section applies shall not be invalid by reason only that the requirements of that subsection are not complied with ; but where any such planning permission is granted without complying with the requirements of that subsection the planning permission shall be deemed to have been granted subject to the conditions attached to the office development permit, or (if any other conditions were imposed by the authority granting the permission) to have been granted subject to the conditions attached to the permit in addition to the other conditions.

Planning
permission
for erection
of building
where no office
development
permit
required.

78.—(1) The provisions of this section shall, subject to subsection (4) of this section, have effect with respect to any planning permission for the erection of a building on land which is within a controlled area when the planning permission is granted and was also within such an area when the application for planning permission was made.

(2) If the case is the following, that is to say—

(a) either the proposed erection of the building is not development to which these provisions apply or it is such development but no office development permit is required for it ; and

(b) the building will have a floor space of twice or more than twice, the prescribed exemption limit,

the planning permission for the erection of the building shall be granted subject to the condition specified in subsection (3)

of this section (in addition to any other conditions imposed by   PART IV
the authority granting the permission).

(3) The said condition is that the use of the building, whether
as originally erected or as subsequently extended or altered,
shall be restricted so that (whether in consequence of a change
of use or otherwise) it does not at any time contain office
premises having an aggregate office floor space which exceeds
the prescribed exemption limit.

(4) In the following two cases this section shall not apply—

  (*a*) where the planning permission is in respect of a building which is wholly residential ; and

  (*b*) where the planning permission is subject to conditions
by virtue of section 70(5) or (6) of this Act and those
conditions either restrict the office floor space which
the building may contain or preclude it from containing any office floor space.

79.—(1) The provisions of this section shall, subject to sub- Planning
section (4) of this section, have effect with respect to any plan- permission
ning permission for the alteration or extension of a building on for alteration
land which is within a controlled area when the planning of building
permission is granted and was also within such an area when where no office
the application for planning permission was made, but shall development
have effect only in the case of a building erected under a plan- permit
ning permission granted on or after 1st April 1969. required

(2) If the case is the following, that is to say—

  (*a*) either the erection of the building was not development
to which these provisions (or Part I of the Act of
1965) applied, or it was such development but no
office development permit was required for it ; and

  (*b*) either the proposed alteration or extension is not
development to which these provisions apply or it is
such development but no office development permit is
required for it ; and

  (*c*) there will result from the proposed alteration or extension a building with an aggregate floor space of twice,
or more than twice, the prescribed exemption limit,

the planning permission for the alteration or extension shall be
granted subject to the condition specified in subsection (3) of
this section (in addition to any other conditions imposed by the
authority granting the permission).

(3) The said condition is that the use of the building as
altered or extended, or as subsequently further altered or
extended, shall be restricted so that (whether in consequence of

a change of use or otherwise) it does not at any time contain office premises having an aggregate office floor space which exceeds the prescribed exemption limit.

(4) In the following two cases this section shall not apply—

    (*a*) where the planning permission is in respect of a building which, after its alteration or extension, will be wholly residential ; and

    (*b*) where the planning permission is subject to conditions by virtue of section 70(5) or (6) of this Act and those conditions either restrict the office floor space which the building as extended or altered may contain or preclude it from containing any office floor space.

Planning permission for erection of two or more buildings where no office development permit required.

80.—(1) The provisions of this section shall have effect with respect to any planning permission for development involving the erection of two or more buildings on land which is within a controlled area when the planning permission is granted and was also within such an area when the application for planning permission was made, except in a case where all the buildings are exempt from this section.

(2) Any one of the said buildings shall be exempt from this section if—

    (*a*) it is wholly residential ; or

    (*b*) the planning permission is subject to conditions by virtue of section 70(5) or (6) of this Act and those conditions either restrict the office floor space which the building may contain or preclude it from containing any office floor space.

(3) If the aggregate floor space of the buildings proposed to be erected (leaving out of account any which are exempt from this section) is twice, or more than twice, the prescribed exemption limit, and either the erection of the buildings is not development to which these provisions apply or it is such development but no office development permit is required for it, the planning permission shall be granted subject to the condition specified in subsection (4) of this section (in addition to any other conditions imposed by the authority granting the permission).

(4) The said condition is that the use of each one of the buildings (excluding any which are exempt from this section) shall be restricted so that (whether in consequence of a change of use or otherwise) it does not at any time contain office premises having an aggregate floor space which exceeds the limit for that building specified in the condition, which limit shall (subject to subsection (5) of this section) be a floor space

bearing such proportion to the building's total floor space as the prescribed exemption limit bears to the aggregate floor space of all the buildings (excluding any which are exempt from this section) for whose erection the planning permission is granted.

(5) The authority granting the planning permission may in doing so specify in the said condition, as it applies to any building, a limit differing from the one provided by subsection (4) of this section, but not so that the total of the limits for all the buildings to which the condition applies exceeds the prescribed exemption limit.

(6) If after the grant of the planning permission a further application for planning permission is made in respect of all or any of the buildings to which the condition specified in subsection (4) of this section applies, and the further application involves a departure from the terms of the said condition as applying to any building, the application shall be subject to section 74(1) of this Act notwithstanding anything in these provisions exempting development from the requirements of that section in particular cases.

81.—(1) Any planning permission with respect to which Provisions section 78, 79 or 80 of this Act has effect shall not be invalid supple- by reason only that the requirements of section 78(2), 79(2) mentary to or 80(3) of this Act, as the case may be, are not complied with; ss. 78 to 80. but in that case the planning permission shall be deemed to have been granted subject to the condition specified in section 78(3), 79(3) or 80(4) of this Act, as the case may be, or (if any other conditions are imposed by the authority granting the permission) to have been granted subject to the condition so specified in addition to the other conditions, and references in those sections to a condition imposed thereunder shall be construed accordingly as including references to a condition deemed to be imposed.

(2) In sections 78, 79 and 80 of this Act—

" controlled area " means an area to which these provisions apply, or, as respects any time before the commencement of this Act, Part I of the Act of 1965 applied;

" the prescribed exemption limit " means that number of square feet which, at the time when the planning permission in question is granted, is for the purposes of section 75 of this Act the prescribed exemption limit in relation to the land to which the planning permission relates, whether—

(a) by virtue of subsection (7) of that section, or

PART IV

    (*b*) if an order under subsection (8) of that section is for the time being in force and applies to the area, or part of an area, in which that land is situated, by virtue of that order ;

" wholly residential " in relation to a building, means for use exclusively as a dwellinghouse or comprising only units of accommodation for such use.

Provisions as to conditions imposed or implied in pursuance of these provisions.

    82.—(1) This section applies to any condition subject to which planning permission is granted in accordance with these provisions or subject to which planning permission is by virtue of these provisions deemed to have been granted, whether or not it is a condition which could have been imposed apart from these provisions.

    (2) If the planning permission is or was granted by the local planning authority, the Secretary of State shall not be required to entertain an appeal under section 36 of this Act from the decision of the local planning authority, in so far as that decision relates or related to any condition to which this section applies.

    (3) Where planning permission is granted subject to a condition to which this section applies, and it appears to the authority granting the permission that the condition could have been imposed apart from these provisions and would have been imposed if these provisions had not been enacted, the decision granting the permission may include a certificate to that effect ; and, where such a certificate is included in a decision of the local planning authority—

    (*a*) the Secretary of State shall not be required to entertain an appeal from the decision in so far as it includes the certificate ; but

    (*b*) subject to the preceding paragraph, section 36 of this Act shall have effect in relation to the certificate as it has effect in relation to any other part of the decision.

    (4) If any condition imposed by an authority granting planning permission is inconsistent with any condition to which this section applies, the last-mentioned condition shall prevail in so far as it is inconsistent with the condition so imposed.

    (5) Where on an application made as mentioned in section 32(1) of this Act (as modified by section 74(2) of this Act) planning permission is granted (either unconditionally or subject to conditions) for a building to be retained, or a use of a building to be continued, without complying with a condition to which this section applies (that condition being one subject to which a previous planning permission was granted or is deemed to

have been granted), nothing in sections 77 to 81 of this Act or PART IV
in the preceding provisions of this section shall be construed
as preventing the subsequent planning permission from operating
so as to extinguish or modify that condition, as the case may be.

83. Schedule 12 to this Act shall have effect as respects Development in
planning permission granted before 5th August 1965 (the date metropolitan region: planning
of the passing of the Act of 1965) in the cases mentioned in permission granted
that Schedule. before passing of Act of 1965.

84. As soon as may be after the end of March in each year Annual
the Secretary of State shall prepare a report on the performance report.
of his functions under these provisions, and shall lay the report
before Parliament.

85.—(1) In these provisions— Interpretation
   " the Act of 1965 " means the Control of Office and of these
      Industrial Development Act 1965 ; provisions.
   " building " includes any structure ; 1965 c. 33.
   " building contract " means a contract (other than a lease)
      which is made in relation to land whereby a person
      undertakes to erect or extend a building on that land
      in the course of the carrying on by him of a business
      consisting wholly or mainly of the execution of build-
      ing operations, or of building operations and
      engineering operations ;
   " erection ", in relation to a building, includes re-erection ;
   " the metropolitan region ", subject to subsection (2) of
      this section, means Greater London together with the
      areas specified in Schedule 13 to this Act :
   " premises " means a part of a building ;
   " these provisions " has the meaning assigned to it by
      section 73(7) of this Act.

(2) For the purposes of these provisions—
   (a) land shall be taken to be, and at all material times to
      have been, in Greater London if it is in the area
      which constituted Greater London on 1st April 1965 ;
   (b) land shall be taken to be, and at all material times to
      have been, in an area specified by name in Schedule
      13 to this Act if it is in the area bearing that name on
      1st April 1965 as that area was constituted on that
      date.

(3) In these provisions " office floor space " means gross floor
space comprised in office premises ; and for the purposes of
these provisions the amount of any such space shall be

PART IV   ascertained by external measurement of that space, whether the office premises in question are or are to be bounded (wholly or partly) by external walls of a building or not.

(4) In these provisions any reference to the granting of planning permission for the carrying out of any development of land is a reference to the granting of planning permission for that development—

(a) either in respect of that land taken by itself or in respect of that land together with other land ; and

(b) either on an ordinary application or on an outline application (that is to say, an application for planning permission subject to subsequent approval on any matters).

(5) In these provisions any reference to a building containing office premises includes a reference to a building of which every part consists or is to consist of office premises ; and in these provisions any reference to the addition of office premises includes a reference to the addition of office premises together with other premises.

(6) In these provisions any reference to land in Greater London, within the metropolitan region, or within any other area to which these provisions apply or, as respects any time before the commencement of this Act, the Act of 1965 applied, shall be construed as a reference to land of which any part is within the area in question.

(7) In these provisions any reference to an application made as mentioned in section 32(1) of this Act includes a reference to an application which by virtue of section 88(7) or 95(6) of this Act is deemed to have been made for such planning permission as is mentioned in the said section 88(7) or, as the case may be, the said section 95(6).

Temporary operation of these provisions.

86.—(1) Unless Parliament otherwise determines, these provisions (other than this section) shall cease to have effect at the end of the period of seven years beginning with 5th August 1965.

(2) Where immediately before the end of that period any planning permission has effect subject to a condition subject to which the planning permission is by virtue of these provisions deemed to have been granted, the planning permission shall, as from the end of that period, have effect free from that condition.

(3) Where immediately before the end of that period any planning permission has effect subject to a condition imposed by the authority granting the permission in circumstances where

that authority was required by these provisions to impose that condition, then unless the condition is the subject of a certificate under section 82(3) of this Act, the planning permission shall, as from the end of that period, have effect free from that condition.

(4) An enforcement notice to which paragraph 4 of Schedule 12 to this Act applies shall not operate so as to prevent or restrict the doing of anything after the end of that period.

(5) Subject to the preceding provisions of this section, at the end of that period section 38(2) of the Interpretation Act 1889 (effect of repeals) shall apply as if these provisions had, as from the end of that period, been repealed by another Act. 1889 c. 63.

PART V
ENFORCEMENT OF CONTROL UNDER PARTS III AND IV
Development requiring planning permission

87.—(1) Where it appears to the local planning authority that there has been a breach of planning control after the end of 1963, then, subject to any directions given by the Secretary of State and to the following provisions of this section, the authority, if they consider it expedient to do so having regard to the provisions of the development plan and to any other material considerations, may serve a notice under this section (in this Act referred to as an " enforcement notice ") requiring the breach to be remedied. Power to serve enforcement notice.

(2) There is a breach of planning control if development has been carried out, whether before or after the commencement of this Act, without the grant of planning permission required in that behalf in accordance with Part III of the Act of 1962 or Part III of this Act, or if any conditions or limitations subject to which planning permission was granted have not been complied with.

(3) Where an enforcement notice relates to a breach of planning control consisting in—

    (a) the carrying out without planning permission of building, engineering, mining or other operations in, on, over or under land ; or

    (b) the failure to comply with any condition or limitation which relates to the carrying out of such operations and subject to which planning permission was granted for the development of that land ; or

    (c) the making without planning permission of a change of use of any building to use as a single dwelling-house,

it may be served only within the period of four years from the date of the breach.

D

(4) An enforcement notice shall be served on the owner and on the occupier of the land to which it relates and on any other person having an interest in that land, being an interest which in the opinion of the authority is materially affected by the notice.

(5) Where planning permission has effect subject to a condition to which section 82 of this Act applies, and by reason of anything done in a particular part of a building that condition is contravened, any enforcement notice relating to the contravention shall be taken to be served on the owner and on the occupier of the land to which it relates if it is served on the owner and on the occupier of that part of the building, whether it is also served on any other person or not.

(6) An enforcement notice shall specify—

(*a*) the matters alleged to constitute a breach of planning control ;

(*b*) the steps required by the authority to be taken in order to remedy the breach, that is to say steps for the purpose of restoring the land to its condition before the development took place or (according to the particular circumstances of the breach) of securing compliance with the conditions or limitations subject to which planning permission was granted ; and

(*c*) the period for compliance with the notice, that is to say the period (beginning with the date when the notice takes effect) within which those steps are required to be taken.

(7) The steps which may be required by an enforcement notice to be taken include the demolition or alteration of any buildings or works, the discontinuance of any use of land, or the carrying out on land of any building or other operations.

(8) Subject to section 88 of this Act, an enforcement notice shall take effect at the end of such period, not being less than twenty-eight days after the service of the notice, as may be specified in the notice.

(9) The local planning authority may withdraw an enforcement notice (without prejudice to their power to serve another) at any time before it takes effect ; and, if they do so, they shall forthwith give notice of the withdrawal to every person who was served with the notice.

Appeal against enforcement notice.   **88.**—(1) A person on whom an enforcement notice is served, or any other person having an interest in the land may, at any time within the period specified in the notice as the period

at the end of which it is to take effect, appeal to the Secretary of
State against the notice on any of the following grounds—

(a) that planning permission ought to be granted for the
development to which the notice relates or, as the case
may be, that a condition or limitation alleged in the
enforcement notice not to have been complied with
ought to be discharged ;

(b) that the matters alleged in the notice do not constitute
a breach of planning control;

(c) in the case of a notice which, by virtue of section 87(3)
of this Act, may be served only within the period of four
years from the date of the breach of planning control to
which the notice relates, that that period has elapsed
at the date of service;

(d) in the case of a notice not falling within paragraph (c)
of this subsection, that the breach of planning control
alleged by the notice occurred before the beginning of
1964 ;

(e) that the enforcement notice was not served as required
by section 87(4) of this Act;

(f) that the steps required by the notice to be taken exceed
what is necessary to remedy any breach of planning
control;

(g) that the specified period for compliance with the notice
falls short of what should reasonably be allowed.

(2) An appeal under this section shall be made by notice
in writing to the Secretary of State, which shall indicate the
grounds of the appeal and state the facts on which it is based ;
and on any such appeal the Secretary of State shall, if either
the appellant or the local planning authority so desire, afford to
each of them an opportunity of appearing before, and being
heard by, a person appointed by the Secretary of State for the
purpose.

(3) Where an appeal is brought under this section, the
enforcement notice shall be of no effect pending the final
determination or the withdrawal of the appeal.

(4) On an appeal under this section—

(a) the Secretary of State may correct any informality,
defect or error in the enforcement notice if he is satisfied
that the informality, defect or error is not material;

(b) in a case where it would otherwise be a ground for
determining the appeal in favour of the appellant that
a person required by section 87(4) of this Act to be
served with the notice was not served, the Secretary

of State may disregard that fact if neither the appellant nor that person has been substantially prejudiced by the failure to serve him.

(5) On the determination of an appeal under this section, the Secretary of State shall give directions for giving effect to his determination, including, where appropriate, directions for quashing the enforcement notice or for varying the terms of the notice in favour of the appellant; and the Secretary of State may—

(a) grant planning permission for the development to which the enforcement notice relates or, as the case may be, discharge any condition or limitation subject to which planning permission for that development was granted;

(b) determine any purpose for which the land may, in the circumstances obtaining at the time of the determination, be lawfully used having regard to any past use thereof and to any planning permission relating to the land.

(6) In considering whether to grant planning permission under subsection (5) of this section, the Secretary of State shall have regard to the provisions of the development plan, so far as material to the subject-matter of the enforcement notice, and to any other material considerations; and any planning permission granted by him under that subsection may—

(a) include permission to retain or complete any buildings or works on the land, or to do so without complying with some condition attached to a previous planning permission;

(b) be granted subject to such conditions as the Secretary of State thinks fit;

and where under that subsection he discharges a condition or limitation, he may substitute another condition or limitation for it, whether more or less onerous.

(7) Where an appeal against an enforcement notice is brought under this section, the appellant shall be deemed to have made an application for planning permission for the development to which the notice relates and, in relation to any exercise by the Secretary of State of his powers under subsection (5) of this section, the following provisions shall have effect—

(a) any planning permission granted thereunder shall be treated as granted on the said application;

(b) in relation to a grant of planning permission or a determination under that subsection, the Secretary of State's decision shall be final; and

(c) for the purposes of section 34 of this Act, the decision
shall be treated as having been given by the Secretary
of State in dealing with an application for planning
permission made to the local planning authority.

(8) On an appeal under this section against an enforcement
notice relating to anything done in contravention of a condition
to which section 71 or 82 of this Act applies, the Secretary of
State shall not be required to entertain the appeal in so far
as the appellant claims that planning permission free from that
condition ought to be granted.

(9) Schedule 9 to this Act applies to appeals under this
section, including appeals under this section as applied by
regulations under any other provision of this Act.

89.—(1) Subject to the provisions of this section, where an
enforcement notice has been served on the person who, at the
time when the notice was served on him, was the owner of the
land to which it relates, then, if any steps required by the notice
to be taken (other than the discontinuance of a use of land)
have not been taken within the period allowed for compliance
with the notice, that person shall be liable on summary conviction to a fine not exceeding £400 or on conviction on indictment
to a fine.

Penalties for
non-
compliance
with
enforcement
notice.

(2) If a person against whom proceedings are brought under
subsection (1) of this section has, at some time before the end
of the period allowed for compliance with the notice, ceased
to be the owner of the land, he shall, upon information duly
laid by him, and on giving to the prosecution not less than three
clear days' notice of his intention, be entitled to have the
person who then became the owner of the land (in this section
referred to as " the subsequent owner ") brought before the
court in the proceedings.

(3) If, after it has been proved that any steps required by the
enforcement notice have not been taken within the period
allowed for compliance with the notice, the original defendant
proves that the failure to take those steps were attributable, in
whole or in part, to the default of the subsequent owner—

(a) the subsequent owner may be convicted of the offence ;
and

(b) the original defendant, if he further proves that he took
all reasonable steps to secure compliance with the
enforcement notice, shall be acquitted of the offence.

(4) If, after a person has been convicted under the preceding
provisions of this section, he does not as soon as practicable

PART V
do everything in his power to secure compliance with the enforcement notice, he shall be guilty of a further offence and liable—

> (*a*) on summary conviction to a fine not exceeding £50 for each day following his first conviction on which any of the requirements of the enforcement notice (other than the discontinuance of the use of land) remain unfulfilled ; or
>
> (*b*) on conviction on indictment to a fine.

(5) Where, by virtue of an enforcement notice, a use of land is required to be discontinued, or any conditions or limitations are required to be complied with in respect of a use of land or in respect of the carrying out of operations thereon, then if any person uses the land or causes or permits it to be used, or carries out those operations or causes or permits them to be carried out, in contravention of the notice, he shall be guilty of an offence, and shall be liable on summary conviction to a fine not exceeding £400, or on conviction on indictment to a fine ; and if the use is continued after the conviction he shall be guilty of a further offence and liable on summary conviction to a fine not exceeding £50 for each day on which the use is so continued, or on conviction on indictment to a fine.

(6) Any reference in this section to the period allowed for compliance with an enforcement notice is a reference to the period specified in the notice for compliance therewith or such extended period as the local planning authority may allow for compliance with the notice.

Power to stop further development pending proceedings on enforcement notice.
90.—(1) Where in respect of any land the local planning authority have served an enforcement notice, they may at any time before the notice takes effect serve a further notice (in this Act referred to as a " stop notice ") referring to, and having annexed to it a copy of, the enforcement notice and prohibiting any person on whom the stop notice is served from carrying out or continuing any specified operations on the land, being operations either alleged in the enforcement notice to constitute a breach of planning control or so closely associated therewith as to constitute substantially the same operations.

(2) The operations which may be the subject of a stop notice shall include the deposit of refuse or waste materials on land where that is a breach of planning control alleged in the enforcement notice.

(3) A stop notice may be served by the local planning authority on any person who appears to them to have an interest in the land or to be concerned with the carrying out or continuance of any operations thereon.

(4) A stop notice—

(*a*) shall specify the date (not being earlier than three nor later than fourteen days from the day on which the notice is first served on any person) when it is to take effect;

(*b*) in relation to any person served with it, shall have effect as from that date or the third day after the date of service on him, whichever is the later; and

(*c*) shall, without prejudice to subsection (7) of this section, cease to have effect when the enforcement notice takes effect or is withdrawn or quashed.

(5) If while a stop notice has effect in relation to him a person carries out, or causes or permits to be carried out, any operations prohibited by the notice, he shall be guilty of an offence and liable on summary conviction to a fine not exceeding £400, or on conviction on indictment to a fine; and if the offence is continued after conviction he shall be guilty of a further offence and liable on summary conviction to a fine not exceeding £50 for each day on which the offence is continued, or on conviction on indictment to a fine.

(6) A stop notice shall not be invalid by reason that the enforcement notice to which it relates was not served as required by section 87(4) of this Act if it is shown that the local planning authority took all such steps as were reasonably practicable to effect proper service.

(7) The local planning authority may at any time withdraw a stop notice (without prejudice to their power to serve another) by serving notice to that effect on persons who were served with the stop notice; and the stop notice shall cease to have effect as from the date of service of the notice under this subsection.

(8) Where a person (in this subsection called "the contractor") is under contract to another person (in this subsection called "the developer") to carry out any operations on land and—

(*a*) a stop notice takes effect (whether in relation to the developer or the contractor, or both) prohibiting the carrying out or continuance of those operations; and

(*b*) the operations are countermanded, or discontinued by the contractor accordingly,

then, unless and in so far as the contract makes provision explicitly to the contrary of this subsection, the developer shall be under the same liability in contract as if the operations had

PART V

been countermanded or discontinued on instructions given by him in breach of the contract.

This subsection applies only to contracts entered into before the end of 1969.

Execution and cost of works required by enforcement notice.

91.—(1) If, within the period specified in an enforcement notice for compliance therewith, or within such extended period as the local planning authority may allow, any steps required by the notice to be taken (other than the discontinuance of a use of land) have not been taken, the local planning authority may enter the land and take those steps, and may recover from the person who is then the owner of the land any expenses reasonably incurred by them in doing so.

(2) Any expenses incurred by the owner or occupier of any land for the purpose of complying with an enforcement notice served in respect of any breach of planning control (as defined in section 87(2) of this Act) and any sums paid by the owner of any land under subsection (1) of this section in respect of expenses incurred by the local planning authority in taking steps required by such a notice to be taken, shall be deemed to be incurred or paid for the use and at the request of the person by whom the breach of planning control was committed.

(3) Regulations made under this Act may provide that, in relation to any steps required to be taken by an enforcement notice, all or any of the enactments specified in subsection (4) of this section shall apply, subject to such adaptations and modifications as may be specified in the regulations, including, in the case of the enactment specified in paragraph (*b*) of that sub-section, adaptations and modifications for the purpose of affording to the owner of land to which an enforcement notice relates the right, as against all other persons interested in the land, to comply with the requirements of the enforcement notice.

1936 c. 49.

(4) The said enactments are the following provisions of the Public Health Act 1936, that is to say—

(*a*) section 276 (power of local authorities to sell materials removed in executing works under that Act subject to accounting for the proceeds of sale) ;

(*b*) section 289 (power to require the occupier of any premises to permit works to be executed by the owner of the premises) ;

(*c*) section 292 (power of local authorities to include a sum in respect of establishment charges in their expenses in executing works) ; and

(*d*) section 294 (limit on liability of persons holding premises as agents or trustees in respect of the expenses recoverable under that Act).

(5) Any regulations made in accordance with subsection (3) of this section may provide for the charging on the land of any expenses recoverable by a local authority under subsection (1) of this section.

92.—(1) If, after the service of an enforcement notice, plan- Effect of ning permission is granted for the retention on land of buildings planning or works, or for the continuance of a use of land, to which the permission on enforcement notice relates, the enforcement notice shall cease notice. to have effect in so far as it requires steps to be taken for the demolition or alteration of those buildings or works, or the discontinuance of that use, as the case may be.

(2) If the planning permission granted as mentioned in sub section (1) of this section is granted so as to permit the retention of buildings or works, or the continuance of a use of land, without complying with some condition subject to which a previous planning permission was granted, the enforcement notice shall cease to have effect in so far as it requires steps to be taken for complying with that condition.

(3) The preceding provisions of this section shall be without prejudice to the liability of any person for an offence in respect of a failure to comply with the enforcement notice before the relevant provision of the enforcement notice ceased to have effect.

93.—(1) Compliance with an enforcement notice, whether in Enforcement respect of— notice to have effect

(a) the demolition or alteration of any buildings or works ; against or subsequent

(b) the discontinuance of any use of land, development.

or in respect of any other requirements contained in the enforcement notice, shall not discharge the enforcement notice.

(2) Without prejudice to subsection (1) of this section, any provision of an enforcement notice requiring a use of land to be discontinued shall operate as a requirement that it shall be discontinued permanently, to the extent that it is in contravention of Part III of this Act ; and accordingly the resumption of that use at any time after it has been discontinued in compliance with the enforcement notice shall to that extent be in contravention of the enforcement notice.

(3) Without prejudice to subsection (1) of this section, if any development is carried out on land by way of reinstating or restoring buildings or works which have been demolished or altered in compliance with an enforcement notice, the notice shall, notwithstanding that its terms are not apt for the purpose, be deemed to apply in relation to the buildings or works as

reinstated or restored as it applied in relation to the buildings or works before they were demolished or altered ; and, subject to subsection (4) of this section, the provisions of section 91(1) and (2) of this Act, shall apply accordingly.

(4) Where, at any time after an enforcement notice takes effect—

    (a) any development is carried out on land by way of reinstating or restoring buildings or works which have been demolished or altered in compliance with the notice ; and

    (b) the local planning authority propose, under section 91(1) of this Act, to take any steps required by the enforcement notice for the demolition or alteration of the buildings or works in consequence of the re-instatement or restoration,

the local planning authority shall, not less than twenty-eight days before taking any such steps, serve on the owner and occupier of the land a notice of their intention to do so.

(5) A person who, without the grant of planning permission in that behalf, carries out any development on land by way of reinstating or restoring buildings or works which have been demolished or altered in compliance with an enforcement notice shall be guilty of an offence, and shall be liable on summary conviction to a fine not exceeding £400 ; and no person shall be liable under any of the provisions of section 89(1) to (4) of this Act for failure to take any steps required to be taken by an enforcement notice by way of demolition or alteration of what has been so reinstated or restored.

Certification of **94.**—(1) For the purposes of this Part of this Act, a use of
established use. land is established if—

    (a) it was begun before the beginning of 1964 without planning permission in that behalf and has continued since the end of 1963 ; or

    (b) it was begun before the beginning of 1964 under a planning permission in that behalf granted subject to conditions or limitations, which either have never been complied with or have not been complied with since the end of 1963 ; or

    (c) it was begun after the end of 1963 as the result of a change of use not requiring planning permission and there has been, since the end of 1963, no change of use requiring planning permission.

(2) Where a person having an interest in land claims that a particular use of it has become established, he may apply to the local planning authority for a certificate (in this Act referred to as an " established use certificate ") to that effect :

Provided that no such application may be made in respect of the use of land as a single dwellinghouse, or of any use not subsisting at the time of the application.

(3) An established use certificate may be granted (either by the local planning authority or, under section 95 of this Act, by the Secretary of State)—

   (a) either for the whole of the land specified in the application, or for a part of it ;

   (b) in the case of an application specifying two or more uses, either for all those uses or for some one or more of them.

(4) On an application to them under this section, the local planning authority shall, if and so far as they are satisfied that the applicant's claim is made out, grant to him an established use certificate accordingly ; and if and so far as they are not so satisfied, they shall refuse the application.

(5) Where an application is made to a local planning authority for an established use certificate, then unless within such period as may be prescribed by a development order, or within such extended period as may at any time be agreed upon in writing between the applicant and the local planning authority, the authority give notice to the applicant of their decision on the application, then, for the purposes of section 95(2) of this Act, the application shall be deemed to be refused.

(6) Schedule 14 to this Act shall have effect with respect to established use certificates and applications therefor and to appeals under section 95 of this Act.

(7) An established use certificate shall, as respects any matters stated therein, be conclusive for the purposes of an appeal to the Secretary of State against an enforcement notice served in respect of any land to which the certificate relates, but only where the notice is served after the date of the application on which the certificate was granted.

(8) If any person, for the purpose of procuring a particular decision on an application (whether by himself or another) for an established use certificate or on an appeal arising out of such an application—

   (a) knowingly or recklessly makes a statement which is false in a material particular ; or

   (b) with intent to deceive, produces, furnishes, sends or otherwise makes use of any document which is false in a material particular ; or

   (c) with intent to deceive, withholds any material information,

he shall be guilty of an offence and liable on summary conviction to a fine not exceeding £400 or, on conviction on indictment, to

PART V

imprisonment for a term not exceeding two years or a fine, or both.

Grant of
certificate
by Secretary
of State
on referred
application
or appeal
against refusal.

95.—(1) The Secretary of State may give directions requiring applications for established use certificates to be referred to him instead of being dealt with by local planning authorities ; and, on any such application being referred to him in accordance with such directions, section 94(4) of this Act shall apply in relation to the Secretary of State as it applies in relation to the local planning authority in the case of an application determined by them.

(2) Where an application is made to a local planning authority for an established use certificate and is refused, or is refused in part, the applicant may by notice under this subsection appeal to the Secretary of State ; and on any such appeal the Secretary of State shall—

> (*a*) if and so far as he is satisfied that the authority's refusal is not well-founded, grant to the appellant an established use certificate accordingly or, as the case may be, modify the certificate granted by the authority on the application ; and
>
> (*b*) if and so far as he is satisfied that the authority's refusal is well-founded, dismiss the appeal.

(3) On an application referred to him under subsection (1) of this section or on an appeal to him under subsection (2) of this section, the Secretary of State may, in respect of any use of land for which an established use certificate is not granted (either by him or by the local planning authority), grant planning permission for that use or, as the case may be, for the continuance of that use without complying with some condition subject to which a previous planning permission was granted.

(4) Before determining an application or appeal under this section the Secretary of State shall, if either the applicant or appellant (as the case may be) or the local planning authority so desire, afford to each of them an opportunity of appearing before, and being heard by, a person appointed by the Secretary of State for the purpose.

(5) The decision of the Secretary of State on an application referred to him, or on an appeal, under this section shall be final.

(6) In the case of any use of land for which the Secretary of State has power to grant planning permission under this section, the applicant or appellant shall be deemed to have made an application for such planning permission ; and any planning permission so granted shall be treated as granted on the said application.

(7) Schedule 9 to this Act applies to appeals under this section.   PART V

Listed buildings

96.—(1) Where it appears to the local planning authority that any works have been, or are being, executed to a listed building in their area and are such as to involve a contravention of section 55(1) or (4) of this Act, then, subject to any directions given by the Secretary of State, they may, if they consider it expedient to do so having regard to the effect of the works on the character of the building as one of special architectural or historic interest, serve a notice—

    (*a*) specifying the alleged contravention ; and

    (*b*) requiring such steps as may be specified in the notice for restoring that building to its former state or, as the case may be, for bringing it to the state it would have been in if the terms and conditions of any listed building consent for the works had been complied with, to be taken within such period as may be so specified.

Power to serve listed building enforcement notice.

(2) A notice under this section is in this Act referred to as a " listed building enforcement notice ".

(3) A listed building enforcement notice shall be served on the owner and on the occupier of the building to which it relates and on any other person having an interest in the building, being an interest which in the opinion of the authority is materially affected by the notice.

(4) Subject to section 97 of this Act, a listed building enforcement notice shall take effect at the end of such period, not being less than twenty-eight days after the service of the notice, as may be specified in the notice.

(5) The local planning authority may withdraw a listed building enforcement notice (without prejudice to their power to serve another) at any time before it takes effect ; and if they do so, they shall forthwith give notice of the withdrawal to every person who was served with the notice.

97.—(1) A person on whom a listed building enforcement notice is served, or any other person having an interest in the building to which it relates, may, at any time within the period specified in the notice as the period at the end of which it is to take effect, appeal to the Secretary of State against the notice on any of the following grounds—

Appeal against listed building enforcement notice.

    (*a*) that the building is not of special architectural or historic interest ;

(*b*) that the matters alleged to constitute a contravention of section 55 of this Act do not involve such a contravention ;

(*c*) that the works were urgently necessary in the interests of safety or health, or for the preservation of the building ;

(*d*) that listed building consent ought to be granted for the works, or that any relevant condition of such consent which has been granted ought to be discharged, or different conditions substituted ;

(*e*) that the notice was not served as required by section 96(3) of this Act ;

(*f*) that the requirements of the notice exceed what is necessary for restoring the building to its condition before the works were carried out ;

(*g*) that the period specified in the notice as the period within which any steps required thereby are to be taken falls short of what should reasonably be allowed ;

(*h*) that the steps required by the notice to be taken would not serve the purpose of restoring the character of the building to its former state.

(2) An appeal under this section shall be made by notice in writing to the Secretary of State, which shall indicate the grounds of appeal and state the facts on which it is based ; and on any such appeal the Secretary of State shall, if either the appellant or the local planning authority so desire, afford to each of them an opportunity of appearing before, and being heard by, a person appointed by the Secretary of State for the purpose.

(3) Where an appeal is brought under this section the notice shall be of no effect pending the final determination or withdrawal of the appeal.

(4) On an appeal under this section,—

(*a*) the Secretary of State may correct any informality, defect or error in the notice if he is satisfied that the informality, defect or error is not material ;

(*b*) in a case where it would otherwise be a ground for determining the appeal in favour of the appellant that a person required by section 96(3) of this Act to be served with the notice was not served, the Secretary of State may disregard that fact if he is satisfied that the person has not been substantially prejudiced by the failure to serve him.

(5) On the determination of an appeal under this section the Secretary of State shall give directions for giving effect to his determination, including, where appropriate, directions for

quashing the listed building enforcement notice or for varying the terms of the notice in favour of the appellant, and the Secretary of State may—

(*a*) grant listed building consent for the works to which the notice relates or, as the case may be, discharge any condition subject to which such consent was granted and substitute any other condition, whether more or less onerous ;

(*b*) in so far as any works already executed constitute development for which planning permission is required, grant such permission in respect of the works ;

(*c*) if he thinks fit, exercise his power under section 54 of this Act to amend any list compiled or approved thereunder by removing from it the building to which the appeal relates or his power under subsection (10) of that section to direct that that subsection shall no longer apply to the building.

(6) Any planning permission granted by the Secretary of State under subsection (5) of this section shall be treated as granted on an application for the like permission under Part III of this Act, and any listed building consent granted by him thereunder shall be treated as granted on an application for the like consent under Part I of Schedule 11 to this Act ; and—

(*a*) in relation to the grant thereunder either of planning permission or of listed building consent, the Secretary of State's decision shall be final ;

(*b*) for the purposes of section 34 of this Act a decision of the Secretary of State to grant planning permission shall be treated as having been given by him in dealing with an application for planning permission made to the local planning authority.

(7) Schedule 9 to this Act applies to appeals under this section.

98.—(1) Subject to the provisions of this section, where a Penalties for listed building enforcement notice has been served on the person non-who, at the time when the notice was served on him, was the compliance owner of the building to which it relates, then, if any steps with listed required by the notice to be taken have not been taken within building the period allowed for compliance with the notice, that person notice. shall be guilty of an offence and liable on summary conviction to a fine not exceeding £400, or on conviction on indictment to a fine.

(2) If a person against whom proceedings have been brought under subsection (1) of this section has, at some time before the

end of the period allowed for compliance with the notice, ceased to be the owner of the building, he shall, upon information duly laid by him, and on giving to the prosecution not less than three clear days' notice of his intention, be entitled to have the person who then became the owner of the building (in this section referred to as " the subsequent owner ") brought before the court in the proceedings.

(3) If, after it has been proved that any steps required by the notice have not been taken within the period allowed for compliance with the notice, the original defendant proves that the failure to take those steps was attributable, in whole or in part, to the default of the subsequent owner—

> (a) the subsequent owner may be convicted of the offence ; and
>
> (b) the original defendant, if he further proves that he took all reasonable steps to secure compliance with the notice, shall be acquitted of the offence.

(4) If, after a person has been convicted under the preceding provisions of this section, he does not as soon as practicable do everything in his power to secure compliance with the notice, he shall be guilty of a further offence and be liable—

> (a) on summary conviction to a fine not exceeding £50 for each day following his first conviction on which any of the requirements of the notice remain unfulfilled ; or
>
> (b) on conviction on indictment to a fine.

(5) Any reference in this section to the period allowed for compliance with a listed building enforcement notice is a reference to the period specified in the notice as that within which the steps specified in the notice are required thereby to be taken, or such extended period as the local planning authority may allow for taking them.

Execution
and cost of
works
required by
listed building
enforcement
notice.

99.—(1) If, within the period specified in a listed building enforcement notice as that within which the steps specified in the notice are required thereby to be taken, or within such extended period as the local planning authority may allow, any steps required by the notice to be taken have not been taken, the authority may enter the land and take those steps, and may recover from the person who is then the owner of the land any expenses reasonably incurred by them in doing so.

(2) Any expenses incurred by the owner or occupier of a building for the purpose of complying with a listed building enforcement notice, and any sums paid by the owner of a building under subsection (1) of this section in respect of expenses incurred by the local planning authority in taking steps required

by such a notice to be taken, shall be deemed to be incurred or paid for the use and at the request of the person who carried out the works to which the notice relates.

(3) The provisions of section 91(3) and (4) of this Act shall apply in relation to a listed building enforcement notice as they apply in relation to an enforcement notice ; and any regulations made by virtue of this subsection may provide for the charging on the land on which the building stands of any expenses recoverable by a local planning authority under subsection (1) of this section.

100.—(1) If it appears to the Secretary of State, after consultation with the local planning authority (and, in Greater London, also with the Greater London Council), to be expedient that a listed building enforcement notice should be served in respect of any land, he may give directions to the local planning authority requiring them to serve such a notice, or may himself serve such a notice ; and any notice so served by the Secretary of State shall have the like effect as a notice served by the local planning authority.

(2) In relation to a listed building enforcement notice served by the Secretary of State, the provisions of section 99 of this Act shall apply as if for any reference therein to the local planning authority there were substituted a reference to the Secretary of State.

101. If it appears to a local authority that any works are urgently necessary for the preservation of any unoccupied building situated in their area which—

(a) is included in a list compiled or approved under section 54 of this Act ; and

(b) is not an excepted building as defined in section 58(2) of this Act,

they may, after giving to the owner of the building not less than seven days' notice in writing of the proposed execution of the works, take such steps as they consider appropriate for executing the works.

Trees

102.—(1) If any person, in contravention of a tree preservation order, cuts down or wilfully destroys a tree, or tops or lops a tree in such a manner as to be likely to destroy it, he shall be guilty of an offence and liable on summary conviction to a fine not exceeding £250 or twice the sum which appears to the court to be the value of the tree, whichever is the greater.

(2) If any person contravenes the provisions of a tree preservation order otherwise than as mentioned in subsection (1) of this section, he shall be guilty of an offence and liable on summary conviction to a fine not exceeding £50.

(3) If, in the case of a continuing offence under this section, the contravention is continued after the conviction, the offender shall be guilty of a further offence and liable on summary conviction to an additional fine not exceeding £2 for each day on which the contravention is so continued.

Enforcement
of duties
as to
replacement
of trees.

103.—(1) If it appears to the local planning authority that the provisions of section 62 of this Act, or any conditions of a consent given under a tree preservation order which require the replacement of trees, are not complied with in the case of any tree or trees, that authority may, at any time within four years from the date of the alleged failure to comply with the said provisions or conditions, serve on the owner of the land a notice requiring him, within such period as may be specified in the notice, to plant a tree or trees of such size and species as may be so specified.

(2) Subject to the following provisions of this section, a notice under this section shall take effect at the end of such period, not being less than twenty-eight days after the service of the notice, as may be specified in the notice.

(3) A person on whom a notice under this section is served may, at any time within the period specified in the notice as the period at the end of which it is to take effect, appeal to the Secretary of State against the notice on any of the following grounds—

   (a) that the provisions of the said section 62 or the conditions aforesaid are not applicable or have been complied with;

   (b) that the requirements of the notice are unreasonable in respect of the period or the size or species of trees specified therein;

   (c) that the planting of a tree or trees in accordance with the notice is not required in the interests of amenity or would be contrary to the practice of good forestry;

   (d) that the place on which the tree is or trees are required to be planted is unsuitable for that purpose;

and the provisions of section 88(2), (3) and (4)(a) of this Act, and of so much of section 88(5) of this Act as enables the Secretary of State to give directions, shall apply in relation to any such appeal as they apply in relation to an appeal against an enforcement notice.

(4) Schedule 9 to this Act applies to appeals under subsection (3) of this section.

(5) In section 91 of this Act, and in regulations in force under that section, references to an enforcement notice and an enforcement notice served in respect of any breach of planning control shall include references to a notice under this section ; and in relation to such a notice the reference in subsection (2) of that section to the person by whom the breach of planning control was committed shall be construed as a reference to any person, other than the owner, responsible for the cutting down, destruction or removal of the original tree or trees.

Waste land

104.—(1) The provisions of this section shall have effect where a notice has been served under section 65 of this Act, and the period within which the steps required by the notice are to be taken has expired.

(2) If at any time after the end of that period any of those steps have not been taken, and any person does anything which has the effect of continuing or aggravating the injury caused by the condition of the land to which the notice relates, he shall be guilty of an offence and liable on summary conviction to a fine not exceeding £50.

105.—(1) A person on whom a notice under section 65 of this Act is served, or any other person having an interest in the land to which the notice relates, may, at any time within the period specified in the notice as the period at the end of which it is to take effect, appeal against the notice on any of the following grounds—

(*a*) that the condition of the land to which the notice relates does not seriously injure the amenity of any part of the area of the local planning authority who served the notice, or of any adjoining area ;

(*b*) that the condition of the land to which the notice relates is attributable to, and such as results in the ordinary course of events from, the carrying on of operations or a use of land which is not in contravention of Part III of this Act ;

(*c*) that the land to which the notice relates does not constitute a garden, vacant site or other open land in the area of the local planning authority who served the notice ;

(*d*) that the requirements of the notice exceed what is necessary for preventing the condition of the land from seriously injuring the amenity of any part of the area of the local planning authority who served the notice, or of any adjoining area ;

(e) that the period specified in the notice as the period within which any steps required by the notice are to be taken falls short of what should reasonably be allowed.

(2) Any appeal under this section shall be made to a magistrates' court acting for the petty sessions area in which the land in question is situated.

(3) Where an appeal is brought under this section, the notice to which it relates shall be of no effect pending the final determination or withdrawal of the appeal.

(4) On an appeal under this section the magistrates' court may correct any informality, defect or error in the notice if satisfied that the informality, defect or error is not material.

(5) On the determination of an appeal under this section the magistrates' court shall give directions for giving effect to their determination, including, where appropriate, directions for quashing the notice or for varying the terms of the notice in favour of the appellant.

Further
appeal to the
Crown Court

106. Where an appeal has been brought under section 105 of this Act, an appeal against the decision of the magistrates' court thereon may be brought to the Crown Court by the appellant or by the local planning authority.

Execution
and cost
of works
required by
notice as to
waste land.

107.—(1) If, within the period specified in a notice under section 65 of this Act in accordance with subsection (1) of that section, or within such extended period as the local planning authority may allow, any steps required by the notice to be taken have not been taken, the local planning authority may enter the land and take those steps, and may recover from the person who is then the owner of the land any expenses reasonably incurred by them in doing so.

(2) Any expenses incurred by the owner or occupier of any land for the purpose of complying with a notice under section 65 of this Act, and any sums paid by the owner of any land under subsection (1) of this section in respect of expenses incurred by the local planning authority in taking steps required by such a notice to be taken, shall be deemed to be incurred or paid for the use and at the request of the person who caused or permitted the land to come to be in the condition in which it was when the notice was served.

(3) The provisions of section 91(3) and (4) of this Act shall apply in relation to a notice under section 65 of this Act as they apply in relation to an enforcement notice ; and regulations made by virtue of this subsection may provide for the charging on the land of any expenses recoverable by a local authority under subsection (1) of this section.

Other controls

108.—(1) Where, by virtue of an order under section 51 of this Act, the use of land for any purpose is required to be discontinued, or any conditions are imposed on the continuance thereof, then if any person, without the grant of planning permission in that behalf, uses the land for that purpose or, as the case may be, uses the land for that purpose in contravention of those conditions, or causes or permits the land to be so used, he shall be guilty of an offence, and shall be liable on summary conviction to a fine not exceeding £400 or on conviction on indictment to a fine ; and if the use is continued after the conviction, he shall be guilty of a further offence and liable—

Enforcement of orders under s. 51.

(a) on summary conviction to a fine not exceeding £50 for each day on which the use is so continued ; or

(b) on conviction on indictment to a fine.

(2) If, within the period specified in that behalf in an order under section 51 of this Act, any steps required by that order to be taken for the alteration or removal of any buildings or works have not been taken, the local planning authority may, and shall if so required by directions of the Secretary of State, enter the land and take those steps ; and section 276 of the Public Health Act 1936 shall apply in relation to any works executed by a local planning authority under this subsection as it applies in relation to works executed by a local authority under that Act.

1936 c. 49.

109.—(1) The matters for which provision may be made by regulations under section 63 of this Act shall include provision for enabling the local planning authority to require the removal of any advertisement which is being displayed in contravention of the regulations, or the discontinuance of the use for the display of advertisements of any site which is being so used in contravention of the regulations, and for that purpose for applying any of the provisions of this Part of this Act with respect to enforcement notices or the provisions of section 177 of this Act, subject to such adaptations and modifications as may be specified in the regulations.

Enforcement of control as to advertisements.

(2) Without prejudice to any provisions included in regulations made under section 63 of this Act by virtue of subsection (1) of this section, if any person displays an advertisement in contravention of the provisions of the regulations he shall be guilty of an offence and liable on summary conviction to a fine of such amount as may be prescribed by the regulations, not exceeding £100 and, in the case of a continuing offence, £5 for each day during which the offence continues after conviction.

PART V

(3) For the purposes of subsection (2) of this section, and without prejudice to the generality thereof, a person shall be deemed to display an advertisement if—

(a) the advertisement is displayed on land of which he is the owner or occupier ; or

(b) the advertisement gives publicity to his goods, trade, business or other concerns:

Provided that a person shall not be guilty of an offence under that subsection by reason only that an advertisement is displayed on land of which he is the owner or occupier, or that his goods, trade, business or other concerns are given publicity by the advertisement, if he proves that it was displayed without his knowledge or consent.

Supplementary provisions

Supplementary provisions as to appeals to Secretary of State under Part V.
1933 c. 51.

110.—(1) Subsection (5) of section 290 of the Local Government Act 1933 (which authorises a government department holding an inquiry under that section to make orders with respect to the costs of the parties) shall apply in relation to any proceedings before the Secretary of State on an appeal under this Part of this Act as if those proceedings were an inquiry held by the Secretary of State under the said section 290.

(2) Where under this Part of this Act any person has appealed to the Secretary of State or (in accordance with section 105 of this Act) to a magistrates' court against a notice, neither that person nor any other shall be entitled, in any other proceedings instituted after the making of the appeal, to claim that the notice was not duly served on the person who appealed.

Recovery of expenses of local planning authorities under Part V.

111. Where by virtue of any of the preceding provisions of this Part of this Act any expenses are recoverable by a local planning authority, those expenses shall be recoverable as a simple contract debt in any court of competent jurisdiction.

PART VI

ACQUISITION AND APPROPRIATION OF LAND AND RELATED PROVISIONS

Acquisition and appropriation of land

Compulsory acquisition of land in connection with development and for other planning purposes.

112.—(1) The Secretary of State may authorise a local authority to whom this section applies to acquire compulsorily any land within their area if he is satisfied—

(a) that the land is required in order to secure the treatment as a whole, by development, redevelopment or improvement, or partly by one and partly by another method, of the land or of any area in which the land is situated ; or

(*b*) that it is expedient in the public interest that the land
should be held together with land so required; or

(*c*) that the land is required for development or redevelopment, or•both, as a whole for the purpose of providing for the relocation of population or industry or the replacement of open space in the course of the redevelopment or improvement, or both, of another area as a whole; or

(*d*) that it is expedient to acquire the land immediately for a purpose which it is necessary to achieve in the interests of the proper planning of an area in which the land is situated.

(2) Where under subsection (1) of this section the Secretary of State has power to authorise a local authority to whom this section applies to acquire any land compulsorily he may, after the requisite consultation, authorise the land to be so acquired by another authority, being a local authority within the meaning of this Act.

(3) Before giving an authorisation under subsection (2) of this section, the Secretary of State shall—

(*a*) where the land is in a county borough, consult with the council of the borough;

(*b*) where the land is in a county district, consult with the councils of the county and the county district;

(*c*) where the land is in a London borough, consult with the council of the borough and with the Greater London Council.

(4) The Acquisition of Land (Authorisation Procedure) Act 1946 c. 49
1946 shall apply to the compulsory acquisition of land under this section and accordingly shall have effect as if this section had been in force immediately before the commencement of that Act.

(5) The local authorities to whom this section applies are the councils of counties, county boroughs, and county districts, the Greater London Council and the councils of London boroughs.

113.—(1) The Secretary of State for the Environment may Compulsory
acquire compulsorily any land necessary for the public service. acquisition
of land by
(2) The power of acquiring land compulsorily under this Secretary of
section shall include power to acquire an easement or other right State for the
over land by the grant of a new right: Environment.

Provided that this subsection shall not apply to an easement or other right over any land which would for the purposes of the Acquisition of Land (Authorisation Procedure) Act 1946

PART VI   form part of a common, open space or fuel or field garden allotment.

(3) The said Act of 1946 shall apply to any compulsory acquisition by the Secretary of State for the Environment under this section as it applies to a compulsory acquisition by another Minister in a case falling within section 1(1) of that Act.

Compulsory acquisition of listed building in need of repair.

114.—(1) Where it appears to the Secretary of State, in the case of a building to which this section applies, that reasonable steps are not being taken for properly preserving it, the Secretary of State may authorise the council of the county, county borough or county district in which the building is situated or, in the case of a building situated in Greater London, the Greater London Council or the London borough council, to acquire compulsorily under this section the building and any land comprising or contiguous or adjacent to it which appears to the Secretary of State to be required for preserving the building or its amenities, or for affording access to it, or for its proper control or management.

(2) Where it appears to the Secretary of State, in the case of a building to which this section applies, that reasonable steps are not being taken for properly preserving it, he may be authorised under this section to acquire compulsorily the building and any land comprising or contiguous or adjacent to it which appears to him to be required for the purpose mentioned in subsection (1) of this section.

(3) This section applies to any listed building, not being an excepted building as defined in section 58(2) of this Act.

(4) The Secretary of State shall not make or confirm a compulsory purchase order for the acquisition of any building by virtue of this section unless he is satisfied that it is expedient to make provision for the preservation of the building and to authorise its compulsory acquisition for that purpose.

1946 c. 49.   (5) The Acquisition of Land (Authorisation Procedure) Act 1946 shall apply to the compulsory acquisition of land under this section and accordingly shall have effect—

(*a*) as if this section had been in force immediately before the commencement of that Act ; and

(*b*) as if references therein to the enactments specified in section 1(1)(*b*) of that Act included references to the provisions of this section.

(6) Any person having an interest in a building which it is proposed to acquire compulsorily under this section may, within twenty-eight days after the service of the notice required by

paragraph 3(1)(*b*) of Schedule 1 to the said Act of 1946, apply
to a magistrates' court acting for the petty sessions area within
which the building is situated for an order staying further
proceedings on the compulsory purchase order ; and, if the court
is satisfied that reasonable steps have been taken for properly
preserving the building, the court shall make an order
accordingly.

(7) Any person aggrieved by the decision of a magistrates'
court on an application under subsection (6) of this section may
appeal against the decision to the Crown Court.

115.—(1) Neither a council nor the Secretary of State shall Repairs
start the compulsory purchase of a building under section 114 notice as
of this Act unless at least two months previously they have preliminary
served on the owner of the building, and not withdrawn, a acquisition
notice under this section (in this section referred to as a " repairs under s. 114.
notice ")—

> (*a*) specifying the works which they consider reasonably
> necessary for the proper preservation of the building ;
> and
>
> (*b*) explaining the effect of sections 114 to 117 of this Act.

(2) Where a council or the Secretary of State have served a
repairs notice, the demolition of the building thereafter shall not
prevent them from being authorised under section 114 of this
Act to acquire compulsorily the site of the building, if the Secretary of State is satisfied that he would have confirmed or, as
the case may be, would have made a compulsory purchase
order in respect of the building had it not been demolished.

(3) A council or the Secretary of State may at any time withdraw a repairs notice served by them ; and if they do so, they
shall forthwith give notice of the withdrawal to the person who
was served with the notice.

(4) For the purposes of this section a compulsory acquisition
is started when the council or the Secretary of State, as the case
may be, serve the notice required by paragraph 3(1)(*b*) of
Schedule 1 to the Acquisition of Land (Authorisation Procedure) 1946 c. 49.
Act 1946.

116. Subject to section 117 of this Act, for the purpose of Compensation
assessing compensation in respect of any compulsory acquisi- on compulsory
tion of land including a building which, immediately before the acquisition
date of the compulsorily purchase order, was listed, it shall be of listed
assumed that listed building consent would be granted for any building
works for the alteration or extension of the building, or for its
demolition, other than works in respect of which such consent
has been applied for before the date of the order and refused by

the Secretary of State, or granted by him subject to conditions, the circumstances having been such that compensation thereupon became payable under section 171 of this Act.

Minimum
compensation
in case of
listed building
deliberately
left derelict.

117.—(1) A council proposing to acquire a building compulsorily under section 114 of this Act, if they are satisfied that the building has been deliberately allowed to fall into disrepair for the purpose of justifying its demolition and the development or re-development of the site or any adjoining site, may include in the compulsory purchase order as submitted to the Secretary of State for confirmation. an application for a direction for minimum compensation ; and the Secretary of State, if he is so satisfied, may include such a direction in the order as confirmed by him.

(2) Subject to the provisions of this section, where the Secretary of State acquires a building compulsorily under section 114 of this Act, he may, if he is satisfied as mentioned in subsection (1) of this section, include a direction for minimum compensation in the compulsory purchase order.

1946 c. 49.

(3) The notice required to be served in accordance with paragraph 3(1)(*b*) of Schedule 1 to the Acquisition of Land (Authorisation Procedure) Act 1946 (notices stating effect of compulsory purchase order or, as the case may be, draft order) shall, without prejudice to so much of that paragraph as requires the notice to state the effect of the order, include a statement that the authority have made application for a direction for minimum compensation or, as the case may be, that the Secretary of State has included such a direction in the draft order prepared by him in accordance with paragraph 7 of that Schedule and shall in either case explain the meaning of the expression " direction for minimum compensation ".

1961 c. 33.

(4) A direction for minimum compensation, in relation to a building compulsorily acquired, is a direction that for the purpose of assessing compensation it is to be assumed, notwithstanding anything to the contrary in the Land Compensation Act 1961 or this Act, that planning permission would not be granted for any development or re-development of the site of the building and that listed building consent would not be granted for any works for the demolition, alteration or extension of the building other than development or works necessary for restoring it to, and maintaining it in, a proper state of repair ; and if a compulsory purchase order is confirmed or made with the inclusion of such a direction, the compensation in respect of the compulsory acquisition shall be assessed in accordance with the direction.

(5) Where the local authority include in a compulsory purchase order made by them an application for a direction for

minimum compensation, or the Secretary of State includes such
a direction in a draft compulsory purchase order prepared by
him, any person having an interest in the building may, within
twenty-eight days after the service of the notice required by
paragraph 3(1)(*b*) of Schedule 1 to the said Act of 1946, apply
to a magistrates' court acting for the petty sessions area in which
the building is situated for an order that the local authority's
application for a direction for minimum compensation be
refused or, as the case may be, that such a direction be not
included in the compulsory purchase order as made by the
Secretary of State ; and if the court is satisfied that the building
has not been deliberately allowed to fall into disrepair for the
purpose mentioned in subsection (1) of this section, the court
shall make the order applied for.

(6) A person aggrieved by the decision of a magistrates' court
on an application under subsection (5) of this section may appeal
against the decision to the Crown Court.

(7) The rights conferred by subsections (5) and (6) of this
section shall not prejudice those conferred by section 114(6)
and (7) of this Act.

118.—(1) Subject to the provisions of this section, upon the Extinguish-
completion by the acquiring authority of a compulsory acquisi- ment of rights
tion of land under this Part of this Act, all private rights of way over land
and rights of laying down, erecting, continuing or maintaining acquired.
any apparatus on, under or over the land shall be extinguished,
and any such apparatus shall vest in the acquiring authority.

(2) Subsection (1) of this section shall not apply to any right
vested in, or apparatus belonging to, statutory undertakers for
the purpose of the carrying on of their undertaking.

(3) In respect of any right or apparatus not falling within
subsection (2) of this section, subsection (1) of this section shall
have effect subject—

(*a*) to any direction given by the acquiring authority before
the completion of the acquisition that subsection (1) of
this section shall not apply to any right or apparatus
specified in the direction ; and

(*b*) to any agreement which may be made (whether before
or after the completion of the acquisition) between the
acquiring authority and the person in or to whom the
right or apparatus in question is vested or belongs.

(4) Any person who suffers loss by the extinguishment of a
right or the vesting of any apparatus under this section shall
be entitled to compensation from the acquiring authority.

(5) Any compensation payable under this section shall be determined in accordance with the Land Compensation Act 1961.

119.—(1) The council of any county, county borough, London borough or county district may acquire by agreement—

    (*a*) any land which they require for any purpose for which a local authority may be authorised to acquire land under section 112 of this Act;

    (*b*) any building appearing to them to be of special architectural or historic interest; and

    (*c*) any land comprising or contiguous or adjacent to such a building which appears to the Secretary of State to be required for preserving the building or its amenities, or for affording access to it, or for its proper control or management.

(2) The powers conferred by subsection (1) of this section shall not be exerciseable by a council except with the consent of the Secretary of State, unless the land which is to be acquired either—

    (*a*) is immediately required by the council for the purpose for which it is to be acquired; or

    (*b*) if it is not so required, is land within the area of the council.

(3) The provisions of Part I of the Compulsory Purchase Act 1965 (so far as applicable), other than sections 4 to 8, section 10 and section 31, shall apply in relation to the acquisition of land under this section.

(4) The powers conferred by this section on the councils of London boroughs shall be exerciseable also by the Greater London Council—

    (*a*) in a London borough, with the consent of the council of the borough; or

    (*b*) in the Inner Temple or the Middle Temple with the consent of the Sub-Treasurer or, as the case may be, Under-Treasurer thereof; or

    (*c*) in any of the areas aforesaid if the appropriate consent aforesaid is withheld, with the consent of the Secretary of State; or

    (*d*) in relation to land in any of the areas aforesaid, without any such consent as aforesaid, if the land is used for the purposes of an industrial or commercial undertaking and is to be acquired incidentally to the removal of that undertaking from Greater London.

120. Without prejudice to the generality of the powers conferred by the preceding provisions of this Part of this Act, any Acquisition
power of a local authority to acquire land thereunder, whether of land for
compulsorily or by agreement, shall include power to acquire purposes of
land required for giving in exchange— exchange.

    (*a*) for land appropriated under section 121 of this Act;
       or

    (*b*) for Green Belt land, within the meaning of the Green 1938 c. xciii.
       Belt (London and Home Counties) Act 1938, appro-
       priated in accordance with that Act for any purpose
       specified in a development plan.

121.—(1) Any local authority may be authorised, by an order Appropriation
made by that authority and confirmed by the Secretary of State, of land
to appropriate for any purpose for which that authority can be forming
authorised to acquire land under any enactment any land for the part of
time being held by them for other purposes, being land which is common etc.
or forms part of a common, open space or fuel or field garden
allotment (including any such land which is specially regulated
by any enactment, whether public general or local or private),
other than land which is Green Belt land within the meaning of
the Green Belt (London and Home Counties) Act 1938.

(2) Paragraph 11 of Schedule 1 to the Acquisition of Land 1946 c. 49.
(Authorisation Procedure) Act 1946 (special provision with
respect to compulsory purchase orders under that Act relating
to land forming part of a common, open space or fuel or field
garden allotment) shall apply to an order under this section
authorising the appropriation of land as it applies to a compulsory purchase order under that Act.

(3) Section 163 of the Local Government Act 1933 (general 1933 c. 51.
provisions as to the appropriation of land by local authorities)
shall not apply to land which a local authority have power to
appropriate under subsection (1) of this section.

(4) Where land appropriated under this section was acquired
under an enactment incorporating the Lands Clauses Acts, any
works executed on the land after the appropriation has been
effected shall, for the purposes of section 68 of the Lands Clauses 1845 c. 18.
Consolidation Act 1845 and section 10 of the Compulsory Pur- 1965 c. 56.
chase Act 1965 be deemed to have been authorised by the
enactment under which the land was acquired.

(5) On an appropriation of land by a local authority under
this section, where—

    (*a*) the authority is not an authority to whom Part II of the
       Act of 1959 applies; or

    (*b*) the land was immediately before the appropriation held
       by the authority for the purposes of a grant-aided

function within the meaning of the Act of 1959, or is appropriated by the authority for the purposes of such a function,

there shall be made in the accounts of the local authority such adjustments as the Secretary of State may direct.

(6) On an appropriation under this section which does not fall within subsection (5) of this section, there shall be made such adjustment of accounts as is required by section 24(1) of the Act of 1959.

Powers exercisable in relation to land held for planning purposes, and other related powers

Appropriation of land held for planning purposes.

122.—(1) Where any land has been acquired or appropriated by a local authority for planning purposes and is for the time being held by the authority for the purposes for which it was so acquired or appropriated, the authority (subject to the following provisions of this section) may appropriate the land for any purpose for which they are or may be authorised in any capacity to acquire land by virtue of or under any enactment not contained in this Part of this Act.

(2) The consent of the Secretary of State shall be requisite to any appropriation under this section—

(a) by an authority which is not an authority to whom Part II of the Act of 1959 applies ; or

(b) of land which, immediately before the appropriation, is land which consists or forms part of a common, or formerly consisted or formed part of a common, and is held or managed by a local authority in accordance with a local Act,

and any such consent may be given either in respect of a particular appropriation or in respect of appropriations of any class, and may be given either subject to or free from any conditions or limitations.

(3) For the purposes of subsection (2) of section 23 of the Act of 1959 (consent of Ministers to appropriations in certain cases) the power of appropriation conferred by subsection (1) of this section shall (except in respect of any exercise thereof in circumstances falling within subsection (2) of this section) be deemed to be a power in relation to which subsection (1) of that section has effect.

(4) In relation to any appropriation under this section—

1933 c. 51.

(a) subsection (2) of section 163 of the Local Government Act 1933 (which relates to the operation of section 68 of the Lands Clauses Consolidation Act 1845 and section 10 of the Compulsory Purchase Act 1965) ; and

1845 c. 18.
1965 c. 56.

(*b*) subsections (5) and (6) of section 121 of this Act,
shall have effect as they have effect in relation to appropriations
under those sections respectively.

(5) In relation to any such land as is mentioned in subsection
(1) of this section, this section shall have effect to the exclusion
of the provisions of section 163(1) of the Local Government Act 1933 c. 51.
1933.

123.—(1) Where any land has been acquired or appropriated Disposal of
by a local authority for planning purposes, and is for the time land held
being held by the authority for the purposes for which it was for planning
so acquired or appropriated, the authority may dispose of the purposes.
land to such person, in such manner and subject to such conditions as may appear to them to be expedient in order to secure
the best use of that or other land and any buildings or works
which have been, or are to be, erected, constructed or carried
out thereon, whether by themselves or by any other person, or
to secure the erection, construction or carrying out thereon of
any buildings or works appearing to them to be needed for the
proper planning of the area of the authority.

(2) The consent of the Secretary of State shall be requisite to
any disposal under this section—

   (*a*) by an authority which is not an authority to whom
       Part II of the Act of 1959 applies ; or

   (*b*) of land acquired or appropriated for planning purposes
       for a reason mentioned in section 112(1)(*a*) to (*c*) of
       this Act ; or

   (*c*) of land which, immediately before the disposal, is land
       which consists or forms part of a common, or formerly
       consisted or formed part of a common, and is held or
       managed by a local authority in accordance with a
       local Act,

and any such consent may be given either in respect of a particular disposal or in respect of disposals of any class, and
may be given either subject to or free from any conditions or
limitations.

(3) For the purposes of subsections (2) and (3) of section 26
of the Act of 1959 (consent of Ministers to disposals in certain
cases), any disposal of land under this section shall be deemed
to be a disposal which, apart from that section, could not be
effected except with the consent of a Minister ; and for the
purposes of subsection (4) of that section (disposals for a price,
consideration or rent less than the best reasonably obtainable)
the power of disposal conferred by subsection (1) of this section
shall (except in respect of any exercise thereof in circumstances

falling within subsection (2) of this section) be deemed to be a power in relation to which subsection (1) of that section has effect.

(4) Subject to subsection (5) of this section, if it appears to the Secretary of State that it is expedient as mentioned in subsection (1) of this section that a local authority should dispose of land under this section to any person, and the authority have refused to dispose of it to him or are unable to reach agreement with him as to the manner in which, or the terms or conditions on or subject to which, it is to be disposed of to him, the Secretary of State may, after consultation with the authority and that person, require the authority to offer to dispose of it to him, and give directions as to the manner of the disposal and as to all or any of the terms or conditions on or subject to which it is to be offered to him.

(5) A local authority shall not be required by any directions given under subsection (4) of this section (except to such extent as may appear to the Secretary of State to be requisite in any particular case for giving effect to subsection (7) of this section) to offer to dispose of land for a money consideration less than the best that can reasonably be obtained, having regard to the other terms and conditions on and subject to which the offer is to be made ; and any difference as to what is the best consideration shall be referred to and determined by an arbitrator agreed between the Secretary of State and the authority, or, in default of such agreement, shall be referred to and determined by the Lands Tribunal.

(6) In estimating the best consideration for the purposes of subsection (5) of this section, any amount which only a particular purchaser might be prepared to offer by reason of special needs of his shall be disregarded.

(7) In relation to land acquired or appropriated for planning purposes for a reason mentioned in section 112(1)(a) to (c) of this Act the powers conferred by this section on a local authority, and on the Secretary of State in respect of the giving of consent to disposals under this section, shall be so exercised as to secure, so far as may be practicable, to persons who were living or carrying on business or other activities on any such land which the authority have acquired as mentioned in subsection (1) of this section, who desire to obtain accommodation on such land, and who are willing to comply with any requirements of the authority as to the development and use of such land, an opportunity to obtain thereon accommodation suitable to their reasonable requirements, on terms settled with due regard to the price at which any such land has been acquired from them.

In this subsection " development " includes redevelopment.

(8) Subject to the provisions of section 27 of the Act of 1959 (which enables capital money in certain cases to be applied without the consent or approval of a Minister which would otherwise be required), section 166 of the Local Government Act 1933 (which relates to the application of capital money received from the disposal of land) shall have effect in relation to capital money received in respect of transactions under this section as it has effect in relation to capital money received in respect of such transactions as are mentioned in that section.

(9) In relation to any such land as is mentioned in subsection (1) of this section, this section shall have effect to the exclusion of sections 164 and 165 of the Local Government Act 1933.

124.—(1) The functions of a local authority shall include power for the authority, notwithstanding any limitation imposed by law on the capacity of the authority by virtue of its constitution, to erect, construct or carry out any building or work on any land to which this section applies, not being a building or work for the erection, construction or carrying out of which, whether by that local authority or by any other person, statutory power exists by virtue of, or could be conferred under, an alternative enactment.

(2) This section applies to any land which has been acquired or appropriated by a local authority for planning purposes and is for the time being held by the authority for the purposes for which it was so acquired or appropriated.

(3) The consent of the Secretary of State shall be requisite to any exercise by a local authority of the power conferred on them by subsection (1) of this section ; and any such consent may be given either in respect of a particular operation or in respect of operations of any class, and either subject to or free from any conditions or limitations.

(4) Where a local authority propose to carry out any operation which they would have power to carry out by virtue only of subsection (1) of this section, they shall notify the Secretary of State of their proposal, and the Secretary of State may direct such advertisement by the authority as appears to him to be requisite for the purposes of subsection (3) of this section.

(5) The functions of a local authority shall include power for the authority, notwithstanding any such limitation as is mentioned in subsection (1) of this section, to repair, maintain and insure any buildings or works on land to which this section applies, and generally to deal therewith in a proper course of management.

E

PART VI

(6) A local authority may, with the consent of the Secretary of State, enter into arrangements with an authorised association for the carrying out by the association of any operation which, apart from the arrangements, the local authority would have power under this section to carry out, on such terms (including terms as to the making of payments or loans by the authority to the association) as may be specified in the arrangements:

Provided that nothing in this section shall be construed as authorising such an association to carry out any operation which they would not have power to carry out apart from this sub-section.

(7) Nothing in this section shall be construed as authorising any act or omission on the part of a local authority which is actionable at the suit of any person on any grounds other than such a limitation as is mentioned in subsection (1) of this section.

(8) In this section " alternative enactment " means any enactment which is not contained in this Part of this Act, in section 2 or 14 of the Local Employment Act 1960, in section 2, 5 or 6 of the Local Authorities (Land) Act 1963, or in section 20 or 21(4) of the Industrial Development Act 1966; and "authorised association " means any society, company or body of persons approved by the Secretary of State whose objects include the promotion, formation or management of garden cities, garden suburbs or garden villages, and the erection, improvement or management of buildings for the working classes and others, and which does not trade for profit or whose constitution forbids the issue of any share or loan capital with interest or dividend exceeding the rate for the time being fixed by the Treasury.

1960 c. 18.
1963 c. 29.
1966 c. 34.

Special provisions as to features and buildings of architectural and historic interest.

125.—(1) In the exercise of the powers of appropriation, disposal and development conferred by the provisions of sections 122, 123 and 124(1) of this Act, a local authority shall have regard to the desirability of preserving features of special architectural or historic interest, and in particular, listed buildings; and the Secretary of State shall not give his consent to the appropriation or disposal thereunder of any land comprising a listed building, or to the erection, construction or carrying out of any building or work on any such land, unless either—

(a) the consent is given subject to such conditions or limitations as in the opinion of the Secretary of State will secure the preservation of the listed building; or

(b) the Secretary of State, after giving the requisite notice of the application for his consent, is satisfied that the purpose which the local authority seek to achieve by the proposed exercise of their powers is one which ought in the public interest to be carried out, and that the carrying out of that purpose, whether by the use of the land in question or otherwise, either—

(i) would be prevented by the preservation of the listed building ; or

(ii) would be so affected by the preservation thereof that, notwithstanding the desirability of preserving the building, it is inexpedient to do so.

(2) For the purposes of subsection (1)(*b*) of this section the requisite notice of an application for the consent of the Secretary of State is a notice which—

(*a*) contains such particulars of the appropriation, disposal or operation for which his consent is sought as appear to him to be requisite ; and

(*b*) not less than twenty-eight days before he gives his decision on the application, is published in the London Gazette and, in each of two successive weeks, in one or more newspapers circulating in the locality in which the land is situated.

(3) In this section " preservation ", in relation to a building, means the preservation thereof either in its existing state or subject only to such alterations or extensions as can be carried out without serious detriment to its character, and " development " includes redevelopment.

(4) This section is without prejudice to the provisions of section 277(5) of this Act.

126.—(1) Where a local authority acquire any building or other land under section 114(1) or 119(1)(*b*) of this Act, they may make such arrangements as to its management, use or disposal as they consider appropriate for the purpose of its preservation.

(2) Where the Secretary of State acquires any building or other land under section 114(2) of this Act, subsection (3) of section 5 of the Historic Buildings and Ancient Monuments Act 1953 (management, custody and disposal), except so much of it as refers to subsection (4) of that section, shall apply in relation thereto as it applies in relation to property acquired under that section.

Management etc. of listed buildings acquired by local authority or Secretary of State.
1953 c. 49.

127.—(1) The erection, construction or carrying out, or maintenance, of any building or work on land which has been acquired or appropriated by a local authority for planning purposes, whether done by the local authority or by a person deriving title under them, is authorised by virtue of this section if it is done in accordance with planning permission, notwithstanding that it involves interference with an interest or right to

Power to override easements and other rights.

which this section applies, or involves a breach of a restriction as to the user of land arising by virtue of a contract:

Provided that nothing in this subsection shall authorise interference with any right of way or right of laying down, erecting, continuing or maintaining apparatus on, under or over land, being a right vested in or belonging to statutory undertakers for the purpose of the carrying on of their undertaking.

(2) This section applies to the following interests and rights, that is to say, any easement, liberty, privilege, right or advantage annexed to land and adversely affecting other land, including any natural right to support.

(3) In respect of any interference or breach in pursuance of subsection (1) of this section, compensation shall be payable under section 63 or 68 of the Lands Clauses Consolidation Act 1845 or under section 7 or 10 of the Compulsory Purchase Act 1965 to be assessed in the same manner and subject to the same rules as in the case of other compensation under those sections in respect of injurious affection where the compensation is to be estimated in connection with a purchase under those Acts or the injury arises from the execution of works on land acquired under those Acts.

(4) Where a person deriving title under the local authority by whom the land in question was acquired or appropriated is liable to pay compensation by virtue of subsection (3) of this section, and fails to discharge that liability, the liability shall be enforceable against the local authority:

Provided that nothing in this subsection shall be construed as affecting any agreement between the local authority and any other person for indemnifying the local authority against any liability under this subsection.

(5) Nothing in this section shall be construed as authorising any act or omission on the part of any person which is actionable at the suit of any person on any grounds other than such an interference or breach as is mentioned in subsection (1) of this section.

Use and development of consecrated land and burial grounds.   **128.**—(1) Any consecrated land, whether or not including a buildings which has been acquired by a Minister, a local authority or statutory undertakers under this Part of this Act or compulsorily under any other enactment, or which has been appropriated by a local authority for planning purpose, may, subject to the following provisions of this section—

(a) in the case of land acquired by a Minister, be used in any manner by him or on his behalf for any purpose for which he acquired the land ; and

(b) in any other case, be used by any person in any manner in accordance with planning permission, notwithstanding any obligation or restriction imposed under ecclesiastical law or otherwise in respect of consecrated land:

Provided that this subsection does not apply to land which consists or forms part of a burial ground.

(2) Any use of consecrated land authorised by subsection (1) of this section, and the use of any land, not being consecrated land, acquired or appropriated as therein mentioned which at the time of acquisition or appropriation included a church or other building used or formerly used for religious worship or the site thereof, shall be subject to compliance with the prescribed requirements with respect to the removal and reinterment of any human remains, and the disposal of monuments and fixtures and furnishings; and, in the case of consecrated land, shall be subject to such provisions as may be prescribed for prohibiting or restricting the use of the land, either absolutely or until the prescribed consent has been obtained, so long as any church or other building used or formerly used for religious worship, or any part thereof, remains on the land.

(3) Any regulations made for the purposes of subsection (2) of this section—

(a) shall contain such provisions as appear to the Secretary of State to be requisite for securing that any use of land which is subject to compliance with the regulations shall, as nearly as may be, be subject to the like control as is imposed by law in the case of a similar use authorised by an enactment not contained in this Act or by a Measure, or as it would be proper to impose on a disposal of the land in question otherwise than in pursuance of an enactment or Measure;

(b) shall contain requirements relating to the disposal of any such land as is mentioned in subsection (2) of this section such as appear to the Secretary of State requisite for securing that the provisions of that subsection shall be complied with in relation to the use of the land; and

(c) may contain such incidental and consequential provisions (including provision as to the closing of registers) as appear to the Secretary of State to be expedient for the purposes of the regulations.

(4) Any land consisting of a burial ground or part of a burial ground, which has been acquired or appropriated as mentioned in subsection (1) of this section, may—

(a) in the case of land acquired by a Minister, be used in any manner by him or on his behalf for any purpose for which he acquired the land; and

E 3

(*b*) in any other case, be used by any person in any manner in accordance with planning permission,

notwithstanding anything in any enactment relating to burial grounds or any obligation or restriction imposed under ecclesiastical law or otherwise in respect of burial grounds :

Provided that this subsection shall not have effect in respect of any land which has been used for the burial of the dead until the prescribed requirements with respect to the removal and reinterment of human remains, and the disposal of monuments, in or upon the land have been complied with.

(5) Provision shall be made by any regulations made for the purposes of subsection (2) of this section and the proviso to subsection (4) of this section—

(*a*) for requiring the persons in whom the land is vested to publish notice of their intention to carry out the removal and reinterment of any human remains or the disposal of any monuments ;

(*b*) for enabling the personal representatives or relatives of any deceased person themselves to undertake the removal and reinterment of the remains of the deceased, and the disposal of any monument commemorating the deceased, and for requiring the persons in whom the land is vested to defray the expenses of such removal, reinterment and disposal, not exceeding such amount as may be prescribed ;

(*c*) for requiring compliance with such reasonable conditions (if any) as may be imposed, in the case of consecrated land, by the bishop of the diocese, with respect to the manner of removal, and the place and manner of reinterment of any human remains, and the disposal of any monuments, and with any directions given in any case by the Secretary of State with respect to the removal and reinterment of any human remains.

(6) Subject to the provisions of any such regulations, no faculty shall be required for the removal and reinterment in accordance with the regulations of any human remains, or for the removal or disposal of any monuments, and the provisions
1857 c. 81. of section 25 of the Burial Act 1857 (prohibition of removal of human remains without the licence of the Secretary of State except in certain cases) shall not apply to a removal carried out in accordance with the regulations.

(7) Nothing in this section shall be construed as authorising any act or omission on the part of any person which is actionable at the suit of any person on any grounds other than contravention of any such obligation, restriction or enactment as is mentioned in subsection (1) or subsection (4) of this section.

(8) In this section " burial ground " includes any churchyard, PART VI cemetery or other ground, whether consecrated or not, which has at any time been set apart for the purposes of interment, and " monument " includes a tombstone or other memorial.

129.—(1) Any land being, or forming part of, a common, open Use and space or fuel or field garden allotment, which has been acquired development by a Minister, a local authority or statutory undertakers under of land for this Part of this Act or compulsorily under any other enactment, open spaces. or which has been appropriated by a local authority for planning purposes, may—

    (a) in the case of land acquired by a Minister, be used in any manner by him or on his behalf for any purpose for which he acquired the land ; and

    (b) in any other case, be used by any person in any manner in accordance with planning permission,

notwithstanding anything in any enactment relating to land of that kind, or in any enactment by which the land is specially regulated.

(2) Nothing in this section shall be construed as authorising any act or omission on the part of any person which is actionable at the suit of any person on any grounds other than contravention of any such enactment as is mentioned in subsection (1) of this section.

130.—(1) Where any land has been acquired or appropriated Displacement for planning purposes and is for the time being held by a local of persons authority for the purposes for which it was acquired or appro- from land priated, and the carrying out of redevelopment on the land will acquired or involve the displacement of persons residing in premises thereon, appropriated. it shall be the duty of the authority, in so far as there is no other residential accommodation suitable to the reasonable require- ments of those persons available on reasonable terms, to secure the provision of such accommodation in advance of the displace- ments from time to time becoming necessary as the redevelop- ment proceeds.

(2) Section 144 of the Housing Act 1957 (obligations as to 1957 c. 56. the provision of housing accommodation where land is acquired under statutory powers) shall not have effect in relation to an acquisition by a local authority under section 112 of this Act.

(3) If the Secretary of State certifies that possession of a house which has been acquired or appropriated by a local authority for planning purposes, and is for the time being held by the authority for the purposes for which it was acquired or

E 4

appropriated, is immediately required for those purposes, nothing in the Rent Act 1968 shall prevent the acquiring or appropriating authority from obtaining possession of the house.

(4) Where any land has been acquired by a Minister or a local authority under this Part of this Act, or has been appropriated by a local authority for planning purposes, that Minister or the local authority in question, as the case may be—

(a) may pay to any person who is displaced in the carrying out of redevelopment on the land such reasonable allowance as he or they think fit towards his expenses in removing ; and

(b) may pay to a person carrying on any business in a building from which he is so displaced such reasonable allowance as he or they think fit towards the loss which, in his or their opinion, that person will sustain by reason of the disturbance to his business consequent on his having to quit the building.

(5) In estimating loss for the purposes of paragraph (b) of subsection (4) of this section, the Minister or local authority in question shall have regard to the period for which the premises occupied by the person referred to in that paragraph might reasonably have been expected to be available for the purpose of that person's business, and to the availability of other premises suitable for that purpose.

Constitution of joint body to hold land acquired for planning purposes. **131.**—(1) If it appears to the Secretary of State, after consultation with the local authorities concerned, to be expedient that any land acquired by a local authority for planning purposes should be held by a joint body, consisting of representatives of that authority and of any other local authority, he may by order provide for the establishment of such a joint body and for the transfer to that body of the land so acquired.

(2) Any order under this section providing for the establishment of a joint body may make such provision as the Secretary of State considers expedient with respect to the constitution and functions of that body, including provisions—

(a) for incorporating the joint body ;

(b) for conferring on them, in relation to land transferred to them as mentioned in subsection (1) of this section, any of the powers conferred on local authorities by this Part of this Act in relation to land acquired and held by such authorities for the purposes of this Part of this Act ;

(c) for determining the manner in which their expenses are to be defrayed.

(3) Regulations under this Act may make such provision consequential upon or supplementary to the provisions of this section as appears to the Secretary of State to be necessary or expedient.

Supplementary provisions

132.—(1) Where it is proposed that land should be acquired compulsorily under section 112 or 113 of this Act, and a compulsory purchase order relating to that land is submitted to the confirming authority in accordance with Part I of Schedule 1 to the Acquisition of Land (Authorisation Procedure) Act 1946, or, as the case may be, is made in draft by the Secretary of State for the Environment in accordance with Part II of that Schedule, the confirming authority or that Secretary of State, as the case may be, may disregard for the purposes of that Schedule any objection to the order or draft which, in the opinion of that authority or Secretary of State, amounts in substance to an objection to the provisions of the development plan defining the proposed use of that or any other land.

Modification of incorporated enactments for purposes of Part VI.
1946 c. 49.

(2). Where a compulsory purchase order authorising the acquisition of any land under section 112 of this Act is submitted to the Secretary of State in accordance with Part I of Schedule 1 to the said Act of 1946, then if the Secretary of State—

(a) is satisfied that the order ought to be confirmed so far as it relates to part of the land comprised therein ; but

(b) has not for the time being determined whether it ought to be confirmed so far as it relates to any other such land,.

he may confirm the order so far as it relates to the land mentioned in paragraph (a) of this subsection, and give directions postponing consideration of the order, so far as it relates to any other land specified in the directions, until such time as may be so specified.

(3) Where the Secretary of State gives directions under subsection (2) of this section, the notices required by paragraph 6 of Schedule 1 to the said Act of 1946 to be published and served shall include a statement of the effect of the directions.

(4) In cónstruing the Compulsory Purchase Act 1965 in relation to any of the provisions of this Part of this Act—

1965 c. 56.

(a) references to the execution of the works shall be construed as including references to any erection, construction or carrying out of buildings or works authorised by section 127 of this Act ;

PART VI

(b) in relation to the erection, construction or carrying out of any buildings or works so authorised, references in section 10 of the said Act of 1965 to the acquiring authority shall be construed as references to the person by whom the buildings or works in question are erected, constructed or carried out; and

(c) references to the execution of the works shall be construed as including also references to any erection, construction or carrying out of buildings or works on behalf of a Minister or statutory undertakers on land acquired by that Minister or those undertakers, where the buildings or works are erected, constructed or carried out for the purposes for which the land was acquired.

Interpretation of Part VI.

133.—(1) In this Part of this Act any reference to the acquisition of land for planning purposes is a reference to the acquisition thereof under section 112 or 119 of this Act or section 68 or 71 of the Act of 1962 and any reference to the appropriation of land for planning purposes is a reference to the appropriation thereof for purposes for which land can be or could have been acquired under those sections.

(2) In relation to a local authority or body corporate, nothing in sections 127 to 129 of this Act shall be construed as authorising any act or omission on their part in contravention of any limitation imposed by law on their capacity by virtue of the constitution of the authority or body.

(3) Any power conferred by section 128 or 129 of this Act to use land in a manner therein mentioned shall be construed as a power so to use the land, whether it involves the erection, construction or carrying out of any building or work, or the maintenance of any building or work, or not.

PART VII

COMPENSATION FOR PLANNING DECISIONS RESTRICTING NEW DEVELOPMENT

Unexpended balance of established development value

Scope of Part VII.

134.—(1) The provisions of this Part of this Act shall have effect for enabling compensation to be claimed in respect of planning decisions whereby permission for the carrying out of new development of land to which this section applies is refused or is granted subject to conditions.

(2) This section applies to any land in respect of which planning permission is refused or is granted subject to conditions, by a planning decision if, at the time of the planning decision, that land, or part of that land, has an unexpended balance of established development value.

(3) In accordance with the proviso to subsection (2) of section 32 of this Act, that subsection does not apply for the purposes of this Part of this Act.

(4) In this Part of this Act " interest " (where the reference is to an interest in land) means the fee simple or a tenancy of the land, and does not include any other interest therein ; and any reference to the local planning authority, in relation to a planning decision made on behalf of that authority by another authority, by virtue of the delegation of any functions of the local planning authority to that other authority, shall be construed as a reference to that other authority.

135.—(1) In determining, for the purposes of this Part of this Act, whether land has an unexpended balance of established development value, regard shall be had to claims made, in pursuance of Part VI of the Act of 1947, for payments under the scheme provided for by section 58 of that Act (that is to say, the scheme which, but for the provisions·of section 2 of the Town and Country Planning Act 1953, would have fallen to be made under the said section 58, providing for payments in respect of interests in land depreciated in value by virtue of the provisions of the Act of 1947).

Derivation of unexpended balance from claims under Part VI of Act of 1947.
1953 c. 16.

(2) Where such a claim was made in respect of an interest in land, that claim shall for the purposes of this Part of this Act be taken to have been established in respect of that land under Part VI of the Act of 1947 if an amount was determined under the said Part VI as being the development value of the interest to which the claim related, and payment in respect of that interest would not have been excluded—

(a) by section 63 of the Act of 1947 (which excluded claims where the development value was small in proportion to the area, or to the restricted value, of the land) ; or

(b) by any of sections 82 to 85 of that Act (which related to certain land belonging to local authorities, development corporations and statutory undertakers, and to land held on charitable trusts) ; or

(c) by section 84 of that Act as applied by regulations under section 90 of that Act (which related to the National Coal Board).

(3) In this Part of this Act " established claim " means a claim which by virtue of subsection (2) of this section is to be taken to have been established as therein mentioned, and references to the establishment of a claim shall be construed accordingly ; and " the claim area ", in relation to an established claim, means the land in respect of which the claim is by virtue of that subsection to be taken to have been established.

(4) References in this Part of this Act to the benefit of an established claim—

    (a) in relation to any time before the passing of the Town and Country Planning Act 1953, whether before or after the making of the claim, or before or after the establishment thereof, shall be construed as references to the prospective right, under and subject to the provisions of the scheme referred to in subsection (1) of this section, to receive a payment in respect of the interest in land to which the claim related ; and

    (b) in relation to any time after the passing of the said Act of 1953, shall be construed as references to such prospective right to the satisfaction of the claim as subsisted by virtue of section 2 of that Act immediately before 1st January 1955 (being the date of the commencement of the Act of 1954) ;

and references to part of the benefit of an established claim shall be construed accordingly.

(5) References in this Part of this Act to the amount of an established claim are references to the amount determined under Part VI of the Act of 1947 as being the development value of the interest in land to which the claim related.

(6) In this section any reference to Part VI of the Act of 1947 includes a reference to the provisions of the said Part VI as modified by Schedule 1 to the Act of 1954.

136.—(1) In this Part of this Act " original unexpended balance of established development value ", in relation to any land, means the unexpended balance of established development value which that land had immediately after the time when, in accordance with section 138 of this Act, the adjustment of claim holdings is deemed to have been completed.

(2) For the purposes of this Part of this Act land shall be taken to have had such a balance if, immediately after the time referred to in subsection (1) of this section—

    (a) there were subsisting one or more claim holdings whose area consisted of that land, or included that land together with other land ; and

(b) there was not subsisting any claim holding whose area consisted of part only of that land, whether with or without other land.

(3) Where subsection (2) of this section applies, there shall be attributed to the land referred to in that subsection—

(a) the value of any claim holding having an area consisting of that land ; and

(b) such fraction of the value of any claim holding whose area included that land as attached to that land,

and the original unexpended balance of established development value of that land shall be taken to have been an amount equal to eight-sevenths of the amount or aggregate amount so attributed.

137.—(1) Subject to the provisions of this section and of section 138 of this Act, in this Part of this Act—

(a) " claim holding " means the benefit of an established claim, references to the area of a claim holding are references to the land which, in relation to the established claim constituting that holding, is the claim area, and references to the value of a claim holding are references to the amount of the established claim constituting that holding ; and

(b) references to the fraction of the value of a claim holding which attached to a part of the area of the holding are references to so much of the amount of the established claim of which that holding represents the benefit or part of the benefit (in this section referred to as " the relevant established claim ") as was properly attributable to that part of the area of the holding.

(2) In the case of a claim holding where—

(a) the area of the holding is the same as the claim area of the relevant established claim ; but

(b) the value of the claim holding is, by virtue of the adjustment of claim holdings, less than the amount of the relevant established claim,

the amount of any such fraction as is referred to in subsection (1)(b) of this section shall be treated as reduced proportionately.

(3) In the case of a claim holding where—

(a) the area of the holding consists of part only of the claim area of the relevant established claim ; and

(b) the value of the holding is, by virtue of the adjustment of claim holdings, less or greater than so much of the

PART VII

amount of the relevant established claim as was properly attributable to the area of the holding,

the amount of any such fraction as is referred to in subsection (1)(*b*) of this section shall be treated as reduced, or (as the case may be) increased, proportionately.

(4) For the purposes of this section, the part of the amount of the relevant established claim which was properly attributable to any land forming part of the claim area shall be taken to have been so much of the amount of that claim as might reasonably be expected to have been attributed to that land if the authority determining that amount had been required to apportion it, in accordance with the same principles as applied to its determination, between that land and the residue of the claim area.

Adjustment of claim holdings.

138.—(1) The provisions of Schedule 15 to this Act shall have effect for the purposes of this Part of this Act; and any reference in this Part of this Act to the adjustment of claim holdings is a reference to the operation of those provisions.

(2) For the purposes of this Part of this Act the adjustment of claim holdings shall be deemed to have been completed on 1st January 1955.

General provision for continuance of original unexpended balance.

139. Where in accordance with section 136 of this Act land had an original unexpended balance of established development value, then, subject to the following provisions of this Part of this Act, that land shall be taken—

(*a*) to have continued to have that balance until the commencement of this Act; and

(*b*) to continue to have that balance at all times thereafter.

Reduction or extinguishment of balance in consequence of compensation.

140.—(1) Where at any time compensation becomes payable under this Part of this Act, or became payable under Part II of the Act of 1954 or Part VI of the Act of 1962, in respect of depreciation of the value of an interest in land by a planning decision, then, for the purpose of determining whether that land or any part thereof has or had an unexpended balance of established development value at any subsequent time, the amount of the compensation shall be deducted from the original unexpended balance of established development value of that land, and the original unexpended balance of that land or that part thereof shall be treated as having been reduced or extinguished accordingly immediately before that subsequent time.

(2) Subsection (1) of this section shall have effect subject to the provisions of this Part of this Act relating to the recovery of compensation on subsequent development.

141.—(1) Where in accordance with section 136 of this Part VII Act land had an original unexpended balance of established Reduction or development value, and at any time on or after the appointed extinguish- day (whether before or after the commencement of this Act) any ment of new development of that land is or was initiated, then (subject to balance on the following provisions of this section) for the purpose of new develop- determining whether that land or any part thereof has or had ment. an unexpended balance of established development value at any subsequent time—

(*a*) if the development relates or related only to that land, the value of that development (ascertained, with reference to that subsequent time, in accordance with the provisions of Schedule 16 to this Act); or

(*b*) if the development relates or related to that land together with other land, so much of the value of that develop- ment (so ascertained) as is or was attributable to that land,

shall be deducted from the original unexpended balance of established development value of that land, and the original unexpended balance of that land or that part thereof shall be treated as having been reduced or extinguished accordingly immediately before that subsequent time.

(2) Subsection (1) of this section shall not apply to any land if, in respect of any interest therein, a payment has become or becomes payable under section 59 of the Act of 1947 (which provided for payments in respect of certain war-damaged land).

(3) For the purposes of subsection (1) of this section no account shall be taken of any development initiated before 1st January 1955, if—

(*a*) a development charge under Part VII of the Act of 1947 was determined to be payable in respect thereof, or would have fallen to be so determined but for any exemption conferred by regulations under that Part of that Act, or by any provisions of Part VIII of that Act; or

(*b*) in a certificate issued under section 58 of the Act of 1954 (which related to monopoly value of licensed premises) it was certified that a development charge could have been determined to be payable in respect of that development if the circumstances referred to in subsection (1)(*a*) or (*b*) of that section had not existed.

PART VII
Reduction or
extinguish-
ment of
balance on
acquisition of
land under
compulsory
powers.

142.—(1) Where in the case of—

(a) a compulsory acquisition to which this section applies; or

(b) a sale of an interest in land by agreement in circumstances corresponding to such an acquisition,

any of the land in which the interest acquired or sold subsists or subsisted has or had an unexpended balance of established development value immediately before the relevant date (in this section referred to as " the relevant balance ") the following provisions of this section shall have effect for the purpose of determining whether that land or any part thereof has or had an unexpended balance of established development value at any subsequent time.

(2) This section applies—

(a) to every compulsory acquisition of an interest in land in pursuance of a notice to treat served on or after 30th October 1958, whether before or after the commencement of this Act; and

(b) to every compulsory acquisition of an interest in land, in pursuance of a notice to treat served on or after 1st January 1955 but before the said 30th October, by an authority possessing compulsory purchase powers, being at that time a government department or local or public authority within the meaning of the Acquisition of Land (Assessment of Compensation) Act 1919, or a person or body of persons to whom that Act applied as it applied to such a department or authority.

1919 c. 57.

(3) Unless, immediately after the acquisition or sale, there is or was outstanding some interest (other than an excepted interest) in the land to which some person other than the acquiring authority is or was entitled, the original unexpended balance of established development value of that land shall be treated as having been extinguished immediately before the subsequent time referred to in subsection (1) of this section.

(4) If, immediately after the acquisition or sale, there is or was such an outstanding interest (other than an excepted interest) as is mentioned in subsection (3) of this section, there shall be deducted from the said original balance an amount equal to any part of the relevant balance which is or was not attributable to any such outstanding interest, and the original unexpended balance of established development value of the land or the part thereof in question shall be treated as having been reduced or extinguished accordingly immediately before that subsequent time.

(5) For the purposes of this section any question as to the portion of the relevant balance which is or was attributable to an interest in land—

(a) in relation to a compulsory acquisition to which this section applies, shall be determined in accordance with the provisions of Schedule 17 to this Act; and

(b) in relation to a sale of an interest in land by agreement in circumstances corresponding to such an acquisition, shall be determined in accordance with the provisions of that Schedule as those provisions would apply if the sale had been a compulsory acquisition in pursuance of a notice to treat served on the relevant date.

(6) Any reference in this section or in section 143 of this Act to a sale of an interest in land by agreement in circumstances corresponding to a compulsory acquisition to which this section applies is a reference to a sale thereof—

(a) to an authority possessing compulsory purchase powers, in pursuance of a contract made on or after 30th October 1958, whether before or after the commencement of this Act; or

(b) to such an authority possessing compulsory purchase powers as is mentioned in subsection (2)(b) of this section, in pursuance of a contract made on or after 1st January 1955 but before the said 30th October.

(7) In this section "the relevant date" means the date of service of the notice to treat or the date of the contract in pursuance of which the interest was sold, as the case may be, and "excepted interest" means the interest of any such person as is mentioned in section 20(1) of the Compulsory Purchase Act 1965 (which relates to persons having no greater interest than as tenant for a year or from year to year).

143.—(1) Where in connection with—

(a) a compulsory acquisition to which section 142 of this Act applies; or

(b) a sale of an interest in land by agreement in circumstances corresponding to such an acquisition,

compensation is or was payable, or an amount is or was included in the purchase price, in respect of an interest in land other than the relevant land (in this section referred to as "the interest affected"), for damage sustained by reason that the relevant land is or was severed from other land held therewith, or that any other land (whether held with the relevant land or not) is or was injuriously affected, then (subject to the following provisions of this section) for the purpose of determining whether that other

PART VII   land or any part thereof has or had an unexpended balance of established development value at any subsequent time, there shall be deducted from the original unexpended balance of established development value of that other land an amount calculated in accordance with the following provisions of this section, and the original unexpended balance of that land, or of the part thereof in question, as the case may be, shall be treated as having been reduced or extinguished accordingly immediately before that subsequent time.

(2) In the case of an acquisition or sale in pursuance of a notice to treat served, or contract made, on or after 30th October 1958, the amount to be deducted, as mentioned in subsection (1) of this section, shall be the amount (if any) by which the compensation payable, or amount included in the purchase price, as therein mentioned exceeds or exceeded the compensation which would have been so payable, or the amount which would have been so included, if the extent of the damage sustained in respect of the other land in question had fallen to be ascertained on the assumption that planning permission would not be granted for any new development of that land, but would be granted for any development thereof other than new development.

(3) The following provisions of this section shall have effect with respect to any such acquisition or sale as is mentioned in subsection (1) of this section, being an acquisition or sale in pursuance of a notice to treat served, or contract made, before 30th October 1958; and any such acquisition or sale is hereinafter referred to as an acquisition or sale to which this subsection applies.

(4) No such deduction as is mentioned in subsection (1) of this section shall be made in the case of an acquisition or sale to which subsection (3) of this section applies unless—

(a) where it was a compulsory acquisition, an amount was paid by way of compensation as mentioned in the said subsection (1);

(b) the amount which was so paid, or, in the case of a sale by agreement, was included in the purchase price as mentioned in the said subsection (1) (hereafter in this section referred to as " the sum paid for severance or injurious affection ") exceeded the loss of immediate value of the interest affected ; and

(c) where it was a sale by agreement, the other land in question was held with the relevant land.

(5) Subject to subsection (4) of this section, the amount to be deducted as mentioned in subsection (1) of this section, in the case of an acquisition or sale to which subsection (3) of this section applies, shall be the amount by which the sum paid for severance or injurious affection exceeded the loss of immediate value of the interest affected.

(6) The following provisions of this subsection shall have effect, in the case of an acquisition or sale to which subsection (3) of this section applies, where so much (if any) of the sum paid for severance or injurious affection as was attributable to the loss of immediate value of the interest affected was less than the depreciation in restricted value of that interest, that is to say—

(a) the amount of the difference shall be ascertained ; and

(b) for the purpose of determining whether, at any time after the acquisition or sale, the land in which the interest affected subsisted or any part thereof had or has an unexpended balance of established development value (whether or not that land or any part thereof would apart from this subsection have had an original unexpended balance of established development value a claim holding with an area consisting of that land and a value equal to seven-eighths of the amount of the difference shall be deemed to have subsisted immediately after the time when the adjustment of claim holdings was completed.

(7) In this section—

" the loss of immediate value " means the amount (if any) by which the difference in the value of the interest affected, immediately before and immediately after the acquisition or sale, exceeded the loss of development value ;

" the loss of development value " means the amount (if any) by which the value of the interest affected immediately before the acquisition or sale, if calculated on the assumption that, until such time as the land in which that interest subsisted might reasonably be expected to become ripe for new development, no use whatever could be made of that land, would have exceeded the value of that interest immediately after the acquisition or sale if calculated on the like assumption ;

" the depreciation in restricted value " means the amount (if any) by which the value of the interest affected, immediately after the acquisition or sale, would have been less than the value of that interest immediately before the acquisition or sale, if both values were calculated on the assumption that planning permission would not be granted for any new development of that land, but would be granted for any development thereof other than new development;

" the relevant land ", in relation to an acquisition or sale, means the land in which the interest acquired or sold subsisted.

Supplementary provisions as to deductions from original balance.

144.—(1) Where, immediately after the time when the adjustment of claim holdings was completed, any land taken as a whole had an original unexpended balance of established development value, and at any time thereafter (whether before or after the commencement of this Act) an act or event occurs or has occurred in relation to part of that land such that, in accordance with any of the preceding provisions of this Part of this Act, an amount is required to be deducted from the original unexpended balance of that part of that land for the purpose of determining whether it has or had an unexpended balance of established development value at any subsequent time, then (without prejudice to the operation of any of the preceding provisions of this Part of this Act with respect to any part of the land taken separately) the land taken as a whole shall be treated as not having (or as not having had) any such balance at that subsequent time.

(2) Where in accordance with any of the preceding provisions of this Part of this Act an amount is required to be deducted from the original unexpended balance of established development value of any land, there shall be attributed to the various parts of that land so much of that amount as might reasonably be expected to have been attributed thereto if the authority determining the amount had been required to apportion it between those parts in accordance with the same principles as applied to its determination.

(3) Where two or more acts or events occur or have occurred in relation to the same land (whether before or after the commencement of this Act) such that, in accordance with any of the preceding provisions of this Part of this Act, an amount is required to be deducted from the original unexpended balance of established development value of that land or any part thereof, those provisions shall apply cumulatively, and the requisite deduction from the original unexpended balance of established development value of that land shall be made by reference to each of those acts or events.

145.—(1) Subject to the provisions of this section, the Secretary of State shall, on application being made to him by any
person, and may if he thinks fit without any such application,
issue a certificate in the prescribed form with respect to any
land stating whether any of that land had an original unexpended
balance of established development value, and, if so— Part VII
Provision of
information
relating to
unexpended
balance.

(a) giving a general statement of what was taken by the
Central Land Board, for the purposes of Part VI of
the Act of 1947, to be the state of that land on the
appointed day ; and

(b) specifying (subject to any outstanding claims under Part
I or Part V of the Act of 1954) the amount of that
original balance.

(2) Any such certificate issued with respect to any land may,
if the Secretary of State thinks fit, contain additional information
with respect to acts or events in consequence of which, in
accordance with any of the preceding provisions of this Part of
this Act, an amount is required to be deducted from the original
unexpended balance of established development value of any
of that land.

(3) Where, at any time on or after 1st January 1955 (whether
before or after the commencement of this Act), a notice to treat
has been served with a view to the compulsory acquisition of an
interest in land by an authority possessing compulsory purchase
powers, that authority may apply to the Secretary of State for,
and shall be entitled to the issue of, a certificate showing the
unexpended balance of established development value (if any) of
any of that land immediately before the service of that notice.

(4) Where the issue of a certificate under this section with
respect to any land involves a new apportionment, or, in the
case of a certificate under subsection (3) of this section, involves
the calculation of a deduction from the original unexpended
balance of established development value by virtue of section
141 of this Act, then—

(a) except in the case of a certificate under subsection (3)
of this section, or of a certificate which the Secretary
of State proposes to issue without any application being
made for it, the certificate shall not be issued otherwise
than on the application of a person who is for the
time being entitled to an interest in that land ;

(b) before issuing the certificate, the Secretary of State shall
give notice in writing to any person entitled to an
interest in land appearing to him to be an interest
which will be substantially affected by the apportionment or calculation, giving particulars of the proposed

apportionment or calculation, and stating that objections or other representations with respect thereto may be made to the Secretary of State within the period of thirty days from the date of the notice ; and

(c) the certificate shall not be issued before the end of that period, and if within that period an objection to the proposed apportionment or calculation has been made by any person to whom notice has been given under paragraph (b) of this subsection, or by any other person who establishes that he is entitled to an interest in land which is substantially affected by the apportionment or calculation, and that objection has not been withdrawn, subsection (5) of this section shall have effect.

(5) Where by virtue of subsection (4)(c) or this section this subsection is to have effect, then—

(a) if within a further period of thirty days the person by whom any such objection was made requires the dispute to be referred to the Lands Tribunal, the dispute shall be so referred, and the certificate shall not be issued until either the Tribunal has decided the matter or the reference to the Tribunal has been withdrawn ;

(b) the certificate may be issued before the end of the said further period if every such objection has been withdrawn ;

(c) the certificate shall be issued at the end of that further period, notwithstanding that every such objection has not been withdrawn, if no requirement has within that period been made under paragraph (a) of this subsection.

(6) Where, on a reference to the Lands Tribunal under this section, it is shown that a new apportionment relates partly to the same matters as a previous apportionment, and is consistent with that previous apportionment in so far as it relates to those matters, the Tribunal shall not vary the new apportionment in such a way as to be inconsistent with the previous apportionment in so far as it relates to those matters.

(7) A certificate under subsection (3) of this section shall be conclusive evidence of the unexpended balance shown therein ; and a certificate under subsection (1) of this section shall be sufficient proof of any facts stated therein unless the contrary is shown.

(8) An application for a certificate under this section shall be made in such form and manner as may be prescribed, and shall

be accompanied by sufficient particulars, including a map if necessary, to enable the land to be identified, and, where a new apportionment will be involved, particulars of the nature of the applicant's interest, and such information as to the nature of any other interest in thé land, and as to the name and address of the person entitled to that other interest, as may be known to the applicant.

(9) On any application under subsection (1) of this section the applicant shall pay in the prescribed manner a fee of twenty-five new pence, and, if the application involves a new apportionment, the certificate shall not be issued until the applicant has paid in the prescribed manner a further fee of seventy-five new pence.

(10) In this section "new apportionment" means an apportionment which relates wholly or partly to any matter to which no previous apportionment related.

Right to compensation

146. Subject to the provisions of this Part of this Act, a person shall be entitled to compensation under this Part of this Act in respect of a planning decision whereby planning permission for the carrying out of new development of land is refused, or is granted subject to conditions, if—

General provision as to right to compensation.

(*a*) at the time of the decision he is entitled to an interest in any land to which the decision relates which has an unexpended balance of established development value ; and

(*b*) the value of that interest, or, in the case of an interest extending to other land, the value of that interest in so far as it subsists in such land as is referred to in the preceding paragraph, is depreciated by the decision.

147.—(1) Compensation under this Part of this Act shall not be payable—

Planning decisions not ranking for compensation.

(*a*) in respect of the refusal of planning permission for any development which consists of or includes the making of any material change in the use of any buildings or other land ; or

(*b*) in respect of any decision made on an application in pursuance of regulations under section 63 of this Act for consent to the display of advertisements.

(2) Compensation under this Part of this Act shall not be payable in respect of the imposition, on the granting of planning permission to develop land, of any condition relating to—

(*a*) the number or disposition of buildings on any land ;

(b) the dimensions, design, structure or external appearance of any building, or the materials to be used in its construction ;

(c) the manner in which any land is to be laid out for the purposes of the development, including the provision of facilities for the parking, loading, unloading or fuelling of vehicles on the land ;

(d) the use of any buildings or other land ; or

(e) the location or design of any means of access to a highway, or the materials to be used in the construction of any such means of access,

or in respect of any condition subject to which permission is granted for the winning and working of minerals.

In this subsection " means of access to a highway " does not include a service road.

(3) Compensation under this Part of this Act shall not be payable in respect of the application to any planning permission of any of the conditions referred to in sections 41 and 42 of this Act or in respect of the imposition of any condition to which section 71 or 82 of this Act applies.

(4) Compensation under this Part of this Act shall not be payable in respect of the application to any planning permission if the reason or one of the reasons stated for the refusal is that development of the kind proposed would be premature by reference to either or both of the following matters, that is to say—

(a) the order of priority (if any) indicated in the development plan for the area in which the land is situated for development in that area ;

(b) any existing deficiency in the provision of water supplies or sewerage services, and the period within which any such deficiency may reasonably be expected to be made good :

Provided that this subsection shall not apply if the planning decision refusing the permission is made on an application made more than seven years after the date of a previous planning decision whereby permission to develop the same land was refused for the same reason, or for reasons which included the same reason.

(5) Compensation under this Part of this Act shall not be payable in respect of the refusal of permission to develop land, if the reason or one of the reasons stated for the refusal is that the land is unsuitable for the proposed development on account of its liability to flooding or to subsidence.

(6) For the purposes of this section, a planning decision whereby permission to develop land is granted subject to a condition prohibiting development on a specified part of that land shall

be treated as a decision refusing the permission with respect to that part of the land.

148.—(1) Compensation under this Part of this Act shall not be payable in respect of a planning decision whereby permission is refused for the development of land if, notwithstanding that refusal, there is available with respect to that land planning permission for development to which this section applies :

No compensation if certain other development permitted.

Provided that, where such permission is available with respect to part only of the land, this section shall have effect only in so far as the interest subsists in that part.

(2) Where a claim for compensation under this Part of this Act is made in respect of an interest in any land, planning permission for development to which this section applies shall be taken for the purposes of this section to be available with respect to that land or a part thereof if, immediately before the Secretary of State gives notice of his findings in respect of that claim, there is in force with respect to that land, or that part thereof, a grant of, or an undertaking by the Secretary of State to grant, planning permission for some such development, subject to no conditions other than such as are mentioned in section 147(2) of this Act.

(3) This section applies to any development of a residential, commercial or industrial character, being development which consists wholly or mainly of the construction of houses, flats, shop or office premises, or industrial buildings (including warehouses), or any combination thereof.

149.—(1) Where an interest in any land has (whether before or after the commencement of this Act) been compulsorily acquired by, or sold to, an authority possessing compulsory purchase powers (not being statutory undertakers or the National Coal Board), that authority, and any person deriving title from that authority under a disposition made by that authority on or at any time after the appointed day, shall not be entitled to compensation under this Part of this Act in respect of a planning decision made after the service of the notice to treat, or after the making of the contract of sale, as the case may be, by reason that the value of that interest, or of any interest created (whether immediately or derivatively) out of that interest, is depreciated by the decision.

Further exclusions from compensation.

(2) Subsection (1) of this section shall apply to land which has at any time on or after the appointed day (whether before or after the commencement of this Act) been appropriated by a local authority for a purpose for which the authority could have been authorised to acquire the land compulsorily, as it applies to land in which an interest has been acquired as mentioned in

PART VII that subsection, with the substitution, for the reference to the service of the notice to treat, of a reference to the appropriation.

(3) Where at the relevant date any land was or is operational land of statutory undertakers, or land of the National Coal Board of a class specified in regulations made under section 90 of the Act of 1947 or under section 273 of this Act, the statutory undertakers or the National Coal Board, as the case may be, and any person deriving title from those undertakers or that Board, shall not be entitled to compensation under this Part of this Act, in respect of a planning decision made after the relevant date, by reason that the value of any interest in that land is depreciated by that decision.

In this subsection " the relevant date ", in relation to land which was such operational land or land of the National Coal Board as is mentioned in this subsection on 1st January 1955, means that day, and, in relation to land which (whether before or after the commencement of this Act) became or becomes such operational land or land of the National Coal Board on a date subsequent to the said 1st January, means that subsequent date.

(4) A person shall not be entitled to compensation under this Part of this Act in respect of depreciation of the value of an interest in land by a planning decision if he is entitled to compensation by virtue of section 165 of this Act in respect of depreciation of the value of that interest by that decision.

Grant of planning permission treated as subject to notional condition.

150.—(1) The provisions of this section shall have effect where—

(*a*) on an application for planning permission for the carrying out of new development of land, a planning decision is made whereby the permission is granted, whether unconditionally or subject to conditions ; and

(*b*) the Secretary of State certifies that he is satisfied that particular buildings or works to which the application related were only included therein because the applicant had reason to believe that permission for the other development to which the application related (in this section referred to as " the principal development ") would not have been granted except subject to a condition requiring the erection or construction of those buildings or works.

(2) Where subsection (1) of this section applies, then for the purposes of this Part of this Act—

(*a*) the application shall be deemed to have included, in place of those buildings or works, such other development of the land on which the buildings or works were to be erected or constructed as might reasonably have

been expected to have been included having regard to
the principal development ; and

(*b*) the permission shall be deemed to have been granted
for the principal development subject to a condition
requiring the erection or construction of those buildings
or works.

151. Where a notice under section 72(1) of this Act is served Notice under
in respect of the whole or part of any land, the provisions of s. 72 treated
this Part of this Act shall have effect as if the application, in decision.
consequence of which the notice is served, had been an effective
application for planning permission, and as if the notice had
been a planning decision of the local planning authority refusing
that permission in respect of that land or that part thereof, as
the case may be.

Measure of compensation

152.—(1) Where a person is entitled to compensation under General
this Part of this Act in respect of depreciation by a planning provisions as
decision of the value of an interest in land, the amount of the compen-
compensation, subject to the following provisions of this section, sation.
shall be whichever is the lesser of the following amounts, that is
to say—

(*a*) the amount by which the value of that interest (if it is
an interest subsisting only in land to which this section
applies), or (if it is an interest extending to other land)
the amount by which the value of the interest in so far
as it subsists in land to which this section applies, is
depreciated by the decision ; and

(*b*) the amount of the unexpended balance of established
development value, immediately before the decision, of
so much of the land in which the interest subsists as is
land to which this section applies.

(2) Land to which this section applies, in relation to a planning
decision, is land which—

(*a*) constitutes or forms part of the decision area ; and

(*b*) at the time of the decision has an unexpended balance
of established development value.

(3) If, in the case of any land to which this section applies,
compensation is payable under this Part of this Act in respect
of two or more interests in that land by reason of the same
planning decision, and the aggregate amount of compensation
payable apart from this subsection in respect of those interests
would exceed the amount mentioned in paragraph (*b*) of subsection (1) of this section, the amount mentioned in that paragraph shall be allocated between those interests in proportion

to the depreciation of the value of each of them respectively, and the amount of the compensation payable in respect of any of those interests shall be the sum so allocated to that interest.

(4) Where the land constituting the decision area, taken as a whole, does not satisfy both of the following conditions, that is to say—

(a) that at the time of the decision it has an unexpended balance of established development value ; and

(b) that every interest subsisting therein, the value of which is depreciated by the decision, subsists in the whole of that land,

the provisions of subsection (5) of this section shall have effect for the purpose of assessing the compensation payable under this Part of this Act in respect of any interest subsisting in that land or any part thereof.

(5) Where this subsection applies in relation to an interest in land—

(a) the depreciation of the value of the interest by the planning decision shall first be ascertained with reference to the whole of the land which constitutes or forms part of the decision area and is land in which that interest subsists ;

(b) the land referred to in paragraph (a) of this subsection shall then be treated as divided into as many parts as may be requisite to ensure that each such part consists of land which either satisfies both of the conditions mentioned in subsection (4) of this section or is not land which, at the time of the decision, has an unexpended balance of established development value ; and

(c) the depreciation of the value of the interest, ascertained in accordance with paragraph (a) of this subsection, shall then be apportioned between those parts, according to the nature of those parts and the effect of the planning decision in relation to each of them,

and the amount of the compensation shall be the aggregate of the amounts which would be payable by virtue of the preceding provisions of this section if the planning decision had been made separately with respect to each of those parts.

(6) In this section " the decision area " in relation to a planning decision means the aggregate of the land to which the decision relates.

Assessment of depreciation.

153.—(1) For the purposes of this Part of this Act, the value of an interest in land, or of an interest in so far as it subsists in particular land, shall be taken to be depreciated by a planning decision (in this section referred to as " the relevant decision ")

if, and to the extent to which, that value, calculated in accordance with the following provisions of this section, falls short of
what that value, so calculated, would have been if the relevant
decision had been a decision to the contrary effect.

(2) Subject to the following provisions of this section, any
such value shall for the purposes of this section be calculated—

    (*a*) as at the time of the relevant decision; but

    (*b*) as affected by that decision, by any grant of planning
        permission made after that decision and in force
        immediately before the Secretary of State gives notice
        of his findings on the claim for compensation in respect
        of that decision, and by any undertaking to grant
        planning permission so in force; and

    (*c*) on the assumption that, after the relevant decision, and
        apart from any such permission or undertaking as is
        mentioned in paragraph (*b*) of this subsection, plan-
        ning permission would not be granted for any new
        development of the land in question, but would be
        granted for any development thereof other than new
        development.

(3) If in consequence of another planning decision or of an
order, being a decision or order made—

    (*a*) before the relevant decision; and

    (*b*) either in respect of the whole or part of the land to
        which the relevant decision relates, or in respect of
        land which includes the whole or part of that land,

compensation to which this subsection applies has become or
becomes payable in respect of that other planning decision or
that order, the calculation to be made under this section shall
be made as if that other planning decision had been a decision
to the contrary effect, or that order had not been made, as the
case may be.

(4) Subsection (3) of this section applies—

    (*a*) to any compensation payable under this Part of this
        Act, or under Part II or Part V of the Act of 1954 or
        Part VI of the Act of 1962; and

    (*b*) to so much of any compensation payable under section
        164 of this Act or section 118 of the Act of 1962, or
        under the provisions of those sections as applied by
        section 165 of this Act or section 119 of the Act of
        1962 respectively, and so much of any compensation
        to which Part IV of the Act of 1954 applied, as is or
        was payable in respect of loss or damage consisting
        of depreciation of the value of an interest in land.

(5) In this section "a decision to the contrary effect"—

(a) in relation to a decision refusing permission, means a decision granting the permission subject to such condition (if any) of a description falling within subsection (2) of section 147 of this Act as the authority making the decision might reasonably have been expected to impose if the permission had not been refused; and

(b) in relation to a decision granting the permission subject to conditions, means a decision granting the permission applied for subject only to such of those conditions (if any) as fell within subsection (2) of that section.

Claims for, and payment of, compensation

General provisions as to claims for compensation.

154.—(1) Compensation under this Part of this Act shall not be payable unless a claim for it is duly made in accordance with the provisions of this section.

(2) A claim for compensation under this Part of this Act shall not have effect unless it is made before the end of the period of six months beginning with the date of the planning decision to which it relates:

Provided that the Secretary of State may in any particular case (either before, on or after the date on which the time for claiming would otherwise have expired) allow an extended, or further extended, period for making such a claim.

(3) Regulations made under this section may—

(a) require claims for compensation under this Part of this Act to be made in a form prescribed by the regulations;

(b) require a claimant to provide such evidence in support of the claim, and such information as to the interest of the claimant in the land to which the claim relates, and as to the interests of other persons therein which are known to the claimant, as may be so prescribed.

(4) Any claim for such compensation in respect of a planning decision shall be sent to the local planning authority; and it shall be the duty of that authority, as soon as may be after receipt of a claim, to transmit the claim to the Secretary of State, and to furnish the Secretary of State with—

(a) any evidence or other information provided by the claimant in accordance with regulations made under this section; and

(b) such other information (if any) as may be required by or under regulations made under this section, being information appearing to the Secretary of State to be

relevant to the exercise of his powers under the provisions of Part III of this Act relating to the review of
planning decisions where compensation is claimed.

(5) Where a claim is transmitted to the Secretary of State
under subsection (4) of this section—

   (a) if it appears to the Secretary of State that the development to which the planning decision related was not
new development, or that at the time of the planning
decision no part of the land to which the claim relates
had an unexpended balance of established development value, or that compensation is excluded by section
147 or 148 of this Act, the Secretary of State shall
notify the claimant accordingly, stating on which of
those grounds it appears to him that compensation is
not payable, and inviting the claimant to withdraw the
claim ;

   (b) unless the claim is withdrawn, the Secretary of State shall
give notice of the claim to every other person (if any)
appearing to him to have an interest in the land to
which the planning decision related.

155.—(1) Where, in accordance with section 39(3) of this Act, Effect on
the Secretary of State gives notice of a direction under section 38 claims of
of this Act to a person who has made a claim for compensation direction
in respect of the planning decision to which that direction relates, under s. 38.
that person, if he does not withdraw the claim, may, at any
time within thirty days after the service on him of the Secretary
of State's notice, give notice to the Secretary of State modifying
the claim.

(2) Subject to any modification by virtue of a notice given by
a claimant under subsection (1) of this section, where the Secretary of State gives a direction under section 38 of this Act in
respect of a decision of a local planning authority, any claim
made in respect of that decision shall have effect as if it had
been made in respect of the decision which, by virtue of the
direction, is substituted for the decision of the authority, or, as
the case may be, as if it had been made in respect of the decision
of the authority as modified by the direction.

156.—(1) Provision shall be made by regulations under this Determin-
section— ation of
claims.
   (a) for requiring claims for compensation under this Part
of this Act to be determined by the Secretary of State
in such manner as may be prescribed by the
regulations ;

   (b) for regulating the practice and procedure to be followed
in connection with the determination of such claims ;

(c) for requiring the Secretary of State, on determining any such claim, to give notice of his findings to the claimant, and to every other person (if any) who has made a claim for compensation under this Part of this Act in respect of the same planning decision, and, if his findings include an apportionment, to give particulars of the apportionment to any other person entitled to an interest in land appearing to the Secretary of State to be an interest substantially affected by the apportionment.

(2) Subject to subsection (3) of this section, provision shall be made by regulations under this section—

(a) for enabling the claimant or any other person to whom notice of the Secretary of State's findings has been given in accordance with subsection (1) of this section, if he wishes to dispute the findings, and any other person to whom particulars of an apportionment included in those findings have been so given, or who establishes that he is entitled to an interest in land which is substantially affected by such an apportionment, if he wishes to dispute the apportionment, to require the findings, or, as the case may be, the apportionment, to be referred to the Lands Tribunal;

(b) for enabling the claimant and every other person to whom notice of any findings or apportionment has been given as mentioned in paragraph (a) of this subsection to be heard by the Tribunal on any reference under this section of those findings or of that apportionment, as the case may be; and

(c) for requiring the Tribunal, on any such reference, either to confirm or to vary the Secretary of State's findings or the apportionment, as the case may be, and to notify the parties of the decision of the Tribunal.

(3) Where on a reference to the Lands Tribunal under this section it is shown that an apportionment relates wholly or partly to the same matters as a previous apportionment, and is consistent with that previous apportionment in so far as it relates to those matters, the Tribunal shall not vary the apportionment in such a way as to be inconsistent with the previous apportionment in so far as it relates to those matters.

Payment of compensation.   **157.** Where compensation is determined under section 156 of this Act to be payable, the Secretary of State shall pay the compensation to the person entitled thereto in accordance with the preceding provisions of this Part of this Act.

Subsequent recovery of compensation

158.—(1) Where, on a claim for compensation under this Part
of this Act in respect of a planning decision, the Secretary of
State determines that compensation is payable and that the
amount of the compensation exceeds £20, the Secretary of State
shall (if it appears to him to be practicable to do so) apportion
the amount of the compensation between different parts of the
land to which the claim for compensation relates, and shall
include particulars of the apportionment in the notice of his
findings under section 156 of this Act.

(2) In carrying out an apportionment under subsection (1)
of this section the Secretary of State shall divide the land into
parts, and shall distribute the compensation between those parts,
according to the way in which the different parts of the land
appear to him to be differently affected by the planning decision.

(3) On a reference to the Lands Tribunal under section 156
of this Act, unless the decision of the Tribunal will not affect
the amount of the compensation or any apportionment thereof
by the Secretary of State, the preceding provisions of this section
shall apply with the substitution, for references to the Secretary
of State, of references to the Lands Tribunal.

(4) Where, on a claim for compensation under this Part of
this Act in respect of a planning decision, compensation has
become payable of an amount exceeding £20, the Secretary of
State shall cause notice of that fact, specifying the planning
decision and the land to which the claim for compensation
relates, and the amount of the compensation and any apportionment thereof under this section, to be deposited with the council
of the county borough, London borough or county district in
which the land is situated, and, if that council is not the local
planning authority, with the local planning authority.

(5) Notices deposited under this section shall be registered
in the register of local land charges in such manner as may be
prescribed by rules made for the purposes of this section under
section 15(6) of the Land Charges Act 1925 by the proper officer
of the council of the county borough, London borough or county
district.

(6) In relation to compensation specified in a notice registered
under this section, references in this Part of this Act to so much
of the compensation as is attributable to a part of the land to
which the notice relates shall be construed in accordance with
the following provisions, that is to say—

    (a) if the notice does not include an apportionment under
        the preceding provisions of this section, the amount
        of the compensation shall be treated as distributed

PART VII

rateably according to area over the land to which the notice relates ;

(b) if the notice includes such an apportionment, the compensation shall be treated as distributed in accordance with that apportionment as between the different parts of the land by reference to which the apportionment is made ; and so much of the compensation as, in accordance with the apportionment, is attributed to a part of the land shall be treated as distributed rateably according to area over that part of the land.

Recovery of compensation on subsequent development.

159.—(1) No person shall carry out any new development to which this section applies, on land in respect of which a notice (hereafter in this Part of this Act referred to as a " compensation notice ") is registered under section 158 of this Act, until such amount (if any) as is recoverable under this section in respect of the compensation specified in the notice has been paid or secured to the satisfaction of the Secretary of State.

(2) Subject to the following provisions of this section, this section applies to any new development—

(a) which is development of a residential, commercial or industrial character and consists wholly or mainly of the construction of houses, flats, shop or office premises, or industrial buildings (including warehouses), or any combination thereof ; or

(b) which consists in the winning and working of minerals ; or

(c) to which, having regard to the probable value of the development, it is in the opinion of the Secretary of State reasonable that this section should apply.

(3) This section shall not apply to any development by virtue of subsection (2)(c) of this section if, on an application made to him for the purpose, the Secretary of State has certified that, having regard to the probable value of the development, it is not in his opinion reasonable that this section should apply thereto.

(4) Where the compensation specified in the compensation notice became payable in respect of the imposition of conditions on the granting of permission to develop land, this section shall not apply to the development for which that permission was granted.

Amount recoverable, and provisions for payment or remission

160.—(1) Subject to the following provisions of this section, the amount recoverable under section 159 of this Act in respect of the compensation specified in a compensation notice—

(a) if the land on which the development is to be carried out (in this subsection referred to as " the development area ") is identical with, or includes (with other land) the whole of, the land comprised in the compensation notice, shall be the amount of compensation specified in that notice ;

(*b*) if the development area forms part of the land comprised in the compensation notice, or includes part of that land together with other land not comprised in that notice, shall be so much of the amount. of the compensation specified in that notice as is attributable to land comprised in that notice and falling within the development area.

(2) Where, in the case of any land in respect of which a compensation notice has been registered, the Secretary of State is satisfied, having regard to the probable value of any proper development of that land, that no such development is likely to be carried out unless he exercises his powers under this sub-section, he may, in the case of any particular development, remit the whole or part of any amount otherwise recoverable under section 159 of this Act ; and where part only of any such amount has been remitted, he shall cause the compensation notice to be amended by substituting therein, for the statement of the amount of the compensation, in so far as it is attributable to that land, a statement of the amount which has been remitted under this subsection.

(3) Where, in connection with the development of any land, an amount becomes recoverable under section 159 of this Act in respect of the compensation specified in a compensation notice, then, except where, and to the extent that, payment of that amount has been remitted under subsection (2) of this section, no amount shall be recoverable under section 159 of this Act in respect of that compensation, in so far as it is attributable to that land, in connection with any subsequent development thereof.

(4) No amount shall be recoverable under section 159 of this Act in respect of any compensation by reference to which a sum has become recoverable by the Secretary of State under section 257 of this Act.

(5) An amount recoverable under section 159 of this Act in respect of any compensation shall be payable to the Secretary of State, and—

(*a*) shall be so payable either as a single capital payment or as a series of instalments of capital and interest combined, or as a series of other annual or periodical payments, of such amounts, and payable at such times, as the Secretary of State may direct, after taking into account any representations made by the person by whom the development is to be carried out ; and

(b) except where the amount is payable as a single capital payment, shall be secured by that person in such manner (whether by mortgage, convenant or otherwise) as the Secretary of State may direct.

(6) If any person initiates any new development to which section 159 of this Act applies in contravention of subsection (1) of that section, the Secretary of State may serve a notice on him specifying the amount appearing to the Secretary of State to be the amount recoverable under that section in respect of the compensation in question, and requiring him to pay that amount to the Secretary of State within such period, not being less than three months after the service of the notice, as may be specified in the notice.

Amount recovered not to be deducted from unexpended balance.

161.—(1) Where an amount has become recoverable under section 159 of this Act in respect of the compensation specified in a compensation notice, the following provisions of this section shall have effect for the purpose of determining any question as to the unexpended balance of established development value of any land at any subsequent time.

(2) Except where, and to the extent that, payment of that amount has been remitted under section 160 of this Act, so much (if any) of that compensation as is attributable to that land shall, for the purpose mentioned in subsection (1) of this section, be treated as not having become payable, and accordingly (notwithstanding anything in section 140 of this Act) shall not be deducted from that balance.

Supplementary provisions

Mortgages, rentcharges and settlements.

162.—(1) Regulations made under this section may make provision as to the exercise of the right to claim compensation under this Part of this Act, and as to the person to whom such compensation or any part thereof is to be paid, and as to the application of any such compensation or any part thereof, in cases where, apart from this section, the right to claim the compensation is exercisable by reference to an interest in land which is subject to a mortgage, or to a rentcharge, or to the trusts of a settlement, or which was so subject at a time specified in the regulations.

(2) In relation to any case where, by virtue of any such regulations, compensation or a part thereof is to be paid to the owner of a rentcharge, the regulations may apply all or any

1943 c. 21.

of the provisions of section 25 of the War Damage Act 1943 (rights of owners of rentcharges as to payments for war damage)

subject to such adaptations and modifications as may be prescribed by the regulations, and may provide for disputes arising
under the regulations, so far as they relate to rentcharges, to be
referred to the Lands Tribunal for determination by that tribunal.

163.—(1) In calculating value for any of the purposes of this Calculation
Part of this Act— of value.

    (*a*) rules (2) to (4) of the rules set out in section 5 of the
        Land Compensation Act 1961 shall apply with the 1961 c. 33.
        necessary modifications ; and

    (*b*) if the interest to be valued is subject to a mortgage, it
        shall be treated as if it were not subject to the mort-
        gage:

Provided that rule (3) of those rules shall not apply for the
purposes of Schedule 16 to this Act.

(2) Where, for the purposes of any of the provisions of this
Part of this Act, value falls to be calculated by reference to the
duration of a tenancy, and, by reason of any option or other
contractual right with respect to the determination, renewal or
continuance of the tenancy, the date of expiry of the tenancy
is not ascertainable with certainty, that date shall be taken to
be such as appears reasonable and probable having regard to
the interests of the party by whom the option is exercisable,
or in whose favour the right operates, and to any other material
considerations subsisting at the time when the calculation of
value falls to be made.

PART VIII

COMPENSATION FOR OTHER PLANNING RESTRICTIONS

Revocation or modification of planning permission

164.—(1) Where planning permission is revoked or modified Compensation
by an order under section 45 of this Act, (other than an order where plan-
which takes effect by virtue of section 46 of this Act and without ning permis-
being confirmed by the Secretary of State), then if, on a claim or modified.
made to the local planning authority within the time and in the
manner prescribed by regulations under this Act, it is shown
that a person interested in the land—

    (*a*) has incurred expenditure in carrying out work which
        is rendered abortive by the revocation or modification ;
        or

    (*b*) has otherwise sustained loss or damage which is directly
        attributable to the revocation or modification,

PART VIII   the local planning authority shall pay to that person compensation in respect of that expenditure, loss or damage.

(2) For the purposes of this section, any expenditure incurred in the preparation of plans for the purposes of any work, or upon other similar matters preparatory thereto, shall be taken to be included in the expenditure incurred in carrying out that work.

(3) Subject to subsection (2) of this section, no compensation shall be paid under this section in respect of any work carried out before the grant of the permission which is revoked or modified, or in respect of any other loss or damage (not being loss or damage consisting of depreciation of the value of an interest in land) arising out of anything done or omitted to be done before the grant of that permission.

(4) In calculating, for the purposes of this section, the amount of any loss or damage consisting of depreciation of the value of an interest in land, it shall be assumed that planning permission would be granted for development of the land of any class specified in Schedule 8 to this Act.

(5) In this Part of this Act any reference to an order under section 45 of this Act includes a reference to an order under the provisions of that section as applied by section 51(2) of this Act.

Application
of s. 164 to
special cases
of refusal
or conditional
grant of
planning
permission.

165.—(1) The provisions of this section shall have effect where—

(a) planning permission for the development of land has been granted by a development order ; and

(b) that permission is withdrawn, whether by the revocation or amendment of the order or by the issue of directions under powers in that behalf conferred by the order ; and

(c) on an application made in that behalf under Part III of this Act, planning permission for that development is refused, or is granted subject to conditions other than those previously imposed by the development order.

(2) In any case falling within subsection (1) of this section, the provisions of section 164 of this Act shall apply as if the planning permission granted by the development order—

(a) had been granted by the local planning authority under Part III of this Act ; and

(b) had been revoked or modified by an order under section 45 of this Act,

and the provisions of section 166 (except subsection (5)(b) thereof) and of sections 167 and 168 of this Act shall apply as if references therein to an order under section 45 of this

Act were references to the planning decision whereby the plan-   PART VIII
ning permission in question is refused, or is granted subject
to conditions other than those previously imposed by the development order.

(3) This section shall not apply in relation to planning permission for the development of operational land of statutory
undertakers.

(4) No compensation shall be payable under this section in
respect of the imposition of any condition to which section 71
or 82 of this Act applies.

166.—(1) Where compensation becomes payable under the   Registration
preceding provisions of this Part of this Act, and includes com-   and apportion-
pensation for depreciation of an amount exceeding £20, the   pensation for
local planning authority shall (if it appears to them to be prac-   depreciation
ticable to do so) apportion the amount of the compensation
for depreciation between different parts of the land to which
the claim for that compensation relates, and give particulars of
any such apportionment to the claimant and to every other
person (if any) entitled to an interest in land which appears to the
authority to be substantially affected by the apportionment.

(2) In carrying out an apportionment under subsection (1)
of this section, the local planning authority shall divide the land
into parts, and shall distribute the compensation for depreciation
between those parts, according to the way in which different parts
of the land appear to the authority to be differently affected by
the order in consequence of which the compensation is payable.

(3) Section 156(2) of this Act, and any regulations made by
virtue thereof, shall have effect with respect to any such apportionment (subject to any necessary modifications) as they have
effect with respect to an apportionment under section 158(1)
of this Act.

(4) On a reference to the Lands Tribunal by virtue of subsection (3) of this section, subsections (1) and (2) of this section,
so far as they relate to the making of an apportionment, shall
apply with the substitution, for references to the local planning
authority, of references to the Lands Tribunal.

(5) Where compensation becomes payable under the preceding
provisions of this Part of this Act, and includes compensation for
depreciation exceeding £20, the local planning authority shall
give notice thereof to the Secretary of State, specifying the
amount of the compensation for depreciation and any apportionment thereof under this section; and subsections (4) to (6) of
section 158 of this Act shall have effect with respect thereto as
they have effect with respect to compensation under Part VII of

this Act, subject, however, to any necessary modifications, and, in particular, with the substitution—

(a) for references to the compensation mentioned in that section, of references to the compensation for depreciation specified in the notice; and

(b) for references to the planning decision, of references to the order under section 45 of this Act in consequence of which the compensation is payable.

(6) In this section and in section 167 of this Act " compensation for depreciation " means so much of any compensation payable under the preceding provisions of this Part of this Act as is payable in respect of loss or damage consisting of depreciation of the value of an interest in land, and " interest " (where the reference is to an interest in land) means the fee simple or a tenancy of the land and does not include any other interest therein.

Contribution by Secretary of State towards compensation in certain cases

167.—(1) Where a notice under section 166 of this Act is given to the Secretary of State in consequence of the making of an order under section 45 of this Act, and the circumstances are such that, if the permission revoked or modified by the order had been refused, or, as the case may be, had been granted as so modified, at the time when it was granted, compensation under Part VII of this Act could have been claimed and would have been payable by the Secretary of State, the Secretary of State may, subject to the provisions of this section, pay to the local planning authority a contribution of the amount appearing to him to be the amount of compensation which would have been so payable by him under Part VII of this Act.

(2) The amount of any such contribution shall not exceed—

(a) the amount of the compensation for depreciation paid by the local planning authority; or

(b) the unexpended balance of established development value, at the date of the making of the order, of the land in respect of which that compensation was paid.

(3) Regulations made under this section shall make provision, in relation to cases where the Secretary of State proposes to pay a contribution under this section—

(a) for requiring the Secretary of State to give notice of his proposal to persons entitled to such interests as may be prescribed in the land to which the proposal relates, and to such other persons (if any) as may be determined in accordance with the regulations to be affected by the proposal;

(b) for enabling persons to whom notice of the proposal is given to object to the proposal, on the grounds that compensation would not have been payable as mentioned in subsection (1) of this section, or that the amount of the compensation so payable would have been less than the amount of the proposed contribution;

(c) for enabling any person making such an objection to require the matter in dispute to be referred to the Lands Tribunal for determination; and

(d) where a contribution under this section is paid, for applying (with any necessary modifications) the provisions of Part VII of this Act as to the reduction or extinguishment of the unexpended balance of established development value of land, as if the contribution had been a payment of compensation under that Part of this Act.

168.—(1) In relation to notices registered under the provisions of section 158 of this Act, as applied by the preceding provisions of this Part of this Act, sections 159 and 160 of this Act shall have effect as they have effect in relation to compensation notices registered as therein mentioned:

Provided that, in a case where the compensation under section 164 of this Act specified in such a notice became payable in respect of an order modifying planning permission, the said sections shall not apply to development in accordance with that permission as modified by the order.

(2) Subject to subsection (3) of this section, any sum recovered by the Secretary of State under section 159 of this Act, as applied by subsection (1) of this section, shall be paid to the local planning authority who paid the compensation to which that sum relates.

(3) In paying any such sum to the local planning authority, the Secretary of State shall deduct therefrom—

(a) the amount of any contribution paid by him under section 167 of this Act in respect of the compensation to which the sum relates;

(b) the amount of any grant paid by him under Part XIII of this Act in respect of that compensation:

Provided that, if the sum recovered by the Secretary of State is an instalment of the total sum recoverable, or is recovered by reference to development of part of the land in respect of which the compensation was payable, any deduction to be made under paragraph (a) or paragraph (b) of this subsection shall be a

PART VIII   deduction of such amount as the Secretary of State may determine to be the proper proportion of the amount referred to in that paragraph.

(4) For the purposes of sections 159 and 160 of this Act, in their application by virtue of this section to compensation calculated under section 164 of this Act, the expression "new development" shall include—

> (a) any development of a class specified in paragraph 1 or 3 of Schedule 8 to this Act which is carried out otherwise than subject to the condition set out in Schedule 18 to this Act ; and
>
> (b) any development excluded by subsection (2) of section 278 of this Act from that Schedule in its application to any determination to which subsection (1) of the said section 278 applies.

Other restrictions

Compensation for planning decisions restricting development other than new development.

169.—(1) The provisions of this section shall have effect where, on an application for planning permission to carry out development of any class specified in Part II of Schedule 8 to this Act, the Secretary of State, either on appeal or on the reference of the application to him for determination, refuses the permission or grants it subject to conditions.

(2) If, on a claim made to the local planning authority within the time and in the manner prescribed by regulations under this Act, it is shown that the value of the interest of any person in the land is less than it would have been if the permission had been granted, or had been granted unconditionally, as the case may be, the local planning authority shall pay to that person compensation of an amount equal to the difference.

(3) In determining, for the purposes of subsection (2) of this section, whether or to what extent the value of an interest in land is less than it would have been if the permission had been granted, or had been granted unconditionally—

> (a) it shall be assumed that any subsequent application for the like planning permission would be determined in the same way ; but
>
> (b) if, in the case of a refusal of planning permission, the Secretary of State, on refusing that permission, undertook to grant planning permission for some other development of the land in the event of an application being made in that behalf, regard shall be had to that undertaking ; and
>
> (c) no account shall be taken of any prospective use which would contravene the condition set out in Schedule 18 to this Act.

(4) Where, on such an application as is mentioned in subsection (1) of this section, planning permission is granted by the
Secretary of State subject to conditions for regulating the design
or external appearance of buildings, or the size or height of
buildings, the Secretary of State, if it appears to him to be
reasonable to do so having regard to the local circumstances, may
direct that those conditions shall be disregarded, either altogether
or to such extent as may be specified in the direction, in assessing the compensation (if any) payable under this section.

(5) Where, in the case of an application for planning permission to carry out any such development as is mentioned in subsection (1) of this section, a notice under section 72(1) of this
Act is served in respect of the whole or part of the land to
which the application relates, the preceding provisions of this
section shall have effect as if the application had been an effective application for planning permission, and as if that permission had been refused, as mentioned in subsection (1) of this
section, in respect of that land or that part thereof, as the case
may be.

(6) For the purposes of subsection (1) of this section—

(*a*) paragraph 3 of Schedule 8 to this Act shall be construed
as not extending to works involving any increase in
the cubic content of a building erected after the
appointed day (including any building resulting from
the carrying out of such works as are described in
paragraph 1 of that Schedule) ; and

(*b*) paragraph 7 of that Schedule shall not apply to any
such building.

(7) For the purposes of this section the conditions referred
to in sections 41 and 42 of this Act shall be disregarded and no
compensation shall be payable under this section in respect of
the imposition of any condition to which section 71 or 82
of this Act applies.

(8) No compensation shall be payable under this section in
respect of an interest in land in respect of which a purchase
notice is served.

170.—(1) The provisions of this section shall have effect where Compensation
an order is made under section 51 of this Act, requiring a use in respect
of land to be discontinued, or imposing conditions on the con- of orders
tinuance thereof, or requiring any buildings or works on land under s. 51.
to be altered or removed.

(2) If, on a claim made to the local planning authority within
the time and in the manner prescribed by regulations under this
Act, it is shown that any person has suffered damage in consequence of the order by depreciation of the value of an interest

in the land to which he is entitled, or by being disturbed in his enjoyment of the land, that authority shall pay to that person compensation in respect of that damage.

(3) Without prejudice to subsection (2) of this section, any person who carries out any works in compliance with the order shall be entitled, on a claim made as mentioned in that subsection, to recover from the local planning authority compensation in respect of any expenses reasonably incurred by him in that behalf.

(4) Any compensation payable to a person under this section by virtue of such an order as is mentioned in subsection (1) of this section shall be reduced by the value to him of any timber, apparatus or other materials removed for the purpose of complying with the order.

Compensation for refusal of consent to alteration, etc. of listed building.

171.—(1) The provisions of this section shall have effect where an application is made for listed building consent for the alteration or extension of a listed building and—

(a) either the works do not constitute development or they do so but the development is such that planning permission therefor is granted by a development order, and

(b) the Secretary of State, either on appeal or on the reference of the application to him, refuses such consent or grants it subject to conditions.

(2) If, on a claim made to the local planning authority within the time and in the manner prescribed by regulations under this Act, it is shown that the value of the interest of any person in the land is less than it would have been if listed building consent had been granted, or had been granted unconditionally, as the case may be, the local planning authority shall pay to that person compensation of an amount equal to the difference.

(3) In determining, for the purposes of subsection (2) of this section, whether or to what extent the value of an interest in land is less than it would have been if the permission had been granted, or had been granted unconditionally—

(a) it shall be assumed that any subsequent application for the like consent would be determined in the same way; but

(b) if, in the case of a refusal of listed building consent, the Secretary of State, on refusing that consent, undertook to grant such consent for some other works to the building in the event of an application being made in that behalf, regard shall be had to that undertaking.

(4) No compensation shall be payable under this section in PART VIII respect of an interest in land in respect of which a purchase notice is served, whether under section 180, 188 or 190 of this Act, being a purchase notice which takes effect.

172.—(1) Where listed building consent is revoked or modi- Compensation fied by an order under paragraph 10 of Schedule 11 to this where listed Act (other than an order which takes effect by virtue of paragraph consent 12 of that Schedule and without being confirmed by the Secre- revoked or tary of State), then if on a claim made to the local planning modified. authority within the time and in the manner prescribed by regulations under this Act, it is shown that a person interested in the building—

(*a*) has incurred expenditure in carrying out works which are rendered abortive by the revocation or modification ; or

(*b*) has otherwise sustained loss or damage which is directly attributable to the revocation or modification,

the authority shall pay to that person compensation in respect of that expenditure, loss or damage.

(2) For the purposes of this section, any expenditure incurred in the preparation of plans for the purposes of any works, or upon other similar matters preparatory thereto, shall be taken to be included in the expenditure incurred in carrying out those works.

(3) Subject to subsection (2) of this section, no compensation shall be paid under this section in respect of any works carried out before the grant of the listed building consent which is revoked or modified, or in respect of any other loss or damage (not being loss or damage consisting of depreciation of the value of an interest in land) arising out of anything done or omitted to be done before the grant of that consent.

173.—(1) The provisions of this section shall have effect as Compensation respects compensation where a building preservation notice is for loss or served. damage caused by

(2) The local planning authority shall not be under any obliga- service of tion to pay compensation under section 171 of this Act, in building respect of any refusal of listed building consent or its grant notice. subject to conditions, unless and until the building is included in a list compiled or approved by the Secretary of State under section 54 of this Act; but this subsection shall not prevent a claim for such compensation being made before the building is so included.

(3) If the building preservation notice ceases to have effect without the building having been included in a list so compiled

PART VIII

or approved, then, subject to a claim in that behalf being made to the local planning authority within the time and in the manner prescribed by regulations under this Act, any person who at the time when the notice was served had an interest in the building shall be entitled to be paid compensation by the authority in respect of any loss or damage directly attributable to the effect of the notice.

(4) The loss or damage in respect of which compensation is payable under subsection (3) of this section shall include a sum payable in respect of a breach of contract caused by the necessity of discontinuing or countermanding any works to the building on account of the building preservation notice being in force with respect thereto.

Compensation in respect of tree preservation orders.

174. The matters for which provision may under section 60 of this Act be made by a tree preservation order include the payment by the local planning authority, subject to such exceptions and conditions as may be specified in the order, of compensation in respect of loss or damage caused or incurred in consequence of the refusal of any consent required under the order, or of the grant of any such consent subject to conditions.

Compensation in respect of requirement as to re-planting of trees.

175.—(1) The provisions of this section shall have effect where, in pursuance of provision made by a tree preservation order, a direction is given, by the local planning authority or the Secretary of State, for securing the replanting of all or any part of a woodland area which is felled in the course of forestry operations permitted by or under the order.

1967 c. 10.

(2) If the Forestry Commissioners decide not to make any advance under section 4 of the Forestry Act 1967 in respect of the replanting and come to that decision on the ground that the direction frustrates the use of the woodland area for the growing of timber or other forest products for commercial purposes and in accordance with the rules or practice of good forestry, the local planning authority exercising functions under the tree preservation order shall be liable, on the making of a claim in accordance with this section, to pay compensation in respect of such loss or damage, if any, as is caused or incurred in consequence of compliance with the direction.

(3) The Forestry Commissioners shall, at the request of the person under a duty to comply with the direction, give a certificate stating whether they have decided not to make any such advance and, if so, the grounds of their decision.

(4) A claim for compensation under this section must be served on the local planning authority within twelve months from the date on which the direction was given, or where an

appeal has been made to the Secretary of State against the decision of the local planning authority, from the date of the decision of the Secretary of State on the appeal, but subject in either case to such extension of that period as the local planning authority may allow.

176. Where, for the purpose of complying with any regulations made under section 63 of this Act, works are carried out by any person—

(*a*) for removing an advertisement which was being displayed on 1st August 1948 ; or

(*b*) for discontinuing the use for the display of advertisements of a site used for that purpose on that date,

that person shall, on a claim made to the local planning authority within the time and in the manner prescribed by regulations under this Act, be entitled to recover from that authority compensation in respect of any expenses reasonably incurred by him in that behalf.

PART VIII

Compensation for restrictions on advertising.

177.—(1) Where a stop notice under section 90 of this Act ceases to have effect, a person who, at the time when it was first served, had an interest in the land to which it relates shall, in any of the circumstances mentioned in subsection (2) of this section, be entitled to be compensated by the local planning authority in respect of any loss or damage directly attributable to the prohibition contained in the notice.

Compensation for loss due to stop notice.

(2) A person shall be entitled to compensation under subsection (1) of this section in respect of a prohibition contained in a stop notice in any of the following circumstances :—

(*a*) the enforcement notice is quashed on any of the grounds mentioned in section 88(1)(*b*), (*c*), (*d*) or (*e*) of this Act ;

(*b*) the allegation in the enforcement notice on which the prohibition in the stop notice is dependent is not upheld by reason that the enforcement notice is varied on one of those grounds ;

(*c*) the enforcement notice is withdrawn by the local planning authority otherwise than in consequence of the grant by them of planning permission for the development to which the notice relates or for its retention or continuance without compliance with a condition or limitation subject to which a previous planning permission was granted ;

(*d*) the stop notice is withdrawn.

(3) A prohibition in a stop notice shall be treated for the purposes of subsection (2) of this section as dependent on an

allegation in an enforcement notice if and to the extent that the operations to which the prohibition in the stop notice relates are the same as those alleged in the enforcement notice to constitute a breach of planning control or are so closely associated therewith as to constitute substantially the same operations.

(4) A claim for compensation under this section shall be made to the local planning authority within the time and in the manner prescribed by regulations under this Act.

(5) The loss or damage in respect of which compensation is payable under this section in respect of a prohibition shall include a sum payable in respect of a breach of contract caused by the taking of action necessary to comply with the prohibition or of any liability arising by virtue of section 90(8) of this Act.

Supplementary provisions

General
provisions
as to com-
pensation for
depreciation
under Part
VIII.
1961 c. 33.

178.—(1) For the purpose of assessing any compensation to which this section applies, the rules set out in section 5 of the Land Compensation Act 1961 shall, so far as applicable and subject to any necessary modifications, have effect as they have effect for the purpose of assessing compensation for the compulsory acquisition of an interest in land.

(2) This section applies to any compensation which, under the preceding provisions of this Part of this Act other than section 174, 175 or 177 is payable in respect of depreciation of the value of an interest in land.

(3) Where an interest in land is subject to a mortgage—

(a) any compensation to which this section applies, which is payable in respect of depreciation of the value of that interest, shall be assessed as if the interest were not subject to the mortgage ;

(b) a claim for any such compensation may be made by any mortgagee of the interest, but without prejudice to the making of a claim by the person entitled to the interest ;

(c) no compensation to which this section applies shall be payable in respect of the interest of the mortgagee (as distinct from the interest which is subject to the mortgage) ; and

(d) any compensation to which this section applies which is payable in respect of the interest which is subject to the mortgage shall be paid to the mortgagee, or, if there is more than one mortgagee, to the first mortgagee, and shall in either case be applied by him as if it were proceeds of sale.

179.—(1) Except in so far as may be otherwise provided by any tree preservation order or by any regulations made under this Act, any question of disputed compensation under this Part of this Act shall be referred to and determined by the Lands Tribunal.

(2) In relation to the determination of any such question, the provisions of sections 2 and 4 of the Land Compensation Act 1961 shall apply, subject to any necessary modifications and to the provisions of any regulations made under this Act.

PART IX

PROVISIONS ENABLING OWNER TO REQUIRE PURCHASE OF HIS INTEREST

Interests affected by planning decisions or orders

180.—(1) Where, on an application for planning permission to develop any land, permission is refused or is granted subject to conditions, then if any owner of the land claims—

(a) that the land has become incapable of reasonably beneficial use in its existing state ; and

(b) in a case where planning permission was granted subject to conditions, that the land cannot be rendered capable of reasonably beneficial use by the carrying out of the permitted development in accordance with those conditions ; and

(c) in any case, that the land cannot be rendered capable of reasonably beneficial use by the carrying out of any other development for which planning permission has been granted or for which the local planning authority or the Secretary of State has undertaken to grant planning permission,

he may, within the time and in the manner prescribed by regulations under this Act, serve on the council of the county borough, London borough or county district in which the land is situated a notice requiring that council to purchase his interest in the land in accordance with the following provisions of this Part of this Act.

(2) Where, for the purpose of determining whether the conditions specified in subsection (1) (a) to (c) of this section are fulfilled in relation to any land, any question arises as to what is or would in any particular circumstances be a reasonably beneficial use of that land, then, in determining that question for that purpose, no account shall be taken of any prospective use of that land which would involve the carrying out of new development or which would contravene the condition set out in Schedule 18 to this Act.

PART IX

(3) In the application of Schedule 8 to this Act for the purposes of any determination under subsection (2) of this section—

(a) paragraph 3 of that Schedule shall be construed as not extending to works involving any increase in the cubic content of a building erected after the appointed day (including any building resulting from the carrying out of such works as are described in paragraph 1 of that Schedule); and

(b) paragraph 7 of that Schedule shall not apply to any such building.

(4) For the purposes of this section the conditions referred to in sections 41 and 42 of this Act shall be disregarded, and no account shall be taken of any condition to which section 71 or 82 of this Act applies.

(5) A person on whom there has been served a repairs notice under section 115 of this Act shall not in any case be entitled to serve a purchase notice under this section in respect of the building in question until the expiration of three months beginning with the date of the service of the repairs notice; and if during that period the council or the Secretary of State start the compulsory acquisition of the building in the exercise of their powers under section 114 of this Act, that person shall not be so entitled unless and until the compulsory acquisition is discontinued.

(6) For the purposes of subsection (5) of this section a compulsory acquisition—

(a) is started when the council or the Secretary of State, as the case may be, serve the notice required by paragraph 3(1)(b) of Schedule 1 to the Acquisition of Land (Authorisation Procedure) Act 1946; and

1946 c. 49.

(b) is discontinued, in the case of acquisition by a council, when they withdraw the compulsory purchase order or the Secretary of State decides not to confirm it and, in the case of acquisition by the Secretary of State, when he decides not to make the compulsory purchase order.

(7) A notice under this section, or under any other provision of this Part of this Act to which this subsection is applied, is in this Act referred to as a " purchase notice ".

Action by council on whom purchase notice is served.

181.—(1) The council on whom a purchase notice is served under section 180 of this Act shall, before the end of the period of three months beginning with the date of service of that notice, serve on the owner by whom the purchase notice was served a notice stating either—

(a) that the council are willing to comply with the purchase notice; or (*b*) that another local authority or statutory undertakers specified in the notice under this subsection have agreed to comply with it in their place ; or

(*c*) that, for reasons specified in the notice under this subsection, the council are not willing to comply with the purchase notice and have not found any other local authority or statutory undertakers who will agree to comply with it in their place, and that they have transmitted a copy of the purchase notice to the Secretary of State, on a date specified in the notice under this subsection, together with a statement of the reasons so specified.

(2) Where the council on whom a purchase notice is served by an owner have served on him a notice in accordance with subsection (1)(*a*) or (*b*) of this section, the council, or the other local authority or statutory undertakers specified in the notice, as the case may be, shall be deemed to be authorised to acquire the interest of the owner compulsorily in accordance with the relevant provisions, and to have served a notice to treat in respect thereof on the date of service of the notice under that subsection.

(3) Where the council on whom a purchase notice is served by an owner propose to serve on him a notice in accordance with subsection (1)(*c*) of this section, they shall transmit a copy of the purchase notice to the Secretary of State, together with a statement of their reasons.

(4) In this section " the relevant provisions " means the provisions of Part VI of this Act or, in the case of statutory undertakers, any statutory provision (however expressed) under which they have power, or may be authorised, to purchase land compulsorily for the purposes of their undertaking.

182.—(1) Where a copy of a purchase notice is transmitted Procedure on to the Secretary of State under section 181(3) of this Act, the reference of Secretary of State shall consider whether to confirm the notice purchase or to take other action under section 183 of this Act in respect notice to thereof. Secretary of State.

(2) Before confirming a purchase notice or taking any other action under section 183 of this Act in respect thereof, the Secretary of State shall give notice of his proposed action—

(*a*) to the person by whom the purchase notice was served ;

(*b*) to the council on whom the purchase notice was served ;

(*c*) to the local planning authority for the area in which the land is situated ; and (*d*) if the Secretary of State proposes to substitute any other local authority or statutory undertakers for the council on whom the purchase notice was served, to that other local authority or those statutory undertakers.

(3) If, within such period as may be specified in a notice under subsection (2) of this section, being a period of not less than twenty-eight days from the service of that notice, any of the persons, authorities or statutory undertakers on whom that notice is served so requires, the Secretary of State, before confirming the purchase notice or taking any other action under section 183 of this Act in respect thereof, shall afford to those persons, authorities and undertakers an opportunity of appearing before, and being heard by, a person appointed by the Secretary of State for the purpose.

(4) Where the Secretary of State has given notice under sub-section (2) of this section of his proposed action, and any of the persons, authorities and statutory undertakers concerned have appeared before and been heard by a person appointed by the Secretary of State for the purpose, and it then appears to the Secretary of State to be expedient to take action under section 183 of this Act otherwise than in accordance with the notice given by him, the Secretary of State may take that action accordingly

Action by
Secretary of
State in
relation to
purchase
notice.
183.—(1) Subject to the following provisions of this section and to section 184 of this Act, if the Secretary of State is satisfied that the conditions specified in section 180(1)(*a*) to (*c*) of this Act are fulfilled in relation to a purchase notice, he shall confirm the notice.

(2) If it appears to the Secretary of State to be expedient to do so, he may, in lieu of confirming the purchase notice, grant planning permission for the development in respect of which the application was made, or, where planning permission for that development was granted subject to conditions, revoke or amend those conditions so far as appears to him to be required in order to enable the land to be rendered capable of reasonably beneficial use by the carrying out of that development.

(3) If it appears to the Secretary of State that the land, or any part of the land, could be rendered capable of reasonably beneficial use within a reasonable time by the carrying out of any other development for which planning permission ought to be granted, he may, in lieu of confirming the purchase notice, or in lieu of confirming it so far as it relates to that part of the land, as the case may be, direct that planning permission for that development shall be granted in the event of an application being made in that behalf.

(4) If it appears to the Secretary of State, having regard to the probable ultimate use of the land, that it is expedient to do so, he may, if he confirms the notice, modify it, either in relation to the whole or in relation to any part of the land to which it relates, by substituting another local authority or statutory undertakers for the council on whom the notice was served.

(5) In section 182 of this Act, any reference to the taking of action by the Secretary of State under this section is a reference to the taking by him of any such action as is mentioned in subsections (1) to (4) of this section, or to the taking by him of a decision not to confirm the purchase notice either on the grounds that any of the conditions referred to in subsection (1) of this section are not fulfilled or by virtue of section 184 of this Act.

184.—(1) This section shall have effect where, on an application for planning permission to develop any land which has a restricted use by virtue of a previous planning permission, permission is refused or granted subject to conditions and an owner of the land serves a purchase notice under section 180 of this Act.

(2) For the purposes of this section, land is to be treated as having a restricted use by virtue of a previous planning permission if it is part of a larger area in respect of which planning permission was previously granted (and has not been revoked) and either—

(a) it remains a condition of the planning permission (however expressed) that that part shall remain undeveloped or be preserved or laid out in a particular way as amenity land in relation to the remainder ; or

(b) the planning permission was granted on an application which contemplated (expressly or by necessary implication) that the part should not be comprised in the development for which planning permission was sought, or should be preserved or laid out as aforesaid.

(3) If a copy of the purchase notice is transmitted to the Secretary of State under section 181(3) of this Act the Secretary of State, although satisfied that the land has become incapable of reasonably beneficial use in its existing state, shall nevertheless not be required under section 183(1) of this Act to confirm the notice if it appears to him that the land ought, in accordance with the previous planning permission, to remain undeveloped or, as the case may be, remain or be preserved or laid out as amenity land in relation to the remainder of the large area for which that planning permission was granted.

PART IX

Power to
refuse to
confirm
purchase
notice in
respect of
office premises.

185.—(1) This section applies to any purchase notice served on or after 5th November 1964 (whether before or after the passing of this Act) in respect of land within the metropolitan region, or served on or after 5th August 1965 (whether before or after the passing of this Act) in respect of land which, at the date of service of the notice, is within a controlled area as defined in section 81(2) of this Act outside the metropolitan region, where either—

(a) planning permission for the carrying out on that land, or part of it, of development to which section 74 of this Act applies was granted before 5th August 1965, but by virtue of paragraph 1(4) of Schedule 12 to this Act that planning permission is for the time being deemed not to have effect ; or

(b) the purpose for which that land, or part of it, is or was used at the date of service of the notice, or was last used before that date, is or was that of a building containing office premises.

(2) In relation to a purchase notice to which this section applies, the provisions of this Act shall have effect as if, after subsection (4) of section 183 of this Act, there were inserted the following subsection—

" (4A) Where the purchase notice is one to which section 185 of this Act applies, the Secretary of State may, if he thinks fit, determine not to confirm the notice without taking any such action as is mentioned in subsections (2) to (4) of this section ",

and as if, in subsection (5) of that section, after the words " by virtue of " there were inserted the words " subsection (4A) of this section or "

(3) Where in pursuance of subsection (4A) of the said section 183 (as modified by subsection (2) of this section) the Secretary of State has determined not to confirm a purchase notice to which this section applies, and on a subsequent date the land to which that notice related ceases to be within an area to which section 74 of this Act applies—

(a) a further purchase notice may be served on or after that date in respect of the planning decision to which the previous notice related ; and

(b) for the purposes of any regulations made under this Act as to the time within which a purchase notice may be served, the service of such a further purchase notice shall not be treated as out of time if it is served within the period which would be applicable in accordance with those regulations if the planning decision referred to in the preceding paragraph had been made on that subsequent date.

(4) In determining, for the purposes of subsection (1)(*b*) of this section, for what purpose any land is used, or was last used, as the case may be, no account shall be taken—

   (*a*) of any use in accordance with planning permission granted for a limited period ; or

   (*b*) of any use in respect of which, before the date of service of the purchase notice, an enforcement notice had been served and had become effective ; or

   (*c*) of any use of land at a time when it is or was not covered by a building.

(5) For the purposes of this section " office premises " has the meaning assigned by section 73(4) of this Act and this section shall have effect as if it were included in sections 73 to 86 of this Act.

(6) Notwithstanding subsection (5) of this section, subsection (3) of this section shall not cease to have effect at the end of the period mentioned in section 86 of this Act ; and in relation to any land which, immediately before the end of that period, is land within an area to which section 74 of this Act applies, any reference in that subsection to the date on which the land ceases to be within such an area shall be construed as a reference to the end of that period.

186.—(1) Where the Secretary of State confirms a purchase Effect of notice, the council on whom the purchase notice was served Secretary (or, if under section 183(4) of this Act the Secretary of State of State's modified the purchase notice by substituting another local action in authority or statutory undertakers for that council, that other relation to local authority or those statutory undertakers) shall be deemed notice. purchase to be authorised to acquire the interest of the owner compulsorily in accordance with the relevant provisions and to have served a notice to treat in respect thereof on such date as the Secretary of State may direct.

(2) If, before the end of the relevant period, the Secretary of State has neither confirmed the purchase notice nor taken any such action in respect thereof as is mentioned in section 183(2) or (3) of this Act, and has not notified the owner by whom the notice was served that he does not propose to confirm the notice, the notice shall be deemed to be confirmed at the end of that period, and the council on whom the notice was served shall be deemed to be authorised to acquire the interest of the owner compulsorily in accordance with the relevant provisions and to have served a notice to treat in respect thereof at the end of that period.

(3) For the purposes of subsection (2) of this section the relevant period is whichever of the following periods first expires, that is to say—

(a) the period of nine months beginning with the date of service of the purchase notice ; and

(b) the period of six months beginning with the date on which a copy of the purchase notice was transmitted to the Secretary of State.

(4) Where the Secretary of State has notified the owner by whom a purchase notice has been served of a decision on his part to confirm, or not to confirm, the notice (including any decision not to confirm the notice in respect of part of the land to which it relates, and including any decision to grant any permission, or give any direction, in lieu of confirming the notice, either wholly or in part) .and that decision of the Secretary of State is quashed under the provisions of Part XII of this Act, the purchase notice shall be treated as cancelled, but the owner may serve a further purchase notice in its place.

(5) For the purposes of any regulations made under this Act as to the time within which a purchase notice may be served, the service of a purchase notice under subsection (4) of this section shall not be treated as out of time if the notice is served within the period which would be applicable in accordance with those regulations if the planning decision, in consequence of which the notice is served, had been made on the date on which the decision of the Secretary of State was quashed as mentioned in subsection (4) of this section.

(6) In this section " the relevant provisions " has the same meaning as in section 181 of this Act.

Special provisions as to compensation where purchase notice served.

187.—(1) Where by virtue of section 164 of this Act compensation is payable in respect of expenditure incurred in carrying out any work on land, then, if a purchase notice is served in respect of an interest in that land, any compensation payable in respect of the acquisition of that interest in pursuance of the purchase notice shall be reduced by an amount equal to the value of the works in respect of which compensation is payable by virtue of that section.

(2) Where a purchase notice served in respect of an interest in land does not take effect, or does not take effect in relation to a part of the land, by reason that the Secretary of State gives a direction under section 183(3) of this Act, then if, on a claim made to the local planning authority within the time and in the manner prescribed by regulations under this Act it is shown that the permitted development value of that interest (or, as the case may be, of that interest so far as it relates to that part of the

land) is less than its existing use value, the local planning authority shall pay to the person entitled to that interest compensation of an amount which (subject to the following provisions of this section) shall be equal to the difference.

(3) If the planning permission which, by the direction referred to in subsection (2) of this section, is required to be granted would be granted subject to conditions for regulating the design or external appearance of buildings, or the size or height of buildings, or for regulating the number of buildings to be erected on the land, the Secretary of State, if it appears to him to be reasonable to do so having regard to the local circumstances, may direct that those conditions shall be disregarded, either altogether or to such extent as may be specified in the direction, in assessing any compensation payable under subsection (2) of this section.

(4) Sections 178 and 179 of this Act shall have effect in relation to compensation under subsection (2) of this section as they have effect in relation to compensation to which those sections apply.

(5) In this section " permitted development value ", in relation to an interest in land in respect of which a direction is given under section 183(3) of this Act, means the value of that interest calculated with regard to that direction, but on the assumption that no planning permission would be granted otherwise than in accordance with that direction, and " existing use value ", in relation to such an interest, means the value of that interest as (for the purpose of ascertaining the compensation payable on an acquisition thereof in pursuance of the purchase notice) that value would have been assessed in accordance with the provisions of the Acquisition of Land (Assessment of Compensation) Act 1919, as modified by the provisions of sections 51 to 54 of the Act of 1947, if no enactment repealing, modifying or superseding any of those provisions had been passed after the passing of the Act of 1947.

1919 c. 57.

188.—(1) Where by an order under section 45 of this Act planning permission in respect of any land is revoked, or is modified by the imposition of conditions, then if any owner of the land claims—

Purchase notice in respect of order revoking or modifying planning permission.

    (a) that the land has become incapable of reasonably beneficial use in its existing state ; and

    (b) in a case where the planning permission was modified by the imposition of conditions, that the land cannot be rendered capable of reasonably beneficial use by the carrying out of the permitted development in accordance with those conditions ; and

(c) in any case, that the land cannot be rendered capable of reasonably beneficial use by the carrying out of any other development for which planning permission has been granted or for which the local planning authority or the Secretary of State has undertaken to grant planning permission,

he may, within the time and in the manner prescribed by regula tions under this Act, serve on the council of the county borough, London borough or county district in which the land is situated a notice requiring that council to purchase his interest in the land in accordance with the preceding provisions of this Part of this Act.

(2) Section 180(7) of this Act shall apply to this section; and, subject to subsection (3) of this section, sections 180(2), 181 to 184, 186 and 187 of this Act shall apply to a notice served by virtue of subsection (1) of this section as they apply to a notice served by virtue of section 180(1) of this Act.

(3) In the application of subsection (2) of section 180 of this Act to a purchase notice served by virtue of subsection (1) of this section, that subsection shall apply as if the words " or which would contravene the condition set out in Schedule 18 to this Act " were omitted ; and in the application of section 183 of this Act to a purchase notice served as aforesaid, that section shall apply as if the following subsection were substituted for subsection (2) thereof—

" (2) If it appears to the Secretary of State to be expedient to do so, he may, in lieu of confirming the purchase notice, cancel the order revoking the planning permission, or, where the order modified the permission by the imposition of conditions, revoke or amend those conditions so far as appears to him to be required in order to enable the land to be rendered capable of reasonably beneficial use by the carrying out of the development in respect of which the permission was granted ".

Purchase notice in respect of order requiring discontinuance of use or alteration or removal of buildings or works.

189.—(1) If any person entitled to an interest in land in respect of which an order is made under section 51 of this Act claims—

(a) that by reason of the order the land is incapable of reasonably beneficial use in its existing state ; and

(b) that it cannot be rendered capable of reasonably beneficial use by the carrying out of any development for which planning permission has been granted, whether by that order or otherwise,

he may, within the time and in the manner prescribed by regulations under this Act, serve on the council of the county borough,

London borough or county district in which the land is situated a notice requiring that council to purchase his interest in the land in accordance with the preceding provisions of this Part of this Act.

(2) Section 180(7) of this Act shall apply to this section ; and, subject to subsection (3) of this section, sections 180(2), 181 to 184, 186 and 187 of this Act shall apply to a notice served by virtue of subsection (1) of this section as they apply to a notice served by virtue of section 180(1) of this Act.

(3) In the application of subsection (2) of section 180 of this Act to a purchase notice served by virtue of subsection (1) of this section, that subsection shall apply as if the words " or which would contravene the condition set out in Schedule 18 to this Act " were omitted ; and in the application of section 183 of this Act to a purchase notice served as aforesaid, that section shall have effect subject to the following modifications, that is to say—

(a) in subsection (1), for the reference to the conditions therein mentioned, there shall be substituted a reference to the conditions specified in subsection (1)(a) and (b) of this section ; and

(b) the following subsection shall be substituted for subsection (2)—

> " (2) If it appears to the Secretary of State to be expedient to do so, he may, in lieu of confirming the purchase notice, revoke the order under section 51 of this Act, or, as the case may be, amend that order so far as appears to him to be required in order to prevent the land from being rendered incapable of reasonably beneficial use by the order "

(4) Where a purchase notice in respect of an interest in land is served in consequence of such an order as is mentioned in subsection (1) of this section, then if—

(a) that interest is acquired in accordance with the preceding provisions of this Part of this Act ; or

(b) compensation is payable in respect of that interest under section 187(2) of this Act,

no compensation shall be payable in respect of that order under section 170 of this Act.

(5) Except as provided by this section, no purchase notice shall be served in respect of an interest in land while the land is incapable of reasonably beneficial use by reason only of such an order as is mentioned in subsection (1) of this section.

PART IX
Purchase
notice on
refusal or
conditional
grant of
listed
building
consent.

190.—(1) Where, on an application for listed building consent in respect of a building, consent is refused or is granted subject to conditions or, by an order under Part II of Schedule 11 to this Act, listed building consent is revoked or modified, then if any owner of the land claims—

(a) that the land has become incapable of reasonably beneficial use in its existing state ; and

(b) in a case where consent was granted subject to conditions with respect to the execution of the works or, as the case may be, was modified by the imposition of such conditions, that the land cannot be rendered capable of reasonably beneficial use by the carrying out of the works in accordance with those conditions ; and

(c) in any case that the land cannot be rendered capable of reasonably beneficial use by the carrying out of any other works for which listed building consent has been granted or for which the local planning authority or the Secretary of State has undertaken to grant such consent,

he may, within the time and in the manner prescribed by regulations under this Act, serve on the council of the county borough, London borough or county district in which the land is situated a notice requiring that council to purchase his interest in the land in accordance with Schedule 19 to this Act.

(2) Where, for the purpose of determining whether the conditions specified in subsection (1)(a) to (c) of this section are satisfied in relation to the land, any question arises as to what is or would in any particular circumstances be a reasonably beneficial use of that land, then in determining that question for that purpose, no account shall be taken of any prospective use of that land which would involve the carrying out of new development or of any works requiring listed building consent which might be executed to the building, other than works for which the local planning authority or the Secretary of State have undertaken to grant such consent.

(3) In this section and in Schedule 19 to this Act, " the land " means the building in respect of which listed building consent has been refused, or granted subject to conditions, or modified by the imposition of conditions, and in respect of which its owner serves a notice under this section, together with any land comprising the building, or contiguous or adjacent to it, and owned with it, being land as to which the owner claims that its use is substantially inseparable from that of the building and that it ought to be treated, together with the building, as a single holding.

(4) Subsections (5) and (6) of section 180 of this Act shall apply to a listed building purchase notice as they apply to a purchase notice under that section.

(5) A notice under this section is in this Act referred to as a " listed building purchase notice "

191.—(1) Sections 180 to 183, 186 and 187 of this Act are provisions falling within subsection (2) of section 60 of this Act; and subsection (1) of the said section 60 and subsection (2) of section 63 of this Act, shall have effect accordingly.

(2) Where, in the case of an application for planning permission, a notice under section 72(1) of this Act is served in respect of the whole or part of the land to which the application relates, the provisions of sections 180 to 183, 186 and 187 of this Act shall have effect as if the application had been an effective application for planning permission, and as if that permission had been refused in respect of that land or that part thereof, as the case may be.

Interests of owner-occupiers affected by planning proposals

192.—(1) The provisions of sections 193 to 207 of this Act shall have effect in relation to land which—

(a) is land indicated in a structure plan in force for the district in which it is situated either as land which may be required for the purposes of any functions of a government department, local authority or statutory undertakers, or of the National Coal Board, or as land which may be included in an action area; or

(b) is land allocated for the purposes of any such functions by a local plan in force for the district or is land defined in such a plan as the site of proposed development for the purposes of any such functions; or

(c) is land indicated in a development plan (otherwise than by being dealt with in a manner mentioned in the preceding paragraphs) as land on which a highway is proposed to be constructed or land to be included in a highway as proposed to be improved or altered; or

(d) is land on or adjacent to the line of a highway proposed to be constructed, improved or altered, as indicated in an order or scheme which has come into operation under the provisions of Part II of the Highways Act 1959 c. 25.

1959 relating to trunk roads or special roads or as indicated in an order which has come into operation under section 1 of the Highways Act 1971, being land in relation to which a power of compulsory acquisition conferred by any of the provisions of Part X of the said Act of 1959 or Part III of the said Act of 1971 (including a power compulsorily to acquire any right by virtue of section 47 of the said Act of 1971) may become exercisable, as being land required for purposes of construction, improvement or alteration as indicated in the order or scheme ; or

(e) is land shown on plans approved by a resolution of a local highway authority as land comprised in the site of a highway as proposed to be constructed, improved or altered by that authority ; or

(f) is land on which the Secretary of State proposes to provide a trunk road or a special road and has given to the local planning authority written notice of his intention to provide the road, together with maps or plans sufficient to identify the proposed route of the road ; or

(g) is land in the case of which—

(i) there is in force a compulsory purchase order made by a highway authority in the exercise of highway land acquisition powers and providing, by virtue of section 47 of the Highways Act 1971, for the acquisition of a right or rights over that land ; and

(ii) the highway authority have power to serve, but have not served, notice to treat in respect of the right or rights ;

(h) is land indicated by information published in pursuance of section 31 of the Housing Act 1969 as land which a local authority propose to acquire in the exercise of their powers under Part II of that Act (general improvement areas) ; or

(i) is land authorised by a special enactment to be compulsorily acquired, or land falling within the limits of deviation within which powers of compulsory acquisition conferred by a special enactment are exercisable ; or

(j) is land in respect of which a compulsory purchase order is in force, where the appropriate authority have power to serve, but have not served, notice to treat in respect of the land.

(2) Paragraph (*a*) of subsection (1) of this section shall not apply to land situated in a district for which a local plan is in force, where that plan—

(*a*) allocates any land in the district for the purposes of such functions as are mentioned in that paragraph; or

(*b*) defines any land in the district as the site of proposed development for the purposes of any such functions.

(3) Interests qualifying for protection under these provisions are either—

(*a*) interests in hereditaments or parts of hereditaments; or

(*b*) interests in agricultural units or parts of agricultural units.

(4) An interest in the whole or part of a hereditament shall be taken to be an interest qualifying for protection under these provisions if, on the date of service of a notice under section 193 of this Act in respect thereof, either—

(*a*) the annual value of the hereditament does not exceed such amount as may be prescribed for the purposes of this paragraph by an order made by the Secretary of State, and the interest in question is the interest of an owner-occupier of the hereditament; or

(*b*) in a case not falling within the preceding paragraph, the interest in question is the interest of a resident owner occupier of the hereditament.

(5) An interest in the whole or part of an agricultural unit shall be taken to be an interest qualifying for protection under these provisions if, on the date of service of a notice under section 193 of this Act in respect thereof, it is the interest of an owner-occupier of the unit.

(6) In this section and in the said sections 193 to 207 " these provisions " means the provisions of this section and of those sections, " the specified descriptions " means the descriptions contained in subsection (1)(*a*) to (*j*) of this section and " blight notice " means a notice served under section 193 or 201 of this Act.

193.—(1) Where the whole or part of a hereditament or agri- Power to serve cultural unit is comprised in land of any of the specified descrip- blight notice. tions, and a person claims that—

(*a*) he is entitled to an interest in that hereditament or unit; and (*b*) the interest is one which qualifies for protection under these provisions ; and

(*c*) since the relevant date he has made reasonable endeavours to sell that interest; and

(*d*) he has been unable to sell it except at a price substantially lower than that for which it might reasonably have been expected to sell if no part of the hereditament or unit were comprised in land of any of the specified descriptions,

he may serve on the appropriate authority a notice in the prescribed form requiring that authority to purchase that interest to the extent specified in, and otherwise in accordance with, these provisions.

(2) Subsection (1) of this section shall apply in relation to an interest in part of a hereditament or agricultural unit as it applies in relation to an interest in the entirety of a hereditament or agricultural unit:

Provided that this subsection shall not enable any person—

(*a*) if he is entitled to an interest in the entirety of a hereditament or agricultural unit, to make any claim or serve any notice under this section in respect of his interest in part of the hereditament or unit ; or

(*b*) if he is entitled to an interest only in part of a hereditament or agricultural unit, to make or serve any such claim or notice in respect of his interest in less than the entirety of that part.

(3) In this section " the relevant date "—

(*a*) in relation to land indicated, allocated or defined as mentioned in paragraph (*a*), (*b*) or (*c*) of subsection (1) of section 192 of this Act, means the date (whether before or after the commencement of this Act) on which the development plan, or the amendment of the development plan, by virtue of which the land was first so indicated, allocated or defined came into operation ;

(*b*) in relation to land falling within paragraph (*d*) of that subsection, means the date (whether before or after the commencement of this Act) of the coming into force of the order or scheme by virtue of which it falls within that paragraph ;

(*c*) in relation to land falling within paragraph (*e*) of that subsection, means the date (whether before or after the commencement of this Act) of the passing of the resolution by virtue of which it falls within that paragraph ;

(*d*) in relation to land falling within paragraph (*f*) of that subsection, means the date (whether before or after the commencement of this Act) on which the Secretary of State gave to the local planning authority the written notice specified in that paragraph ;

(*e*) in relation to land falling within paragraph (*g*) of that subsection, means the date (whether before or after the commencement of this Act) on which the order for the compulsory acquisition of the right or rights over the land was confirmed or made by the Secretary of State ;

(*f*) in relation to land falling within paragraph (*h*) of that subsection, means the date (whether before or after the commencement of this Act) on which the information in question was first published ;

(*g*) in relation to land falling within paragraph (*i*) of that subsection, means the date (whether before or after the commencement of this Act) on which the special enactment in question came into operation ;

(*h*) in relation to land falling within paragraph (*j*) of that subsection, means the date (whether before or after the commencement of this Act) on which the order for its compulsory purchase was confirmed or made by the Secretary of State.

(4) In these provisions " the claimant ", in relation to a blight notice, means the person who served that notice, and any reference to the interest of the claimant, in relation to such a notice, is a reference to the interest which the notice requires the appropriate authority to purchase as mentioned in subsection (1) of this section.

194.—(1) Where a blight notice has been served in respect Objection to of a hereditament or an agricultural unit, the appropriate blight notice. authority, at any time before the end of the period of two months beginning with the date of service of that notice, may serve on the claimant a counter-notice in the prescribed form objecting to the notice.

(2) Subject to the following provisions of this section, the grounds on which objection may be made in a counter-notice to a notice served under section 193 of this Act are—

(*a*) that no part of the hereditament or agricultural unit to which the notice relates is comprised in land of any of the specified descriptions ;

(*b*) that the appropriate authority (unless compelled to do so by virtue of these provisions) do not propose to acquire any part of the hereditament, or (in the case

G

of an agricultural unit) any part of the affected area, in the exercise of any relevant powers ;

(c) that the appropriate authority propose in the exercise of relevant powers to acquire a part of the hereditament or (in the case of an agricultural unit) a part of the affected area specified in the counter-notice, but (unless compelled to do so by virtue of these provisions) do not propose to acquire any other part of that hereditament or area in the exercise of any such powers ;

(d) that (in the case of land falling within paragraph (a) or (c) but not (d), (e) or (f) of section 192(1) of this Act) the appropriate authority (unless compelled to do so by virtue of these provisions) do not propose to acquire in the exercise of any relevant powers any part of the hereditament or (in the case of an agricultural unit) any part of the affected area during the period of fifteen years from the date of the counter-notice or such longer period from that date as may be specified in the counter-notice ;

(e) that, on the date of service of the notice under section 193 of this Act, the claimant was not entitled to an interest in any part of the hereditament or agricultural unit to which the notice relates ;

(f) that (for reasons specified in the counter-notice) the interest of the claimant is not an interest qualifying for protection under these provisions ;

(g) that the conditions specified in paragraphs (c) and (d) of section 193(1) of this Act are not fulfilled.

(3) An objection may not be made on the grounds mentioned in paragraph (d) of subsection (2) of this section if it may be made on the grounds mentioned in paragraph (b) of that subsection.

(4) Where the appropriate enactment is one of the enactments conferring highway land acquisition powers, subsection (2) of this section shall have effect as if—

(a) in paragraph (b) after the word " acquire " there were inserted the words " or to acquire any rights over " ;

(b) in paragraph (c) for the words " do not propose to acquire " there were substituted the words " propose neither to acquire, nor to acquire any right over " ;

(c) in paragraph (d) after the words " affected area " there were inserted " or to acquire any right over any part thereof ".

(5) Any counter-notice served under this section in respect of a blight notice shall specify the grounds (being one or more of the grounds mentioned in the preceding provisions of this section or, as relevant, in section 201(6) of this Act) on which the appropriate authority object to the notice.

(6) In this section "relevant powers", in relation to any land
falling within any of the specified descriptions, means any powers
under which the appropriate authority are or could be
authorised—

 (a) to acquire that land compulsorily as being land falling
 within that description ; or

 (b) to acquire that land compulsorily for any of the relevant
 purposes ;

and, where the appropriate enactment is one of the enactments
conferring highway land acquisition powers, any such powers as
extending to the acquisition of rights over land ; and "the
relevant purposes", in relation to any such land, means the
purposes for which, in accordance with the circumstances by
virtue of which that land falls within the description in question,
it is liable to be acquired or is indicated as being proposed to be
acquired.

195.—(1) Where a counter-notice has been served under section 194 of this Act objecting to a blight notice, the claimant, at
any time before the end of the period of two months beginning
with the date of service of the counter-notice, may require the
objection to be referred to the Lands Tribunal.

(2) On any such reference, if the objection is not withdrawn,
the Lands Tribunal shall consider the matters set out in the
notice served by the claimant and the grounds of the objection
specified in the counter-notice ; and, subject to subsection (3) of
this section, unless it is shown to the satisfaction of the Tribunal
that the objection is not well-founded, the Tribunal shall uphold
the objection.

(3) An objection on the grounds mentioned in section 194(2)
(b), (c) or (d) of this Act shall not be upheld by the Tribunal
unless it is shown to the satisfaction of the Tribunal that the
objection is well-founded.

(4) If the Tribunal determines not to uphold the objection,
the Tribunal shall declare that the notice to which the counter-
notice relates is a valid notice.

(5) If the Tribunal upholds the objection, but only on the
grounds mentioned in section 194(2)(c) of this Act, the Tribunal
shall declare that the notice is a valid notice in relation to the
part of the hereditament or (in the case of an agricultural unit)
of the affected area specified in the counter-notice as being the
part which the appropriate authority propose to acquire as
therein mentioned, but not in relation to any other part of the
hereditament or affected area.

(6) In any case falling within subsection (4) or subsection (5)
of this section, the Tribunal shall give directions specifying the
date on which notice to treat (as mentioned in section 196 of
this Act) is to be deemed to have been served.

196.—(1) Where a blight notice has been served, and either—

(a) no counter-notice objecting to that notice is served in accordance with these provisions ; or

(b) where such a counter-notice has been served, the objection is withdrawn, or, on a reference to the Lands Tribunal, is not upheld by the Tribunal,

the appropriate authority shall be deemed to be authorised to acquire compulsorily under the appropriate enactment the interest of the claimant in the hereditament, or (in the case of an agricultural unit) the interest of the claimant in so far as it subsists in the affected area, and to have served a notice to treat in respect thereof on the date mentioned in subsection (2) of this section.

(2) The said date—

(a) in a case where, on a reference to the Lands Tribunal, the Tribunal determines not to uphold the objection, is the date specified in directions given by the Tribunal in accordance with section 195(6) of this Act ;

(b) in any other case, is the date on which the period of two months beginning with the date of service of the blight notice comes to an end.

(3) Where the appropriate authority have served a counter-notice objecting to a blight notice on the grounds mentioned in section 194(2)(c) of this Act, then if either—

(a) the claimant, without referring that objection to the Lands Tribunal, and before the time for so referring it has expired, gives notice to the appropriate authority that he accepts the proposal of the authority to acquire the part of the hereditament or affected area specified in the counter-notice, and withdraws his claim as to the remainder of that hereditament or area ; or

(b) on a reference to the Lands Tribunal, the Tribunal makes a declaration in accordance with section 195(5) of this Act in respect of that part of the hereditament or affected area,

the appropriate authority shall be deemed to be authorised to acquire compulsorily under the appropriate enactment the interest of the claimant in so far as it subsists in the part of the hereditament or affected area specified in the counter-notice (but not in so far as it subsists in any other part of that hereditament or area) and to have served a notice to treat in respect thereof on the date mentioned in subsection (4) of this section.

(4) The said date—

(a) in a case falling within paragraph (a) of subsection

(3) of this section, is the date on which notice is given PART IX
in accordance with that paragraph; and

(*b*) in a case falling within paragraph (*b*) of that subsection,
is the date specified in directions given by the Lands
Tribunal in accordance with section 195(6) of this Act.

197. Where an interest in land is acquired in pursuance of a Compensation
blight notice and the interest is one— for compulsory

(*a*) in respect of which a compulsory purchase order is in purchase of
force under section 1 of the Acquisition of Land historic
(Authorisation Procedure) Act 1946 (as applied by buildings and of land in
section 114 of this Act) containing a direction for mini- clearance
mum compensation under section 117 of this Act; areas.
or

(*b*) in respect of which a compulsory purchase order is in
force under Part III of the Housing Act 1957; 1957 c. 56.

the compensation payable for the acquisition shall, in a case
falling within paragraph (*a*) of this section, be assessed in accordance with the direction mentioned in that paragraph and, in
a case falling with paragraph (*b*) of this section, be assessed
in accordance with Part III of the said Act of 1957, in either
case as if the notice to treat deemed to have been served in
respect of the interest under section 196 of this Act had been
served in pursuance of the compulsory purchase order.

198.—(1) Subject to subsection (2) of this section, the person Withdrawal
by whom a blight notice has been served may withdraw the of blight
notice at any time before the compensation payable in respect notice.
of a compulsory acquisition in pursuance of the notice has been
determined by the Lands Tribunal, or at any time before the end
of the period of six weeks beginning with the date on which the
compensation is so determined; and, where such a notice is
withdrawn by virtue of this subsection, any notice to treat
deemed to have been served in consequence thereof shall be
deemed to have been withdrawn.

(2) A person shall not be entitled by virtue of subsection (1)
of this section to withdraw a notice after the appropriate
authority have exercised a right of entering and taking possession of land in pursuance of a notice to treat deemed to have
been served in consequence of that notice.

(3) No compensation shall be payable in respect of the withdrawal of a notice to treat which is deemed to have been
withdrawn by virtue of subsection (1) of this section.

G 3

PART IX
Effect on
powers of
compulsory
acquisition of
counter-
notice dis-
claiming
intention to
acquire.

199.—(1) The provisions of subsection (2) of this section shall have effect where the grounds of objection specified in a counter-notice served under section 194 of this Act consist of or include the grounds mentioned in paragraph (*b*) or (*d*) of subsection (2) of that section, and either—

(*a*) the objection on the grounds mentioned in that paragraph is referred to and upheld by the Lands Tribunal ; or

(*b*) the time for referring that objection to the Lands Tribunal expires without its having been so referred.

(2) If a compulsory purchase order has been made under the appropriate enactment in respect of land which consists of or includes the whole or part of the hereditament or agricultural unit to which the counter-notice relates, or if the land in question falls within section 192(1)(*i*) of this Act, any power conferred by that order, or by special enactment, as the case may be, for the compulsory acquisition of the interest of the claimant in the hereditament or agricultural unit or any part thereof shall cease to have effect.

(3) The provisions of subsection (4) of this section shall have effect where the grounds of objection specified in a counter-notice under section 194 of this Act consist of or include the grounds mentioned in paragraph (*c*) of subsection (2) of that section, and either—

(*a*) the objection on the grounds mentioned in that paragraph is referred to and upheld by the Lands Tribunal ; or

(*b*) the time for referring that objection to the Lands Tribunal expires without its having been so referred ;

and in subsection (4) of this section any reference to " the part of the hereditament or affected area not required " is a reference to the whole of that hereditament or area except the part specified in the counter-notice as being the part which the appropriate authority propose to acquire as mentioned in the counter-notice.

(4) If a compulsory purchase order has been made under the appropriate enactment in respect of land which consists of or includes any of the part of the hereditament or affected area not required, or if the land in question falls within section 192(1)(*i*) of this Act, any power conferred by that order, or by the special enactment, as the case may be, for the compulsory acquisition of the interest of the claimant in any land comprised in the part of the hereditament or affected area not required shall cease to have effect.

200.—(1) In relation to any time after the death of a person who has served a blight notice, the provisions mentioned in subsection (2) of this section shall apply as if any reference therein to the claimant were a reference to the claimant's personal representatives.

(2) The said provisions are sections 194(1), 195(1) and 196(3) of this Act.

201.—(1) Where the whole or part of a hereditament or agricultural unit is comprised in land falling within any of the specified descriptions and a person claims that—

  (*a*) he is entitled as mortgagee (by virtue of a power which has become exercisable) to sell an interest in the hereditament or unit, giving immediate vacant possession of the land ; and

  (*b*) since the relevant date (within the meaning of section 193 of this Act) he has made reasonable endeavours to sell that interest ; and

  (*c*) he has been unable to sell it except at a price substantially lower than that for which it might reasonably have been expected to sell if no part of the hereditament or unit were comprised in land of any of the said descriptions,

then, subject to the provisions of this section, he may serve on the appropriate authority a notice in the prescribed form requiring that authority to purchase that interest to the extent specified in, and otherwise in accordance with, these provisions.

(2) Subsection (1) of this section shall apply in relation to an interest in part of a hereditament or agricultural unit as it applies in relation to an interest in the entirety of a hereditament or agricultural unit:

Provided that this subsection shall not enable a person—

  (*a*) if his interest as mortgagee is in the entirety of a hereditament or agricultural unit, to make any claim or serve any notice under this section in respect of any interest in part of the hereditament or unit ; or

  (*b*) if his interest as mortgagee is only in part of a hereditament or agricultural unit, to make or serve any such notice or claim in respect of any interest in less than the entirety of that part.

(3) Notice under this section shall not be served unless one or other of the following conditions is satisfied with regard to the interest which the mortgagee claims he has the power to sell—

  (*a*) the interest could be the subject of a notice under section 193 of this Act served by the person entitled thereto

G 4

on the date of service of the notice under this section ;
or

(b) the interest could have been the subject of such a notice
served by that person on a date not more than six
months before the date of service of the notice under
this section.

(4) No notice under this section shall be served in respect of
a hereditament or agricultural unit, or any part of a
hereditament or agricultural unit, at a time when a notice
already served under section 193 of this Act is outstanding with
respect to the hereditament, unit or part ; and no notice shall
be so served under that section at a time when a notice already
served under this section is so outstanding.

(5) For the purposes of subsection (4) of this section, a notice
served under this section or section 193 of this Act shall be
treated as outstanding with respect to a hereditament or agricultural unit, or to part of a hereditament or agricultural unit,
until—

(a) it is withdrawn in relation to the hereditament, unit or
part ; or

(b) an objection to the notice having been made by a
counter-notice under section 194 of this Act, either—

(i) the period of two months specified in section
195 of this Act elapses without the claimant having
required the objection to be referred to the Lands
Tribunal under that section ; or

(ii) the objection, having been so referred to the
Lands Tribunal, is upheld by the Tribunal with
respect to the hereditament, unit or part.

(6) The grounds on which objection may be made in a
counter-notice under section 194 of this Act to a notice under
this section are those specified in paragraphs (a) to (c) of subsection (2) of that section and, in a case to which it applies,
the grounds specified in paragraph (d) of that subsection and
also the following grounds—

(a) that, on the date of service of the notice under this
section, the claimant had no interest as mortgagee
in any part of the hereditament or agricultural unit
to which the notice relates ;

(b) that (for reasons specified in the counter-notice) the
claimant had not on that date the power referred to in
subsection (1)(a) of this section ;

(c) that the conditions specified in subsection (1)(b) and (c)
of this section are not fulfilled ;

(*d*) that (for reasons specified in the counter-notice) neither   PART IX
of the conditions specified in subsection (3) of this
section was, on the date of service of the notice under
this section, satisfied with regard to the interest
referred tò in that subsection.

202.—(1) The provisions of sections 194(2)(*c*), 195(5), 196(3)   Saving for
and 199(3) and (4) of this Act relating to hereditaments shall   claimant's
not affect the right of a claimant under section 92 of the Lands   right to sell
Clauses Consolidation Act 1845 to sell the whole of the heredita-   whole heredi-
ment, or (in the case of an agricultural unit) the whole of the   tament, etc.
affected area, which he has required the authority to purchase.   1845 c. 18.

(2) The said provisions shall not affect the right of a claim-   1965 c. 56.
ant under section 8 of the Compulsory Purchase Act 1965 to
sell (unless the Lands Tribunal otherwise determines) the whole
of the hereditament, or (in the case of an agricultural unit) the
whole of the affected area, which he has required the authority
to purchase ; and accordingly in determining whether or not to
uphold an objection relating to a hereditament on the grounds
mentioned in section 194(2)(*c*) of this Act the Tribunal shall
consider (in addition to the other matterf which they are required
to consider) whether—

(*a*) in the case of a house, building or manufactory, the
part proposed to be acquired can be taken without
material detriment to the house, building or manufactory ; or

(*b*) in the case of a park or garden belonging to a house,
the part proposed to be acquired can be taken without
seriously affecting the amenity or convenience of the
house.

203.—(1) Subject to the following provisions of this section,   Meaning of
in these provisions " owner-occupier ", in relation to a heredita-   " owner-
ment, means a person who—   occupier "
    and "resident
(*a*) occupies the whole or a substantial part of the heredita-   owner-
ment in right of an owner's interest therein, and has   occupier "
so occupied the hereditament or that part thereof
during the whole of the period of six months ending
with the date of service ; or

(*b*) occupied, in right of an owner's interest, the whole or
a substantial part of the hereditament during the
whole of a period of six months ending not more than
twelve months before the date of service, the hereditament, or that part thereof, as the case may be, having
been unoccupied since the end of that period.

(2) Subject to the following provisions of this section, in these provisions " owner-occupier ", in relation to an agricultural unit, means a person who—

(a) occupies the whole of that unit, and has occupied it during the whole of the period of six months ending with the date of service ; or

(b) occupied the whole of that unit during the whole of a period of six months ending not more than twelve months before the date of service,

and, at all times material for the purposes of paragraph (a) or paragraph (b) of this subsection, as the case may be, has been entitled to an owner's interest in the whole or part of that unit.

(3) In these provisions " resident owner-occupier ", in relation to a hereditament, means an individual who—

(a) occupies the whole or a substantial part of the hereditament as a private dwelling in right of an owner's interest therein, and has so occupied the hereditament or that part thereof, as the case may be, during the whole of the period of six months ending with the date of service ; or

(b) occupied, in right of an owner's interest, the whole or a substantial part of the hereditament as a private dwelling during the whole of a period of six months ending not more than twelve months before the date of service, the hereditament, or that part thereof, as the case may be, having been unoccupied since the end of that period.

(4) In this section " owner's interest ", in relation to a hereditament or agricultural unit, means a freehold interest therein or a tenancy thereof granted or extended for a term of years certain of which, on the date of service, not less than three years remain unexpired ; and " date of service ", in relation to a hereditament or agricultural unit, means the date of service of a notice in respect thereof under section 193 of this Act.

Special
provisions
as to partner-
ships.

204.—(1) The provisions of this section shall have effect for the purposes of the application of these provisions to a hereditament or agricultural unit occupied for the purposes of a partnership firm.

(2) Occupation for the purposes of the firm shall be treated as occupation by the firm, and not as occupation by any one or more of the partners individually, and the definitions of " owner-occupier " in section 203(1) and (2) of this Act shall apply in relation to the firm accordingly.

(3) If, after the service by the firm of a blight notice, any change occurs (whether by death or otherwise) in the constitution of the firm, any proceedings, rights or obligations consequential upon that notice may be carried on or exercised by or against, or (as the case may be) shall be incumbent upon, the partners for the time being constituting the firm.

(4) Nothing in this section or elsewhere in these provisions shall be construed as indicating an intention to exclude the operation of section 19 of the Interpretation Act 1889 (whereby, unless the contrary intention appears, " person " includes any body of persons corporate or unincorporate) in relation to any of these provisions.

1889 c. 63.

(5) Subsection (2) of this section shall not affect the definition of " resident owner-occupier " in section 203(3) of this Act.

205.—(1) Subject to the following provisions of this section, in these provisions " the appropriate authority ", in relation to any land, means the government department, local authority or other body by whom, in accordance with the circumstances by virtue of which the land falls within any of the specified descriptions, the land is liable to be acquired or is indicated as being proposed to be acquired or, as the case may be, any right over the land is proposed to be acquired.

" Appropriate authority " for purposes of these provisions.

(2) If any question arises—

    (*a*) whether the appropriate authority in relation to any land for the purpose of these provisions is the Secretary of State or a local highway authority ; or

    (*b,* which of two or more local highway authorities is the appropriate authority in relation to any land for those purposes ; or

    (*c*) which of two or more local authorities is the appropriate authority in relation to any land for those purposes,

that question shall be referred to the Secretary of State, whose decision shall be final.

(3) If any question arises which authority is the appropriate authority for the purposes of these provisions—

    (*a*) section 194(1) of this Act shall have effect as if the reference to the date of service of the blight notice were a reference to that date or the date on which that question is determined, whichever is the later;

    (*b*) section 201(3)(*b*) of this Act shall apply with the substitution for the period of six months of a reference to that period extended by so long as it takes to obtain a determination of the question ; and

(c) section 203(1)(*b*), (2)(*b*) and (3)(*b*) of this Act shall apply with the substitution for the reference to twelve months before the date of service of a reference to that period extended by so long as it takes to obtain a determination of the question.

" Appropriate enactment " for purposes of these provisions.

206.—(1) Subject to the following provisions of this section, in these provisions " the appropriate enactment ", in relation to land falling within any of the specified descriptions, means the enactment which provides for the compulsory acquisition of land as being land falling within that description or, as respects the description contained in paragraph (*g*) of section 192(1) of this Act, the enactment under which the compulsory purchase order·referred to in that paragraph was made.

(2) In relation to land falling within the description contained in section 192(1)(*b*) of this Act an enactment shall, for the purposes of subsection (1) of this section be taken to be an enactment which provides for the compulsory acquisition of land as being land falling within that description if—

> (*a*) the enactment provides for the compulsory acquisition of land for the purposes of the functions which are indicated in the development plan as being the functions for the purposes of which the land is allocated or is proposed to be developed ; or
>
> (*b*) where no particular functions are so indicated in the development plan, the enactment provides for the compulsory acquisition of land for the purposes of any of the functions of the government department, local authority or other body for the purposes of whose functions the land is allocated or is defined as the site of proposed development.

(3) Where, in accordance with the circumstances by virtue of which any land falls within any of the specified descriptions, it is indicated that the land is proposed to be acquired for highway purposes, any enactment under which a highway authority are or (subject to the fulfilment of the relevant conditions) could be authorised to acquire that land compulsorily for highway purposes shall, for the purposes of subsection (1) of this section, be taken to be an enactment providing for the compulsory acquisition of that land as being land falling within the description in question.

(4) In subsection (3) of this section the reference to the fulfilment of the relevant conditions is a reference to such one or more of the following as are applicable to the circumstances in question, that is to say—

> (*a*) the coming into operation of any requisite order under the provisions of Part II of the Highways Act 1959 relating to trunk roads ;

(*b*) the coming into operation of any requisite scheme or
order under the provisions of the said Part II relating
to special roads ;

(*c*) the coming into operation of the requisite scheme under
section 3 of the Highways (Miscellaneous Provisions)
Act 1961 ;

(*d*) the coming into operation of the requisite order under
section 1 of the Highways Act 1971 ;

(*e*) the making or approval of any requisite plans.

(5) If, apart from this subsection, two or more enactments
would be the appropriate enactment in relation to any land for
the purposes of these provisions, the appropriate enactment for
those purposes shall be taken to be that one of those enactments
under which, in the circumstances in question, it is most likely
that (apart from these provisions) the land would have been
acquired by the appropriate authority.

(6) If any question arises as to which enactment is the appropriate enactment in relation to any land for the purposes of
these provisions, that question shall be referred—

(*a*) where the appropriate authority are a government
department, to the Minister or Board in charge of
that department ;

(*b*) where the appropriate authority are statutory undertakers, to the appropriate Minister ; and

(*c*) in any other case, to the Secretary of State,

and the decision of the Minister, Secretary of State or Board
to whom a question is referred under this subsection shall be
final.

207.—(1) Subject to the following provisions of this section,
in these provisions the following expressions have the meanings
hereby assigned to them respectively, that is to say:—

General
interpretation
of these
provisions.

" the affected area ", in relation to an agricultural unit,
means so much of that unit as, on the date of service,
consists of land falling within any of the specified
descriptions ;

" agricultural unit " means land which is occupied as a unit
for agricultural purposes, including any dwellinghouse
or other building occupied by the same person for the
purpose of farming the land ;

" annual value ", in relation to a hereditament, means the
value which, on the date of service, is shown in the
valuation list as the rateable value of that hereditament,
except that, where the rateable value differs from the
net annual value, it means the value which on that
date is shown in the valuation list as the net annual
value thereof ;

" the claimant " has the meaning assigned to it by section 193(4) of this Act ;

" hereditament " means the aggregate of the land which forms the subject of a single entry in the valuation list for the time being in force for a rating area ;

" highway land acquisition powers " means powers in respect of the acquisition of land which are exercisable by a highway authority under section 214, 215, 218, 219, 220 or 221 of the Highways Act 1959 or under section 44 or 47(3) of the Highways Act 1971 ;

" special enactment " means a local enactment, or a provision contained in an Act other than a local or private Act, being a local enactment or provision authorising the compulsory acquisition of land specifically identified therein ; and in this definition " local enactment " means a local or private Act, or an order confirmed by Parliament or brought into operation in accordance with special parliamentary procedure ;

" these provisions ", " the specified descriptions " and " blight notice " have the meanings assigned to them respectively by section 192(6) of this Act.

(2) Where any land is on the boundary between two or more rating areas, and accordingly—

(a) different parts of that land form the subject of single entries in the valuation lists for the time being in force for those areas respectively ; but

(b) if the whole of that land had been in one of those areas, it would have formed the subject of a single entry in the valuation list for that area,

the whole of that land shall be treated, for the purposes of the definition of " hereditament " in subsection (1) of this section, as if it formed the subject of a single entry in the valuation list for a rating area.

(3) Land which forms the subject of an entry in the valuation list by reason only that it is land over which any shooting, fishing or other sporting rights are exercisable, or that it is land over which a right of exhibiting advertisements is let out or reserved, shall not be taken to be a hereditament within the said definition

(4) Where, in accordance with subsection (2) of this section, land whereof different parts form the subject of single entries in the valuation lists for the time being in force for two or more rating areas is treated as if it formed the subject of a single entry in the valuation list for a rating area, the definition of " annual value " in subsection (1) of this section shall apply as if any reference therein to a value shown in the valuation list were a reference to the aggregate of the values shown (as rateable

values or as net annual values, as the case may be) in those valuation lists in relation to the different parts of that land.

(5) In this section " date of service " has the same meaning as in section 203 of this Act.

Supplementary provisions

208. Without prejudice to the provisions of section 198(1) of this Act, the power conferred by section 31 of the Land Compensation Act 1961 to withdraw a notice to treat shall not be exercisable in the case of a notice to treat which is deemed to have been served by virtue of any of the provisions of this Part of this Act. No withdrawal of constructive notice to treat. 1961 c. 33.

PART X
HIGHWAYS
Stopping up and diversion of highways

209.—(1) The Secretary of State may by order authorise the stopping up or diversion of any highway if he is satisfied that it is necessary to do so in order to enable development to be carried out in accordance with planning permission granted under Part III of this Act, or to be carried out by a government department. Highways affected by development: orders by Secretary of State.

(2) Any order under this section may make such provision as appears to the Secretary of State to be necessary or expedient for the provision or improvement of any other highway, and may direct—

(a) that any highway so provided or improved shall for the purposes of the Highways Act 1959 be a highway maintainable at the public expense ; 1959 c. 25.

(b) that the Secretary of State, or any local authority specified in that behalf in the order, shall be the highway authority for that highway ;

(c) in the case of a highway for which the Secretary of State is to be the highway authority, that the highway shall, on such date as may be specified in the order, become a trunk road within the meaning of the Highways Act 1959.

(3) Any order made under this section may contain such incidental and consequential provisions as appear to the Secretary of State to be necessary or expedient, including in particular—

(a) provision for authorising the Secretary of State, or requiring any other authority or person specified in the order—

(i) to pay, or to make contributions in respect of, the cost of doing any work provided for by the order or any increased expenditure to be incurred which is attributable to the doing of any such work ; or

(ii) to repay, or to make contributions in respect of, any compensation paid by the highway authority in respect of restrictions imposed under section 1 or
2 of the Restriction of Ribbon Development Act 1935 in relation to any highway stopped up or diverted under the order ;

(*b*) provision for the preservation of any rights of statutory undertakers in respect of any apparatus of theirs which immediately before the date of the order is under, in, on, over, along or across the highway to which the order relates.

(4) An order may be made under this section authorising the stopping up or diversion of any highway which is temporarily stopped up or diverted under any other enactment.

(5) The provisions of this section shall have effect without prejudice to—

(*a*) any power conferred on the Secretary of State by any other enactment to authorise the stopping up or diversion of a highway ;

(*b*) the provisions of section 3 of the Acquisition of Land (Authorisation Procedure) Act 1946 ; or

(*c*) the provisions of section 214(1)(*a*) of this Act.

210.—(1) Subject to section 217 of this Act, a competent authority may by order authorise the stopping up or diversion of any footpath or bridleway if they are satisfied as mentioned in section 209(1) of this Act.

(2) An order under this section may, if the competent authority are satisfied that it should do so, provide—

(*a*) for the creation of an alternative highway for use as a replacement for the one authorised by the order to be stopped up or diverted, or for the improvement of an existing highway for such use ;

(*b*) for authorising or requiring works to be carried out in relation to any footpath or bridleway for whose stopping up or diversion, creation or improvement, provision is made by the order ;

(*c*) for the preservation of any rights of statutory under-takers in respect of apparatus of theirs which immediately before the date of the order is under, in, on, over, along or across any such footpath or bridleway ;

(*d*) for requiring any person named in the order to pay, or make contributions in respect of, the cost of carrying out any such works.

(3) An order may be made under this section authorising the stopping up or diversion of a footpath or bridleway which is temporarily stopped up or diverted under any other enactment.

(4) The competent authorities for the purposes of this section are—

    (a) the local planning authority; and

    (b) in relation to development for which planning permission was granted by another authority to whom had been delegated the power of granting it, that other authority.

211.—(1) If planning permission is granted under Part III of this Act for constructing or improving, or the Secretary of State proposes to construct or improve, a highway (hereafter in this section referred to as " the main highway "), the Secretary of State may by order authorise the stopping up or diversion of any other highway which crosses or enters the route of the main highway or which is, or will be, otherwise affected by the construction or improvement of the main highway, if it appears to the Secretary of State expedient to do so—

    (a) in the interests of the safety of users of the main highway; or

    (b) to facilitate the movement of traffic on the main highway.

(2) Subsections (2) to (5) of section 209 of this Act shall apply to an order under this section as they apply to an order under that section.

Conversion of highway into footpath or bridleway

212.—(1) The provisions of this section shall have effect where a local planning authority by resolution adopt a proposal for improving the amenity of part of their area, being a proposal which involves a highway in that area (being a highway over which the public have a right of way with vehicles, but not a trunk road or a road classified as a principal road for the purposes of advances under section 235 of the Highways Act 1959) being changed to a footpath or bridleway.

(2) The Secretary of State may, on an application made by the local planning authority after consultation with the highway authority (if different), by order provide for the extinguishment of any right which persons may have to use vehicles on that highway.

(3) An order made under subsection (2) of this section may include such provision as the Secretary of State (after consultation with the highway authority) thinks fit for permitting the

use on the highway of vehicles (whether mechanically propelled or not) in such cases as may be specified in the order, notwithstanding the extinguishment of any such right as is mentioned in that subsection; and any such provision may be framed by reference to particular descriptions of vehicles, or to particular persons by whom, or on whose authority, vehicles may be used, or to the circumstances in which, or the times at which, vehicles may be used for particular purposes.

(4) No provision contained in, or having effect under, any enactment, being a provision prohibiting or restricting the use of footpaths, footways or bridleways shall affect any use of a vehicle on a highway in relation to which an order made under subsection (2) of this section has effect, where the use is permitted in accordance with provisions of the order included by virtue of subsection (3) of this section.

(5) Any person who, at the time of an order under subsection (2) of this section coming into force, has an interest in land having lawful access to a highway to which the order relates shall be entitled to be compensated by the local planning authority in respect of any depreciation in the value of his interest which is directly attributable to the order and of any other loss or damage which is so attributable.

In this subsection " lawful access " means access authorised by planning permission granted under this Act, the Act of 1947 or the Act of 1962, or access in respect of which no such permission is necessary.

(6) A claim for compensation under subsection (5) of this section shall be made to the local planning authority within the time and in the manner prescribed by regulations under this Act.

(7) Sections 178 and 179 of this Act shall have effect in relation to compensation under subsection (5) of this section as they have effect in relation to compensation to which those sections apply.

(8) Without prejudice to section 287(3) of this Act, the Secretary of State may, on an application made by the local planning authority after consultation with the highway authority (if different) by order revoke an order made by him in relation to a highway under subsection (2) of this section; and the effect of the order shall be to reinstate any right to use vehicles on the highway, being a right which was extinguished by virtue of the order under that subsection.

(9) Subsections (2), (3) and (5) of section 209 of this Act shall apply to an order under this section as they apply to an order under that section.

213.—(1) Where in relation to a highway an order has been made under section 212(2) of this Act, a competent authority may carry out and maintain any such works on or in the highway, or place on or in it any such objects or structures, as appear to them to be expédient for the purposes of giving effect to the order or of enhancing the amenity of the highway and its immediate surroundings or to be otherwise desirable for a purpose beneficial to the public.

(2) The powers exercisable by a competent authority under this section shall extend to laying out any part of the highway with lawns, trees, shrubs and flower-beds and to providing facilities for recreation or refreshment.

(3) A competent authority may so exercise their powers under this section as to restrict the access of the public to any part of the highway, but shall not so exercise them as—

(a) to prevent persons from entering the highway at any place where they could enter it before the order under section 212 of this Act was made ; or

(b) to prevent the passage of the public along the highway ; or

(c) to prevent normal access by pedestrians to premises adjoining the highway ; or

(d) to prevent any use of vehicles which is permitted by an order made under the said section 212 and applying to the highway ; or

(e) to prevent statutory undertakers from having access to any works of theirs under, in, on, over, along or across the highway.

(4) An order under section 212(8) of this Act may make provision requiring the removal of any obstruction of the highway resulting from the exercise by a competent authority of their powers under this section.

(5) The competent authorities for the purposes of this section are—

(a) the councils of counties, county boroughs and county districts ; and

(b) in Greater London, the Greater London Council and the councils of London boroughs ;

but such an authority shall not exercise any powers conferred by this section unless they have obtained the consent of the local planning authority and the highway authority (in a case where they are themselves not that authority).

Extinguish-
ment of public
rights of way
over land
held for
planning
purposes.

Extinguishment of rights of way

214.—(1) Where any land has been acquired or appropriated for planning purposes and is for the time being held by a local authority for the purposes for which it was acquired or appropriated—

(a) the Secretary of State may by order extinguish any public right of way over the land if he is satisfied that an alternative right of way has been or will be provided or that the provision of an alternative right of way is not required ;

(b) subject to section 217 of this Act, the local authority may by order extinguish any such right over the land, being a footpath or bridleway, if they are satisfied as aforesaid.

(2) In this section any reference to the acquisition or appropriation of land for planning purposes shall be construed in accordance with section 133(1) of this Act as if this section were in Part VI of this Act.

Procedure for making and confirming orders

Procedure for
making of
orders by
Secretary of
State.

215.—(1) Before making an order under section 209, 211, 212 or 214(1)(a) of this Act the Secretary of State shall publish in at least one local newspaper circulating in the relevant area, and in the London Gazette, a notice—

(a) stating the general effect of the order ;

(b) specifying a place in the relevant area where a copy of the draft order and of any relevant map or plan may be inspected by any person free of charge at all reasonable hours during a period of twenty-eight days from the date of the publication of the notice ; and

(c) stating that, within that period, any person may by notice to the Secretary of State object to the making of the order.

(2) Not later than the date on which that notice is so published, the Secretary of State—

(a) shall serve a copy of the notice, together with a copy of the draft order and of any relevant map or plan, on every local authority in whose area any highway or, as the case may be, any land to which the order relates is situated, and on any water, hydraulic power, gas or electricity undertakers having any cables, mains, pipes or wires laid along, across, under or over any highway to be stopped up or diverted or, as the case may be, any land over which a right of way is to be extinguished, under the order ; and

(*b*) shall cause a copy of the notice to be displayed in a   PART X
prominent position at the ends of so much of any
highway as is proposed to be stopped up or diverted
or, as the case may be, of the right of way proposed
to be extinguished under the order.

(3) If before the end of the said period of twenty-eight days
an objection is received by the Secretary of State from any
local authority or undertakers on whom a notice is required to
be served under subsection (2) of this section, or from any
other person appearing to him to be affected by the order, and
the objection is not withdrawn, the Secretary of State shall cause
a local inquiry to be held:

Provided that, if the objection is made by a person other than
such a local authority or undertakers, the Secretary of State
may dispense with such an inquiry if he is satisfied that in the
special circumstances of the case the holding of such an inquiry
is unnecessary.

(4) Subsections (2) to (5) of section 290 of the Local 1933 c. 51
Government Act 1933 (evidence and costs at local inquiries) shall
apply in relation to an inquiry caused to be held by the Secretary
of State under subsection (3) of this section as they apply in
relation to an inquiry caused to be held by a department under
subsection (1) of the said section 290, with the substitution for
the references to a department of references to the Secretary of
State.

(5) After considering any objections to the order which are
not withdrawn, and, where a local inquiry is held, the report
of the person who held the inquiry, the Secretary of State
(subject to subsection (6) of this section) may make the order
either without modification or subject to such modifications as
he thinks fit.

(6) Where the order contains a provision requiring any such
payment, repayment or contribution as is mentioned in section
209(3)(*a*) of this Act, and objection to that provision is duly made,
in accordance with subsection (3) of this section, by an authority
or person who would be required thereby to make such a payment, repayment or contribution, and the objection is not withdrawn, the order shall be subject to special parliamentary
procedure.

(7) Immediately after the order has been made, the Secretary
of State shall publish, in the manner specified in subsection
(1) of this section, a notice stating that the order has been made,
and naming a place where a copy of the order may be seen at
all reasonable hours; and the provisions of subsection (2) of
this section shall have effect in relation to any such notice as
they have effect in relation to a notice under subsection (1) of
this section.

PART X

(8) In this section " the relevant area ", in relation to an order, means the area in which any highway or land to which the order relates is situated, and " local authority " means the council of a county, county borough, county district or parish, or of a borough included in a rural district, the Greater London Council, the council of a London borough, and the parish meeting of a rural parish not having a separate parish council.

Procedure in anticipation of planning permission, etc.

216.—(1) Where the Secretary of State would, if planning permission for any development had been granted under Part III of this Act, have power to make an order under section 209 or 211 of this Act authorising the stopping-up or diversion of a highway in order to enable that development to be carried out, then, notwithstanding that such permission has not been granted, the Secretary of State may, in the circumstances specified in subsections (2) to (4) of this section, publish notice of the draft of such an order in accordance with section 215 of this Act.

(2) The Secretary of State may publish such a notice as aforesaid where the relevant development is the subject of an application for planning permission and either—

    (a) that application is made by a local authority or statutory undertakers or the National Coal Board ; or

    (b) that application stands referred to the Secretary of State in pursuance of a direction under section 35 of this Act ; or

    (c) the applicant has appealed to the Secretary of State under section 36 of this Act against a refusal of planning permission or of approval required under a development order, or against a condition of any such permission or approval.

(3) The Secretary of State may publish such a notice as aforesaid where—

    (a) the relevant development is to be carried out by a local authority, statutory undertakers or the National Coal Board and requires, by virtue of an enactment, the authorisation of a government department ; and

    (b) the developers have made application to the department for that authorisation and also requested a direction under section 40 of this Act or, in the case of the National Coal Board, under section 2 of the Opencast Coal Act 1958, that planning permission be deemed to be granted for that development.

1958 c. 69.

(4) The Secretary of State may publish such a notice as aforesaid where the council of a county or county borough, the Greater London Council, the council of a London borough, a joint planning board, or the Inner London Education Authority certify that they have begun to take such steps, in accordance

with regulations made by virtue of section 270 of this Act, as are requisite in order to enable them to obtain planning permission for the relevant development.

(5) Section 215(5) of this Act shall not be construed as authorising the Secretary of State to make an order under section 209 or 211 of this Act of which notice has been published by virtue of subsection (1) of this section until planning permission is granted for the development which occasions the making of the order.

217.—(1) An order made under section 210 or 214(1)(*b*) of this Act shall not take effect unless confirmed by the Secretary of State, or unless confirmed, as an unopposed order, by the authority who made it.

(2) The Secretary of State shall not confirm any such order unless satisfied as to every matter of which the authority making the order are required under section 210 or 214(1)(*b*) (as the case may be) to be satisfied.

(3) The time specified—

(*a*) in an order under section 210 as the time from which a footpath or bridleway is to be stopped up or diverted ; or

(*b*) in an order under section 214(1)(*b*) as the time from which a right of way is to be extinguished,

shall not be earlier than confirmation of the order.

(4) Schedule 20 to this Act shall have effect with respect to the confirmation of orders under section 210 or 214(1)(*b*) of this Act and the publicity for such orders after they are confirmed.

Supplementary provisions

218.—(1) The Secretary of State or a local highway authority may be authorised to acquire land compulsorily—

(*a*) for the purpose of providing or improving any highway which is to be provided or improved in pursuance of an order under section 209, 211 or 212 of this Act or for any other purpose for which land is required in connection with such an order ; or

(*b*) for the purpose of providing any public right of way which is to be provided as an alternative to a right of way extinguished under 214(1)(*a*) of this Act.

(2) The Acquisition of Land (Authorisation Procedure) Act 1946 shall apply to the acquisition of land under this section, and accordingly shall have effect—

(*a*) as if this section had been in force immediately before the commencement of that Act ; and

PART X

(b) as if this section were included among the enactments specified in section 1(1)(b) of that Act.

Concurrent proceedings in connection with highways.

219.—(1) In relation to orders under sections 209, 211 and 212 of this Act, regulations made under this Act may make provision for securing that any proceedings required to be taken for the purposes of the acquisition of land under section 218 of this Act (as mentioned in subsection (1)(a) of that section) may be taken concurrently with any proceedings required to be taken for the purposes of the order.

(2) In relation to orders under section 214(1)(a) of this Act, regulations made under this Act may make provision for securing—

(a) that any proceedings required to be taken for the purposes of such an order may be taken concurrently with any proceedings required to be taken for the purposes of the acquisition of the land over which the right of way is to be extinguished; or

(b) that any proceedings required to be taken for the purposes of the acquisition of any other land under section 218 of this Act (as mentioned in subsection (1)(b) of that section) may be taken concurrently with either or both of the proceedings referred to in the preceding paragraph.

Provisions as to telegraphic lines.

220.—(1) Where in pursuance of an order under section 209, 211 or 212 of this Act a highway is stopped up or diverted, and, immediately before the date on which the order became operative, there was under, in, on, over, along or across the highway a telegraphic line belonging to or used by the Post Office, the Post Office shall have the same powers in respect of that line as if the order had not become operative:

Provided that if any person entitled to land over which the highway subsisted requires that the telegraphic line should be altered, paragraphs (1) to (8) of section 7 of the Telegraph

1878 c. 76.

Act 1878 shall apply to the alteration, and accordingly shall have effect, subject to any necessary modifications, as if references therein to undertakers included references to the person so requiring the line to be altered.

(2) Where any such order provides for the improvement of a highway, other than a trunk road, and, immediately before the date on which the order became operative, there was under, in, on, over, along or across the highway a telegraphic line belonging to or used by the Post Office, then if the local highway authority require that that line should be altered, paragraphs (1) to (8) of the said section 7 shall apply to the alteration, and

accordingly shall have effect, subject to any necessary modifica-   PART X
tions, as if references therein to undertakers included references
to the local highway authority:

Provided that those paragraphs shall not apply by virtue of
this subsection to the alteration of a telegraphic line for the
purpose of the authority's works as defined in Part II of the 1950 c. 39.
Public Utilities Street Works Act 1950.

(3) Where an order under section 214(1)(*a*) of this Act extinguishing a public right of way is made on the application of a
local authority, and at the time of the publication of the notice
required by section 215(1) of this Act there was under, in, on,
over, along or across the land over which the right of way subsisted a telegraphic line belonging to or used by the Post Office—

(*a*) the power of the Post Office to remove the line shall,
notwithstanding the making of the order, be exercisable
at any time not later than the end of the period of
three months from the date on which the right of way
is extinguished, and shall be exercisable in respect of
the whole or any part of the line after the end of that
period if before the end of that period the Post Office
has given notice to the local authority of its intention
to remove the line or that part thereof, as the case
may be;

(*b*) the Post Office may by notice given in that behalf to
the local authority not later than the end of the said
period of three months abandon the telegraphic line
or any part thereof;

(*c*) subject to paragraph (*b*) of this subsection, the Post
Office shall be deemed at the end of that period to
have abandoned any part of the line which it has then
neither removed nor given notice of its intention to
remove;

(*d*) the Post Office shall be entitled to recover from the
local authority the expense of providing, in substitution
for the line and any telegraphic line connected therewith which is rendered useless in consequence of the
removal or abandonment of the line, a telegraphic
line in such other place as the Post Office may require;

(*e*) where under the preceding provisions of this subsection
the Post Office has abandoned the whole or any
part of a telegraphic line, it shall vest in the local
authority, and the provisions of the Telegraph Acts
1863 to 1916 shall not apply in relation to the line
or that part thereof with respect to anything done or
omitted after the abandonment thereof.

PART X

(4) As soon as practicable after the making of an order under section 214(1)(a) of this Act extinguishing a public right of way in circumstances in which subsection (3) of this section applies, the Secretary of State shall give notice to the Post Office of the making of the order.

1878 c. 76.

(5) In this section " telegraphic line " and " alter " have the same meanings as in the Telegraph Act 1878.

Application of s. 32 of Mineral Workings Act 1951 to orders under Part X.

1951 c. 60.

221.—(1) In subsections (1) and (2) of section 32 of the Mineral Workings Act 1951 (power of Ministers to make temporary order for stopping up or diversion of highway in connection with working of surface minerals)—

(a) references to section 209 of this Act (except the reference to subsection (3) of that section) shall include references to section 210 of this Act ;

(b) the reference to the said subsection (3) shall include a reference to subsection (2) of the said section 210 ; and

(c) references to the Secretary of State shall include references to a competent authority for the purposes of the said section 210.

(2) In subsection (3) of the said section 32 (rights of statutory undertakers in respect of their apparatus where order is made under section 209 of this Act) the reference to section 209 of this Act shall include a reference to section 211 of this Act.

(3) This section has effect in lieu of the amendments of the said section 32 made by sections 91(4) and 94(5) of the Act of 1968.

PART XI

STATUTORY UNDERTAKERS

Preliminary

Meaning of " operational land ".

222. In this Act " operational land " means, in relation to statutory undertakers—

(a) land which is used for the purpose of carrying on their undertaking ; and

(b) land in which an interest is held for that purpose,

not being land which, in respect of its nature and situation, is comparable rather with land in general than with land which is used, or in which interests are held, for the purpose of the carrying on of statutory undertakings.

223.—(1) Where an interest in land is held by statutory undertakers for the purpose of carrying on their undertaking and—
  (a) the interest was acquired by them on or after 6th
    December 1968 ; or
  (b) it was held by them immediately before that date but the
    circumstances were then such that the land did not
    fall to be treated as operational land for the purposes
    of the Act of 1962,

then subsection (2) of this section shall have effect for the purpose
of determining whether the land is to be treated as operational
land for the purposes of this Act and shall so have effect notwithstanding the definition of operational land in section 222 of this
Act.

(2) The land shall not be treated as operational land for the
purposes of this Act unless one or both of the following conditions are satisfied with respect to it, namely—
  (a) there is, or at some time has been, in force with respect
    to the land a specific planning permission for its
    development and that development, if carried out,
    would involve or have involved the use of the land
    for the purpose of the carrying on of the statutory
    undertakers' undertaking ; or
  (b) the undertakers' interest in the land was acquired by
    them as the result of a transfer under the provisions
    of the Transport Act 1968 from other statutory under-
    takers and the land was, immediately before transfer,
    operational land of those other undertakers.

(3) A specific planning permission for the purpose of subsection (2)(a) of this section is a planning permission—
  (a) granted on an application in that behalf under Part III
    of this Act or the enactments previously in force
    and replaced by that Part of this Act ; or
  (b) granted by provisions of a development order granting
    planning permission generally for development which
    has received specific parliamentary approval ; or
  (c) granted by a special development order in respect of
    development specifically described in the order ; or
  (d) deemed to be granted by virtue of a direction of a
    government department under section 40 of this Act,
    section 41 of the Act of 1962 or section 35 of the
    Act of 1947 ;

and the reference in paragraph (b) of this subsection to development which has received specific parliamentary approval shall
be construéd as referring to development authorised by a local
or private Act of Parliament or by an order approved by both

PART XI

1945 c. 18
(9 & 10 Geo. 6).

Houses of Parliament or by an order which has been brought into operation in accordance with the provisions of the Statutory Orders (Special Procedure) Act 1945, being an Act or order which designates specifically both the nature of the development thereby authorised and the land upon which it may be carried out.

Meaning of
" the
appropriate
Minister "

224.—(1) In this Act " the appropriate Minister "—

(a) in relation to statutory undertakers carrying on an under- taking for the supply of electricity, gas or hydraulic power, means the Secretary of State for Trade and Industry ;

(b) in relation to statutory undertakers carrying on a light- house undertaking, means the said Secretary of State or the Board of Trade ;

(c) in relation to statutory undertakers carrying on an under- taking for the supply of water, means, in the applica- tion of this Act to Wales, the Secretary of State for Wales ; and

(d) in relation to any other statutory undertakers, means the Secretary of State for the Environment.

(2) This Act shall have effect as if references to the Secretary of State and the appropriate Minister—

(a) were references to the Secretary of State and the appro- priate Minister, if the appropriate Minister is not the one concerned as the Secretary of State ; and

(b) were references to the one concerned as the Secretary of State alone, if he is also the appropriate Minister ;

and similarly with references to a Minister and the appropriate Minister and with any provision requiring the Secretary of State to act jointly with the appropriate Minister.

General provisions

Applications
for planning
permission
by statutory
undertakers.

225.—(1) Where—

(a) an application for planning permission to develop land to which this subsection applies is made by statutory undertakers and is referred to the Secretary of State under Part III of this Act ; or

(b) an appeal is made to the Secretary of State under Part III of this Act from the decision on such an applica- tion ; or

(c) such an application is deemed to be made under sub- section (7) of section 88 of this Act on an appeal under that section by statutory undertakers,

the application or appeal shall be dealt with by the Secretary of State and the appropriate Minister.

(2) Subsection (1) of this section applies—

(a) to operational land ; and

(b) to land in which the statutory undertakers hold, or propose to acquire, an interest with a view to its being used for the purpose of carrying on their undertaking where the planning permission, if granted on the application or appeal, would be for development involving the use of the land for that purpose.

(3) An application for planning permission which is deemed to have been made by virtue of section 95(6) of this Act shall be determined by the Secretary of State and the appropriate Minister.

(4) Notwithstanding anything in Part III of this Act, planning permission to develop operational land of statutory undertakers shall not, except with their consent, be granted subject to conditions requiring that any buildings or works authorised by the permission shall be removed, or that any use of the land so authorised shall be discontinued, at the end of a specified period.

(5) Subject to the provisions of this Part of this Act as to compensation, the provisions of this Act shall apply to an application which is dealt with under this section by the Secretary of State and the appropriate Minister as if it had been dealt with by the Secretary of State.

226.—(1) Where the authorisation of a government department is required in respect of any development of operational land, then, except where that authorisation has been granted without any direction as to the grant of planning permission, the Secretary of State and the appropriate Minister shall not be required to deal with an application for planning permission under section 225(1) of this Act. Development requiring authorisation of government department.

(2) The provisions of subsection (3) of section 40 of this Act shall have effect for the purposes of this section as they have effect for the purposes of that section.

227. In relation to any planning permission, granted on the application of statutory undertakers, for the development of operational land, the provisions of Part III of this Act with respect to the revocation and modification of planning permission shall have effect as if, for any reference therein to the Secretary of State, there were substituted a reference to the Secretary of State and the appropriate Minister. Revocation or modification of permission to develop operational land.

228. The provisions of Part III of this Act with respect to the making of orders requiring the discontinuance of any use of land or imposing conditions on the continuance thereof, or requiring buildings or works on land to be altered or removed, Order requiring discontinuance of use etc. of operational land.

PART XI shall have effect, in relation to operational land of statutory undertakers, as if, for any reference therein to the Secretary of State, there were substituted a reference to the Secretary of State and the appropriate Minister.

Acquisition of land of statutory undertakers. 1946 c. 49.

229.—(1) Notwithstanding anything in paragraph 10 of Schedule 1 to the Acquisition of Land (Authorisation Procedure) Act 1946, a compulsory purchase order to which this section applies may be confirmed or made without the appropriate Minister's certificate.

(2) This section applies to any compulsory purchase order under this Act authorising the acquisition of land which has been acquired by statutory undertakers for the purposes of their undertaking.

(3) Except where the appropriate Minister's certificate is given, a compulsory purchase order to which this section applies shall be of no effect unless it is confirmed or made by the appropriate Minister jointly with the Minister or Ministers who would apart from this subsection have power to make or confirm it.

(4) In this section " the appropriate Minister's certificate " means such a certificate as is mentioned in paragraph 10 of Schedule 1 to the said Act of 1946.

Extinguishment of rights of way, and rights as to apparatus, of statutory undertakers.

230.—(1) Where any land has been acquired by a Minister, a local authority or statutory undertakers under Part VI of this Act or compulsorily under any other enactment, or has been appropriated by a local authority for planning purposes, and—

> (a) there subsists over that land a right vested in or belonging to statutory undertakers for the purpose of the carrying on of their undertaking, being a right of way or a right of laying down, erecting, continuing or maintaining apparatus on, under or over the land ; or
>
> (b) there is on, under or over the land apparatus vested in or belonging to statutory undertakers for the purpose of the carrying on of their undertaking,

the acquiring or appropriating authority, if satisfied that the extinguishment of the right or, as the case may be, the removal of the apparatus, is necessary for the purpose of carrying out any development with a view to which the land was acquired or appropriated, may serve on the statutory undertakers a notice stating that, at the end of the period of twenty-eight days from the date of service of the notice or such longer period as may be specified therein, the right will be extinguished or requiring that, before the end of such period as aforesaid, the apparatus shall be removed.

(2) The statutory undertakers on whom a notice is served under subsection (1) of this section may, before the end of the period of twenty-eight days from the service of the notice, serve a counter-notice on the acquiring or appropriating authority stating that they óbject to all or any of the provisions of the notice and specifying the grounds of their objection.

(3) If no counter-notice is served under subsection (2) of this section—

(a) any right to which the notice relates shall be extinguished at the end of the period specified in that behalf in the notice ; and

(b) if, at the end of the period so specified in relation to any apparatus, any requirement of the notice as to the removal of the apparatus has not been complied with, the acquiring or appropriating authority may remove the apparatus and dispose of it in any way the authority may think fit.

(4) If a counter-notice is served under subsection (2) of this section on a local authority or on statutory undertakers, the authority or undertakers may either withdraw the notice (without prejudice to the service of a further notice) or may apply to the Secretary of State and the appropriate Minister for an order under this section embodying the provisions of the notice, with or without modification.

(5) If a counter-notice is served under subsection (2) of this section on a Minister, he may withdraw the notice (without prejudice to the service of a further notice) or he and the appropriate Minister may make an order under this section embodying the provisions of the notice, with or without modification.

(6) In this section any reference to the appropriation of land for planning purposes shall be construed in accordance with section 133(1) of this Act as if this section were in Part VI of this Act.

231.—(1) Where a Minister and the appropriate Minister propose to make an order under section 230(5) of this Act, they shall prepare a draft of the order.

Orders under s. 230.

(2) Before making an order under subsection (4) or subsection (5) of section 230 of this Act, the Ministers proposing to make the order—

(a) shall afford to the statutory undertakers on whom notice was served under subsection (1) of that section an opportunity of objecting to the application for, or proposal to make, the order ; and

(b) if any objection is made, shall consider the objection and afford to those statutory undertakers (and, in a case falling within subsection (4) of that section, to the local authority or statutory undertakers on whom the counter-notice was served) an opportunity of appearing before, and being heard by, a person appointed by the Secretary of State and the appropriate Minister for the purpose,

and may then, if they think fit, make the order in accordance with the application or in accordance with the draft order, as the case may be, either with or without modification.

(3) Where an order is made under section 230 of this Act—

(a) any right to which the order relates shall be extinguished at the end of the period specified in that behalf in the order ; and

(b) if, at the end of the period so specified in relation to any apparatus, any requirement of the order as to the removal of the apparatus has not been complied with, the acquiring or appropriating authority may remove the apparatus and dispose of it in any way the authority may think fit.

Notice for same purposes as s. 230 but given by statutory undertakers to developing authority.

232.—(1) Subject to the provisions of this section, where land has been acquired or appropriated as mentioned in section 230(1) of this Act, and—

(a) there is on, under or over the land any apparatus vested in or belonging to statutory undertakers ; and

(b) the undertakers claim that development to be carried out on the land is such as to require, on technical or other grounds connected with the carrying on of their undertaking, the removal or re-siting of the apparatus affected by the development,

the undertakers may serve on the acquiring or appropriating authority a notice claiming the right to enter on the land and carry out such works for the removal or re-siting of the apparatus or any part of it as may be specified in the notice.

(2) Where, after the land has been acquired or appropriated as aforesaid, development of the land is begun to be carried out, no notice under this section shall be served later than twenty-one days after the beginning of the development.

(3) Where a notice is served under this section, the authority on whom it is served may, before the end of the period of twenty-eight days from the date of service, serve on the statutory undertakers a counter-notice stating that they object to all or

any of the provisions of the notice and specifying the grounds of their objection.

(4) If no counter-notice is served under subsection (3) of this section, the statutory undertakers shall, after the end of the period of twenty-eight days therein mentioned, have the rights claimed in their notice.

(5) If a counter-notice is served under subsection (3) of this section, the statutory undertakers who served the notice under this section may either withdraw it or may apply to the Secretary of State and the appropriate Minister for an order under this section conferring on the undertakers the rights claimed in the notice or such modified rights as the Secretary of State and the appropriate Minister think it expedient to confer on them.

(6) Where, by virtue of this section or of an order of Ministers thereunder, statutory undertakers have the right to execute works for the removal or re-siting of apparatus, they may arrange with the acquiring or appropriating authority for the works to be carried out by that authority, under the superintendence of the undertakers, instead of by the undertakers themselves.

233.—(1) The powers conferred by this section shall be Extension or exercisable where, on a representation made by statutory under- modification takers, it appears to the Secretary of State and the appropriate of functions Minister to be expedient that the powers and duties of those undertakers. undertakers should be extended or modified, in order—

(a) to secure the provision of services which would not otherwise be provided, or satisfactorily provided, for any purpose in connection with which a local authority or Minister may be authorised under Part VI of this Act to acquire land or in connection with which any such person may compulsorily acquire land under any other enactment ; or

(b) to facilitate an adjustment of the carrying on of the undertaking necessitated by any of the acts and events mentioned in subsection (2) of this section.

(2) The said acts and events are—

(a) the acquisition under Part VI of this Act or compulsorily under any other enactment of any land in which an interest was held, or which was used, for the purpose of the carrying on of the undertaking of the statutory undertakers in question ;

(b) the extinguishment of a right or the imposition of any requirement by virtue of section 230 of this Act ;

(c) a decision on an application made by the statutory undertakers for planning permission to develop any

H

such land as is mentioned in paragraph (*a*) of this subsection ;

(*d*) the revocation or modification of planning permission granted on any such application ;

(*e*) the making of an order under section 51 of this Act in relation to any such land.

(3) The powers conferred by this section shall also be exercisable where, on a representation made by a local authority or Minister, it appears to the Secretary of State and the appropriate Minister to be expedient that the powers and duties of statutory undertakers should be extended or modified, in order to secure the provision of new services, or the extension of existing services, for any purpose in connection with which the local authority or Minister making the representation may be authorised under Part VI of this Act to acquire land or in connection with which the local authority or Minister may compulsorily acquire land under any other enactment.

(4) Where the powers conferred by this section are exercisable, the Secretary of State and the appropriate Minister may, if they think fit, by order provide for such extension or modification of the powers and duties of the statutory undertakers as appears to them to be requisite in order to secure the services in question, as mentioned in subsection (1)(*a*) or (3) of this section, or to secure the adjustment in question, as mentioned in subsection (1)(*b*) of this section, as the case may be.

(5) Without prejudice to the generality of subsection (4) of this section, an order under this section may make provision—

(*a*) for empowering the statutory undertakers to acquire (whether compulsorily or by agreement) any land specified in the order, and to erect or construct any buildings or works so specified ;

(*b*) for applying, in relation to the acquisition of any such land or the construction of any such works, enactments relating to the acquisition of land and the construction of works ;

(*c*) where it has been represented that the making of the order is expedient for the purposes mentioned in subsection (1)(*a*) or (3) of this section, for giving effect to such financial arrangements between the local authority or Minister and the statutory undertakers as they may agree, or as, in default of agreement, may be determined to be equitable in such manner and by such tribunal as may be specified in the order ;

(*d*) for such incidental and supplemental matters as appear to the Secretary of State and the appropriate Minister to be expedient for the purposes of the order.

234.—(1) As soon as may be after making such a representa- PART XI
tion as is mentioned in subsection (1) or subsection (3) of section Procedure
233 of this Act— in relation
to orders
    (a) the statutory undertakers, in a case falling within sub- under s. 233.
        section (1) of that section ; or

    (b) the local authority or Minister making the representa-
        tion, in a case falling within subsection (3) thereof,

shall publish, in such form and manner as may be directed by
the Secretary of State and the appropriate Minister, a notice
giving such particulars as may be so directed of the matters to
which the representation relates, and specifying the time within
which, and the manner in which, objections to the making of an
order on the representation may be made, and shall also, if it is so
directed by the Secretary of State and the appropriate Minister,
serve a like notice on such persons, or persons of such classes, as
may be so directed.

(2) Orders under section 233 of this Act shall be subject
to special parliamentary procedure.

235,—(1) Where, on a representation made by statutory under- Relief of
takers, the appropriate Minister is satisfied that the fulfilment statutory
of any obligation incurred by those undertakers in connection undertakers
with the carrying on of their undertaking has been rendered from
impracticable by an act or event to which this subsection applies, rendered
the appropriate Minister may, if he thinks fit, by order direct impracticable.
that the statutory undertakers shall be relieved of the fulfilment
of that obligation, either absolutely or to such extent as may
be specified in the order.

(2) Subsection (1) of this section applies to the following acts
and events, that is to say—

    (a) the compulsory acquisition under Part VI of this Act
        or under any other enactment of any land in which
        an interest was held, or which was used, for the purpose
        of the carrying on of the undertaking of the statutory
        undertakers ; and

    (b) the acts and events specified in section 233(2)(b) to (e)
        of this Act.

(3) As soon as may be after making a representation to the
appropriate Minister under subsection (1) of this section, the
statutory undertakers shall, as may be directed by the appro
priate Minister, either publish (in such form and manner as may
be so directed) a notice giving such particulars as may be so
directed of the matters to which the representation relates, and
specifying the time within which, and the manner in which,
objections to the making of an order on the representation may

be made, or serve such a notice on such persons, or persons of such classes, as may be so directed, or both publish and serve such notices.

(4) If any objection to the making of an order under this section is duly made and is not withdrawn before the order is made, the order shall be subject to special parliamentary procedure.

(5) Immediately after an order is made under this section by the appropriate Minister, he shall publish a notice stating that the order has been made and naming a place where a copy of it may be seen at all reasonable hours, and shall serve a like notice—

(a) on any person who duly made an objection to the order and has sent to the appropriate Minister a request in writing to serve him with the notice required by this subsection, specifying an address for service ; and

(b) on such other persons (if any) as the appropriate Minister thinks fit.

(6) Subject to subsection (7) of this section, and to the provisions of Part XII of this Act, an order under this section shall become operative on the date on which the notice required by subsection (5) of this section is first published.

(7) Where in accordance with subsection (4) of this section the order is subject to special parliamentary procedure, subsection (6) of this section shall not apply.

Objections to orders under ss. 233 and 235. **236.**—(1) For the purposes of sections 233 and 235 of this Act, an objection to the making of an order thereunder shall not be treated as duly made unless—

(a) the objection is made within the time and in the manner specified in the notice required by the section under which the order is proposed to be made ; and

(b) a statement in writing of the grounds of the objection is comprised in or submitted with the objection.

(2) Where an objection to the making of such an order is duly made in accordance with subsection (1) of this section and is not withdrawn, the following provisions of this section shall have effect in relation thereto:

Provided that, in the application of those provisions to an order under section 233 of this Act, any reference to the appropriate Minister shall be construed as a reference to the Secretary of State and the appropriate Minister.

(3) Unless the appropriate Minister decides apart from the objection not to make the order, or decides to make a modification which is agreed to by the objector as meeting the objection, the appropriate Minister, before making a final decision, shall consider the grounds of the objection as set out in the statement, and may, if he thinks fit, require the objector to submit within a specified period a further statement in writing as to any of the matters to which the objection relates.

(4) In so far as the appropriate Minister, after considering the grounds of the objection as set out in the original statement and in any such further statement, is satisfied that the objection relates to a matter which can be dealt with in the assessment of compensation, the appropriate Minister may treat the objection as irrelevant for the purpose of making a final decision.

(5) If, after considering the grounds of the objection as set out in the original statement and in any such further statement, the appropriate Minister is satisfied that, for the purpose of making a final decision, he is sufficiently informed as to the matters to which the objection relates, or if, where a further statement has been required, it is not submitted within the specified period, the appropriate Minister may make a final decision without further investigation as to those matters.

(6) Subject to subsections (4) and (5) of this section, the appropriate Minister, before making a final decision, shall afford to the objector an opportunity of appearing before, and being heard by, a person appointed for the purpose by the appropriate Minister ; and if the objector avails himself of that opportunity, the appropriate Minister shall afford an opportunity of appearing and being heard on the same occasion to the statutory undertakers, local authority or Minister on whose representation the order is proposed to be made, and to any other persons to whom it appears to the appropriate Minister to be expedient to afford such an opportunity.

(7) Notwithstanding anything in the preceding provisions of this section, if it appears to the appropriate Minister that the matters to which the objection relates are such as to require investigation by public local inquiry before he makes a final decision, he shall cause such an inquiry to be held ; and where he determines to cause such an inquiry to be held, any of the requirements of those provisions to which effect has not been given at the time of that determination shall be dispensed with.

(8) In this section any reference to making a final decision, in relation to an order, is a reference to deciding whether to make the order or what modification (if any) ought to be made.

H 3

PART XI

Right to
compensation
in respect
of certain
decisions
and orders.

Compensation

237.—(1) Statutory undertakers shall, subject to the following provisions of this Part of this Act, be entitled to compensation from the local planning authority—

(*a*) in respect of any decision made in accordance with section 225 of this Act whereby planning permission to develop operational land of those undertakers is refused or is granted subject to conditions where—

(i) planning permission for that development would have been granted by a development order but for a direction given under such an order that planning permission so granted should not apply to the development ; and

(ii) it is not development which has received specific parliamentary approval (within the meaning given to that expression by section 223(3) of this Act) ;

(*b*) in respect of any order under section 45 of this Act, as modified by section 227 thereof, whereby planning permission, granted on the application of those undertakers for the development of any such land, is revoked or modified.

(2) Where, by virtue of section 230 of this Act, any right vested in or belonging to statutory undertakers is extinguished, or any requirement is imposed on statutory undertakers, those undertakers shall be entitled to compensation from the acquiring or appropriating authority at whose instance the right was extinguished or the requirement imposed.

(3) Where works are carried out for the removal or re-siting of statutory undertakers' apparatus, being works which the undertakers have the right to carry out by virtue of section 232 of this Act or an order of Ministers thereunder, the undertakers shall be entitled to compensation from the acquiring or appropriating authority.

(4) Notwithstanding anything in subsection (1) of this section, if the decision or order in question relates to land acquired by the statutory undertakers after 7th January 1947, and the Secretary of State and the appropriate Minister are satisfied, having regard to the nature, situation and existing development of the land and of any neighbouring land, and to any other material considerations, that it is unreasonable that compensation should be recovered in respect of that decision or order, they may include therein a direction that subsection (1) of this section shall not apply to that decision or order.

(5) For the purposes of this section the conditions referred to in sections 41 and 42 of this Act shall be disregarded and

no compensation shall be payable under this section in respect
of the imposition of any condition to which section 71 or 82 of
this Act applies.

238.—(1) Where statutory undertakers are entitled to com- Measure of
pensation— compensation
                                                         to statutory

    (a) as mentioned in subsection (1), (2) or (3) of section undertakers.
237 of this Act ; or

    (b) under the provisions of section 170 in respect of an
order made under section 51 of this Act as modified
by section 228 thereof ; or

    (c) in respect of a compulsory acquisition of land which
has been acquired by those undertakers for the purposes of their undertaking, where the first-mentioned
acquisition is effected under a compulsory purchase
order confirmed or made without the appropriate
Minister's certificate,

the amount of the compensation shall (subject to section 239
of this Act) be an amount calculated in accordance with the
following provisions of this section.

(2) The said amount, subject to subsections (3) and (4) of this
section, shall be the aggregate of the following amounts, that is
to say—

    (a) the amount of any expenditure reasonably incurred in
acquiring land, providing apparatus, erecting buildings
or doing work for the purpose of any adjustment of the
carrying on of the undertaking rendered necessary by
the proceeding giving rise to compensation ;

    (b) whichever of the following is applicable, namely—

        (i) where such an adjustment is made, the esti-
mated amount of any decrease in net receipts from
the carrying on of the undertaking pending the
adjustment, in so far as the decrease is directly attributable to the proceeding giving rise to compensation, together with such amount as appears reasonable compensation for any estimated decrease in net
receipts from the carrying on of the undertaking in
the period after the adjustment has been completed,
in so far as the decrease is directly attributable to the
adjustment ;

        (ii) where no such adjustment is made, such
amount as appears reasonable compensation for any
estimated decrease in net receipts from the carrying
on of the undertaking which is directly attributable
to the proceeding giving rise to compensation ;

H 4

   (c) where the compensation is under section 237(2) of this
       Act, and is in respect of the imposition of a require-
       ment to remove apparatus, the amount of any expendi-
       ture reasonably incurred by the statutory undertakers
       in complying with the requirement, reduced by the
       value after removal of the apparatus removed.

(3) Where any such adjustment as is mentioned in paragraph
(a) of subsection (2) of this section is made, the aggregate amount
mentioned in that subsection shall be reduced by such amount (if
any) as appears to the Lands Tribunal to be appropriate to
offset—

   (a) the estimated value of any property (whether moveable
       or immoveable) belonging to the statutory undertakers
       and used for the carrying on of their undertaking which,
       in consequence of the adjustment, ceases to be so used,
       in so far as the value of the property has not been taken
       into account under paragraph (c) of that subsection;
       and

   (b) the estimated amount of any increase in net receipts
       from the carrying on of the undertaking in the period
       after the adjustment has been completed, in so far as
       that amount has not been taken into account under
       paragraph (b) of that subsection and is directly attribut-
       able to the adjustment,

and by any further amount which appears to the Lands Tribunal
to be appropriate, having regard to any increase in the capital
value of immoveable property belonging to the statutory undertakers which is directly attributable to the adjustment, allowance
being made for any reduction made under paragraph (b) of this
subsection.

(4) Where the compensation is under section 237(3) of this
Act and the acquiring or appropriating authority carry out the
works, then, in addition to any reduction falling to be made
under subsection (3) of this section, the aggregate amount
mentioned in subsection (2) of this section shall be reduced
by the actual cost to the authority of carrying out the works.

(5) References in this section to a decrease in net receipts
shall be construed as references to the amount by which a
balance of receipts over expenditure is decreased, or a balance
of expenditure over receipts is increased, or, where a balance
of receipts over expenditure is converted into a balance of expenditure over receipts, as references to the aggregate of the two
balances ; and references to an increase in net receipts shall be
construed accordingly.

(6) In this section—

" proceeding giving rise to compensation " means—

(a) except in relation to compensation under section 237(3) of this Act, the particular action (that is to say, the decision, order, extinguishment of a right, imposition of a requirement, or acquisition) in respect of which compensation falls to be assessed, as distinct from any development or project in connection with which that action may have been taken ;

(b) in relation to compensation under the said section 237(3), the circumstances making it necessary for the apparatus in question to be removed or re-sited ;

" the appropriate Minister's certificate " has the same meaning as in section 229 of this Act.

239.—(1) Where statutory undertakers are entitled to compensation in respect of such a compulsory acquisition as is mentioned in section 238(1)(c) of this Act, the statutory undertakers may by notice in writing under this section elect that the compensation shall be ascertained in accordance with the enactments (other than rule (5) of the rules set out in section 5 of the Land Compensation Act 1961) which would be applicable apart from section 238 of this Act ; and if the undertakers so elect the compensation shall be ascertained accordingly.

Exclusion of s. 238 at option of statutory undertakers.

1961 c. 33.

(2) An election under this section may be made either in respect of the whole of the land comprised in the compulsory acquisition in question or in respect of part of that land.

(3) Any notice under this section shall be given to the acquiring authority before the end of the period of two months from the date of service of notice to treat in respect of the interest of the statutory undertakers.

240.—(1) Where the amount of any such compensation as is mentioned in subsection (1) of section 238 of this Act falls to be ascertained in accordance with the provisions of that section, the compensation shall, in default of agreement, be assessed by the Lands Tribunal, if apart from this section it would not fall to be so assessed.

Procedure for assessing compensation where s. 238 applies.

(2) For the purposes of any proceedings arising before the Lands Tribunal in respect of compensation falling to be ascertained as mentioned in subsection (1) of this section, the provisions of sections 2 and 4 of the Land Compensation Act 1961 shall apply as they apply to proceedings on a question referred

PART XI   to the Tribunal under section 1 of that Act, but with the substitution in section 4 of that Act, for references to the acquiring authority, of references to the person from whom the compensation is claimed.

Supplementary provisions

Special
provisions as
to display of
advertisements
on operational
land.

241.—(1) The provisions of this Part of this Act specified in subsection (2) of this section do not apply in relation to the display of advertisements on operational land of statutory undertakers.

(2) The said provisions are sections 225 to 228 and 237(1) and (4) of this Act.

PART XII

VALIDITY OF PLANNING INSTRUMENTS AND DECISIONS AND PROCEEDINGS RELATING THERETO

Validity of
development
plans and
certain orders,
decisions and
directions.

242.—(1) Except as provided by the following provisions of this Part of this Act, the validity of—

(a) a structure plan, a local plan or any alteration, repeal or replacement of any such plan, whether before or after the plan, alteration, repeal or replacement has been approved or adopted ; or

(b) an order under any provision of Part X of this Act except section 214(1)(a), whether before or after the order has been made ; or

(c) an order under section 235 of this Act, whether before or after the order has been made ; or

(d) any such order as is mentioned in subsection (2) of this section, whether before or after it has been confirmed ; or

(e) any such action on the part of the Secretary of State as is mentioned in subsection (3) of this section,

shall not be questioned in any legal proceedings whatsoever.

(2) The orders referred to in subsection (1)(d) of this section are orders of any of the following descriptions, that is to say—

(a) any order under section 45 of this Act or under the provisions of that section as applied by or under any other provision of this Act ;

(b) any order under section 51 of this Act ;

(c) any tree preservation order ;

(d) any order made in pursuance of section 63(4) of this Act ;

(e) any order under Part II of Schedule 11 to this Act.

(3) The action referred to in subsection (1)(*e*) of this section is action on the part of the Secretary of State of any of the following descriptions, that is to say—

(*a*) any decision of the Secretary of State on an application for planning permission referred to him under section 35 of this Act;

(*b*) any decision of the Secretary of State on an appeal under section 36 of this Act;

(*c*) the giving by the Secretary of State of any direction under section 38 of this Act;

(*d*) any decision by the Secretary of State to confirm a completion notice under section 44 of this Act;

(*e*) any decision of the Secretary of State relating to an application for consent under a tree preservation order, or relating to an application for consent under any regulations made in accordance with section 63 of this Act, or relating to any certificate or direction under any such order or regulations, whether it is a decision of the Secretary of State on appeal or a decision on an application referred to him for determination in the first instance;

(*f*) any decision of the Secretary of State to grant planning permission under section 88(5)(*a*) of this Act;

(*g*) any decision of the Secretary of State on an application for an established use certificate referred to him under subsection (1) of section 95 of this Act or on an appeal under subsection (2) of that section;

(*h*) any decision of the Secretary of State under subsection (5)(*a*) of section 97 of this Act to grant listed building consent for any works or under subsection (5)(*b*) of that section to grant planning permission in respect of any works;

(*i*) any decision of the Secretary of State to confirm a purchase notice or listed building purchase notice;

(*j*) any decision of the Secretary of State not to confirm a purchase notice or listed building purchase notice, including any decision not to confirm such a notice in respect of part of the land to which it relates, and including any decision to grant any permission, or give any direction, in lieu of confirming such a notice, either wholly or in part;

(*k*) any decision of the Secretary of State on an application referred to him under paragraph 4 of Schedule 11 to this Act (being an application for listed building consent for any works) or on an appeal under paragraph 8 of that Schedule.

(4) Nothing in this section shall affect the exercise of any jurisdiction of any court in respect of any refusal or failure on the part of the Secretary of State to take any such action as is mentioned in subsection (3) of this section.

Validity of
enforcement
notices and
similar notices.

243.—(1) Subject to the provisions of this section—

(a) the validity of an enforcement notice shall not, except by way of an appeal under Part V of this Act, be questioned in any proceedings whatsoever on any of the grounds specified in section 88(1)(b) to (e) of this Act ;

(b) the validity of a listed building enforcement notice shall not, except by way of an appeal under Part V of this Act, be questioned in any proceedings whatsoever on any of the grounds specified in section 97(1)(b) or (e) of this Act.

(2) Subsection (1)(a) of this section shall not apply to proceedings brought under section 89(5) of this Act against a person who—

(a) has held an interest in the land since before the enforcement notice was served under Part V of this Act ; and

(b) did not have the enforcement notice served on him thereunder ; and

(c) satisfies the court that—

(i) he did not know and could not reasonably have been expected to know that the enforcement notice had been served ; and

(ii) his interests have been substantially prejudiced by the failure to serve him.

(3) Subject to subsection (4) of this section, the validity of a notice which has been served under section 65 of this Act on the owner and occupier of the land shall not, except by way of an appeal under Part V of this Act, be questioned in any proceedings whatsoever on any of the grounds specified in section 105(1)(a) to (c) of this Act.

(4) Subsection (3) of this section shall not apply to proceedings brought under section 104 of this Act against a person on whom the notice referred to in that subsection was not served, but who has held an interest in the land since before that notice was served on the owner and occupier of the land, if he did not appeal against the notice under Part V of this Act.

(5) The validity of a notice purporting to be an enforcement notice shall not depend on whether any non-compliance to which the notice relates was a non-compliance with conditions, or with limitations, or with both ; and any reference in such a notice to non-compliance with conditions or limitations (whether both

expressions are used in the notice or only one of them) shall be construed as a reference to non-compliance with conditions, or with limitations, or both with conditions and limitations, as the case may require.

244.—(1) If any person aggrieved by a structure plan or local plan or by any alteration, repeal or replacement of any such plan desires to question the validity of the plan, alteration, repeal or replacement on the ground that it is not within the powers conferred by Part II of this Act, or that any requirement of the said Part II or of any regulations made thereunder has not been complied with in relation to the approval or adoption of the plan, alteration, repeal or replacement, he may, within six weeks from the date of the publication of the first notice of the approval or adoption of the plan, alteration, repeal or replacement required by regulations under section 18 (1) of this Act, make an application to the High Court under this section.

(2) On any application under this section the High Court—

>   (*a*) may by interim order wholly or in part suspend the operation of the plan, alteration, repeal or replacement, either generally or in so far as it affects any property of the applicant, until the final determination of the proceedings ;

>   (*b*) if satisfied that the plan, alteration, repeal or replacement is wholly or to any extent outside the powers conferred by Part II of this Act, or that the interests of the applicant have been substantially prejudiced by the failure to comply with any requirement of the said Part II or of any regulations made thereunder, may wholly or in part quash the plan, alteration, repeal or replacement, as the case may be, either generally or in so far as it affects any property of the applicant.

(3) The preceding provisions of this section shall apply, subject to any necessary modifications, to an order under section 209, 211, 212 or 214(1)(*a*) of this Act as they apply to a structure plan, and as if, in subsection (1) of this section, for the reference to the notice therein mentioned, there were substituted a reference to the notice required by section 215(7) of this Act.

(4) The said provisions shall apply, subject to any necessary modifications, to an order under section 210 or 214(1)(*b*) of this Act as they apply to a structure plan, and as if, in subsection (1) of this section, for the reference to the date on which the notice therein mentioned is first published there were substituted a reference to the date on which the notice required by para-

graph 6 of Schedule 20 to this Act is first published in accordance with that paragraph.

(5) Subsections (1) and (2) of this section shall apply, subject to any necessary modifications, to an order under section 235 of this Act as they apply to a structure plan.

Proceedings
for questioning
validity of
other orders,
decisions and
directions.

245.—(1) If any person—

(a) is aggrieved by any order to which this section applies and desires to question the validity of that order, on the grounds that the order is not within the powers of this Act, or that any of the relevant requirements have not been complied with in relation to that order ; or

(b) is aggrieved by any action on the part of the Secretary of State to which this section applies and desires to question the validity of that action, on the grounds that the action is not within the powers of this Act, or that any of the relevant requirements have not been complied with in relation to that action,

he may, within six weeks from the date on which the order is confirmed or the action is taken, as the case may be, make an application to the High Court under this section.

(2) Without prejudice to subsection (1) of this section, if the authority directly concerned with any order to which this section applies, or with any action on the part of the Secretary of State to which this section applies, desire to question the validity of that order or action on any of the grounds mentioned in subsection (1) of this section, the authority may, within six weeks from the date on which the order is confirmed or the action is taken, as the case may be, make an application to the High Court under this section.

(3) This section applies to any such order as is mentioned in subsection (2) of section 242 of this Act and to any such action on the part of the Secretary of State as is mentioned in subsection (3) of that section.

(4) On any application under this section the High Court—

(a) may by interim order suspend the operation of the order or action, the validity whereof is questioned by the application, until the final determination of the proceedings ;

(b) if satisfied that the order or action in question is not within the powers of this Act, or that the interests of the applicant have been substantially prejudiced by a failure to comply with any of the relevant require-

ments in relation thereto, may quash that order or
action:

Provided that paragraph (*a*) of this subsection shall not apply
to applications questioning the validity of tree preservation
orders.

(5) In relation to a tree preservation order, or to an order
made in pursuance of section 63(4) of this Act, the powers conferred on the High Court by subsection (4) of this section shall be
exercisable by way of quashing or (where applicable) suspending
the operation of the order either in whole or in part, as the
court may determine.

(6) References in this section to the confirmation of an order
include the confirmation of an order subject to modifications
as well as the confirmation of an order in the form in which it
was made.

(7) In this section " the relevant requirements ", in relation
to any order or action to which this section applies, means
any requirements of this Act or of the Tribunals and Inquiries
Act 1971 (or any enactment replaced thereby), or of any order, 1971 c. 62.
regulations or rules made under this Act or under that Act (or
any such enactment) which are applicable to that order or
action, and any reference to the authority directly concerned
with any order or action to which this section applies—

(*a*) in relation to an order made by a local authority other
than the local planning authority, and in relation to
any decision of the Secretary of State on appeal from
a decision made by such a local authority, is a reference
to that local authority ;

(*b*) in relation to any such decision as is mentioned in
section 242(3)(*i*) or (*j*) of this Act, is a reference
to the council on whom the notice in question was
served, and, in a case where the Secretary of State
has modified such a notice, wholly or in part, by
substituting another local authority or statutory undertakers for that council, includes a reference to that
local authority or those statutory undertakers ;

(*c*) in any other case, is a reference to the local planning
authority :

Provided that if, in a case falling within paragraph (*a*) of this
subsection, the order or decision in question was made in the
exercise of functions delegated to the other local authority by
the local planning authority, and it is agreed between the two
authorities that the local planning authority shall act in the
matter, the reference shall be construed as a reference to the
local planning authority.

PART XII
Appeals to
High Court
relating to
enforcement
notices and
similar
notices.

246.—(1) Where the Secretary of State gives a decision in proceedings on an appeal under Part V of this Act against—

(a) an enforcement notice ;

(b) a listed building enforcement notice ; or

(c) a notice under section 103 of this Act,

the appellant or the local planning authority or any person (other than the appellant) on whom the notice was served may, according as rules of court may provide, either appeal to the High Court against the decision on a point of law or require the Secretary of State to state and sign a case for the opinion of the High Court.

(2) At any stage of the proceedings on any such appeal as is mentioned in subsection (1) of this section, the Secretary of State may state any question of law arising in the course of the proceedings in the form of a special case for the decision of the High Court ; and a decision of the High Court on a case stated by virtue of this subsection shall be deemed to be a judgment of the court within the meaning of section 27 of the Supreme Court of Judicature (Consolidation) Act 1925 (jurisdiction of the Court of Appeal to hear and determine appeals from any judgment of the High Court).

1925 c. 49.

(3) In relation to any proceedings in the High Court or the Court of Appeal brought by virtue of this section the power to make rules of court shall include power to make rules—

(a) prescribing the powers of the High Court or the Court of Appeal with respect to the remitting of the matter with the opinion or direction of the court for re-hearing and determination by the Secretary of State ; and

(b) providing for the Secretary of State, either generally or in such circumstances as may be prescribed by the rules, to be treated as a party to any such proceedings and to be entitled to appear and to be heard accordingly.

(4) Rules of court relating to any such proceedings as are mentioned in subsection (3) of this section may provide for excluding so much of section 63(1) of the said Act of 1925 as requires appeals to the High Court to be heard and determined by a Divisional Court ; but no appeal to the Court of Appeal shall be brought by virtue of this section except with the leave of the High Court or the Court of Appeal.

(5) In this section " decision " includes a direction or order, and references to the giving of a decision shall be construed accordingly.

247.—(1) If, in the case of any decision to which this section
applies, the person who made the application to which the decision relates, or the local planning authority, is dissatisfied with
the decision in point of law, that person or the local planning
authority (as the case may be) may, according as rules of court
may provide, either appeal against the decision to the High
Court or require the Secretary of State to state and sign a case
for the opinion of the High Court.

(2) This section applies to any decision of the Secretary of
State—

> (a) on an application under section 53 of this Act which
> is referred to the Secretary of State under the provisions
> of section 35 of this Act as applied by that section;
> or

> (b) on an appeal from a decision of the local planning
> authority under section 53 of this Act, being an appeal
> brought under the provisions of section 36 of this
> Act as so applied.

(3) Where an application under section 53 of this Act is
made as part of an application for planning permission, the
preceding provisions of this section shall have effect in relation
to that application in so far as it is an application under the
said section 53, but not in so far as it is an application for
planning permission.

(4) In relation to proceedings in the High Court or the Court
of Appeal brought by virtue of this section, the power to make
rules of court shall include power to make rules prescribing the
powers of the High Court or the Court of Appeal with respect
to—

> (a) the giving of any decision which might have been given
> by the Secretary of State;

> (b) the remitting of the matter, with the opinion or direction
> of the court, for re-hearing and determination by the
> Secretary of State;

> (c) the giving of directions to the Secretary of State.

(5) Rules of court relating to such proceedings as are mentioned in subsection (4) of this section may provide for excluding
so much of section 63(1) of the Supreme Court of Judicature
(Consolidation) Act 1925 as requires appeals to the High Court
to be heard and determined by a Divisional Court; but no
appeal to the Court of Appeal shall be brought by virtue of this
section except with the leave of the High Court or the Court
of Appeal.

(6) Without prejudice to the preceding provisions of this
section, the power to make rules of court in relation to proceedings in the High Court or the Court of Appeal brought by virtue

of this section shall include power to make rules providing for the Secretary of State, either generally or in such circumstances as may be prescribed by the rules, to be treated as a party to any such proceedings and to be entitled to appear and to be heard accordingly.

Special
provisions as
to decisions
relating to
statutory
undertakers.

248. In relation to any action which—

(a) apart from the provisions of Part XI of this Act, would fall to be taken by the Secretary of State, and, if so taken, would be action falling within section 242(3) of this Act ; but

(b) by virtue of Part XI of this Act, is required to be taken by the Secretary of State and the appropriate Minister,

the provisions of sections 242 and 245 of this Act shall have effect (subject to section 249 of this Act) as if any reference in those provisions to the Secretary of State were a reference to the Secretary of State and the appropriate Minister.

Special
Provisions as
to orders
subject to
special
parliamentary
procedure.
1945 c. 18
(9 & 10 Geo. 6).

249.—(1) Where an order under section 209, 211, 212 or 235 of this Act is subject to special parliamentary procedure, then—

(a) if the order is confirmed by Act of Parliament under section 6 of the Statutory Orders (Special Procedure) Act 1945, the provisions of sections 242 and 244 of this Act shall not apply to the order ;

(b) in any other case, section 244 of this Act shall have effect in relation to the order as if, in subsection (1) of that section, for the reference to the date therein mentioned there were substituted a reference to the date on which the order becomes operative under section 6 of the said Act of 1945.

(2) Where by virtue of Part XI of this Act any such action as is mentioned in section 248 of this Act is required to be embodied in an order, and that order is subject to special parliamentary procedure, then—

(a) if the order in which the action is embodied is confirmed by Act of Parliament under section 6 of the said Act of 1945, the provisions of sections 242 and 245 of this Act shall not apply ;

(b) in any other case, the provisions of section 245 of this Act shall apply with the substitution, for any reference to the date on which the action is taken, of a reference to the date on which the order becomes operative under section 6 of the said Act of 1945.

PART XIII

FINANCIAL PROVISIONS

Grants for development etc.

250.—(1) The Secretary of State may with the consent of Grants for
the Treasury and after consultation with such associations of development
local authorities as appear to the Secretary of State to be con- etc.
cerned and with any local authority with whom consultation
appears to him to be desirable, make regulations providing for
the payment to local authorities for any year of grants of such
amounts, and payable over such periods and subject to such
conditions, as may be determined by or under the regulations
in respect of expenditure incurred by those authorities (whether
before or after the passing of this Act) in or in connection
with the acquisition of land approved for the purposes of the
regulations, being land required for or in connection with—

   (a) the development or redevelopment as a whole of any
   area (whether or not defined in a development plan
   as an area of comprehensive development) ; or

   (b) the relocation of population or industry, or the replacement of open space, in the course or in consequence
   of such development or redevelopment,

or in respect of expenditure so incurred in or in connection with
the clearing or preliminary development of such land.

(2) For the purposes of regulations under this section land
appropriated by a local authority (whether before or after the
passing of this Act) for use for purposes described in subsection (1) of this section may be treated as acquired by that
authority for those purposes at a cost of such amount, and
defrayed in such manner, as may be determined by or under
the regulations.

(3) Provision may be made by regulations under this section—

   (a) for the inclusion, in the expenditure incurred by local
   authorities in the acquisition of land approved for the
   purposes of the regulations, of any sums or part of
   sums paid by those authorities in connection with any
   restriction imposed on the development or use of the
   land by or under any enactment (whether by way of
   compensation or by way of contribution towards
   damage or expense incurred in consequence of the
   restriction) ;

   (b) for the calculation of grants payable under the regulations by reference to the amount of the annual costs

incurred or treated as being incurred by local authorities in respect of the borrowing of money to defray the expenditure in respect of which the grants are made, or by reference to the excess of such annual costs over receipts of those authorities which are attributable to such expenditure, or over the annual value of such receipts, or by reference to such other considerations as may be prescribed by the regulations ;

(c) for the payment of capital sums in substitution for any periodical grants payable under the regulations in respect of such annual costs ;

and for the purposes of this section " clearing " and " preliminary development " means the carrying out of such works as may be prescribed by or determined under the regulations.

(4) In this section " year " means a period of twelve months beginning with the first day of April.

251.—(1) Subject to the following provisions of this section, the amount of any grant paid to a local authority in accordance with regulations made under section 250 of this Act—

(a) where that amount is calculated by reference to annual costs incurred or treated as incurred by the authority in respect of the borrowing of money to defray expenditure in respect of which the grant is made, or by reference to the excess of such annual costs over the receipts, or the annual value of receipts, mentioned in subsection (3)(b) of that section, shall not exceed an amount equal to fifty per cent. of those costs, or of that excess, as the case may be ;

(b) in any other case, shall not exceed an amount equal to fifty per cent. of the amount of the expenditure in respect of which the grant is made.

(2) In respect of land of any of the following descriptions, that is to say—

(a) land comprised in a compulsory purchase order made by a local authority under the Act of 1944 or the Act of 1947, and confirmed before 26th February 1954, being land acquired for war-damage redevelopment ;

(b) land acquired by agreement for war-damage redevelopment with the consent of the Minister of Housing and Local Government given before that date ;

(c) land appropriated by a local authority for war-damage redevelopment before that date ; and

(*d*) land acquired or appropriated for war-damage
redevelopment (whether before or after that date),
being land contiguous or adjacent to land falling within
any of the preceding paragraphs,

subsection (1)(*a*) of this section shall apply (subject to subsection
(3) of this section) as if for the words " fifty per cent." there were
substituted the words " ninety per cent.".

(3) Subsection (2) of this section shall not authorise the payment, in the case of any land, of a grant at a higher rate in
respect of a year or part of a year which, together with the
preceding years or parts of years in respect of which grants at
a higher rate have been paid in the case of that land, would
extend beyond a total period of eight years.

(4) In this section " war-damage redevelopment " means the
redevelopment as a whole of an area of extensive war damage,
and includes the relocation of population or industry, or the
replacement of open space, in the course of such redevelopment.

(5) In this section references to a grant at a higher rate are
references to a grant of an amount which—

(*a*) was or would have been authorised by section 93 of
the Act of 1947 as that section had effect or would have
had effect apart from section 50 of the Act of 1954
and the Local Government Act 1958 and this Act ; 1958 c. 55.
but

(*b*) otherwise than by virtue of the provisions of the Act
of 1954 corresponding to subsections (2) and (3) of
this section, was not or would not have been authorised
by the provisions substituted by the Act of 1954 for the
said section 93.

252.—(1) Any approval of the Secretary of State required for Supplementary
the purposes of the payment of grant under section 250 of this provisions
Act in connection with the acquisition of land may be given as to grants
subject to compliance with requirements imposed by the under s. 250.
Secretary of State for securing that any negotiations for the
acquisition of the land by the local authority will be carried
out by the Valuation Office, and that any valuation of the land
for the purposes of the acquisition, or for any purposes of the
regulations, will be made by that office.

(2) Subject to subsection (1) of this section, any regulations
made for the purposes of section 250 of this Act may make
provision whereby the payment of grants in pursuance of the
regulations is dependent upon the fulfilment of such conditions

PART XIII   as may be determined by or in accordance with the regulations, and may also make provision for requiring local authorities to whom grants have been so paid to comply with such requirements as may be so determined.

Grants for research and education

Grants for research and education.

253. The Secretary of State may, with the consent of the Treasury, make grants for assisting establishments engaged in promoting or assisting research relating to, and education with respect to, the planning and design of the physical environment.

Contributions to certain expenditure

Contributions by Ministers towards compensation paid by local authorities.

254. Where compensation is payable by a local authority under this Act in consequence of any decision or order given or made under—

(a) Part III or Part IV of this Act ;

(b) sections 87 to 100 of this Act ;

(c) the provisions of Part IX of this Act relating to purchase notices ;

(d) Schedule 9 to this Act,

then if that decision or order was given or made wholly or partly in the interest of a service which is provided by a government department and the cost of which is defrayed out of moneys provided by Parliament, the Minister responsible for the administration of that service may pay to that authority a contribution of such amount as he may with the consent of the Treasury determine.

Contributions by local authorities and statutory undertakers. 1959 c. 25.

255.—(1) Without prejudice to the provisions of section 238(1) and (3) of the Highways Act 1959 (contributions by certain local authorities towards expenses incurred in connection with highways), any local authority may contribute towards any expenses incurred by a local highway authority in the acquisition of land under Part VI of this Act, or in the construction or improvement of roads on land so acquired, or in connection with any development required in the interests of the proper planning of the area of the local authority.

(2) Any local authority and any statutory undertakers may contribute towards—

(a) any expenses incurred by a local planning authority in or in connection with the carrying out of a survey or the preparation of a structure plan or local plan under Part II of this Act ;

(*b*) any expenses incurred by a local planning authority, PART XIII
or by the council of a county district, in or in connection with the performance of any of their functions
under Part III (except section 28), Part IV, Part V
(except sections 101 and 103) or Part VI (except
section 126) of this Act, under the provisions of Part
IX of this Act relating to purchase notices and listed
building purchase notices or under Schedule 11 to
this Act.

(3) Where any expenses are incurred by a local authority in
the payment of compensation payable in consequence of anything done under—

(*a*) Part III or Part IV of this Act ;

(*b*) sections 87 to 100 of this Act ;

(*c*) the provisions of Part IX of this Act relating to purchase
notices and listed building purchase notices ;

the Secretary of State may, if it appears to him to be expedient
to do so, require any other local authority to contribute towards
those expenses such sum as appears to him to be reasonable,
having regard to any benefit accruing to that authority by
reason of the proceeding giving rise to the compensation.

(4) The provisions of subsection (3) of this section shall apply
in relation to payments made by a local authority to any statutory undertakers in accordance with financial arrangements to
which effect is given under section 233(5)(*c*) of this Act, as they
apply in relation to compensation payable by such an authority
in consequence of anything done under Part III or Part IV of
this Act, and the reference in subsection (3) of this section to the
proceeding giving rise to the compensation shall be construed
accordingly.

(5) For the purposes of this section, contributions made by a
local planning authority towards the expenditure of a joint
advisory committee shall be deemed to be expenses incurred
by that authority for the purposes for which that expenditure
is incurred by the committee.

256. The council of a county, county borough, London Assistance
borough or county district or the Greater London Council may, for acquisition
subject to such conditions as may be approved by the Secretary of property
of State, advance money to any person for the purposes of where
enabling him to acquire a hereditament or agricultural unit in made to
respect of which a counter-notice has been served under section blight notice
194 of this Act specifying the grounds mentioned in sub- in certain
section (2)(*d*) of that section as, or as one of, the grounds of cases.
objection if, in the case of a hereditament, its annual value
does not exceed such amount as may be prescribed for the
purposes of section 192(4)(*a*) of this Act.

Recovery of compensation etc.

Recovery from   **257.**—(1) Where an interest in land is compulsorily acquired,
acquiring   or is sold to an authority possessing compulsory purchase
authorities of   powers, and any of the land comprised in the acquisition or sale
sums paid by   is land in respect of which a notice to which this section applies
way of   is registered (whether before or after the completion of the
compensation.   acquisition or sale) in respect of a planning decision or order
made before the service of the notice to treat, or the making of
the contract, in pursuance of which the acquisition or sale is
effected, the Secretary of State shall, subject to the following
provisions of this section, be entitled to recover from the
acquiring authority a sum equal to so much of the amount of
the compensation specified in the notice as (in accordance with
section 158(6) of this Act) is to be treated as attributable to that
land.

(2) This section applies to notices registered under subsection
(5) of section 158 of this Act and to notices registered under
the provisions of that subsection as applied by section 166(5)
of this Act.

(3) If, immediately after the completion of the acquisition or
sale, there is outstanding some interest in the land comprised
therein to which a person other than the acquiring authority is
entitled, the sum referred to in subsection (1) of this section shall
not accrue due until that interest either ceases to exist or
becomes vested in the acquiring authority.

(4) No sum shall be recoverable under this section in the case
of a compulsory acquisition or sale where the Secretary of
State is satisfied that the interest in question is being acquired
for the purposes of the use of the land as a public open space.

(5) Where by virtue of the preceding provisions of this section
the Secretary of State recovers a sum in respect of any land,
by reason that it is land in respect of which a notice is registered
under the provisions of section 158(5) of this Act as applied
by section 166 of this Act, section 168(2) and (3) of this Act
shall have effect in relation to that sum as if it were a sum
recovered as mentioned in section 168(2) of this Act.

(6) In this section and in section 258 of this Act "interest"
(where the reference is to an interest in land) means the fee
simple or a tenancy of the land, and does not include any other
interest therein.

Recovery from   **258.**—(1) Where an interest in land is compulsorily acquired
acquiring   by, or sold to, an authority possessing compulsory purchase
authorities of   powers, and a payment exceeding £20 has become or becomes
sums paid   payable under section 59 of the Act of 1947 in respect of that
in respect of   interest, the Secretary of State shall, subject to the following
war-damaged
land.

provisions of this section, be entitled to recover the amount of PART XIII
the payment from the acquiring authority.

(2) If, before 18th November 1952, operations were begun in,
on, over or under the land, or a use of the land was instituted,
being operations or a use—

    (a) in respect of which a development charge has at any
        time been determined to be payable, or it has at any
        time been determined that no development charge was
        payable ; or

    (b) comprised in a scheme of development exempt from
        development charge,

subsection (1) of this section shall not apply to so much of any
payment referred to in that subsection as was attributable to
any land in relation to which the determination was made or,
as the case may be, which is included in that scheme of development.

(3) No amount shall be recoverable under this section in
respect of any land in relation to which an amount has become
recoverable by the Secretary of State under the provisions of
section 159 of this Act as applied by section 279 of this Act.

(4) If the acquisition or sale in question does not extend to
the whole of the land to which the payment under the said
section 59 related, the amount recoverable under this section
shall be so much of that payment as, in accordance with subsection (5) of this section, is to be treated as apportioned to the
land in which the interest acquired or sold subsists.

(5) For the purposes of this section a payment under section
59 of the Act of 1947 shall be treated as apportioned, as between
different parts of the land to which it related, in the way in
which it might reasonably be expected to have been so apportioned if, under the scheme made under that section, the
authority determining the amount of the payment had been
required (in accordance with the same principles as applied to
the determination of that amount) to apportion it between
different parts of that land.

(6) In this section references to a scheme of development
exempt from development charge are references to a scheme of
development such that, if the operations and uses of land comprised in the scheme had all been begun or instituted before
18th November 1952, all those operations and uses would have
been exempt from the provisions of Part VII of the Act of 1947
by virtue of regulations made thereunder ; and references to the
amount of a payment shall be construed as including any interest
payable on the principal amount of the payment.

PART XIII
Sums recoverable from acquiring authorities reckonable for purposes of grant.

259. Where a sum is recoverable from an authority under section 257 or 258 of this Act by reference to an acquisition or purchase of an interest in land, and in respect thereof, or of a subsequent appropriation of the land, a grant became or becomes payable to that or some other authority under an enactment, the power conferred by that enactment to pay the grant shall include, and shall be deemed always to have included, power to pay a grant in respect of that sum as if it had been expenditure incurred by the acquiring authority in connection with the acquisition or purchase.

Expenses and receipts of Ministers

Expenses of government departments.

260.—(1) The following expenses of the Secretary of State shall be paid out of moneys provided by Parliament, that is to say—

(a) any expenses incurred by the Secretary of State under subsection (2) of section 50 of this Act or under that subsection as applied by subsection (7) of section 63 of this Act, or in the payment of expenses of any committee established under the said section 63 ;

(b) any sums necessary to enable the Secretary of State to make any payments becoming payable by him under Part VII or Part VIII of this Act ;

(c) any expenses incurred by the Secretary of State under Part X of this Act ;

(d) any expenses incurred by the Secretary of State in the making of grants in accordance with regulations made under section 250 of this Act or grants under section 253 of this Act ;

(e) subject to the provisions of subsection (4) of section 261 of this Act, any instalment payable by the Secretary of State under subsections (2) and (3) of that section ;

(f) any administrative expenses incurred by the Secretary of State for the purposes of this Act.

(2) There shall be paid out of moneys provided by Parliament any expenses incurred by any government department (including the Secretary of State)—

(a) in the acquisition of land under Part VI of this Act ;

(b) in the payment of compensation under section 118(4), 237(2) or 281 of this Act ;

(c) under section 128(5)(b) of this Act ; or

(d) under section 254 of this Act.

261.—(1) The Secretary of State shall pay out of moneys provided by Parliament any payments falling to be made by him on or after 1st April 1968 under—

(*a*) section 59 of the Act of 1947 (war-damaged land); or

(*b*) any provision of Part I or Part V of the Act of 1954.

(2) The aggregate of the sums issued to the Minister of Housing and Local Government or the Central Land Board out of the Consolidated Fund in any financial year ending before the said 1st April under section 64(1) of the Act of 1954 (sums required for making payments under Part I or Part V of the Act of 1954) shall be repaid by the Secretary of State into the National Loans Fund, as mentioned in subsection (3) of this section, with interest thereon at such rate as the Treasury may determine, such interest accruing, in respect of the whole aggregate, from such date in the financial year in which the sums were issued as the Treasury may determine.

(3) The said aggregate shall be repaid by twenty equal annual instalments, of principal and interest combined, falling due on the anniversary of the date determined under subsection (2) of this section, the first such instalment falling due in the financial year next following the financial year in which the sums in question were issued.

(4) Any sums received by the Secretary of State by virtue of—

(*a*) the provisions of section 159 of this Act, as applied by Schedule 24 to this Act to compensation paid under Part V of the Act of 1954; or

(*b*) the provisions of section 257 of this Act as so applied

shall be paid into the Consolidated Fund.

262. Without prejudice to section 261 of this Act, and subject to the provisions of section 168 of this Act, any sums received by the Secretary of State under any provision of this Act shall be paid into the Consolidated Fund.

Expenses of county councils and Greater London Council

263.—(1) The council of a county may direct that any expenses incurred by them under the provisions of this Act specified in Parts I and II of Schedule 21 to this Act shall be treated as expenses for special county purposes chargeable upon such part of the county as may be specified in the directions.

(2) The Greater London Council may direct that any expenses incurred by them under—

    (*a*) Part II of this Act;

    (*b*) Schedule 3 to this Act;

    (*c*) Part II of Schedule 5 to this Act;

    (*d*) any of the provisions of this Act specified in Part I of Schedule 21 to this Act;

    (*e*) any other provision of this Act conferring functions on local authorities,

shall be treated as expenses for special London purposes chargeable upon such part of Greater London as may be specified in the directions.

PART XIV

APPLICATION OF ACT TO SPECIAL CASES

Minerals

Power to modify Act in relation to minerals.
    264.—(1) In relation to development consisting of the winning and working of minerals, the provisions of this Act specified in Parts I and II of Schedule 21 to this Act shall have effect subject to such adaptations and modifications as may be prescribed by regulations made under this Act with the consent of the Treasury.

(2) In relation to interests in land consisting of or comprising minerals (being either the fee simple or tenancies of such land) and in relation to claims established (as mentioned in section 135(2) of this Act) wholly or partly in respect of such land, the provisions of this Act specified in Part III of Schedule 21 to this Act shall have effect subject to such adaptations and modifications as may be prescribed by regulations made under this Act with the consent of the Treasury.

(3) Regulations made for the purposes of this section shall be of no effect unless they are approved by resolution of each House of Parliament.

(4) Any regulations made by virtue of subsection (1) of this section shall not apply—

    (*a*) to the winning and working, on land held or occupied with land used for the purposes of agriculture, of any minerals reasonably required for the purposes of that use, including the fertilisation of the land so used and the maintenance, improvement or alteration of buildings or works thereon which are occupied or used for those purposes ; or

(*b*) to development consisting of the winning and working PART XIV
of any minerals vested in the National Coal Board,
being development to which any of the provisions of
this Act relating to operational land of statutory undertakers apply by virtue of regulations made under section
273 of this Act;

and nothing in subsection (1) of this section or in this subsection
shall be construed as affecting the prerogative right of Her
Majesty (whether in right of the Crown or of the Duchy
of Lancaster) or of the Duke of Cornwall to any gold or silver
mine.

265.—(1) Where a development plan provides that any land Modification
is to be used for the purpose of securing the winning and working of Mines
of any minerals comprised therein, the provisions of the Mines (Working
(Working Facilities and Support) Act 1966 shall have effect in Support)
relation to the land subject to such modifications as may be Act 1966.
prescribed by regulations made under this Act by the Secretary 1966 c. 4.
of State for the Environment and the Secretary of State for
Trade and Industry.

(2) Regulations made for the purposes of this section may in
particular provide for securing—

(*a*) that a right to work any minerals in the land may be
granted by the High Court under the said Act of 1966
to any person who is desirous of working them, either
by himself or through his lessees, and who is unable
to obtain the necessary rights by agreement on reasonable terms;

(*b*) that for the purposes of the determination by the court
of an application for any such right, it shall be assumed
that the winning and working of the minerals is expedient in the national interest; and

(*c*) that the compensation or consideration in respect of
any such right which is granted by the court shall be
assessed having regard to the amount of the compensation which would be payable in respect of a compulsory
acquisition of the minerals under Part VI of this Act.

(3) Subsections (3) and (4) of section 264 of this Act shall
apply to the provisions of this section and to any regulations
made thereunder as they apply to the provisions of subsection (1)
of that section and to regulations made by virtue of that
subsection.

Crown land

266.—(1) Notwithstanding any interest of the Crown in Crown land, but subject to the following provisions of this section—

(a) a plan approved, adopted or made under Part II of this Act or the Greater London development plan may include proposals relating to the use of Crown land, and any power to acquire land compulsorily under Part VI of this Act may be exercised in relation to any interest therein which is for the time being held otherwise than by or on behalf of the Crown ;

(b) any restrictions or powers imposed or conferred by Part III, Part IV or Part V of this Act, by the provisions of Part IX of this Act relating to purchase notices and listed building purchase notices, or by any of the provisions of sections 225 to 228 of this Act, shall apply and be exercisable in relation to Crown land, to the extent of any interest therein for the time being held otherwise than by or on behalf of the Crown ;

(c) a building which for the time being is Crown land may be included in a list compiled or approved by the Secretary of State under section 54 of this Act.

(2) Except with the consent of the appropriate authority—

(a) no order or notice shall be made or served under any of the provisions of sections 51, 60, 65, 87 or 96 of this Act or under any of those provisions as applied by any order or regulations made under Part IV of this Act, in relation to land which for the time being is Crown land ;

(b) no interest in land which for the time being is Crown land shall be acquired compulsorily under Part VI of this Act.

(3) No enforcement notice shall be served under section 87 of this Act in respect of development carried out by or on behalf of the Crown after the appointed day on land which was Crown land at the time when the development was carried out.

(4) No listed building enforcement notice shall be served in respect of works executed by or on behalf of the Crown in respect of a building which was Crown land at the time when the works were executed.

(5) No purchase notice or listed building purchase notice shall be served in relation to any interest in Crown land unless an offer has been previously made by the owner of that interest to dispose of it to the appropriate authority on terms that the price payable for it shall be equal to (and shall, in default of agreement, be determined in like manner as) the

compensation which would be payable in respect of that interest PART XIV
if it were acquired in pursuance of a purchase notice, and that
offer has been refused by the appropriate authority.

(6) The rights conferred by the provisions of sections 192 to
207 of this Act shall be exercisable by a person who (within the
meaning of those provisions) is an owner-occupier of a hereditament or agricultural unit which is Crown land, or is a resident
owner-occupier of a hereditament which is Crown land, in
the same way as they are exercisable in respect of a hereditament
or agricultural unit which is not Crown land, and those provisions shall apply accordingly.

(7) In this Part of this Act " Crown land " means land in
which there is a Crown interest or a Duchy interest; " Crown
interest " means an interest belonging to Her Majesty in right
of the Crown, or belonging to a government department, or held
in trust for Her Majesty for the purposes of a government
department; " Duchy interest " means an interest belonging to
Her Majesty in right of the Duchy of Lancaster, or belonging
to the Duchy of Cornwall; and for the purposes of this section
and section 267 of this Act " the appropriate authority ", in
relation to any land—

(a) in the case of land belonging to Her Majesty in right
of the Crown and forming part of the Crown Estate,
means the Crown Estate Commissioners, and, in relation to any other land belonging to Her Majesty in
right of the Crown, means the government department
having the management of that land;

(b) in relation to land belonging to Her Majesty in right
of the Duchy of Lancaster, means the Chancellor of
the Duchy;

(c) in relation to land belonging to the Duchy of Cornwall,
means such person as the Duke of Cornwall, or the
possessor for the time being of the Duchy of Cornwall,
appoints;

(d) in the case of land belonging to a government department or held in trust for Her Majesty for the purposes
of a government department, means that department;

and, if any question arises as to what authority is the appropriate
authority in relation to any land, that question shall be referred
to the Treasury, whose decision shall be final.

267.—(1) The appropriate authority and the local planning Agreements
authority for the area in which any Crown land is situated may relating to
make agreements for securing the use of the land, so far as may Crown land.
be prescribed by any such agreement, in conformity with the

PART XIV   provisions of the development plan applicable thereto ; and any such agreement may contain such consequential provisions, including provisions of a financial character, as may appear to be necessary or expedient having regard to the purposes of the agreement.

(2) An agreement made under this section by a government department shall not have effect unless it is approved by the Treasury.

(3) In considering whether to make or approve an agreement under this section relating to land belonging to a government department, or held in trust for Her Majesty for the purposes of a government department, the department and the Treasury shall have regard to the purposes for which the land is held by or for the department.

Supplementary
provisions as
to Crown
and Duchy
interests.

268.—(1) Subject to the following provisions of this section—

(a) where there is a Crown interest in any land, the provisions of Part VII of this Act and of sections 166 to 168 thereof, and the provisions of Schedules 15, 16 and 17 to this Act and the provisions of Schedule 24 to this Act in so far as they relate to Part VII or to sections 166 to 168 of this Act, shall have effect in relation to any private interest or Duchy interest as if the Crown interest were a private interest ; and

(b) where there is a Duchy interest in any land, those provisions shall have effect in relation to that interest, and to any private interest, as if the Duchy interest were a private interest.

(2) References in this Act to claims established under Part VI of the Act of 1947 include references to claims so established in accordance with arrangements made under section 88(2) of that Act (which provided for the application of Part VI of that Act to Duchy interests and for the payment of sums in lieu of development charges in respect of such interests) ; references to development charges include references to sums determined in accordance with such arrangements to be appropriate in substitution for development charges ; and references to the amount of an established claim or of a development charge shall be construed accordingly.

(3) Where, in accordance with an agreement under section 267 of this Act, the approval of a local planning authority is required in respect of any development of land in which there is a Duchy interest, the provisions of this Act referred to in subsection (1)(a) of this section shall have effect in relation

to the withholding of that approval, or the giving thereof sub-   PART XIV
ject to conditions, as if it were a refusal of planning permission,
or a grant of planning permission subject to conditions, as
the case may be.

(4) In this section " private interest " means an interest which
is neither a Crown interest nor a Duchy interest.

Isles of Scilly

269.—(1) The Secretary of State shall, after consultation with Application
the Council of the Isles of Scilly, by order provide for the applica- of Act to
tion to those Isles of the provisions of this Act specified in Isles of Scilly.
Parts I and II of Schedule 21 to this Act as if those Isles were a
separate county.

(2) In relation to land in the Isles of Scilly, the provisions
of this Act specified in Part III of the said Schedule shall have
effect as if those Isles were a county district and the Council of
the Isles were the council of that district.

(3) The Secretary of State, may, after consultation with the
Council of the Isles of Scilly, by order provide for the application
to those Isles of the provisions of this Act specified in Part IV
of the said Schedule as if those Isles were a separate county or
county district.

(4) Any order under subsection (1) or (3) of this section may
provide for the application of the provisions there mentioned
to the Isles subject to such modifications as may be specified
in the order.

Local planning authorities

270.—(1) In relation to land of local planning authorities, Application
and to the development by local authorities of land in respect of to local
which they are the local planning authorities, the provisions of planning
this Act specified in Part V of Schedule 21 to this Act shall have provisions
effect subject to such exceptions and modifications as may be as to planning
prescribed by regulations made under this Act. control and
enforcement.

(2) Subject to the provisions of section 40 of this Act, any
such regulations may in particular provide for securing—

> (a) that any application by such an authority for planning
> permission to develop such land, or for any other
> consent required in relation to such land under the
> said provisions, shall be made to the Secretary of State
> and not to the local planning authority ;

I

PART XIV

(b) that any order or notice authorised to be made or served under those provisions in relation to such land shall be made or served by the Secretary of State and not by the local planning authority.

(3) Sections 26, 27 and 29(2) and (3) of this Act shall apply, with the necessary modifications, in relation to applications made to the Secretary of State in pursuance of regulations made for the purposes of subsection (1) of this section, as they apply in relation to applications for planning permission which fall to be determined by the local planning authority.

Application to local planning authorities of provisions as to listed buildings.

271.—(1) In relation to buildings of local planning authorities which are listed, and to the execution of works for their demolition, alteration or extension, the provisions of this Act specified in Part VI of Schedule 21 to this Act shall have effect subject to such exceptions and modifications as may be prescribed by regulations made under this Act.

(2) Any such regulations may in particular provide for securing—

(a) that any application by such an authority for listed building consent shall be made to the Secretary of State and not to the local planning authority ;

(b) that any notice authorised to be served under the said provisions in relation to a listed building belonging to a local planning authority shall be served by the Secretary of State and not by that authority.

Special provisions as to statutory undertakers who are local planning authorities.

272. In relation to statutory undertakers who are local planning authorities, section 241 of this Act and the provisions specified in subsection (2) of that section shall have effect subject to such exceptions and modifications as may be prescribed by regulations made under this Act.

Other special cases

National Coal Board.

273.—(1) Regulations made under this Act by the Secretary of State for the Environment and the Secretary of State for Trade and Industry with the consent of the Treasury may direct that any of the provisions of this Act specified in Part I of Schedule 21 to this Act or of section 223 of this Act, being provisions relating to statutory undertakers and to land of such undertakers, shall apply, subject to such adaptations, modifications and exceptions as may be specified in the regulations, in relation to the National Coal Board, and in relation to land (including mines) of that Board of any such class as may be specified in the regulations, as if the Board were statutory undertakers and as if land of any class so specified were operational land.

(2) Without prejudice to the generality of subsection (1) of PART XIV
this section, any regulations made thereunder may in particular
provide that any compensation payable to the National Coal
Board by virtue of any of the provisions applied by the regulations, being compensation which, in the case of statutory
undertakers, would be assessable in accordance with the provisions of section 238 of this Act, shall, instead of being assessed
in accordance with that section, be assessed in accordance with
the provisions of the regulations.

274.—(1) Without prejudice to the provisions of the Acquisi- Ecclesiastical
tion of Land (Authorisation Procedure) Act 1946 with respect property.
to notices served under that Act, where under any of the provi- 1946 c. 49.
sions of this Act a notice is required to be served on an owner of
land, and the land is ecclesiastical property, a like notice shall be
served on the Church Commissioners.

(2) Where the fee simple of any ecclesiastical property is in
abeyance—

    (a) if the property is situated elsewhere than in Wales, then
        for the purposes of the provisions of this Act specified
        in Part VII of Schedule 21 to this Act the fee simple
        shall be treated as being vested in the Church Com-
        missioners ;

    (b) in any case, the fee simple shall, for the purposes of a
        compulsory acquisition of the property under Part VI
        of this Act, be treated as being vested in the Church
        Commissioners, and any notice to treat shall be served,
        or be deemed to have been served, accordingly.

(3) Any compensation payable under Part VIII (except
sections 171, 172 and 175) or section 212 of this Act in respect
of land which is ecclesiastical property shall be paid to the
Church Commissioners, to be applied for the purposes for which
the proceeds of a sale by agreement of the land would be
applicable under any enactment or Measure authorising, or dis-
posing of the proceeds of, such a sale.

(4) Any sum which under any of the provisions of this Act
specified in Part III of Schedule 21 to this Act is payable in
relation to land which is, or on the appointed day was,
ecclesiastical property, and apart from this subsection would be
payable to an incumbent, shall be paid to the Church Commissioners, to be applied for the purposes mentioned in subsection (3) of this section ; and where any sum is recoverable under
section 159, 168 or 279 of this Act in respect of any such land,

PART XIV   the Church Commissioners may apply any money or securities held by them in the payment of that sum.

(5) In this section "ecclesiastical property" means land belonging to an ecclesiastical benefice, or being or forming part of a church subject to the jurisdiction of a bishop of any diocese or the site of such a church, or being or forming part of a burial ground subject to such jurisdiction.

Settled land, and land of universities and colleges.
1925 c. 18.
1925 c. 20.
1925 c. 24.

275.—(1) The purposes authorised for the application of capital moneys—

  (a) by section 73 of the Settled Land Act 1925 and by that section as applied by section 28 of the Law of Property Act 1925 in relation to trusts for sale ; and

  (b) by section 26 of the Universities and College Estates Act 1925,

and the purposes authorised by section 71 of the Settled Land Act 1925, by that section as so applied, and by section 30 of the Universities and College Estates Act 1925 as purposes for which moneys may be raised by mortgage, shall include the payment of any sum recoverable under section 159, 168 or 279 of this Act.

(2) The classes of works specified in Part II of Schedule 3 to the Settled Land Act 1925 (which specifies improvements which may be paid for out of capital money, subject to provisions under which repayment out of income may be required to be made) shall include works specified by the Secretary of State as being required for properly maintaining a listed building which is settled land within the meaning of that Act.

PART XV

MISCELLANEOUS AND SUPPLEMENTARY PROVISIONS

Default powers of Secretary of State.

276.—(1) If it appears to the Secretary of State, after consultation with the local planning authority, to be expedient that any order to which this subsection applies should be made, he may give directions to the local planning authority requiring them to submit to him such an order for his confirmation, or may himself make such an order ; and any order so made by the Secretary of State shall have the like effect as if it had been made by the local planning authority and confirmed by the Secretary of State under Part III or IV of this Act.

(2) Subsection (1) of this section applies to the following
orders, that is to say—

   (a) orders under section 45 of this Act, or under the provisions of that section as applied by any order or regulations made under Part IV of this Act;

   (b) orders under section 51 of this Act;

   (c) tree preservation orders and orders amending or revoking them.

(3) The provisions of Part III or Part IV of this Act, and of any regulations made thereunder, with respect to the procedure to be followed in connection with the submission by the local planning authority of any order to which subsection (1) of this section applies, with respect to the confirmation of such an order by the Secretary of State, and with respect to the service of copies thereof as so confirmed, shall have effect, subject to any necessary modifications, in relation to any proposal by the Secretary of State to make such an order by virtue of subsection (1) of this section, in relation to the making thereof by the Secretary of State, and in relation to the service of copies thereof as so made.

(4) Without prejudice to subsection (3) of this section, where the Secretary of State proposes under subsection (1) of this section to make any such order as is mentioned in subsection (2)(a) or (b) of this section he shall serve a notice of the proposal on the local planning authority; and if within such period as may be specified in the notice (not being less than twenty-eight days from the date of service) the authority so require, the Secretary of State before making the order shall afford to the authority an opportunity of appearing before, and being heard by, a person appointed by him for the purpose.

(5) If it appears to the Secretary of State, after consultation with the local planning authority, to be expedient that—

   (a) a completion notice under section 44 of this Act; or

   (b) a notice under section 65 of this Act; or

   (c) an enforcement notice under section 87 of this Act, or under the provisions of that section as applied by regulations under section 63 of this Act; or

   (d) a stop notice under section 90 of this Act; or

   (e) a listed building enforcement notice,

should be served in respect of any land, he may give directions to the local planning authority requiring them to serve such a notice, or may himself serve such a notice; and any notice so served by the Secretary of State shall have the like effect as a notice served by the local planning authority:

Provided that, in relation to an enforcement notice under section 87 of this Act or a listed building enforcement notice which is served by the Secretary of State, the provisions of sections 89 and 91 to 93, or, as the case may be, of sections 98 and 99 of this Act shall apply as if for any reference therein to the local planning authority there were substituted a reference to the Secretary of State.

(6) If the Secretary of State is satisfied, after holding a local inquiry—

> (a) that the council of a county, county borough, London borough or county district have failed to take steps for the acquisition of any land which, in the opinion of the Secretary of State, ought to be acquired by that council under section 112 of this Act for a purpose which it is necessary to achieve in the interests of the proper planning of an area in which the land is situated; or
>
> (b) that a local authority have failed to carry out, on land acquired by them under section 68 of the Act of 1962 or section 112 of this Act or appropriated by them under section 121 of this Act, any development which, in the opinion of the Secretary of State, ought to be carried out,

the Secretary of State may by order require the council or authority to take such steps as may be specified in the order for acquiring the land, or carrying out the development, as the case may be.

(7) Any order under subsection (6) of this section shall be enforceable, on the application of the Secretary of State, by mandamus.

Designation of conservation areas.

277.—(1) Every local planning authority shall from time to time determine which parts of their area are areas of special architectural or historic interest the character or appearance of which it is desirable to preserve or enhance, and shall designate such areas as conservation areas.

(2) The Secretary of State may, after consultation with a local planning authority, give to that authority such directions as he thinks necessary with respect to the exercise of their functions under subsection (1) of this section; and it shall be the duty of the authority to comply with any such directions.

(3) Before making a determination under this section, a local planning authority in Greater London shall consult with the other local planning authority or authorities for the area to which the proposed determination relates, and a local planning authority outside Greater London shall consult with the council

of each county district of which any part is included in that PART XV
area.

(4) The local planning authority shall give notice to the
Secretary of State of the designation of any conservation area,
and of any variation or cancellation of any such designation,
with sufficient particulars to identify the area affected, and shall
cause the like notice to be published in the London Gazette
and in at least one newspaper circulating in the area of the local
planning authority.

(5) Where any area is for the time being designated as a
conservation area, special attention shall be paid to the
desirability of preserving or enhancing its character or appearance in the exercise, with respect to any buildings or other land
in that area, of any powers under this Act, Part I of the Historic 1953 c. 49.
Buildings and Ancient Monuments Act 1953 or the Local 1962 c. 36.
Authorities (Historic Buildings) Act 1962.

(6) The local planning authority for the purpose of this
section shall, in Greater London, be the Greater London Council
and also, in relation to a London borough, the council of that
borough.

278.—(1) In any case where the value or depreciation in Assumptions
value of an interest in land falls to be determined on the assump- as to planning
tion that planning permission would be granted for develop- permission in
ment of any class specified in Schedule 8 to this Act, it shall value of
be further assumed, as regards development of any class specified interests
in paragraph 1 or 3 of that Schedule, that such permission in land.
would be granted subject to the condition set out in Schedule 18
to this Act.

(2) In the application of the said Schedule 8 for the purposes
of any determination to which subsection (1) of this section
applies—

    (*a*) paragraph 3 of that Schedule shall be construed as
        not extending to works involving any increase in the
        cubic content of a building erected after the appointed
        day (including any building resulting from the carrying
        out of such works as are described in paragraph 1 of
        that Schedule) ; and

    (*b*) paragraph 7 of that Schedule shall not apply to any
        such building.

(3) For the purposes of subsections (1) and (2) of this section,
so far as applicable to any determination of existing use value
as defined in section 187(5) of this Act, references to Schedule 8
to this Act, and to paragraphs 1, 3 and 7 of that Schedule,
shall be construed as references to Schedule 3 to the Act of
1947 and to the corresponding paragraphs of that Schedule ;
and that Schedule shall have effect as if it contained a paragraph corresponding to paragraph 13 of Schedule 8 to this Act.

PART XV

(4) Except as provided in section 168(4) of this Act, nothing in the preceding provisions of this section or in paragraph 13 of Schedule 8 affects the meaning of " new development " in this Act or any determination to be made for the purpose of Part VII of this Act.

(5) For the avoidance of doubt it is hereby declared that where, under any provision of this Act, the value of an interest in land is required to be assessed on the assumption that planning permission would be granted for development of any class specified in Schedule 8 to this Act, that assumption is to be made on the footing that any such development must comply with the provisions of any enactment, other than this Act, which would be applicable to it.

Recovery, on subsequent development, of payments in respect of war-damaged land.

279.—(1) In relation to notices registered under section 57 of the Act of 1954 (which provided for the registration of notices of payments made under section 59 of the Act of 1947) the provisions of sections 159 and 160 of this Act shall have effect (subject to the following provisions of this section) as they have effect in relation to notices registered under section 158 of this Act.

(2) The said provisions shall have effect as mentioned in subsection (1) of this section, but as if—

    (a) any reference therein to the compensation specified in a notice were a reference to the payment so specified ; and

    (b) section 159 of this Act applied to every description of new development.

(3) No amount shall be recoverable by the Secretary of State by virtue of this section in respect of any land in relation to which an amount has become recoverable under section 258 of this Act.

(4) Subsection (5) of section 258 of this Act shall apply for the purposes of this section as it applies for the purposes of that section.

Rights of entry.

280.—(1) Any person duly authorised in writing by the Secretary of State or by a local planning authority may at any reasonable time enter any land for the purpose of surveying it in connection with—

    (a) the preparation, approval, adoption, making or amendment of a structure plan or local plan relating to the land under Part II of this Act, including the carrying out of any survey under that Part ;

    (b) any application under Part III or sections 60 or 63 of this Act, or under any order or regulations made thereunder, for any permission, consent or determination

to be given or made in connection with that land or　PART XV
any other land under Part III or either of those sections
of this Act or under any such order or regulations ;
(c) any proposal by the local planning authority or by the
Secretary of State to make or serve any order or notice
under Part III (other than section 44), Part IV or Part
V of this Act, or under any order or regulations made
thereunder or any notice under section 115 of this
Act.

(2) Any person duly authorised in writing by the Secretary
of State may at any reasonable time enter any land for the
purpose of surveying any building thereon in connection with a
proposal to include the building in, or exclude it from, a list
compiled or approved under section 54 of this Act.

(3) Any person duly authorised in writing by the Secretary of
State or a local planning authority may at any reasonable time
enter any land for the purpose of ascertaining whether, with
respect to any building on the land, an offence has been, or is
being, committed under section 55 or 98 of, or Schedule 11 to,
this Act, or whether the building is being maintained in a proper
state of repair.

(4) Any person duly authorised in writing by the Secretary of
State or a local authority may at any reasonable time enter any
land for the purpose of ascertaining whether—
(a) an offence appears to have been committed under section
57 of this Act ; or
(b) any of the functions conferred by section 101 or 103 of
this Act should or may be exercised in connection with
the land,
or for the purpose of exercising any of those functions in
connection with the land.

(5) Any person, being an officer of the Valuation Office or a
person duly authorised in writing by the Secretary of State, may
at any reasonable time enter any land for the purpose of surveying it, or estimating its value, in connection with a claim for
compensation under Part VII of this Act in respect of that land
or any other land.

(6) Any person, being an officer of the Valuation Office or a
person duly authorised in writing by a local planning authority,
may at any reasonable time enter any land for the purpose of
surveying it, or estimating its value, in connection with a claim
for compensation in respect of that land or any other land, being
compensation payable by the local planning authority under
Part VIII of this Act (other than section 175), under section
212(5) of this Act or under Part XI of this Act (other than
section 237(2) or 238(1)(c)).

PART XV   (7) Any person, being an officer of the Valuation Office or a person duly authorised in writing by a local authority or Minister authorised to acquire land under section 112 or 113 of this Act, and any person duly authorised in writing by a local authority having power to acquire land under Part VI of this Act, may at any reasonable time enter any land for the purpose of surveying it, or estimating its value, in connection with any proposal to acquire that land or any other land, or in connection with any claim for compensation in respect of any such acquisition.

(8) Any person duly authorised in writing by the Secretary of State or by a local planning authority may at any reasonable time enter any land in respect of which an order or notice has been made or served as mentioned in subsection (1)(c) of this section, for the purpose of ascertaining whether the order or notice has been complied with.

(9) Subject to the provisions of section 281 of this Act, any power conferred by this section to survey land shall be construed as including power to search and bore for the purpose of ascertaining the nature of the subsoil or the presence of minerals therein.

Supplementary provisions as to rights of entry.   **281.**—(1) A person authorised under section 280 of this Act to enter any land shall, if so required, produce evidence of his authority before so entering, and shall not demand admission as of right to any land which is occupied unless twenty-four hours' notice of the intended entry has been given to the occupier.

(2) Any person wno wilfully obstructs a person acting in the exercise of his powers under section 280 of this Act shall be guilty of an offence and liable on summary conviction to a fine not exceeding £20.

(3) If any person who, in compliance with the provisions of section 280 of this Act, is admitted into a factory, workshop or workplace discloses to any person any information obtained by him therein as to any manufacturing process or trade secret, he shall, unless the disclosure is made in the course of performing his duty in connection with the purpose for which he was authorised to enter the premises, be guilty of an offence and liable on summary conviction to a fine not exceeding £400 or on conviction on indictment to imprisonment for a term not exceeding two years or a fine, or both.

(4) Where any land is damaged in the exercise of a right of entry conferred under section 280 of this Act, or in the making of any survey for the purpose of which any such right of entry has been so conferred, compensation in respect of that damage may be recovered by any person interested in the land from the Secretary of State or authority on whose behalf the entry was effected.

(5) The provisions of section 179 of this Act shall apply in relation to compensation under subsection (4) of this section as they apply in relation to compensation under Part VIII of this Act.

(6) Where under section 280 of this Act a person proposes to carry out any works authorised by virtue of subsection (9) of that section—

- (a) he shall not carry out those works unless notice of his intention to do so was included in the notice required by subsection (1) of this section ; and
- (b) if the land in question is held by statutory undertakers, and those undertakers object to the proposed works on the grounds that the carrying out thereof would be seriously detrimental to the carrying on of their undertaking, the works shall not be carried out except with the authority of the appropriate Minister.

282.—(1) The Secretary of State may cause a local inquiry to Local be held for the purposes of the exercise of any of his functions inquiries. under any of the provisions of this Act.

(2) The provisions of subsections (2) to (5) of section 290 of the .Local Government Act 1933 (which relate to the giving 1933 c. 51. of evidence at, and defraying the cost of, local inquiries) shall have effect with respect to any inquiry held by virtue of this section as if the Secretary of State were a department for the purposes of that section.

283.—(1) Subject to the provisions of this section, any notice Service or other document required or authorised to be served or given of notices. under this Act may be served or given either—

- (a) by delivering it to the person on whom it is to be served or to whom it is to be given ; or
- (b) by leaving it at the usual or last known place of abode of that person, or, in a case where an address for service has been given by that person, at that address ; or
- (c) by sending it in a prepaid registered letter, or by the recorded delivery service, addressed to that person at his usual or last known place of abode, or, in a case where an address for service has been given by that person, at that address ; or
- (d) in the case of an incorporated company or body, by delivering it to the secretary or clerk of the company or body at their registered or principal office, or sending it in a prepaid registered letter, or by the recorded delivery service, addressed to the secretary or clerk of the company or body at that office.

(2) Where the notice or document is required or authorised to be served on any person as having an interest in premises,

PART XV   and the name of that person cannot be ascertained after reasonable inquiry, or where the notice or document is required or authorised to be served on any person as an occupier of premises, the notice or document shall be taken to be duly served if—

(a) being addressed to him either by name or by the description of " the owner " or " the occupier ", as the case may be, of the premises (describing them) it is delivered or sent in the manner specified in subsection (1)(a), (b) or (c) of this section ; or

(b) being so addressed, and marked in such manner as may be prescribed by regulations under this Act for securing that it shall be plainly identifiable as a communication of importance, it is sent to the premises in a prepaid registered letter or by the recorded delivery service and is not returned to the authority sending it, or is delivered to some person on those premises, or is affixed conspicuously to some object on those premises.

(3) Where the notice or other document is required to be served on or given to all persons having interests in, or being occupiers of, premises comprised in any land, and it appears to the authority required or authorised to serve or give the notice or other document that any part of that land is unoccupied, the notice or document shall be taken to be duly served on all persons having interests in, and on any occupiers of, premises comprised in that part of the land (other than a person who has given to that authority an address for the service of the notice or document on him) if it is addressed to " the owners and any occupiers " of that part of the land (describing it) and is affixed conspicuously to some object on the land.

Power to require information as to interests in land.

284.—(1) For the purpose of enabling the Secretary of State or a local authority to make an order or serve any notice or other document which, by any of the provisions of this Act, he or they are authorised or required to make or serve, the Secretary of State or the local authority may require the occupier of any premises and any person who, either directly or indirectly, receives rent in respect of any premises to state in writing the nature of his interest therein, and the name and address of any other person known to him as having an interest therein, whether as a freeholder, mortgagee, lessee or otherwise.

(2) Any person who, having been required in pursuance of this section to give any information, fails to give that information shall be guilty of an offence and liable on summary conviction to a fine not exceeding £100.

(3) Any person who, having been so required to give any information, knowingly makes any misstatement in respect thereof shall be guilty of an offence and liable on summary conviction to a fine not exceeding £400 or on conviction on

ındictment to imprisonment for a term not exceeding two years   PART XV
or to a fine, or both.

285.—(1) Where an offence under this Act (other than section Offences by
57 or paragraph 4 of Schedule 12) which has been committed by corporations.
a body corporate is proved to have been committed with the
consent or connivance of, or to be attributable to any neglect on
the part of, a director, manager, secretary or other similar officer
of the body corporate, or any person who was purporting to act
in any such capacity, he, as well as the body corporate, shall
be guilty of that offence and be liable to be proceeded against
accordingly.

(2) In subsection (1) of this section the expression " director ",
in relation to any body corporate established by or under an
enactment for the purpose of carrying on under national owner-
ship an industry or part of an industry or undertaking, being
a body corporate whose affairs are managed by the members
thereof, means a member of that body corporate.

286.—(1) Regulations made under this Act may provide for Combined
the combination in a single document, made in such form and applications.
transmitted to such authority as may be prescribed by the
regulations, of—

    (*a*) an application for planning permission in respect of any
        development; and

    (*b*) an application required, under any enactment specified
        in the regulations, to be made to a local authority in
        respect of that development.

(2) Before making any regulations under this section, the
Secretary of State shall consult with such local authorities or
associations of local authorities as appear to him to be
concerned.

(3) Different provision may be made by any such regulations
in relation to areas in which different enactments are in force.

(4) An application required to be made to a local authority
under an enactment specified in any such regulations shall, if
made in accordance with the provisions of the regulations, be
valid notwithstanding anything in that enactment prescribing,
or enabling any authority to prescribe, the form in which, or the
manner in which, such an application is to be made.

(5) Subsection (4) of this section shall have effect without
prejudice to—

    (*a*) the validity of any application made in accordance with
        the enactment in question ; or

    (*b*) any provision of that enactment enabling a local
        authority to require further particulars of the matters
        to which the application relates.

(6) In this section " application " includes a submission.

287.—(1) The Secretary of State may make regulations under this Act—

>   (a) for prescribing the form of any notice, order or other document authorised or required by any of the provisions of this Act to be served, made or issued by any local authority;

>   (b) for any purpose for which regulations are authorised or required to be made under this Act, not being a purpose for which regulations are authorised or required to be made by another Minister.

(2) Any power conferred by this Act to make regulations shall be exercisable by statutory instrument; and any statutory instrument containing regulations made under this Act (except regulations which, by virtue of any provision of this Act, are of no effect unless approved by a resolution of each House of Parliament) shall be subject to annulment in pursuance of a resolution of either House of Parliament.

(3) Any power conferred by any of the provisions of this Act to make an order shall include power to vary or revoke any such order by a subsequent order.

(4) The power to make orders under sections 1(2), 21, 22(2)(*f*), 24, 55(3), 69, 73(6), 74(4)(*b*), 75(8), 192(4)(*a*) and 269 of this Act shall be exercisable by statutory instrument.

(5) Any statutory instrument—

>   (a) which contains an order under subsection (2) of section 1 of this Act which has been made after a local inquiry has been held in accordance with the proviso to that subsection; or

>   (b) which contains a development order or an order under section 69, 73(6), 75(8) or 192(4)(*a*) of this Act,

shall be subject to annulment in pursuance of a resolution of either House of Parliament.

(6) Without prejudice to subsection (5) of this section, where a development order makes provision for excluding or modifying any enactment contained in a public general Act (other than any of the enactments specified in Schedule 22 to this Act) the order shall not have effect until that provision is approved by a resolution of each House of Parliament.

(7) Any order under this Act which designates an area for the purposes of section 74(4)(*b*) of this Act shall cease to have effect at the end of the period of twenty-eight days beginning with the day on which the order is made (but without prejudice to anything previously done under the order or to the making of a new order) unless before the end of that period the order is approved by a resolution of each House of Parliament.

(8) In reckoning any period for the purposes of subsection (7) of this section, no account shall be taken of any time during which Parliament is dissolved or prorogued or during which both Houses are adjourned for more than four days.

(9) Any order under section 69, 73(6), 74(4)(*b*) or 75(8) of this Act may contain such supplementary and incidental provisions as may appear to the Secretary of State to be appropriate.

(10) Any power (exercisable in accordance with section 294(2) of this Act) to make regulations or orders under this Act before the date of the commencement of this Act shall include power, by any regulations or order so made, to revoke any regulations or order made under any of the enactments which, as from that date, are repealed by this Act or having effect by virtue of any of those enactments as if made thereunder.

288.—(1) Where the united district for which, by an order Licensing under section 1 of this Act, a joint planning board is constituted planning comprises a licensing planning area, or the whole or part of areas. such a united district is included in a licensing planning area, the Secretary of State may by order revoke or vary any order in force under Part VII of the Licensing Act 1964 so far as may 1964 c. 26. be necessary or expedient in consequence of the order under section 1 of this Act.

(2) Subject to subsection (1) of this section, nothing in any order made under section 1 of this Act shall affect the validity of any order in force under Part VII of the Licensing Act 1964 if made before the date of the order under section 1 of this Act.

289. For the avoidance of doubt it is hereby declared that Act not the provisions of this Act, and any restrictions or powers thereby excluded by imposed or conferred in relation to land, apply and may be special exercised in relation to any land notwithstanding that provision enactments. is made by any enactment in force at the passing of the Act of 1947, or by any local Act passed at any time during the Session of Parliament held during the regnal years 10 & 11 Geo. 6, for authorising or regulating any development of the land.

290.—(1) In this Act, except in so far as the context other- Interpretation. wise requires and subject to the transitional provisions hereinafter contained, the following expressions have the meanings hereby assigned to them respectively, that is to say :—

" acquiring authority ", in relation to the acquisition of an interest in land (whether compulsorily or by agreement) or to a proposal so to acquire such an interest, means the government department, local authority or other body by whom the interest is, or is proposed to be, acquired ;

" the Act of 1944 " means the Town and Country Planning 1944 c. 47. Act 1944 ;

PART XV
1947 c. 51.

1954 c. 72.

1959 c. 53.

1962 c. 38.

1968 c. 72.

" the Act of 1947 " means the Town and Country Planning
Act 1947 ;

" the Act of 1954 " means the Town and Country Planning
Act 1954 ;

" the Act of 1959 " means the Town and Country Planning
Act 1959 ;

" the Act of 1962 " means the Town and Country Planning
Act 1962 ;

" the Act of 1968 " means the Town and Country Planning
Act 1968 ;

" advertisement " means any word, letter, model, sign,
placard, board, notice, device or representation,
whether illuminated or not, in the nature of, and em-
ployed wholly or partly for the purposes of, advertisement, announcement or direction, and (without
prejudice to the preceding provisions of this definition),
includes any hoarding or similar structure used, or
adapted for use, for the display of advertisements, and
references to the display of advertisements shall be
construed accordingly ;

" agriculture " includes horticulture, fruit growing, seed
growing, dairy farming, the breeding and keeping of
livestock (including any creature kept for the produc-
tion of food, wool, skins or fur, or for the purpose of
its use in the farming of land), the use of land as
grazing land, meadow land, osier land, market gardens
and nursery grounds, and the use of land for woodlands where that use is ancillary to the farming of land
for other agricultural purposes, and " agricultural "
shall be construed accordingly ;

" the appointed day " means 1st July 1948 ;

" the appropriate Minister " has the meaning assigned to it
by section 224 of this Act ;

" area of extensive war damage " and " area of bad layout
or obsolete development " mean respectively an area
consisting of land shown to the satisfaction of the
Secretary of State to have sustained war damage or,
as the case may be, to be badly laid out or of obsolete
development, or consisting of such land together with
other land contiguous or adjacent thereto, being in
each case land comprised in an area which is defined
by a development plan as an area of comprehensive
development ;

" authority possessing compulsory purchase powers ", in
relation to the compulsory acquisition of an interest in
land, means the person or body of persons effecting the
acquisition, and, in relation to any other transaction
relating to an interest in land, means any person or

body of persons who could be or have been authorised
to acquire that interest compulsorily for the purposes
for which the transaction is or was effected, or a body
(being a parish council or parish meeting or the
council of a borough included in a rural district) on
whose behalf a county council could be or have been
so authorised;

" authority to whom Part II of the Act of 1959 applies "
means a body of any of the descriptions specified in
Part I of Schedule 4 to the Act of 1959;

" bridleway " has the same meaning as in the Highways Act 1959 c. 25.
1959;

" building " (except in sections 73 to 86 of this Act and
Schedule 12 thereto) includes any structure or erection,
and any part of a building, as so defined, but does not
include plant or machinery comprised in a building;

" buildings or works " includes waste materials, refuse and
other matters deposited on land, and references to the
erection or construction of buildings or works shall be
construed accordingly;

" building operations " includes rebuilding operations,
structural alterations of or additions to buildings, and
other operations normally undertaken by a person
carrying on business as a builder;

" caravan site " has the meaning assigned to it by section
1(4) of the Caravan Sites and Control of Development 1960 c. 62.
Act 1960;

" clearing ", in relation to land, means the removal of
buildings or materials from the land, the levelling of
the surface of the land, and the carrying out of such
other operations in relation thereto as may be
prescribed;

" common " includes any land subject to be enclosed
under the Inclosure Acts 1845 to 1882, and any town
or village green;

" compulsory acquisition " does not include the vesting in a
person by an Act of Parliament of property previously
vested in some other person;

" conservation area " means an area designated under
section 277 of this Act;

" development " has the meaning assigned to it by section
22 of this Act, and " develop " shall be construed
accordingly;

" development order " has the meaning assigned to it by
section 24 of this Act;

" development plan " (subject to section 21 of, and paragraphs 1 and 8 of Schedule 6 to, this Act) shall be construed in accordance with section 20 of this Act ;

" disposal " means disposal by way of sale, exchange or lease, or by way of the creation of any easement, right or privilege, or in any other manner, except by way of appropriation, gift or mortgage, and " dispose of " shall be construed accordingly ;

" enactment " includes an enactment in any local or private Act of Parliament, and an order, rule, regulation, byelaw or scheme made under an Act of Parliament ;

" enforcement notice " means a notice under section 87 of this Act ;

" engineering operations " includes the formation or laying out of means of access to highways ;

" erection ", in relation to buildings as defined in this subsection, includes extension, alteration and re-erection ;

" established use certificate " has the meaning assigned to it by section 94 of this Act ;

1959 c. 25.

" footpath " has the same meaning as in the Highways Act 1959 ;

" fuel or field garden allotment " means any allotment set out as a fuel allotment, or a field garden allotment, under an Inclosure Act ;

" functions " includes powers and duties ;

" government department " includes any Minister of the Crown ;

" the Greater London development plan " (except in Part II of Schedule 5 to this Act) means the development plan submitted to the Minister of Housing and Local Government under section 25 of the London Government Act 1963 and approved by the Secretary of State under section 5 of the Act of 1962 or the corresponding provision of this Act ;

1963 c. 33.

" highway " has the same meaning as in the Highways Act, 1959 ;

" improvement ", in relation to a highway, has the same meaning as in the Highways Act 1959 as amended by the Highways Act 1971 ;

1971 c. 41.

" industrial development certificate " has the meaning assigned to it by section 67 of this Act ;

" joint planning board " has the meaning assigned to it by section 1 of this Act ;

" land " means any corporeal hereditament, including a building, and, in relation to the acquisition of land under Part VI of this Act, includes any interest in or right over land ;

" lease " includes an underlease and an agreement for a
lease or underlease, but does not include an option to
take a lease or a mortgage, and " leasehold interest "
means the interest of the tenant under a lease as so
defined ;

" listed building " has the meaning assigned to it by section
54(9) of this Act ;

" listed building consent " has the meaning assigned to it
by section 55(2) of this Act ;

" listed building enforcement notice " has the meaning
assigned to it by section 96 of this Act ;

" listed building purchase notice " has the meaning assigned
to it by section 190 of this Act ;

" local authority " (except in section 215 of this Act) means
the council of a county, county borough or county
district, the Greater London Council, the council of a
London borough and any other authority (except the
Receiver for the Metropolitan Police District) who are
a local authority within the meaning of the Local 1875 c. 83.
Loans Act 1875 and includes any river authority, any
drainage board and any joint board or joint committee
if all the constituent authorities are local authorities
within the meaning of that Act ;

" local highway authority " means a highway authority
other than the Secretary of State ;

" local planning authority " has the meaning assigned to it
by section 1 of, and Schedule 3 to, this Act ;

" London borough " includes the City of London, references
to the council of a London borough or the clerk to such
a council being construed, in relation to the City, as
references to the Common Council of the City and the
town clerk of the City respectively ;

" means of access " includes any means of access, whether
private or public, for vehicles or for foot passengers,
and includes a street ;

" minerals " includes all minerals and substances in or under
land of a kind ordinarily worked for removal by underground or surface working, except that it does not
include peat cut for purposes other than sale ;

" Minister " means any Minister of the Crown or other
government department ;

" mortgage " includes any charge or lien on any property
for securing money or money's worth ;

" new development " has the meaning assigned to it by
section 22(5) of this Act ;

" open space " means any land laid out as a public garden, or used for the purposes of public recreation, or land which is a disused burial ground ;

" operational land " has the meaning assigned to it by section 222 of this Act ;

" owner ", in relation to any land, means (except in sections 27 and 29 of this Act) a person, other than a mortgagee not in possession, who, whether in his own right or as trustee for any other person, is entitled to receive the rack rent of the land, or, where the land is not let at a rack rent, would be so entitled if it were so let ;

" planning decision " means a decision made on an application under Part III of this Act ;

" planning permission " means permission under Part III of this Act, and in construing references to planning permission to develop land or to carry out any development of land, or to applications for such permission, regard shall be had to section 32(2) of this Act ;

" planning permission granted for a limited period " has the meaning assigned to it by section 30(2) of this Act ;

" prescribed " (except in relation to matters expressly required or authorised by this Act to be prescribed in some other way) means prescribed by regulations under this Act ;

" previous apportionment ", in relation to an apportionment for any of the purposes of the relevant provisions, means an apportionment made before the apportionment in question, being—

(a) an apportionment for any of the purposes of the relevant provisions as made, confirmed or varied by the Lands Tribunal on a reference to that Tribunal ; or

(b) an apportionment for any of those purposes which might have been referred to the Lands Tribunal by virtue of any of the relevant provisions, where the time for such a reference has expired without its being required to be so referred, or where, after it had been so referred, the reference was withdrawn before the Tribunal gave their decision thereon ; or

(c) an apportionment made by or with the approval of the Central Land Board in connection with the approval by the Board, under section 2(2)

of the Town and Country Planning Act 1953 of an assignment of part of the benefit of an established claim (as defined by section 135(4) of this Act),

and in this definition " the relevant provisions " means any of the provisions of Part VII of this Act or of Part

VI of the Act of 1962, any of those provisions as
applied by any other provision of this Act or that Act,
and any of the provisions of the Act of 1954 ;

" purchase nôtice " has the meaning assigned to it by section
180 of this Act ;

" relocation of population or industry ", in relation to any
area, means the rendering available elsewhere than in
that area (whether in an existing community or a community to be newly established) of accommodation for
residential purposes or for the carrying on of business
or other activities, together with all appropriate public
services, facilities for public worship, recreation and
amenity, and other requirements, being accommodation
to be rendered available for persons or undertakings
who are living or carrying on business or other activities
in that area or who were doing so but by reason of
war circumstances are no longer for the time being
doing so, and whose continued or resumed location in
that area would be inconsistent with the proper planning thereof ;

" replacement of open space ", in relation to any area,
means the rendering of land available for use as an
open space, or otherwise in an undeveloped state, in
substitution for land in that area which is so used ;

" statutory undertakers " means persons authorised by any
enactment, to carry on any railway, light railway, tram-
way, road transport, water transport, canal, inland
navigation, dock, harbour, pier or lighthouse undertaking, or any undertaking for the supply of electricity,
gas, hydraulic power or water, and " statutory undertaking " shall be construed accordingly ;

" stop notice " has the meaning assigned to it by section
90 of this Act ;

" tenancy " has the same meaning as in the Landlord and
Tenant Act 1954 ;   1954 c. 56.

" tree preservation order " has the meaning assigned to it
by section 60 of this Act ;

" use ", in relation to land, does not include the use of land
for the carrying out of any building or other operations
thereon ;

" Valuation Office " means the Valuation Office of the
Inland Revenue Department ;

" Wales " includes Monmouthshire and references to
England shall be construed accordingly ;

" war damage " has the same meaning as in the War
Damage Act 1943.   1943 c. 21.

(2) If, in relation to anything required or authorised to be done under this Act, any question arises as to which Minister is or was the appropriate Minister in relation to any statutory undertakers, that question shall be determined by the Treasury; and if any question so arises whether land of statutory undertakers is operational land, that question shall be determined by the Minister who is the appropriate Minister in relation to those undertakers.

(3) Words in this Act importing a reference to service of a notice to treat shall be construed as including a reference to the constructive service of such a notice which, by virtue of any enactment, is to be deemed to be served.

(4) With respect to references in this Act to planning decisions—

> (a) in relation to a decision altered on appeal by the reversal or variation of the whole or part thereof, such references shall be construed as references to the decision as so altered;

> (b) in relation to a decision upheld on appeal, such references shall be construed as references to the decision of the local planning authority and not to the decision of the Secretary of State on the appeal;

> (c) in relation to a decision given on an appeal in the circumstances mentioned in section 37 of this Act, such references shall be construed as references to the decision so given;

> (d) the time of a planning decision, in a case where there is or was an appeal, shall be taken to be or have been the time of the decision as made by the local planning authority (whether or not that decision is or was altered on that appeal) or, in the case of a decision given on an appeal in the circumstances mentioned in section 37 of this Act, the time when in accordance with that section notification of a decision of the local planning authority is deemed to have been received.

(5) Subject to section 43(1) of this Act, for the purposes of this Act development of land shall be taken to be initiated—

> (a) if the development consists of the carrying out of operations, at the time when those operations are begun;

> (b) if the development consists of a change in use, at the time when the new use is instituted;

> (c) if the development consists both of the carrying out of operations and of a change in use, at the earlier of the times mentioned in the preceding paragraphs.

(6) In relation to the sale or acquisition of an interest in land, references in this Act to a contract are references to a contract in writing, or a contract attested by a memorandum or note

thereof in writing signed by the parties thereto or by some other person or persons authorised by them in that behalf, and, where the interest is or was conveyed or assigned without a preliminary contract, are references to the conveyance or assignment; and references to the making of a contract are references to the execution thereof or (if it was not in writing) to the signature of the memorandum or note by which it was attested.

(7) In this Act—

   (a) references to a person from whom title is derived by another person include references to any predecessor in title of that other person;

   (b) references to a person deriving title from another person include references to any successor in title of that other person;

   (c) references to deriving title are references to deriving title either directly or indirectly.

(8) References in this Act to any of the provisions in Part V or VI of Schedule 21 to this Act include, except where the context otherwise requires, references to those provisions as modified under section 270 or 271 of this Act.

(9) References in this Act to any enactment shall, except where the context otherwise requires, be onstrued as references to that enactment as amended by or under any other enactment, including this Act.

291.—(1) The enactments specified in Schedule 23 to this Act Consequential shall have effect subject to the amendments specified in that amendments. Schedule, being amendments consequential upon the provisions of this Act.

(2) References in any Act to the acquisition of land under Part V of the Act of 1962 or to land acquired thereunder (including references which, by Schedule 14 to that Act, are to be construed as such) shall be respectively construed as, or as including (according as the context requires) references to the acquisition of land under Part VI of this Act and to land acquired thereunder.

292.—(1) The transitional provisions and savings contained Transitional in Schedule 24 to this Act shall have effect. provisions, savings

(2) Subject to the provisions of that Schedule, the enactments and repeals. specified in Schedule 25 to this Act are hereby repealed to the extent specified in the third column of that Schedule.

293. The inclusion in this Act of any express savings, transi- Saving for tional provision or amendment shall not be taken as prejudicing Interpretation the operation of section 38 of the Interpretation Act 1889 (which Act 1889 s. 38. relates to the effect of repeals). 1889 c. 63.

PART XV
Commence-
ment.

294.—(1) Except as provided in section 21 of this Act and subject to the following provisions of this section, this Act shall come into operation on 1st April 1972 (in this section referred to as " the commencement date ").

1889 c. 63.

(2) This section, any provisions of this Act which confer any power to make regulations or orders, or which (whether expressly or as construed in accordance with section 32(3) of the Interpretation Act 1889) confer any power to revoke or vary any regulations or orders, and any provisions of this Act relating to the exercise of any such power, shall come into operation on the passing of this Act ; but no regulations or order shall be made under this Act so as to come into operation before the commencement date.

(3) In subsection (2) of this section the reference to provisions of this Act relating to the exercise of any such power as is therein mentioned includes a reference to any provisions of this Act whereby statutory instruments containing regulations or an order are subject to annulment in pursuance of a resolution of either House of Parliament, or whereby any regulations or order or any provisions thereof require the approval of each of those Houses.

(4) Any reference in this Act to the commencement of this Act is a reference to the coming into operation of so much of this Act as comes into operation on the commencement date, and any reference to the date of the commencement of this Act is a reference to that date ; and if any Act passed after the passing of this Act refers to the commencement of this Act, subsections (2) and (3) of this section and section 21 of this Act shall be disregarded for the purpose of construing that reference in accordance with section 36 of the Interpretation Act 1889 (which relates to the meaning of " commencement " with reference to an Act).

(5) The preceding provisions of this section shall have effect without prejudice to the generality of section 37 of the Interpretation Act 1889 (which relates to the exercise of statutory powers between the passing and the commencement of an Act).

Short title and
extent.

295.—(1) This Act may be cited as the Town and Country Planning Act 1971.

1957 c. 20.

(2) This Act, except so far as it relates to the House of Commons Disqualification Act 1957 or (by Schedule 23) amends any enactment which extends to Scotland or Northern Ireland, extends to England and Wales only.

SCHEDULES

SCHEDULE 1   Section 1.

JOINT PLANNING BOARDS

1. A joint planning board constituted by an order under section 1 of this Act shall consist of such number of members as may be determined by the order, to be appointed by the constituent councils.

2. A joint planning board so constituted shall be a body corporate, with perpetual succession and a common seal.

3. An order constituting a joint planning board and any order amending or revoking any order constituting a joint planning board—

   (a) may, without prejudice to the provisions of section 293 of the Local Government Act 1933 (which authorises the 1933 c. 51. application of the provisions of that Act to joint boards), provide for regulating the appointment, tenure of office and vacation of office of members of the board, for regulating the meetings and proceedings of the board, and for the payment of the expenses of the board by the constituent councils ;

   (b) may provide for the transfer and compensation of officers, the transfer of property and liabilities, and the adjustment of accounts and apportionments of liabilities ;

   (c) may contain such other provisions as appear to the Secretary of State to be expedient for enabling the board to exercise their functions ; and

   (d) may apply to the board, with any necessary modifications and adaptations, any of the provisions of Schedule 2 to this Act.

SCHEDULE 2   Section 2.

PLANNING COMMITTEES AND JOINT ADVISORY COMMITTEES

PART I

PLANNING COMMITTEES

1. A local planning authority may establish such planning committees as they think it expedient to establish for the efficient discharge of their functions as a local planning authority, and may authorise any such committee to exercise on their behalf any of those functions, except the power to borrow money or to levy or issue a precept for a rate.

2. A planning committee of a local planning authority may, subject to any restrictions imposed by the local planning authority—

   (a) appoint such sub-committees constituted in such manner as the committee may determine ; and

   (b) authorise any such sub-committee to exercise any of the functions of the committee on their behalf.

SCH. 2   3. A majority of every planning committee of a local planning authority shall be members of the authority, and a majority of every sub-committee of any such committee shall be members either of the local planning authority or of the councils of county districts comprised in the area of that authority.

4. Any power conferred by this Part of this Schedule to establish or appoint committees or sub-committees, or to authorise such committees or sub-committees to exercise any functions, shall include power to dissolve or alter the constitution of such committees or sub-committees, and to revoke or vary any such authorisation.

PART II
JOINT ADVISORY COMMITTEES

5. Any two or more local planning authorities may, with the approval of the Secretary of State, concur in establishing a joint advisory committee for the purpose of advising those authorities as to the preparation of structure plans and local plans and generally as to the planning of development in their areas ; and any such committee shall be constituted in such manner as may be determined by the authorities by whom it was established :

Provided that a majority of the members of any such committee shall be members of one or other of those authorities.

6. If it appears to the Secretary of State to be expedient that a joint advisory committee of any two or more local planning authorities should be established in accordance with paragraph 5 of this Schedule, he may, after consultation with those authorities, by order establish such a committee, and any such order may—

(a) provide for the reference to the committee of such matters as may be specified in the order ;

(b) make such incidental and consequential provisions (including provision for the payment of expenses of the committee and the transfer and compensation of officers) as appear to the Secretary of State to be expedient.

7. Any power conferred by this Part of this Schedule to establish committees or to authorise such committees to exercise any functions shall include power to dissolve or alter the constitution of such committees, and to revoke or vary any such authorisation.

1933 c. 51.   8. The provisions of this Part of this Schedule shall be in addition to and not in substitution for the provisions of the Local Government Act 1933 with respect to the appointment by local authorities of joint committees.

Section 5.   ## SCHEDULE 3

LOCAL PLANNING AUTHORITIES IN GREATER LONDON
Local planning authorities

1. Subject to paragraphs 2 and 5 of this Schedule, the Greater London Council is the local planning authority for Greater London as a whole.

2.—(1) Subject to paragraph 3 of this Schedule, to Schedule 4 and to Part II of Schedule 5 to this Act, for all purposes of this Act the local planning authority as respects any London borough is the council of the borough ; and—

(*a*) any application uner Part III of this Act for planning permission for any development ; and

(*b*) any application uner Part IV of this Act for listed building consent,

shall be made to, and, subject to paragraph 3 of this Schedule, section 35 of this Act and paragraph 4 of Schedule 11 to this Act, shall be determined by such as may be appropriate of those councils.

(2) Except in any case or class of cases with respect to which the Greater London Council otherwise direct, the council of each London borough shall cause a copy of every decision made by them on an application mentioned in this paragraph to be sent to the Greater London Council, together with a copy of the application and such other information relating thereto and to the decision as the Greater London Council may reasonably require.

3.—(1) This paragraph applies to development of such a class, in such area of Greater London, as may be prescribed.

(2) In relation to development to which this paragraph applies, the Greater London Council shall be the local planning authority for all relevant purposes of this Act other than—

(*a*) sections 94 and 95 ; and

(*b*) the reception of applications for, or with respect to the need for, planning permission for such development.

(3) Subject to paragraph 5 of this Schedule, a council by whom there is received—

(*a*) any application for planning permission for development to which this paragraph applies ; or

(*b*) any application under section 53 of this Act in a case in which it appears to that council that the proposed action to which the application relates would constitute or involve such development if it constituted or involved development at all,

shall forward the application to the Greater London Council, who shall deal with it in like manner as if it had been made to them.

(4) Development to which this paragraph applies by the Greater London Council shall be deemed, for the purposes of section 270 of this Act, to be development by the Council of land in respect of which they are the local planning authority.

(5) Without prejudice to paragraph 5 of this Schedule, the Greater London Council may in any particular case by instrument in writing authorise the council of a London borough to discharge on their behalf any functions under sections 87 to 95 and section 177 of this Act with respect to development to which this paragraph applies.

SCH. 3

4. The Greater London Council shall, as respects any London borough, have concurrently with the local planning authority the functions of a local planning authority under sections 58, 96 to 100, 173 and 271 of this Act, and references in those provisions to the local planning authority shall be construed accordingly.

Delegation of functions

1963 c. 33.

5. Section 5(1) of the London Government Act 1963 shall not apply to any functions of the Greater London Council under this Act, but the Greater London Council may, with the consent of the Secretary of State, and shall if so required by the Secretary of State, delegate to the council of a London borough any of those functions so far as exerciseable in that borough, and any council to whom functions are so delegated shall perform those functions on behalf of the Greater London Council.

6. The Greater London Council may agree with the council of a London borough for the transfer to the council of the borough of any liability of the Greater London Council to pay compensation under this Act in respect of anything done by the council of the borough in the exercise of functions delegated to them under paragraph 5 of this Schedule and for the transfer of any officers of any of those councils ; and any such agreement shall include provisions in accordance with section 85(3) of the London Government Act 1963 for the protection of the interests of such officers.

Reference of applications for planning permission to Secretary of State and Greater London Council

7. Without prejudice to his powers by virtue of section 31(1) or 35 of this Act, the Secretary of State may by regulations make with respect to applications for planning permission for development in Greater London provision for particular applications or applications of a particular class to be referred before they are dealt with by the local planning authority—

(a) in the case of an application falling to be dealt with by the Greater London Council, to the Secretary of State ;

(b) in the case of an application falling to be dealt with by the council of a London borough—

(i) to the Greater London Council ;

(ii) in such cases as the regulations may prescribe, to the Secretary of State ;

(c) in the case of an application referred to the Greater London Council by virtue of sub-paragraph (b)(i) of this paragraph, to the Secretary of State,

and for the giving to the referring council by the Greater London Council or, as the case may be, the Secretary of State, of directions as to the manner in which the application is to be dealt with.

Interpretation of references to local planning authorities Sch. 3
in other enactments

8. In relation to land in a London borough—

(a) references to local planning authorities in any of the following enactments, that is to say—

(i) sections 33 and 34 of, and Schedule 2 to, the Elec- 1957 c. 48.
tricity Act 1957 ;

(ii) section 108 of, and Schedule 12 to, the Highways 1959 c. 25.
Act 1959 ;

(iii) Schedule 1 to the Pipe-lines Act 1962, 1962 c. 58.

shall be construed as including references to the Greater
London Council but not to the council of a London
borough ;

(b) the reference in section 86(4) of the Transport Act 1962 1962 c. 46.
to the local planning authority to whom application is
made for permission for the development in question shall
be construed as a reference to the local planning authority
by whom that application falls to be dealt with ;

(c) references in section 3(2) of the Acquisition of Land 1946 c. 49.
(Authorisation Procedure) Act 1946, as applied by section
15 of the Opencast Coal Act 1958, to the local planning 1958 c. 69.
authority shall be construed as including references both to
the Greater London Council and the council of the London
borough ;

(d) any reference in section 17 or 20 of the Caravan Sites and 1960 c. 62.
Control of Development Act 1960 to the local planning
authority shall be construed as a reference to the council
of a London borough ;

(e) any reference in Part III of the Land Compensation Act 1961 c. 33.
1961 to the local planning authority shall be construed as
a reference to the council of a London borough, but that
council shall consult with the Greater London Council
before issuing a certificate under section 17 of that Act
in any case where an application for planning permission
for any development to which the certificate would relate
would fall to be dealt with by the Greater London Council.

SCHEDULE 4 Section 19.

DEVELOPMENT PLANS: GREATER LONDON

Survey of planning areas

1. The matters to be examined and kept under review under section 6 of this Act by the Greater London Council shall be such of the
matters mentioned in that section as they think fit, or, in the case of
a fresh survey under section 6(2) of this Act instituted in pursuance
of a direction of the Secretary of State, such matters as may be
specified in the direction.

2. The matters to be so examined or kept under review by a London borough council shall be such of the matters mentioned in the said section 6 as have not been examined or kept under review by the Greater London Council, such other matters as they may be required by the Greater London Council to examine or keep under review or, in the case of a fresh survey under the said section 6(2) instituted in pursuance of a direction of the Secretary of State, such matters as may be specified in the direction.

3. Any survey by a London borough council under section 6 of this Act shall be carried out on such lines as the Greater London Council may direct.

Structure plans

4. The Greater London development plan shall be treated for the purposes of this Act as a structure plan for Greater London approved under section 9 of this Act and may be altered under section 10 of this Act accordingly ; and the Secretary of State may direct that any area or part of an area indicated by the plan (as originally approved under section 5 of the Act of 1962 or the corresponding provision of this Act) as an area intended for comprehensive development, redevelopment or improvement as a whole shall be treated for those purposes as an action area.

5. The structure plan required by section 7 of this Act to be prepared for any area by a London borough council shall include a restatement of so much of the provisions of the Greater London development plan, with any alterations and additions consistent with the latter plan which appear to them to be necessary or expedient, as is applicable to that area.

6. A London borough council shall send any report and structure plan prepared by them under the said section 7 to the Greater London Council for submission to the Secretary of State, and the Greater London Council shall send them on to the Secretary of State within such period as he may allow, with any observations of theirs thereon.

7. The information on which a London borough council's policy and general proposals formulated under section 7(3) of this Act are based shall include any information which the council obtain in pursuance of a direction of the Greater London Council.

8. The inclusion in the Greater London development plan of an area wholly or partly within a London borough which is to be treated as an action area shall not preclude a London borough council from selecting any other part of the borough as an action area.

9. Before giving a direction to a London borough council under section 7(4) of this Act the Secretary of State shall consult the Greater London Council and the London borough council with respect to the proposed direction.

Alterations to structure plans

10. A direction under section 10(1) of this Act to a London borough council may, instead of being given by the Secretary of State, be given by the Greater London Council with the approval of the Secretary of State.

11. Before giving such a direction the Secretary of State or Greater
London Council, as the case may be, shall consult the council to
whom the direction is proposed to be given.

12. The report required by section 10 of this Act to be sent by a
London borough council with the proposals submitted by them
under that section shall include a report of any review by the
Greater London Council of the relevant matters on which the
proposals are based.

13. Paragraphs 5, 6 and 7 of this Schedule shall apply with any
necessary modifications in relation to proposals for the amendment of
any structure plan for the whole or part of a London borough as
they apply in relation to the plan to be amended.

Local plans

14. Notwithstanding anything in Schedule 3 to this Act, the Greater
London Council shall not under section 11 of this Act prepare a local
plan for any part of Greater London other than a plan for an action
area, but the foregoing provision shall not be construed as precluding
them from preparing a local plan for any area by virtue of section
17 of this Act.

15. The council of a London borough any part of which is indicated
by the Greater London development plan as an action area or is to
be treated as an action area shall, if it falls to them and not to the
Greater London Council to prepare a local plan for that area, prepare
such a plan as soon as practicable after the approval of the Greater
London development plan, notwithstanding that the council of that
borough have not prepared a structure plan for that area.

16. References in section 11(6) and (9) of this Act to a structure
plan shall, in relation to a local plan prepared for an action area or
for an area which is to be treated as an action area by a London
borough council, be construed as including references to the Greater
London development plan.

17. The duty of the Secretary of State under section 11(10) of
this Act to consult a local planning authority with respect to a
direction which he proposes to give them shall, where the authority
is a London borough council, include a duty to consult the Greater
London Council with respect to the direction.

18. On sending a copy of a local plan to the Secretary of State
under section 12(2) of this Act a London borough council shall also
send a copy of the plan to the Greater London Council.

19. Section 15(3) of this Act shall, in its application to proposals
made by a London borough council for the alteration of a local
plan, have effect as if the reference to a provision of section 11 or 12
of this Act were a reference to that provision as modified by paragraphs 16 to 18 of this Schedule.

SCHEDULE 5

Development Plans: Provisions in Force until Superseded
by Part II of this Act

Part I

General

Surveys of planning areas and preparation of development plans

1.—(1) Any local planning authority who have not submitted
to the Secretary of State a development plan for their area shall
carry out a survey of their area and shall, within such period as
the Secretary of State may in any particular case allow, submit to
the Secretary of State a report of the survey together with a development plan for their area.

(2) Subject to the following provisions of this Part of this Schedule,
in this Act " development plan " means a plan indicating the manner
in which a local planning authority propose that land in their area
should be used, whether by the carrying out thereon of development
or otherwise, and the stages by which any such development should
be carried out.

(3) Subject to the provisions of any regulations made under this
Act for regulating the form and content of development plans, any
such plan shall include such maps and such descriptive matter as
may be necessary to illustrate the proposals in question with such
degree of particularity as may be appropriate to different parts of
the area ; and any such plan may in particular define the sites of
proposed roads, public and other buildings and works, airfields,
parks, pleasure grounds, nature reserves and other open spaces, or
allocate areas of land for use for agricultural, residential, industrial
or other purposes of any class specified in the plan.

(4) For the purposes of this paragraph, a development plan may
define as an area of comprehensive development any area which,
in the opinion of the local planning authority, should be developed
or redeveloped as a whole for any one or more of the following
purposes, that is to say—

(a) for the purposes of dealing satisfactorily with extensive war
damage or conditions of bad lay-out or obsolete development ; or

(b) for the purpose of providing for the relocation of population or industry or the replacement of open space in the
course of the development or redevelopment of any other
area ; or

(c) for any other purpose specified in the plan ;

and land may be included in any area so defined whether or not
provision is made by the plan for the development or redevelopment
of that particular land.

(5) At any time before a development plan with respect to the
whole of the area of a local planning authority has been approved
by the Secretary of State, that authority may, with the consent of

the Secretary of State, and shall, if so required by directions of the Secretary of State, prepare and submit to him a development plan relating to part of that area ; and the preceding provisions of this paragraph shall apply in relation to any such plan as they apply in relation to a plan relating to the whole of the area of a local planning authority.

Approval of development plans

2. The Secretary of State may approve any development plan submitted to him under paragraph 1 of this Schedule, either without modification or subject to such modifications as he considers expedient.

Amendment of development plans

3.—(1) At least once in every five years after the date on which a development plan for any area was approved by the Secretary of State, the local planning authority shall carry out a fresh survey of that area, and (subject to paragraph 1 of Schedule 7 to this Act) submit to the Secretary of State a report of the survey, together with proposals for any alterations or additions to the plan which appear to them to be required having regard thereto.

(2) Without prejudice to the provisions of sub-paragraph (1) of this paragraph, any local planning authority may (subject to paragraph 1 of Schedule 7 to this Act) at any time, and shall if so required by directions of the Secretary of State, submit to the Secretary of State proposals for such alterations or additions to the development plan for their area or any part thereof as appear to them to be expedient, or as may be required by those directions, as the case may be.

(3) Where proposals for alterations or additions to a development plan are submitted to the Secretary of State under this paragraph, the Secretary of State may amend that plan to such extent as he considers expedient having regard to those proposals and to any other material considerations.

(4) Where in accordance with the provisions of paragraph 1(5) of this Schedule a development plan has been prepared for part of the area of a local planning authority, and has been approved by the Secretary of State, then (without prejudice to the provisions of sub-paragraph (2) of this paragraph) the periods of five years mentioned in sub-paragraph (1) of this paragraph shall run from the date on which development plans in respect of the whole of the area have been approved by the Secretary of State.

Additional powers of Secretary of State with respect to development plans

4.—(1) Where, by virtue of any of the preceding provisions of this Schedule or of any directions of the Secretary of State thereunder, any development plan, report or proposals for alterations or

K

additions to a development plan are required to be submitted to the Secretary of State, then—

(a) if within the period allowed in that behalf under those provisions or directions no such plan, report or proposals, or no such plan or proposals satisfactory to the Secretary of State, have been so submitted ; or

(b) if at any time the Secretary of State is satisfied, after holding a local inquiry, that the local planning authority are not taking the steps necessary to enable them to submit such a plan, report or proposals within that period,

the Secretary of State may, after carrying out any survey which appears to him to be expedient for the purpose, make such development plan, or, as the case may be, amend the development plan to such extent, as he considers expedient.

(2) Where, under sub-paragraph (1) of this paragraph, the Secretary of State has power to make or amend a development plan, he may, if he thinks fit, authorise the local planning authority for any neighbouring area, or any other local planning authority which appears to the Secretary of State to have an interest in the proper planning of the area concerned, to submit such a plan to him for his approval, or as the case may be, to submit to him proposals for the amendment of the plan, and to carry out any survey of the land which appears to him to be expedient for the purpose.

(3) The Secretary of State may approve any plan submitted to him under sub-paragraph (2) of this paragraph, either without modification or subject to such modifications as he considers expedient, or, as the case may be, may amend any development plan, with respect to which proposals for amendment have been submitted to him under that sub-paragraph to such extent as he considers expedient having regard to those proposals and to any other material considerations.

(4) The preceding provisions of this Schedule shall, so far as applicable, apply to the making, approval or amendment of development plans under this paragraph, and to plans so made, approved or amended, as they apply to the approval or amendment of development plans under those provisions, and to plans approved or amended thereunder.

(5) Where the Secretary of State incurs expenses under this paragraph in connection with the making or amendment of a plan with respect to the area, or any part of the area, of a local planning authority, so much of those expenses as may be certified by the Secretary of State to have been incurred in the performance of functions of that authority shall on demand be repaid by that authority to the Secretary of State.

(6) Where, under this paragraph, a plan, or proposals for the amendment of a plan, are authorised to be submitted to the Secretary of State by the local planning authority for any area other than the area in which the land is situated, any expenses reasonably incurred in that behalf by that authority, as certified by the Secretary of State, shall be repaid to that authority by the local planning authority for the area in which the land is situated.

Incorporation in development plans of orders and schemes relating   Sch. 5
to highways and new towns

5.—(1) Where the Secretary of State—

(*a*) makes an order under section 7 of the Highways Act 1959   1959 c. 25.
directing that a highway proposed to be constructed by
him shall become a trunk road ; or

(*b*) makes or confirms an order or scheme under section 9, 11
or 13 of that Act,

any development plan approved or made under this Schedule which
relates to land on which a highway is to be constructed or altered
in accordance with that order or scheme shall have effect as if the
provisions of that order or scheme were included in the plan.

(2) Where an order is made by the Secretary of State under section
1 of the New Towns Act 1965 designating an area as the site of a   1965 c. 59.
new town under that Act, any development plan approved or made
under this Schedule which relates to land in that area shall have
effect as if the provisions of that order were included in the plan.

(3) Nothing in this paragraph shall be construed as prohibiting
the inclusion in a development plan, as approved or made by the
Secretary of State or as for the time being amended, of provisions—

(*a*) defining the line of a highway proposed to be constructed
or altered in accordance with any such order or scheme
as is mentioned in sub-paragraph (1) of this paragraph ; or

(*b*) defining an area designated as the site of a new town by any
such order as is mentioned in sub-paragraph (2) of this
paragraph ; or

(*c*) defining land as likely to be made the subject of any such
order or scheme as is mentioned in either of those sub-
paragraphs.

(4) Provision may be made by regulations under this Act for
enabling any proceedings preliminary to the making of any such
order as is mentioned in sub-paragraph (1)(*a*) or (2) of this paragraph, to be taken concurrently with proceedings required under this
Schedule to be taken in connection with the approval or making of
a development plan relating to land to which any such order applies,
or in connection with any amendment of a development plan rendered necessary or desirable in consequence of any such order.

Supplementary provisions as to development plans

6.—(1) A local planning authority, before preparing a development
plan relating to any land in a county district, or proposals for
alterations or additions to any such plan, shall consult with the
council of that district, and shall, before submitting any such plan
or proposals to the Secretary of State, give to that council an opportunity to make representations with respect thereto and shall consider
any representations so made.

(2) Provision may be made by regulations under this Act with
respect to the form and content of development plans, and with
respect to the procedure to be followed in connection with the

K 2

SCH. 5   preparation, submission, approval, making and amendment of such plans ; and such regulations shall in particular make provision for securing—

> (a) that notice shall be given by advertisement in the London Gazette, and in at least one newspaper circulating in the area concerned, of the submission to the Secretary of State of any such plan, or of proposals for the amendment of any such plan, and of any proposal by the Secretary of State to make or amend such a plan, and of the place or places where copies of the plan or proposals as so submitted, or of any such proposal of the Secretary of State, may be inspected ;

> (b) that objections and representations duly made in accordance with the regulations shall be considered, and that such local inquiries or other hearings as may be prescribed shall be held, before such a plan is approved, made or amended by the Secretary of State ; and

> (c) that copies of any such plan as approved or made by the Secretary of State, including any amendments thereof, shall be available for inspection by the public, and that copies thereof (including reproductions, on such scale as may be appropriate, of any relevant maps) shall be available for sale to the public at a reasonable cost.

(3) If, as the result of any objections or representations considered, or local inquiry or other hearing held, in connection with a development plan or proposals for amendment of such a plan submitted to or prepared by the Secretary of State under this Schedule, the Secretary of State is of opinion that the local planning authority, or any other authority or person, ought to be consulted before he decides whether to approve or make the plan, either with or without modifications, or to amend the plan, as the case may be, he shall consult that authority or person but shall not be under any obligation to consult any other authority or person, or to afford any opportunity for further objections or representations, or to cause any further local inquiry or other hearing to be held.

(4) Subject to the preceding provisions of this paragraph, the Secretary of State may give directions to any local planning authority, or to local planning authorities generally—

> (a) for formulating the procedure for the carrying out of their functions under the preceding provisions of this Schedule ;

> (b) for requiring them to give him such information as he may require for the purpose of the exercise of any of his functions under those provisions.

Publication and date of operation of development plans

7.—(1) Immediately after a development plan has been approved or made or amended by the Secretary of State under this Schedule, the local planning authority shall publish, in such manner as may be prescribed, a notice stating that the plan has been approved, made or amended, as the case may be, and naming a place where a copy of the

plan or of the plan as amended, may be seen at all reasonable hours,   Sᴄʜ. 5
and shall serve a like notice—

   (*a*) on any person who duly made an objection to, or representation with respect to, the proposed plan or amendment, and has sent to the local planning authority a request
in writing to serve him with the notice required by this
sub-paragraph, specifying an address for service ; and

   (*b*) on such other persons (if any) as may be required by general
or special directions given by the Secretary of State.

(2) Subject to the provisions of Part XII of this Act as to the
validity of development plans and of amendments of such plans, a
development plan, or an amendment of a development plan, shall
become operative on the date on which the notice required by sub-
paragraph (1) of this paragraph is first published.

PART II

Gʀᴇᴀᴛᴇʀ Lᴏɴᴅᴏɴ

Development plans

8.—(1) In the application of this Schedule to Greater London,
paragraphs 1(1) and (5) and 3(1) and (2) shall ˈnot apply but the
provisions of this and the next following paragraph shall have
effect in place thereof.

(2) Subject to the provisions of any order under section 84ˈof the
London Government Act 1963, any development plans under the 1963 c. 33.
Act of 1962 operative on 31st March 1965 which relate, or so far
as they relate, to any part of Greater London shall together constitute as from 1st April 1965 the initial development plan for Greater
London.

(3) The Greater London Council shall cause to be carried out
a survey of Greater London and shall, within such period as the
Secretary of State may allow, submit to the Secretary of State a report
of that survey and a general development plan for Greater London,
to be known as the Greater London development plan, which, subject
to any regulations made (by virtue of paragraph 10(5)(*e*) of this
Schedule) under paragraph 6 of this Schedule, shall lay down considerations of general policy with respect to the use of land in the
various parts of Greater London, including in particular guidance as
to the future road system, and may make any necessary consequential modifications in the initial development plan aforesaid ; and as
from the date when the Greater London development plan becomes
operative, that plan and the initial development plan aforesaid with
any modifications therein made by the Greater London development
plan shall together constitute the interim development plan for
Greater London.

K 3

SCH. 5   (4) Within such period as the Secretary of State may allow after the Greater London development plan becomes operative, each London borough council shall as respects their borough carry out on behalf of the Greater London Council such further survey, if any, as the borough council may consider necessary or as the Greater London Council may direct, and submit to the Greater London Council a report on any such further survey and a local development plan which, subject to any such regulations as aforesaid, shall restate as respects the borough the relevant provisions of the initial development plan aforesaid as modified by the Greater London development plan with any alterations and additions appearing to them necessary or expedient which are consistent with the Greater London development plan ; and, without prejudice to paragraph 10(1) of this Schedule, the Greater London Council shall within such further period as the Secretary of State may allow forward any such reports and those local development plans to the Secretary of State with any observations thereon by that Council.

(5) The development plan for the purposes of this Act for any London borough shall be the following, as amended from time to time by virtue of any provision of paragraphs 9 and 10 of this Schedule, that is to say—

(a) as from 1st April 1965 until the Greater London development plan becomes operative, the relevant provisions of the initial development plan aforesaid ;

(b) as from the date when the Greater London development plan becomes operative until the date when the local development plan submitted by the borough council becomes operative, the relevant provisions of the interim development plan aforesaid ;

(c) as from the date when the said local development plan becomes operative, that plan together with the Greater London development plan.

Amendment of development plans

9.—(1) The Greater London Council shall from time to time cause fresh surveys of Greater London to be carried out and, not less than once in every five years after the approval of the Greater London development plan by the Secretary of State (but subject to paragraph 1 of Schedule 7 to this Act), submit to the Secretary of State a report of any such surveys together with proposals for any alterations or additions to that plan which appear to that Council to be required having regard to those surveys.

(2) Without prejudice to the provisions of the foregoing sub-paragraph, the Greater London Council may (subject to paragraph 1 of the said Schedule 7) at any time, and shall at any time when so directed by the Secretary of State, submit to the Secretary of State proposals for such alterations or additions as appear to the Council to be expedient or as may be required by that direction—

(a) in the case of proposals made before the date of the Secretary of State's approval of the Greater London development plan, to the initial development plan referred to in paragraph 8(2) of this Schedule ; or

(*b*) in the case of proposals made after that date, to the Greater London development plan.

(3) After the Greater London development plan has become operative, the council of any London borough may (subject to paragraph 1 of the said Schedule 7) at any time, and shall at any time when so directed by the Secretary of State or, with the approval of the Secretary of State, by the Greater London Council, after carrying out on behalf of the Greater London Council such, if any, fresh survey of the borough as may appear to the borough council to be expedient or as may be required by that direction, submit to the Greater London Council proposals for such alterations or additions as may appear expedient or as may be so required—

(*a*) in the case of proposals made before the date of the Secretary of State's approval of their local development plan under paragraph 8(4) of this Schedule, to the initial development plan aforesaid as modified by the Greater London development plan ; or

(*b*) in the case of proposals made after that date, to that local development plan ;

and, without prejudice to paragraph 10(1) of this Schedule, the Greater London Council shall, within such time as the Secretary of State may allow, forward any such proposals to the Secretary of State together with any observations thereon by that Council.

Supplementary provisions as to development plans

10.—(1) If any local development plan submitted to the Greater London Council under paragraph 8(4) of this Schedule, or any proposal so submitted under paragraph 9(3) of this Schedule, contains any provision which in the opinion of the Greater London Council involves a departure from the Greater London development plan, that Council may, if they think fit, require the council submitting the plan or proposal to reconsider that provision within such period as may be specified in the requirement, and thereupon—

(*a*) unless within the period so specified the submitting council agree that the provision involves such a departure, the question shall be referred to the Secretary of State for decision ;

(*b*) if the submitting council agree as aforesaid, or if on such a reference to the Secretary of State the Secretary of State decides that the provision involves such a departure, the Greater London Council may if they think fit cause that provision to be struck out from the local development plan or proposal for the purpose of its consideration by the Secretary of State ;

(*c*) if on such a reference to the Secretary of State the Secretary of State decides that the provision does not involve such a departure, the provision shall be included in the local development plan or proposal for the purpose of its consideration by the Secretary of State, but the Secretary of

K 4

State, if so required by the Greater London Council, shall afford that Council an opportunity to make further observations thereon.

(2) Any survey under paragraph 8(3) or 9(1) of this Schedule shall, unless for special reasons the Greater London Council decide to carry it out themselves, be carried out on behalf of that Council by the London borough councils as respects their respective areas ; and subject to sub-paragraph (6) of this paragraph any such survey and any survey under paragraph 8(4) or 9(3) of this Schedule shall be carried out on such lines as the Greater London Council may direct.

(3) The Greater London Council, before preparing the Greater London development plan or any proposals under paragraph 9(1) or (2) of this Schedule, shall consult with the London borough councils or, in the case of any such proposals, with such of those councils as are affected by the proposals, and before submitting the plan or proposals to the Secretary of State shall give to each of those councils an opportunity to make representations with respect to the plan or proposals and shall consider any representations so made.

(4) A London borough council—

(a) when preparing their local development plan under paragraph 8(4) or any proposal under paragraph 9(3) of this Schedule shall give to the Greater London Council any information which that Council may require with respect to the matters to be included in that plan or proposal ; and

(b) before submitting that plan or proposal to the Greater London Council shall give that Council an opportunity to make representations in the light of that information and shall consider any representations so made.

(5) The following provisions of Part I of this Schedule, that is to say—

(a) paragraph 1(2), (3) and (4) ;

(b) paragraph 2 ;

(c) paragraph 3(3) ;

(d) paragraph 4 ;

(e) paragraph 6(2) and (3) ;

(f) paragraph 7,

shall apply for the purposes of paragraphs 8 and 9 of this Schedule with the modifications specified in sub-paragraph (7) of this paragraph as if any report or plan submitted or forwarded under paragraph 8(3) or (4) of this Schedule were a report or plan submitted under paragraph 1(1) of this Schedule and any report or proposal submitted or forwarded under paragraph 9 of this Schedule were a report or proposal submitted under paragraph 3 of this Schedule.

(6) Paragraph 6(4) of this Schedule shall not apply to Greater London but, subject to any express provision contained in or having

effect by virtue of this paragraph or paragraphs 8 or 9 of this SCH. 5
Schedule, the Secretary of State may give directions—

(*a*) to the Greater London Council with respect to the form and
content of any directions by the Greater London Council
under sub-paragraph (2) of this paragraph ;

(*b*) to that Council and to any London borough council—

(i) with respect to the procedure for the carrying
out of the functions exercisable under or by virtue of
those paragraphs by any of those councils ; and

(ii) with respect to the furnishing to the Secretary of
State by those councils of information required for the
purpose of the functions exercisable under or by virtue of
those paragraphs by the Secretary of State.

(7) In the application by virtue of sub-paragraph (5) of this
paragraph of the provisions of this Schedule hereinafter mentioned—

(*a*) any reference in paragraph 1(4) to the opinion of the local
planning authority shall be construed as a reference to the
opinion of either the Greater London Council or the council
of the London borough in which the land in question is
situated ;

(*b*) the reference in paragraph 4(1)(*b*) to the local planning
authority shall be construed as a reference to any of the
following councils, that is to say, the Greater London
Council and the London borough councils, by whom there
fall to be taken the steps necessary to enable the plan,
report or proposal in question to be submitted within the
period in question ;

(*c*) the reference in paragraph 4(4) to the preceding provisions
of this Schedule shall be construed as including a reference
to the provisions of paragraphs 8 and 9 of this Schedule
and sub-paragraphs (1) to (4) of this paragraph ;

(*d*) any reference in paragraph 6(2) or (3) to objections or
representations shall be construed as a reference only to
objections or representations arising from—

(i) any addition, modification or alteration to the
initial development plan referred to in paragraph 8(2)
of this Schedule which is proposed to be effected by the
Greater London development plan or which is proposed
under paragraph 9(2)(*a*) of this Schedule ;

(ii) any addition or alteration to the initial development plan aforesaid as modified by the Greater London
development plan which is proposed to be effected by any
local development plan forwarded to the Secretary of State
under paragraph 8(4) of this Schedule or which is proposed
under paragraph 9(3)(*a*) thereof ;

(iii) any alteration or addition to the Greater London
development plan proposed under paragraph 9(1) or
(2)(*b*) of this Schedule ;

(iv) any alteration or addition to such a local development plan as aforesaid proposed under paragraph 9(3)(*b*) of this Schedule ;

(*e*) the reference in paragraph 7(1) to the local planning authority shall be construed—

(i) in relation to any amendment of the initial development plan aforesaid made before the Greater London development plan becomes operative or made by the Greater London development plan, as a reference to the Greater London Council ;

(ii) in relation to any amendment of the provisions with respect to any London borough of the initial development plan aforesaid as modified by the Greater London development plan, as a reference to the council of that borough ;

(iii) in relation to the Greater London development plan, as a reference to the Greater London Council ;

(iv) in relation to a local development plan under paragraph 8(4) of this Schedule, as a reference to the council of the London borough in question.

SCHEDULE 6

DEVELOPMENT PLANS: MODIFICATIONS OF THIS ACT
PENDING REPEAL OF SCHEDULE 5

1. After section 147(5) there shall be inserted the following subsection : —

" (5A) Except in relation to Greater London, the reference in subsection (4) of this section to the development plan for the area in which the land is situated is a reference to the development plan for that area as approved by the Secretary of State or, if the plan so approved has been amended by the Secretary of State, to that plan as so amended."

2. For section 242(1)(*a*) there shall be substituted : —

" (*a*) a development plan or an amendment of a development plan, whether before or after it has been approved or made ; or ".

3. For subsections (1) and (2) of section 244 there shall be substituted :—

" (1) If any person aggrieved by a development plan, or by an amendment of a development plan, desires to question the validity thereof or of any provision contained therein on the grounds that it is not within the powers of this Act, or that any requirement of this Act or of any regulation made thereunder has not been complied with in relation to the approval or making of the plan, or, as the case may be, in relation to the making of the amendment, he may, within six weeks from the date on which the notice required by paragraph 7(1) of Schedule 5 to this Act is first published, make an application to the High Court under this section.

(2) On any application under this section the High Court—

    (*a*) may by interim order suspend the operation of the plan or amendment, as the case may be, or of any provision contained therein, either generally or in so far as it affects any property of the applicant, until the final determination of the proceedings ;

    (*b*) if satisfied that the plan or amendment, or any provision contained therein, is not within the powers of this Act, or that the interests of the applicant have been substantially prejudiced by a failure to comply with any requirement of this Act or of any regulation made thereunder, may quash the plan or amendment or any provision contained therein, either generally or in so far as it affects any property of the applicant."

and in subsections (3), (4) and (5) of the said section 244 for the words " structure plan " there shall be substituted the words " development plan ".

4. In section 255(2)(*a*) for the words " a structure plan or local plan under Part II of this Act " there shall be substituted the words " a development plan under Schedule 5 to this Act ".

5. For section 266(1)(*a*) there shall be substituted : —

    " (*a*) a development plan approved or made under Part I of Schedule 5 to this Act or the Greater London development plan may include proposals relating to the use of Crown land and any power to acquire land compulsorily under Part VI of this Act may be exercised in relation to any interest therein which is for the time being held otherwise than by or on behalf of the Crown ; "

6. After section 279 there shall be inserted the following sections : —

    " 279A. Where, in accordance with the provisions of Part III, Part IV or Part V of this Act, a local planning authority are required to have regard to the provisions of the development plan in relation to the exercise of any of their functions, then, in relation to the exercise of those functions during any period before such a plan has become operative with respect to the area of that authority, the authority—

    (*a*) shall have regard to any directions which may be or have been given to them by the Secretary of State as to the provisions to be included in such a plan ; and

    (*b*) subject to any such directions, shall have regard to the provisions which in their opinion will be required to be so included for securing the proper planning of their area."

and section 3(6) of this Act shall have effect in relation to any reference to the local planning authority in the said section 279A.

7. For section 280(1)(*a*) there shall be substituted : —

    " (*a*) the preparation, approval, making or amendment of a development plan relating to the land under Schedule 5 to this Act, including the carrying out of any survey under that Schedule ; "

SCH. 6

8. In section 290(1), for the definition of " development plan there shall be substituted: —
> " ' development plan ' has the meaning assigned to it by paragraphs 1 and 8 of Schedule 5 to this Act, and includes a plan made in accordance with sub-paragraph (5) of the said paragraph 1 ; "

9. In Schedule 2, in paragraph 5, for the words " structure plans and local plans " there shall be substituted the words " development plans ".

10. In Schedule 3, in paragraph 7, there shall be added at the end the words " ; and in particular the Secretary of State shall make regulations under this paragraph with respect to any application which the local planning authority consider should be granted for permission for development inconsistent with the Greater London development plan referred to in paragraph 8(3) (or, as respects any period before that plan becomes operative, with the initial development plan referred to in paragraph 8(2)) of Schedule 5 to this Act ".

11. In Part I of Schedule 21 after the words " Schedules 1 and 2 " there shall be inserted the words " Part I of Schedule 5 ".

SCHEDULE 7

DEVELOPMENT PLANS: TRANSITION FROM SCHEDULE 5 TO PART II OF THIS ACT

1. Until the repeal of Part I of Schedule 5 to this Act and, where applicable, paragraph 8 of that Schedule as respects any district (whether the whole or part of the area of a local planning authority), proposals for any alterations or additions to a development plan in force in the area consisting of or comprising that district shall not without the approval of the Secretary of State be submitted to him under paragraph 3 or 9 of that Schedule.

2. On the repeal of the said Part I and, where applicable, the said paragraph 8 as respects any district, the development plan which was in force in the area consisting of or comprising that district immediately before the repeal takes effect (hereafter in this Schedule referred to as " the old development plan ") shall, subject to the following provisions of this Schedule, continue in force as respects that district and be treated for the purposes of this Act, any other enactment relating to town and country planning, the Land Compensation Act 1961, the Land Commission Act 1967 and the Highways Act 1959 as being comprised in, or as being, the development plan therefor.

1961 c. 33.
1967 c. 1.
1959 c. 25.

3. Subject to the following provisions of this Schedule, where by virtue of paragraph 2 of this Schedule the old development plan for any district is treated as being comprised in a development plan for that district and there is a conflict between any of its provisions and those of the structure plan for that district, the provisions of the structure plan shall be taken to prevail for the purposes of Parts III, IV, V, VI, VII and IX of this Act and Schedule 11 to this Act.

4. Where a structure plan is in force in any district, but no local Sch. 7 plan is in force in that district, a street authorisation map prepared in pursuance of the Town and Country Planning (Development S.I. 1965/1453. Plans) Regulations 1965 or the Town and Country Planning (De- S.I. 1966/48. velopment Plans for Greater London) Regulations 1966 for any area consisting of or comprising that district shall—

(a) if in force immediately before the structure plan comes into force be treated for the purposes of this Act as having been adopted as a local plan by the local planning authority ;

(b) if immediately before the structure plan comes into force it was under consideration by the Secretary of State be treated for those purposes as having been so adopted on being approved by the Secretary of State.

5. Where a structure plan is in force in any district, but no local plan is in force in that district, then, for any of the purposes of the Land Compensation Act 1961— 1961 c. 33.

(a) the development plan or current development plan shall as respects that district be taken as being whichever of the following plans gives rise to those assumptions as to the grant of planning permission which are more favourable to the owner of the land acquired, for that purpose, that is to say, the structure plan, so far as applicable to the district, and any alterations thereto, together with the Secretary of State's notice of approval of the plan and alterations, and the old development plan ;

(b) land situated in an area defined in the current development plan as an area of comprehensive development shall be taken to be situated in whichever of the following areas leads to such assumptions as aforesaid, that is to say, any area wholly or partly within that district selected by the structure plan as an action area and the area so defined in the old development plan.

6. Subject to paragraph 7 of this Schedule, the Secretary of State may by order wholly or partly revoke a development plan continued in force under this Schedule whether in its application to the whole of the area of a local planning authority or in its application to part of that area and make such consequential amendments to the plan as appear to him to be necessary or expedient.

7. Before making an order with respect to a development plan under paragraph 6 of this Schedule, the Secretary of State shall consult with the local planning authority for the area to which the plan relates or, where the area is a London borough, with the council of that borough and the Greater London Council.

8. Any reference in the preceding provisions of this Schedule to a development plan shall as respects any district in Greater London, be construed as a reference to the initial development plan within the meaning of paragraph 8 of Schedule 5 to this Act, the Greater London development plan and any development plan prepared for the area consisting of or comprising that district by the council of the relevant London borough.

SCH. 7   9. Any reference in paragraphs 1 and 2 of this Schedule to the repeal of Part I of Schedule 5 to this Act or paragraph 8 of that Schedule shall, in a case where that repeal is brought into force by an order under section 21 of this Act on different days, be construed as a reference to a repeal of such of the provisions of the said Part I or the said paragraph 8 as may be specified in the order.

10. In relation to any development plan continued in force by virtue of this Schedule, sections 242 and 244 of this Act shall have effect with the same substitutions as are specified in paragraphs 2 and 3 of Schedule 6 to this Act.

Sections 22, 43, 164, 169, 180 and 278.

SCHEDULE 8

DEVELOPMENT NOT CONSTITUTING NEW DEVELOPMENT

PART I

DEVELOPMENT NOT RANKING FOR COMPENSATION UNDER S. 169

1. The carrying out of any of the following works, that is to say—

   (a) the rebuilding, as often as occasion may require, of any building which was in existence on the appointed day, or of any building which was in existence before that day but was destroyed or demolished after 7th January 1937, including the making good of war damage sustained by any such building ;

   (b) the rebuilding, as often as occasion may require, of any building erected after the appointed day which was in existence at a material date ;

   (c) the carrying out of works for the maintenance, improvement or other alteration of any building, being works which affect only the interior of the building, or which do not materially affect the external appearance of the building and (in either case) are works for making good war damage,

so long as (in the case of works falling within any of the preceding sub-paragraphs) the cubic content of the original building is not exceeded—

   (i) in the case of a dwellinghouse, by more than one-tenth or 1,750 cubic feet, whichever is the greater ; and

   (ii) in any other case, by more than one-tenth.

2. The use as two or more separate dwellinghouses of any building which at a material date was used as a single dwellinghouse.

PART II

DEVELOPMENT RANKING FOR COMPENSATION UNDER S. 169

3. The enlargement, improvement or other alteration, as often as occasion may require, of any such building as is mentioned in paragraph 1(a) or (b) of this Schedule, or any building substituted for

such a building by the carrying out of any such operations as are mentioned in that paragraph, so long as the cubic content of the original building is not increased or exceeded—

(a) in the case of a dwellinghouse, by more than one-tenth or 1,750 cubic feet, whichever is the greater ; and

(b) in any other case, by more than one-tenth.

4. The carrying out, on land which was used for the purposes of agriculture or forestry at a material date, of any building or other operations required for the purposes of that use, other than operations for the erection, enlargement, improvement or alteration of dwellinghouses or of buildings used for the purposes of market gardens, nursery grounds or timber yards or for other purposes not connected with general farming operations or with the cultivation or felling of trees.

5. The winning and working, on land held or occupied with land used for the purposes of agriculture, of any minerals reasonably required for the purposes of that use, including the fertilisation of the land so used and the maintenance, improvement or alteration of buildings or works thereon which are occupied or used for those purposes.

6. In the case of a building or other land which, at a material date,. was used for a purpose falling within any general class specified in the Town and Country Planning (Use Classes for Third S.I. 1948/955. Schedule Purposes) Order 1948, or which having been unoccupied on and at all times since the appointed day, was last used (otherwise than before 7th January 1937) for any such purpose, the use of that building or land for any other purpose falling within the same general class.

7. In the case of any building or other land which, at a material date, was in the occupation of a person by whom it was used as to part only for a particular purpose, the use for that purpose of any additional part of the building or land not exceeding one-tenth of the cubic content of the part of the building used for that purpose on the appointed day, or on the day thereafter when the building began to be so used, or, as the case may be, one-tenth of the area of the land so used on that day.

8. The deposit of waste materials or refuse in connection with the working of minerals, on any land comprised in a site which at a material date was being used for that purpose, so far as may be reasonably required in connection with the working of those minerals.

PART III

SUPPLEMENTARY PROVISIONS

9. Any reference in this Schedule to the cubic content of a building shall be construed as a reference to that content as ascertained by external measurement.

10. Where, after the appointed day, any buildings or works have been erected or constructed, or any use of land has been instituted,

SCH. 8   and any condition imposed under Part III of this Act, limiting the period for which those buildings or works may be retained, or that use may be continued, has effect in relation thereto, this Schedule shall not operate except as respects the period specified in that condition.

11. For the purposes of paragraph 3 of this Schedule—

(*a*) the erection, on land within the curtilage of any such building as is mentioned in that paragraph, of an additional building to be used in connection with the original building shall be treated as the enlargement of the original building ; and

(*b*) where any two or more buildings comprised in the same curtilage are used as one unit for the purposes of any institution or undertaking, the reference in that paragraph to the cubic content of the original building shall be construed as a reference to the aggregate cubic content of those buildings.

12. In this Schedule " at a material date " means at either of the following dates, that is to say—

(*a*) the appointed day ; and

(*b*) the date by reference to which this Schedule falls to be applied in the particular case in question :

Provided that sub-paragraph (*b*) of this paragraph shall not apply in relation to any buildings, works or use of land in respect of which, whether before or after the date mentioned in that sub-paragraph, an enforcement notice served before that date has become or becomes effective.

13.—(1) In relation to a building erected after the appointed day, being a building resulting from the carrying out of any such works as are described in paragraph 1 of this Schedule, any reference in this Schedule to the original building is a reference to the building in relation to which those works were carried out and not to the building resulting from the carrying out of those works.

(2) This paragraph has effect subject to section 278(4) of this Act.

Sections 36, 88, 95, 97 and 103 and paragraph 8 of Schedule 11.

SCHEDULE 9

DETERMINATION OF CERTAIN APPEALS BY PERSON APPOINTED BY SECRETARY OF STATE

Determination of appeals by appointed person

1.—(1) An appeal to which this Schedule applies, being an appeal of a prescribed class, shall, except in such classes of case as may for the time being be prescribed or as may be specified in directions given by the Secretary of State, be determined by a person appointed by the Secretary of State for the purpose instead of by the Secretary of State.

(2) Regulations made for the purpose of this paragraph may provide for the giving of publicity to any directions given by the Secretary of State under this paragraph.

(3) This paragraph shall not affect any provision contained in this Act or any instrument thereunder that an appeal shall lie to, or a notice of appeal shall be served on, the Secretary of State.

Powers and duties of person determining appeal

2.—(1) A person appointed under this Schedule to determine an appeal shall have the like powers and duties in relation to the appeal as the Secretary of State under whichever are relevant of the following provisions, that is to say—

(a) in relation to appeals under section 36 subsections (3) and (5) of that section ;

(b) in relation to appeals under section 88 subsections (4) to (6) of that section ;

(c) in relation to appeals under section 95 subsections (2) and (3) of that section ;

(d) in relation to appeals under section 97 subsections (4) and (5) of that section ;

(e) in relation to appeals under section 103 sections 88(4) and (5) of this Act ;

(f) in relation to appeals under paragraph 8 of Schedule 11 to this Act, sub-paragraph (3) of that paragraph.

(2) The provisions of sections 36(4), 88(2), 95(4), 97(2) and paragraph 8(4) of Schedule 11 to this Act relating to the affording of an opportunity of appearing before, and being heard by, a person appointed by the Secretary of State, shall not apply to an appeal which falls to be determined by a person appointed under this Schedule but before the determination of any such appeal the Secretary of State shall, unless (in the case of an appeal under section 36) the appeal is referred to a Planning Inquiry Commission under section 48 of this Act, ask the applicant or appellant, as the case may require, and the local planning authority whether they wish to appear before and be heard by the person so appointed, and—

(a) the appeal may be determined without a hearing of the parties if both of them express a wish not to appear and be heard as aforesaid ; and

(b) the person so appointed shall, if either of the parties expresses a wish to appear and be heard, afford to both of them an opportunity of so doing.

(3) Where an appeal to which this Schedule applies has been determined by a person appointed under this Schedule, his decision shall be treated as that of the Secretary of State and—

(a) except as provided by Part XII of this Act, the validity of his decision shall not be questioned in any proceedings whatsoever ;

(b) it shall not be a ground of application to the High Court under section 245 of this Act, or of appeal to the High Court under section 246 or 247 thereof, that the appeal ought to have been determined by the Secretary of State and not by that person, unless the challenge to the person's power to determine the appeal was made (either by the appellant or the local planning authority) before his decision on the appeal was given.

(4) Where in any enactment (including this Act) there is a reference to the Secretary of State in a context relating or capable of relating to an appeal to which this Schedule applies, or to any thing done or authorised or required to be done by, to or before the Secretary of State on or in connection with any such appeal, then so far as the context permits it shall be construed, in relation to an appeal determined or falling to be determined by a person appointed under this Schedule, as a reference to that person.

Determination of appeals by Secretary of State

3.—(1) The Secretary of State may, if he thinks fit, direct that an appeal, which by virtue of paragraph 1 of this Schedule and apart from this sub-paragraph, falls to be determined by a person appointed by the Secretary of State shall instead be determined by the Secretary of State.

(2) A direction under this paragraph shall state the reasons for which it is given and shall be served on the person, if any, so appointed, the applicant or appellant, the local planning authority and any person who has made representations relating to the subject matter of the appeal which the authority are required to take into account under section 29(3)(*a*) of this Act.

(3) Where in consequence of a direction under this paragraph an appeal to which this Schedule applies falls to be determined by the Secretary of State, the provisions of this Act which are relevant to the appeal shall, subject to the following provisions of this paragraph, apply to the appeal as if this Schedule had never applied to it.

(4) Where in consequence of a direction under this paragraph the Secretary of State determines an appeal himself, he shall, unless (in the case of an appeal under section 36) the appeal is referred to a Planning Inquiry Commission under section 48 of this Act, afford to the applicant or appellant, the local planning authority and any person who has made any such representations as aforesaid an opportunity of appearing before and being heard by a person appointed by the Secretary of State for that purpose either—

(*a*) if the reasons for the direction raise matters with respect to which either the applicant or appellant, or the local planning authority or any such person, have not made representations ; or

(*b*) if the applicant or appellant or the local planning authority had not been asked in pursuance of paragraph 2(2) of this Schedule whether they wished to appear before and be heard by a person appointed to hear the appeal, or had been asked that question and had expressed no wish in answer thereto, or had expressed a wish to appear and be heard as aforesaid, but had not been afforded an opportunity of doing so.

(5) Except as provided by sub-paragraph (4) of this paragraph, where the Secretary of State determines an appeal in consequence of a direction under this paragraph he shall not be obliged to afford any person an opportunity of appearing before and being heard by a person appointed for the purpose, or of making fresh representations or making or withdrawing any representations already made ; and in determining the appeal the Secretary of State may take into account any report made to him by any person previously appointed to determine it.

Appointment of another person to determine appeal

4.—(1) Where the Secretary of State has appointed a person to determine an appeal under this Schedule the Secretary of State may, at any time before the determination of the appeal, appoint another person to determine it instead of the first-mentioned person.

(2) If before the appointment of a person under this paragraph to determine an appeal, the Secretary of State had with reference to the person previously appointed, asked the question referred to in paragraph 2(2) of this Schedule, the question need not be asked again with reference to the person appointed under this paragraph and any answers to the question shall be treated as given with reference to him, but—

(a) the consideration of the appeal or any inquiry or other hearing in connection therewith, if already begun, shall be begun afresh ; and

(b) it shall not be necessary to afford any person an opportunity of making fresh representations or modifying or withdrawing any representations already made.

Local inquiries and hearings

5.—(1) A person appointed under this Schedule to determine an appeal may (whether or not the parties have asked for an opportunity to appear and be heard) hold a local inquiry in connection with the appeal and shall hold such an inquiry if the Secretary of State directs him to do so.

(2) Subject to sub-paragraph (3) of this paragraph, the costs—

(a) of any hearing held by virtue of paragraph 2(2)(b) of this Schedule ; and

(b) of any inquiry held by virtue of this paragraph,

shall be defrayed by the Secretary of State.

(3) Subsections (2) to (5) of section 290 of the Local Government Act 1933 (evidence and costs at local inquiries) shall apply in relation to an inquiry held under this paragraph as they apply in relation to an inquiry caused to be held by a department under subsection (1) of that section, with the substitution for references to a department (other than the first reference in subsection (4)) of references to the Secretary of State.

SCH. 9

Stopping of appeals

6. If before or during the determination of an appeal under section 36 of this Act which is to be or is being determined in accordance with paragraph 1 of this Schedule, the Secretary of State forms the opinion mentioned in subsection (7) of that section, he may direct that the determination shall not be begun or proceeded with.

Supplementary provisions

1971 c. 62.

7.—(1) The Tribunals and Inquiries Act 1971 shall apply to a local inquiry or other hearing held in pursuance of this Schedule as it applies to a statutory inquiry held by the Secretary of State, but as if in section 12(1) of that Act (statement of reasons for decisions) the reference to any decision taken by the Secretary of State were a reference to a decision taken by a person appointed to determine the relevant appeal under this Schedule.

(2) The functions of determining an appeal and doing anything in connection therewith conferred by this Schedule on a person appointed to determine an appeal thereunder who is an officer of the Department of the Environment or the Welsh Office shall be

1967 c. 13.

treated for the purposes of the Parliamentary Commissioner Act 1967—

(a) if he was appointed by the Secretary of State for the time being having general responsibility in planning matters in relation to England, as functions of that Department; and

(b) if he was appointed by the Secretary of State for the time being having general responsibility in planning matters in relation to Wales, as functions of the Welsh Office.

Section 48.

SCHEDULE 10

CONSTRUCTION OF REFERENCES IN SECTIONS 48 AND 49 TO " THE RESPONSIBLE MINISTER OR MINISTERS "

1. In relation to matters specified in the first column of the Table below (being in each case a matter mentioned in subsection (1)(a), (b), (c) or (d) of section 48 of this Act as one which may be referred to a Planning Inquiry Commission under that section) " the responsible Minister or Ministers " for the purposes of sections 48 and 49 of this Act—

(a) in the case of a matter affecting England only, are those specified opposite in the second column of the Table;

(b) in the case of a matter affecting Wales only, are those specified opposite in the third column of the Table; and

(c) in the case of a matter affecting both England and Wales, are those specified opposite in the fourth column of the Table.

2. Where an entry in the second, third or fourth columns of the Table specifies two or more Ministers, that entry shall be construed as referring to those Ministers acting jointly.

TABLE

Referred matter	Affecting England only	Affecting Wales only	Affecting both England and Wales
1. Application for planning permission or appeal under section 36 of this Act—			
(a) relating to land to which section 225(1) of this Act applies;	The Secretary of State for the time being having general responsibility in planning matters in relation to England and the appropriate Minister (if different).	The Secretary of State for the time being having general responsibility in planning matters in relation to Wales and the appropriate Minister (if different).	The Secretaries of State for the time being having general responsibility in planning matters in relation to England and in relation to Wales and the appropriate Minister (if different).
(b) relating to other land.	The Secretary of State for the time being having general responsibility in planning matters in relation to England.	The Secretary of State for the time being having general responsibility in planning matters in relation to Wales.	The Secretaries of State for the time being having general responsibility in planning matters in relation to England and in relation to Wales.
2. Proposal that a government department should give a direction under section 40 of this Act or that development should be carried out by or on behalf of a government department.	The Secretary of State for the time being having general responsibility in planning matters in relation to England and the Minister (if different) in charge of the government department concerned.	The Secretary of State for the time being having general responsibility in planning matters in relation to Wales and the Minister (if different) in charge of the government department concerned.	The Secretaries of State for the time being having general responsibility in planning matters in relation to England and in relation to Wales and the Minister (if different) in charge of the government department concerned.

SCHEDULE 11

CONTROL OF WORKS FOR DEMOLITION, ALTERATION OR
EXTENSION OF LISTED BUILDINGS

PART I

APPLICATIONS FOR LISTED BUILDING CONSENT

Form of application and effect of consent

1.—(1) Provision may be made by regulations under this Act with respect to the form and manner in which applications for listed building consent are to be made, the manner in which such applications are to be advertised and the time within which they are to be dealt with by local planning authorities or, as the case may be, by the Secretary of State.

Sch. 11

(2) Any listed building consent shall (except in so far as it otherwise provides) enure for the benefit of the building and of all persons for the time being interested therein.

2.—(1) Regulations under this Act may provide that an application for listed building consent, or an appeal against the refusal of such an application, shall not be entertained unless it is accompanied by a certificate in the prescribed form and corresponding to one or other of those described in section 27(1)(a) to (d) of this Act and any such regulations may—

(a) include requirements corresponding to sections 27(2) and (4) and 29(3) of this Act; and

(b) make provision as to who, in the case of any building, is to be treated as the owner for the purposes of any provision of the regulations made by virtue of this subparagraph.

(2) If any person issues a certificate which purports to comply with the requirements of regulations made by virtue of this paragraph and which contains a statement which he knows to be false or misleading in a material particular, or recklessly issues a certificate which purports to comply with those requirements and which contains a statement which is false or misleading in a material particular, he shall be guilty of an offence and liable on summary conviction to a fine not exceeding £100.

Directions as to manner of dealing with applications

3. The provisions of section 31(2) and (3) of this Act shall apply to an application for listed building consent for any works for the demolition, alteration or extension of a building in a conservation area as they apply to an application of the kind therein mentioned.

Reference of applications to Secretary of State or Greater London Council

4.—(1) The Secretary of State may give directions requiring applications for listed building consent to be referred to him instead of being dealt with by the local planning authority.

(2) A direction under this paragraph may relate either to a particular application, or to applications in respect of such buildings as may be specified in the direction.

(3) An application in respect of which a direction under this paragraph has effect shall be referred to the Secretary of State accordingly.

(4) Before determining an application referred to him under this paragraph, the Secretary of State shall, if either the applicant or the authority so desire, afford to each of them an opportunity of appearing before, and being heard by, a person appointed by the Secretary of State.

(5) The decision of the Secretary of State on any application referred to him under this paragraph shall be final.

5.—(1) Subject to the following provisions of this paragraph, a   Sch. 11
local planning authority (other than a London borough council)
to whom application is made for listed building consent shall not
grant such consent, unless they have notified the Secretary of State
of the application (giving particulars of the works for which the
consent is required) and either—

> (a) a period of twenty-eight days has expired, beginning with
> the date of the notification, without the Secretary of State
> having directed the reference of the application to him ; or

> (b) the Secretary of State has notified the authority that he does
> not intend to require the reference of the application.

(2) The Secretary of State may at any time before the said period
expires give notice to the authority that he requires further time in
which to consider whether to require the reference of the application
to him and sub-paragraph (1) of this paragraph shall then have effect
with the substitution for a period of twenty-eight days of such longer
period as may be specified in the Secretary of State's notice.

6.—(1) Subject to the following provisions of this paragraph,
where application for listed building consent is made to a local
planning authority, being a London borough council, and the
authority do not determine to refuse it, they shall notify the Greater
London Council of the application (giving particulars of the works
for which the consent is required) and shall not grant such consent
unless authorised or directed to do so under sub-paragraph (2) of
this paragraph.

(2) On receipt of notification under sub-paragraph (1) of this paragraph the Greater London Council may either—

> (a) authorise the local planning authority to grant or refuse the
> application, as they think fit ; or

> (b) give them directions as to how they are to determine it.

(3) The Greater London Council shall not authorise the local
planning authority as mentioned in sub-paragraph (2)(a) of this paragraph, nor under sub-paragraph (2)(b) of this paragraph direct them to
grant listed building consent, unless the Council have notified the
Secretary of State of the application made to the local planning
authority (giving particulars of the works for which the consent is
required) and either—

> (a) a period of twenty-eight days has expired, beginning with
> the date of the notification, without the Secretary of State
> having directed the reference of the application to him ; or

> (b) the Secretary of State has notified the Council that he does
> not intend to require the reference of the application.

(4) The Secretary of State may at any time before the said period
of twenty-eight days expires give notice to the Council that he
requires further time in which to consider whether to require the
reference of the application to him and sub-paragraph (3) of this
paragraph shall then have effect with the substitution for the period
of twenty-eight days of such longer period as may be specified in
the Secretary of State's notice.

7.—(1) The Secretary of State may give directions that, in the case of such descriptions of applications for listed building consent as he may specify, other than such consent for the demolition of a building, paragraphs 5 and 6 of this Schedule shall not apply; and accordingly, so long as the directions are in force local planning authorities may determine applications of such descriptions in any manner they think fit, without notifying the Secretary of State or, as the case may be, the Greater London Council.

(2) Without prejudice to the preceding provisions of this Schedule, the Secretary of State may give directions to local planning authorities requiring them, in such cases or classes of case as may be specified in the directions, to notify to him and to such other persons as may be so specified any applications made to them for listed building consent, and the decisions taken by the authorities thereon.

Appeal against decision

8.—(1) Where an application is made to the local planning authority for listed building consent and the consent is refused by the authority or is granted by them subject to conditions, the applicant, if he is aggrieved by the decision, may by notice served in the prescribed manner within such period as may be prescribed, not being less than twenty-eight days from the receipt by him of notification of the decision, appeal to the Secretary of State.

(2) A person appealing under this paragraph may include in his notice thereunder, as the ground or one of the grounds of his appeal, a claim that the building is not of special architectural or historic interest and ought to be removed from any list compiled or approved by the Secretary of State under section 54 of this Act, or—

> (a) in the case of a building to which subsection (10) of that section applies, that the Secretary of State should give a direction under that subsection with respect to the building ; or

> (b) in the case of a building subject to a building preservation notice under section 58 of this Act, that the building should not be included in a list compiled or approved under the said section 54.

(3) Subject to the following provisions of this paragraph, the Secretary of State may allow or dismiss an appeal thereunder, or may reverse or vary any part of the decision of the authority, whether the appeal relates to that part thereof or not, and—

> (a) may deal with the application as if it had been made to him in the first instance ; and

> (b) may, if he thinks fit, exercise his power under section 54 of this Act to amend any list compiled or approved thereunder by removing from it the building to which the appeal relates or his power under subsection (10) of that section to direct that that subsection shall no longer apply to the building.

(4) Before determining an appeal under this paragraph, the Secretary of State shall, if either the applicant or the local planning

authority so desire, afford to each of them an opportunity of appearing before, and being heard by, a person appointed by the Secretary of State for the purpose.

(5) The decision of the Secretary of State on any appeal under this paragraph shall be final.

(6) Schedule 9 to this Act applies to appeals under this paragraph.

Appeal in default of decision

9. Where an application is made to the local planning authority for listed building consent, then unless within the prescribed period from the date of the receipt of the application, or within such extended period as may at any time be agreed upon in writing between the applicant and the authority, the authority either—

 (a) give notice to the applicant of their decision on the application ; or

 (b) give notice to him that the application has been referred to the Secretary of State in accordance with directions given under paragraph 4 of this Schedule,

the provisions of paragraph 8 of this Schedule shall apply in relation to the application as if listed building consent had been refused by the authority and as if notification of their decision had been received by the applicant at the end of the prescribed period or at the end of the said extended period, as the case may be.

PART II

REVOCATION OF LISTED BUILDING CONSENT

10.—(1) If it appears to the local planning authority, having regard to the development plan and to any other material considerations, that it is expedient to revoke or modify listed building consent in respect of any works to a building, being consent granted on an application made under Part I of this Schedule, the authority, subject to the following provisions of this paragraph, may by order revoke or modify the consent to such extent as (having regard to those matters), they consider expedient.

(2) Except as provided in paragraph 12 of this Schedule, an order under this paragraph shall not take effect unless it is confirmed by the Secretary of State ; and the Secretary of State may confirm any such order submitted to him either without modification or subject to such modifications as he considers expedient.

(3) Where a local planning authority submit an order to the Secretary of State for confirmation under this paragraph, the authority shall serve notice on the owner and on the occupier of the building affected and on any other person who in their opinion will be affected by·the order ; and if within such period as may be specified in that notice (not being less than twenty-eight days after the service thereof) any person on whom the notice is served so requires, the Secretary of State, before confirming the order, shall afford to that person and to the local planning authority an opportunity of appearing before, and being heard by, a person appointed by the Secretary of State for the purpose.

(4) The power conferred by this paragraph to revoke or modify listed building consent in respect of any works may be exercised at any time before those works have been completed, but the revocation or modification shall not affect so much of those works as has been previously carried out.

11.—(1) If it appears to the Secretary of State, after consultation with the local planning authority, to be expedient that an order under paragraph 10 of this Schedule should be made, he may give directions to the authority requiring them to submit to him such an order for his confirmation, or may himself make such an order ; and any order so made by the Secretary of State shall have the like effect as if it had been made by the authority and confirmed by the Secretary of State under that paragraph.

(2) The provisions of paragraph 10 of this Schedule shall have effect, subject to any necessary modifications, in relation to any proposal by the Secretary of State to make such an order by virtue of this paragraph, in relation to the making thereof by the Secretary of State and in relation to the service of copies thereof as so made.

12.—(1) The following provisions shall have effect where the local planning authority have made an order under paragraph 10 of this Schedule but have not submitted the order to the Secretary of State for confirmation by him, and—

> (a) the owner and occupier of the land and all persons who in the authority's opinion will be affected by the order have notified the authority in writing that they do not object to the order ; and

> (b) it appears to the authority that no claim for compensation is likely to arise under section 172 of this Act on account of the order.

(2) The authority shall advertise in the prescribed manner the fact that the order has been made, and the advertisement shall specify—

> (a) the period (not being less than twenty-eight days from the date on which the advertisement first appears) within which persons affected by the order may give notice to the Secretary of State that they wish for an opportunity of appearing before, and being heard by, a person appointed by the Secretary of State for the purpose ; and

> (b) the period (not being less than fourteen days from the expiration of the period referred to in paragraph (a) of this sub-paragraph) at the expiration of which. if no such notice is given to the Secretary of State, the order may take effect by virtue of this paragraph and without being confirmed by the Secretary of State.

(3) The authority shall also serve notice to the same effect on the persons mentioned in sub-paragraph (1)(a) of this paragraph, and the notice shall include a statement to the effect that no compensation is payable under section 172 of this Act in respect of an order under paragraph 10 of this Schedule which takes effect by virtue of this paragraph and without being confirmed by the Secretary of State.

(4) The authority shall send a copy of any advertisement published under sub-paragraph (2) of this paragraph to the Secretary of State, not more than three days after the publication.

(5) If within the period referred to in sub-paragraph (2)(*a*) of this paragraph no person claiming to be affected by the order has given notice to the Secretary of State as aforesaid and the Secretary of State has not directed that the order be submitted to him for confirmation, the order shall, at the expiration of the period referred to in sub-paragraph (2)(*b*) of this paragraph, take effect by virtue of this paragraph and without being confirmed by the Secretary of State as required by paragraph 10(2) of this Schedule.

(6) This paragraph does not apply to an order revoking or modifying a listed building consent granted by the Secretary of State.

PART III

PROVISIONS APPLICABLE ON LAPSE OF BUILDING PRESERVATION NOTICE

13. The provisions of this Part of this Schedule apply where a building preservation notice ceases to be in force by virtue of section 58(3) of this Act, otherwise than by reason of the building to which it relates being included in a list compiled or approved under section 54 of this Act.

14. The fact that the building preservation notice has ceased to be in force shall not affect the liability of any person to be prosecuted and punished for an offence under section 55 or 98 of this Act committed by him with respect to the said building while the notice was in force.

15. Any proceedings on or arising out of an application for listed building consent made while the building preservation notice was in force shall lapse and any listed building consent granted with respect to the building, while the notice was in force, shall also lapse.

16. Any listed building enforcement notice served by the local planning authority while the building preservation notice was in force shall cease to have effect and any proceedings thereon under sections 96 and 97 of this Act shall lapse, but section 99(1) and (2) of this Act shall continue to have effect as respects any expenses incurred by the local authority, owner or occupier as therein mentioned and with respect to any sums paid on account of such expenses.

SCHEDULE 12

OFFICE DEVELOPMENT IN METROPOLITAN REGION: PLANNING
PERMISSION GRANTED BEFORE PASSING OF ACT OF 1965

Certain planning permissions treated as of no effect

1.—(1) Where before 5th August 1965 an application was made
to the local planning authority for planning permission for development consisting of or including the erection on land in Greater
London of a building containing office premises, or consisting of or
including the extension of a building on land in Greater London
by the addition of office premises, and on that application planning
permission for such development was granted before that date, then,
unless that planning permission was granted before 5th November
1964 and either—

(a) a building was before the said 5th November erected, or (as
the case may be) the building was before the said
5th November extended, in accordance with that planning
permission ; or

(b) a building contract was made before the said 5th November
which specifically related to the land, or part of the land,
in respect of which the planning permission was granted
and which provided for the erection thereon of such a
building, or the making of such an extension, in accordance
with that planning permission,

the provisions of sub-paragraph (4) of this paragraph shall (except
where sub-paragraph (3) of this paragraph or paragraph 3 of this
Schedule applies) have effect in relation to that planning permission.

(2) Where before 5th August 1965 an application was made to the
local planning authority for planning permission—

(a) to carry out, on land in Greater London, development to
which these provisions apply, other than such development
as is mentioned in sub-paragraph (1) of this paragraph ; or

(b) to carry out any development to which these provisions apply
on land within the metropolitan region but outside Greater
London,

and on that application planning permission to carry out the
development in question was granted before that date, then, unless
the planning permission was granted before 5th November 1964, the
provisions of sub-paragraph (4) of this paragraph shall (except where
sub-paragraph (3) of this paragraph applies) have effect in relation
to that planning permission.

(3) Notwithstanding anything in sub-paragraph (1) or (2) of this
paragraph, the provisions of sub-paragraph (4) of this paragraph shall
not have effect in relation to planning permission for any development
if the office floor space to be created by that development does not
exceed 3,000 square feet.

(4) Where in accordance with sub-paragraphs (1) to (3) of this
paragraph the provisions of this sub-paragraph are to have effect in
relation to planning permission granted for carrying out development

on land within the metropolitan region, then, subject to paragraph 2 of this Schedule—

> (a) the planning permission shall by virtue of this paragraph be deemed not to have effect so long as that land continues to be land within an area to which these provisions apply ;
>
> (b) for the purposes of Part V of this Act anything done before the passing of this Act, as well as anything done after the passing of this Act at a time when that land continues to be land within such an area, shall, in so far as (apart from this sub-paragraph) it was development authorised by that planning permission, be deemed to have been done without the grant of planning permission ; and
>
> (c) for the purposes of section 75(3)(a) of this Act that planning permission shall be disregarded.

(5) Where in any proceedings (whether civil or criminal) it falls to be determined whether the provisions of sub-paragraph (4) of this paragraph have effect in relation to a grant of planning permission, and the question arises whether a building contract was made as mentioned in sub-paragraph (1)(b) of this paragraph, the burden of proving that a building contract was so made shall be on the party who alleges it.

Effect of grant of office development permit

2.—(1) Where, in accordance with the provisions of paragraph 1 of this Schedule, sub-paragraph (4)(a) and (b) of that paragraph have effect in relation to planning permission granted for carrying out development on land within the metropolitan region, and an office development permit in respect of that development is issued under these provisions, the said sub-paragraph (4)(a) and (b) shall thereupon cease to have effect in relation to that planning permission.

(2) Where planning permission for carrying out development on land within the metropolitan region having been granted before 5th August 1965, an office development permit in respect of that development is issued in the circumstances specified in sub-paragraph (1) of this paragraph and conditions are attached to that permit, the planning permission shall be deemed to have been granted subject to the conditions attached to the office development permit, or (if any other conditions were imposed by the authority granting the permission) to have been granted subject to the conditions attached to the permit in addition to the other conditions.

(3) Section 82 of this Act shall have effect as if in subsection (5) the reference to sections 77 to 81 of this Act included a reference to this paragraph.

Mixed industrial and office development

3. Where before 5th August 1965 an application was made to the local planning authority for planning permission for development consisting of or including the erection on land in Greater London of a building containing office premises or consisting of or including the

SCH. 12   extension of a building on land in Greater London by the addition
of office premises together with other premises, and—

    (a) in accordance with sections 38 and 39 of the Act of 1962 an
industrial development certificate was required for that
development and such a certificate was issued in respect of
it by the Board of Trade ; and

    (b) planning permission for the development was granted before
5th November 1964,

then, notwithstanding that neither of the conditions specified in sub-
paragraph (1)(a) and (b) of paragraph 1 of this Schedule is fulfilled,
the provisions of sub-paragraph (4) of that paragraph shall not have
effect in relation to that planning permission.

Enforcement notices

4.—(1) This paragraph applies to any enforcement notice which—

    (a) relates to the carrying out of development consisting of or
including the erection or extension of a building on land in
Greater London ; and

    (b) states that it is served on the grounds that, notwithstanding
that planning permission for that development was granted
before 5th August 1965, the development is by virtue of
paragraph 1(4) of this Schedule deemed to have been carried
out without the grant of planning permission.

(2) An enforcement notice to which this paragraph applies shall
not be served except by the Secretary of State or in pursuance of
directions given by the Secretary of State under section 276(5) of
this Act.

(3) An enforcement notice to which this paragraph applies—

    (a) may be served on any person who, in pursuance of a build-
ing contract to which he is a party, is engaged in carrying
out operations for the erection or extension of the building
in question, in addition to any other persons on whom (by
virtue of section 87(4) of this Act) the notice is required or
authorised to be served ;

    (b) may require any such operations to be discontinued forth-
with, either instead of, or in addition to, any other steps
which (in accordance with section 87(6)(b) and (7) of this
Act) may be required by the notice to be taken.

(4) In so far as an enforcement notice to which this paragraph
applies requires any operations to be discontinued forthwith—

    (a) the notice, notwithstanding anything in section 87(8) of this
Act, shall take effect immediately on its being served ; and

    (b) section 88(3) of this Act shall not apply to the notice ;

but nothing in this sub-paragraph shall affect the operation of section
87(8) or 88(3) of this Act in relation to such a notice in so far as
the notice requires any other steps to be taken.

(5) An enforcement notice to which this paragraph applies shall
specify a period (not being less than twenty-eight days after the

service thereof) within which an appeal may be brought against the notice ; and in relation to such a notice section 88(1) of this Act shall have effect with the substitution, for the words " the period at the end of which it is to take effect ", of the words " the period within which an appeal may be brought against the notice."

(6) In relation to any enforcement notice to which this section applies, the grounds on which an appeal may be brought under section 88 of this Act shall not include those specified in paragraphs (*a*) and (*b*) of subsection (1) of that section, but shall include the grounds specified in sub-paragraph (7) of this paragraph ; and the grounds specified in that sub-paragraph shall be deemed to be included among those mentioned in section 243(1)(*a*) of this Act.

(7) The grounds referred to in sub-paragraph (6) of this paragraph are the following—

(*a*) that the development to which the enforcement notice relates does not consist of or include the erection on land in Greater London of a building containing office premises, or the extension of a building on land in Greater London by the addition of office premises ;

(*b*) that a building was erected before 5th November 1964, or (as the case may be) the building in question was before that date extended, in accordance with planning permission for the development to which the enforcement notice relates ;

(*c*) that a building contract was made before that date which specifically related to the land, or part of the land, in respect of which planning permission was granted for the development to which the enforcement notice relates and which provided for the erection thereon of such a building as is mentioned in paragraph (*a*) of this sub-paragraph, or for the making of such an extension as is mentioned in that paragraph, in accordance with that planning permission ;

(*d*) that the office floor space to be created by the development to which the enforcement notice relates does not exceed 3,000 square feet ;

(*e*) that an industrial development certificate was required for development consisting of or including the development to which the enforcement notice relates and that such a certificate was issued in respect of it by the Board of Trade.

(8) Where an enforcement notice to which this paragraph applies requires any operations to be discontinued, any person on whom the notice has been served who continues those operations, or causes or permits them to be continued, in contravention of the notice shall be guilty of an offence and liable on summary conviction to a fine not exceeding £100.

(9) If, after a person has been convicted of an offence under sub-paragraph (8) of this paragraph, he further continues the operations (whether immediately or after an interval) in contravention of the notice, or causes or permits them to be so continued, he shall be guilty of a further offence and liable on summary conviction to a fine not

exceeding £20 for each day on which he so continues the operations or causes or permits them to be so continued.

(10) Where an enforcement notice to which this paragraph applies has been served, and either of the following events occurs, that is to say—

> (a) an office development permit is issued in respect of the development to which the notice relates ; or
>
> (b) planning permission for any development of the land to which the notice relates is granted authorising (either unconditionally or subject to conditions) the operations to which the notice relates to be continued,

the enforcement notice shall not have effect in so far as it would prevent or restrict the doing of anything after that event occurs.

Power to require information as to building contracts

5.—(1) Where it appears to the Secretary of State that, in accordance with planning permission granted before 5th November 1964, operations for the erection on land in Greater London of a building containing office premises, or for the extension of a building on land in Greater London by the addition of office premises, have been begun on or after that date (whether before or after the passing of this Act) or had been begun but not completed before that date or are about to begin, and no office development permit in respect of the erection or extension of that building has been issued, the Secretary of State may serve on any person who is—

> (a) the applicant on whose application the planning permission was granted ; or
>
> (b) the owner of the land ; or
>
> (c) the person carrying out or about to carry out the operations,

a notice under this paragraph requiring him to furnish to the Secretary of State such information, and to produce for examination on behalf of the Secretary of State documents in that person's custody or under his control of any such description, as may be specified in the notice for the purpose of enabling the Secretary of State to ascertain whether a building contract for the erection or extension of the building was made before 5th November 1964 and who is the owner of the land.

(2) A notice under this paragraph may require the information to which it relates to be furnished within such time as may be specified in the notice, and may require the documents to which it relates to be produced at such time and place as may be so specified:

Provided that the time specified in such a notice for furnishing any information or producing any document shall not be earlier than the end of the period of twenty-eight days after the service of the notice.

(3) If any person on whom a notice is served under this paragraph fails without reasonable excuse to comply with a requirement imposed

by the notice, he shall be guilty of an offence and liable on summary
conviction to a fine not exceeding £100 ; and if any such person—

(a) in furnishing any information required by the notice, makes
a statement which he knows to be false in a material
particular, or recklessly makes a statement which is false in
a material particular ; or

(b) produces for examination in accordance with the notice a
document which to his knowledge has been wilfully falsified,

he shall be guilty of an offence and liable on summary conviction to a
fine not exceeding £100 or imprisonment for a term not exceeding
three months or both, or on conviction on indictment to a fine or
imprisonment for a term not exceeding two years or both.

Planning permission to retain buildings or continue use of land

6.—(1) In relation to any planning permission granted before
5th August 1965 in accordance with section 32(2) of this Act (in this
section referred to as a "section 32 permission") relating to land
within the metropolitan region, where the circumstances are such that
any of the provisions specified in sub-paragraph (2) of this paragraph
would have had effect in relation thereto if it had been a corresponding
grant of planning permission for development, those provisions shall
have effect as if it had been a corresponding grant of planning
permission for development.

(2) The provisions referred to in sub-paragraph (1) of this paragraph are paragraphs 1, 2(1), 4 and 5 of this Schedule ; and in that
sub-paragraph "corresponding grant of planning permission for
development", in relation to a section 32 permission, means a
grant of planning permission to construct or carry out the building
or works, or to institute the use of land, of which the section 32
permission authorises the retention or continuance or (as the case
may be) authorises the retention or continuance without complying
with a condition previously imposed.

Planning permission where no office development permit required

7.—(1) This paragraph applies to any planning permission granted
on or after 5th November 1964 but before 5th August 1965 for the
erection of a building on land within the metropolitan region where
either the erection of that building is not development to which these
provisions apply or it is such development but no office development
permit is required for it.

(2) Any planning permission to which this paragraph applies
shall be deemed to have been granted subject to the following
condition (in addition to any other conditions imposed by the
authority granting the permission), that is to say, that the use of the
building, whether as originally erected or as subsequently extended or
altered, shall be restricted so that (whether in consequence of a change
of use or otherwise) it does not at any time contain office premises
having an aggregate office floor space which exceeds 3,000 square
feet.

L

(3) Section 82 of this Act shall have effect as if in subsection (5) the reference to sections 77 to 81 of this Act included a reference to this paragraph.

(4) For the purposes of this paragraph " office premises " has the meaning assigned by section 73(4) of this Act.

Section 85.

SCHEDULE 13

OFFICE DEVELOPMENT: METROPOLITAN REGION OUTSIDE
GREATER LONDON

1. In Bedfordshire—
the borough of Dunstable,
the urban district of Leighton-Linslade,
the rural district of Luton.

2. In Berkshire—
the boroughs of Maidenhead, New Windsor and Wokingham,
the rural districts of Bradfield, Cookham, Easthampstead, Windsor and Wokingham.

3. In Buckinghamshire—
the boroughs of Aylesbury, High Wycombe and Slough,
the urban districts of Beaconsfield, Bletchley, Chesham, Eton, and Marlow,
the rural districts of Amersham, Aylesbury, Eton, Wing and Wycombe.

4. In Essex—
the borough of Chelmsford,
the urban districts of Basildon, Benfleet, Brentwood, Canvey Island, Epping, Harlow, Rayleigh, Thurrock, Waltham Holy Cross and Chigwell,
the rural districts of Chelmsford, Epping and Ongar and Rochford.

5. In Hampshire—
the borough of Aldershot,
the urban districts of Farnborough and Fleet,
the rural district of Hartley Wintney.

6. The administrative county of Hertfordshire.

7. In Kent—
the boroughs of Chatham, Dartford, Gravesend, Gillingham, Maidstone, Rochester and Royal Tunbridge Wells,
the urban districts of Northfleet, Sevenoaks, Southborough, Swanscombe and Tonbridge,
the rural districts of Dartford, Maidstone, Malling, Sevenoaks, Strood and Tonbridge.

8. In Oxfordshire—
the borough of Henley-on-Thames,
the rural district of Henley.

9. The administrative county of Surrey.

10. In East Sussex—
the urban districts of Burgess Hill, Cuckfield and East
Grinstead,
the rural districts of Cuckfield and Uckfield.

11. In West Sussex—
the urban districts of Crawley and Horsham,
the rural district of Horsham.

12. The county borough of Luton.

13. The county borough of Reading.

14. The county borough of Southend-on-Sea.

SCHEDULE 14

PROVISIONS AS TO ESTABLISHED USE CERTIFICATES

*Application for certificate and appeal against
refusal thereof*

1. An application for an established use certificate shall be
made in such manner as may be prescribed by a development
order, and shall include such particulars, and be verified by such
evidence, as may be required by such an order or by any directions
given thereunder, or by the local planning authority or, in the case
of an application referred to the Secretary of State, by him.

2. Provision may be made by a development order for
regulating the manner in which applications for established use
certificates are to be dealt with by local planning authorities, and, in
particular—

   (*a*) for requiring the authority to give to any applicant for such
   a certificate, within such time as may be prescribed by the
   order, such notice as may be so prescribed as to the manner
   in which his application has been dealt with ;

   (*b*) for requiring the authority to give to the Secretary of State
   and to such other persons as may be prescribed by or under
   the order, such information as may be so prescribed with
   respect to applications for such certificates made to the
   authority, including information as to the manner in which
   any such application has been dealt with.

3.—(1) A development order may provide that an application
for an established use certificate, or an appeal against the refusal
of such an application, shall not be entertained unless it is

SCH. 14   accompanied by a certificate in such form as may be prescribed by
the order and corresponding to one or other of those described in
section 27(1)(a) to (d) of this Act ; and any such order may—

    (a) include requirements corresponding to section 27(2), (3) and
       (4), and section 29(3) of this Act ; and

    (b) make provision as to who, in the case of any land, is to be
       treated as the owner for the purposes of any provision
       of the order made by virtue of this sub-paragraph.

(2) If any person issues a certificate which purports to comply
with any provision of a development order made by virtue of sub-
paragraph (1) above and which contains a statement which he knows
to be false or misleading in a material particular, or recklessly
issues a certificate which purports to comply with those requirements
and which contains a statement which is false or misleading in a
material particular, he shall be guilty of an offence and liable on
summary conviction to a fine not exceeding £100.

Provisions with respect to grant of certificate

4. An established use certificate shall be in such form as may
be prescribed by a development order and shall specify—

    (a) the land to which the certificate relates and any use thereof
       which is certified by the certificate as established ;

    (b) by reference to the paragraphs of section 94(1) of this Act,
       the grounds on which that use is so certified ; and

    (c) the date on which the application for the certificate was
       made, which shall be the date at which the use is certified
       as established.

5. Where the Secretary of State grants an established use certificate,
he shall give notice to the local planning authority of that fact.

6. In section 34 of this Act references to applications for planning
permission shall include references to applications for established
use certificates ; and the information which may be prescribed as
being required to be contained in a register kept under that section
shall include information with respect to established use certificates
granted by the Secretary of State.

Section 138.

SCHEDULE 15

ADJUSTMENT OF CLAIM HOLDINGS

PART 1

ADJUSTMENT OF CLAIM HOLDINGS PLEDGED TO CENTRAL LAND BOARD
AS SECURITY FOR DEVELOPMENT CHARGES

1.—(1) In this Part of this Schedule references to the pledging of
a claim holding to the Central Land Board are references to any
transaction whereby—

    (a) the holder of the claim holding mortgaged it to the Central
       Land Board as security, or part of the security, for one
       or more development charges determined, or thereafter to
       be determined, by the Board ; or

(*b*) the holder and the Central Land Board agreed that a development charge determined by the Board should be set off against any payment which might thereafter become payable to the holder by reference to that holding ; or

(*c*) the Central Land Board refrained from determining a development charge, which would otherwise have fallen to be determined by them, in consideration of a mortgage of the holding, with or without other claim holdings.

(2) All pledges of claim holdings to the Central Land Board made by the same person, whether or not made at the same time, other than any pledge to which paragraph 2(1) of this Schedule applies, shall for the purposes of this Part of this Schedule be treated collectively as a single pledge made at the time when the last of those pledges was made.

(3) Where a development charge covered by a pledge to the Central Land Board was determined in respect of land consisting of, or forming part of, the area of a claim holding—

(*a*) which was not comprised in the pledge ; but

(*b*) whose holder immediately before the time of completion was the person who would, apart from the pledge, have been liable to pay the unpaid balance of the development charge,

then, for the purposes of this Part of this Schedule, that claim holding shall be deemed to have been comprised in the pledge.

(4) In this Part of this Schedule references to the determination of a development charge in respect of any land are references to a determination of the Central Land Board that the charge was payable in respect of the carrying out of operations in, on, over or under that land, or in respect of the use of that land.

(5) For the purposes of this Part of this Schedule the amount of a development charge—

(*a*) in a case where the Central Land Board determined that amount as a single capital payment, shall be taken to have been the amount of that payment ; and

(*b*) in a case where the Board determined that amount otherwise than as a single capital payment, shall be taken to have been the amount of the single capital payment which would have been payable if the Board had determined the amount as such a payment ;

and references in this Part of this Schedule to the unpaid balance of a development charge are references to the amount of the charge, if no sum was actually paid to the Board on account of the charge, or if any sum was so paid, are references to the amount of the charge reduced by the amount or aggregate amount of the sum or sums so paid, other than any sum paid by way of interest.

L 3

(6) In relation to the pledging of a claim holding to the Central Land Board, references in this Part of this Schedule to a development charge covered by the pledge are references to a development charge the payment of which was secured, or partly secured, by the pledge, or, as the case may be, which was agreed to be set off against any payment which might become payable by reference to that claim holding.

(7) References in this Part of this Schedule to a mortgage of a claim holding do not include a mortgage which was subsequently discharged.

2.—(1) Where a claim holding was pledged to the Central Land Board in accordance with the special arrangements relating to owners of single house plots, that claim holding shall, subject to sub-paragraph (2) of this paragraph, be deemed to have been extinguished as from the time when it was pledged to the Board.

(2) Where a claim holding (in this sub-paragraph referred to as " the original holding ") was pledged as mentioned in sub-paragraph (1) of this paragraph but was so pledged by reference to a plot of land which did not extend to the whole of the area of the original holding, that sub-paragraph shall not apply, but there shall be deemed to have been substituted for the original holding, as from the time of the pledge, a claim holding with an area consisting of so much of the area of the original holding as was not comprised in that plot of land, and with a value equal to that fraction of the value of the original holding which then attached to so much of the area of the original holding as was not comprised in that plot.

3. Without prejudice to paragraph 2 of this Schedule, where a pledge to the Central Land Board comprised one or more claim holdings, and the unpaid balance of the development charge covered by the pledge, or (if more than one) the aggregate of the unpaid balances of the development charges so covered, was equal to or greater than the value of the claim holding, or the aggregate value of the claim holdings, as the case may be, the holding or holdings shall be deemed to have been extinguished as from the time of the pledge.

4. Where a pledge to the Central Land Board comprised only a single claim holding with an area of which every part either consisted of, or formed part of, the land in respect of which some development charge covered by the pledge was determined, and paragraph 3 of this Schedule does not apply, the value of that claim holding shall be deemed to have been reduced, as from the time of the pledge, by the unpaid balance of the development charge covered by the pledge, or (if more than one) by the aggregate of the unpaid balances of all the development charges covered by the pledge.

5.—(1) The provisions of this paragraph shall have effect in the case of a pledge of one or more claim holdings to the Central Land Board to which neither paragraph 3 nor paragraph 4 of this Schedule applies.

(2) Any claim holding comprised in the pledge with an area of which every part either consisted of, or formed part of, the land in respect of which some development charge covered by the pledge was determined shall be allocated to the development charge in question, or (if more than one) to those development charges collectively.

(3) Any claim holding comprised in the pledge with an area part of which did, and part of which did not, consist of, or form part of, such land as is mentioned in sub-paragraph (2) of this paragraph shall be treated as if, at the time of the pledge, the claim holding (in this sub-paragraph referred to as " the parent holding ") had been divided into two separate claim holdings, that is to say—

(a) a claim holding with an area consisting of so much of the area of the parent holding as consisted of, or formed part of, such land as is mentioned in sub-paragraph (2) of this paragraph, and with a value equal to that fraction of the value of the parent holding which then attached to that part of the area of the parent holding ; and

(b) a claim holding with an area consisting of the residue of the area of the parent holding, and with a value equal to that fraction of the value of the parent holding which then attached to the residue of the area of the parent holding,

and the claim holding referred to in head (a) of this sub-paragraph shall be allocated to the development charge in question, or (if more than one) to those development charges collectively.

(4) Paragraph 3 or paragraph 4 of this Schedule shall then apply in relation to each claim holding (if any) allocated in accordance with sub-paragraph (2) or sub-paragraph (3) of this paragraph to any development charge, or to any development charges collectively, as if the pledge had comprised only that claim holding and had covered only that development charge or those development charges.

(5) If, after the application of the preceding provisions of this paragraph, there remains outstanding any claim holding not allocated in accordance with those provisions, or any claim holding which (having been so allocated) is deemed to have been reduced in value but not extinguished, an amount equal to the aggregate of—

(a) the unpaid balance of any development charge covered by the pledge to which no claim holding was so allocated ; and

(b) the amount (if any) by which the value of any claim holding so allocated which is deemed to have been extinguished falls short of the unpaid balance of the development charge, or the aggregate of the unpaid balances of the development charges, to which it was so allocated,

SCH. 15   shall be treated as having been deducted from the value of the claim holding so remaining outstanding, or (if more than one) as having been deducted rateably from the respective values of those claim holdings, and the value of any such holding shall be deemed to have been reduced accordingly as from the time of the pledge.

PART II

ADJUSTMENT BY REFERENCE TO PAYMENTS IN RESPECT OF WAR-DAMAGED LAND

6.—(1) The provisions of this Part of this Schedule shall have effect where a payment under the scheme has become, or becomes payable in respect of an interest in land, and a claim holding related (or would, apart from this Part of this Schedule, have related) to the like interest in the whole or part of that land, with or without any other land.

(2) In this Part of this Schedule " the scheme " means the scheme made under section 59 of the Act of 1947, " the date of the scheme " means 12th December 1949, and " payment under the scheme " means a payment which has become, or becomes, payable by virtue of the scheme.

(3) In relation to any payment under the scheme " the payment area ", in this Part of this Schedule, means the land in respect of which the payment became or becomes payable, and references to the amount of the payment shall be construed as references to the principal amount thereof, excluding any interest payable thereon in accordance with section 65(3) of the Act of 1947.

7. If the payment area is identical with the area of the claim holding, then—

    (a) in the case of a payment of an amount equal to the value of the claim holding, the claim holding shall be deemed to have been extinguished as from the date of the scheme ;

    (b) in the case of a payment of an amount less than the value of the claim holding, the value of the claim holding shall be deemed to have been reduced, as from the date of the scheme, by the amount of the payment.

8.—(1) If the payment area forms part of the area of the claim holding, the holding (in this paragraph referred to as " the parent holding ") shall be treated, as from the date of the scheme, as having been divided into two claim holdings, that is to say—

    (a) a claim holding with an area consisting of that part of the area of the parent holding which constituted the payment area, and with a value equal to that fraction of the value of the parent holding which attached to that part of the area of the parent holding ; and

(b) a claim holding with an area consisting of the residue of the area of the parent holding, and with a value equal to that fraction of the value of the parent holding which attached to the residue of the area of the parent holding.

(2) Where sub-paragraph (1) of this paragraph applies, paragraph 7 of this Schedule shall have effect in relation to the claim holding referred to in sub-paragraph (1)(a) of this paragraph as if it were the parent holding.

9. If the payment area includes the area of the claim holding together with other land, paragraph 7 of this Schedule shall apply as if—

    (a) the payment area had been identical with the area of the claim holding ; but

    (b) the amount of the payment had been so much of the actual amount thereof, as might reasonably be expected to have been attributed to the area of the claim holding if, under the scheme, the authority determining the amount of the payment had been required (in accordance with the same principles as applied to the determination of that amount) to apportion it between the area of the claim holding and the rest of the payment area.

10. If the payment area includes part of the area of the claim holding together with other land not comprised in the area of the claim holding—

    (a) paragraph 8 of this Schedule shall apply as if the part of the payment area comprised in the area of the claim holding had been the whole of the payment area ; and

    (b) paragraph 9 of this Schedule shall apply as if the part of the area of the claim holding comprised in the payment area had been the whole of the area of the claim holding.

PART III

ADJUSTMENT IN CASES OF PARTIAL DISPOSITION OF CLAIM HOLDINGS

11. The provisions of this Part of this Schedule shall have effect where, by virtue of a disposition of part of the benefit of an established claim, not being a mortgage made otherwise than by way of assignment (in this Part of this Schedule referred to as " the relevant disposition "), different persons became entitled to different parts of the benefit of that established claim.

12. As from the date of the relevant disposition, each of those different parts shall be treated as having constituted a separate claim holding.

13. The area and value of any such separate claim holding at any time after the relevant dispositon shall be taken to have been such as may, in the requisite manner, be or have been determined to be just and appropriate in all the circumstances.

14. In paragraph 13 of this Schedule the reference to determination in the requisite manner of the area and value of a claim holding is a reference to the determination thereof on the occasion of an apportionment affecting that holding which fell or falls to be made for any of the purposes of the Act of 1954, of Part VI of the Act of 1962 or Schedule 5 thereto, of Part VII of this Act or of this Schedule, being a determination made—

(a) by the authority making that apportionment ; or

(b) where, under the Act of 1954, Part VI of the Act of 1962 or Part VII of this Act, that authority's findings were or are referred to the Lands Tribunal, by that Tribunal,

having regard in particular to the principles mentioned in paragraph 15 of this Schedule.

15.—(1) The said principles are those set out in the following provisions of this paragraph.

(2) The aggregate of the values of all claim holdings representing parts of the benefit of the same established claim must not exceed the amount of the established claim.

(3) Subject to sub-paragraph (2) of this paragraph, where a claim holding representing part only of the benefit of an established claim was pledged to the Central Land Board, otherwise than as mentioned in paragraph 2 of this Schedule, and by virtue of Part I of this Schedule the value of that claim holding is deemed to have been reduced by reference to an amount due by way of development charge, the value of that holding at the time of the pledge is not to be taken to have been less than the amount credited for the purposes of the pledge by reference to the holding.

(4) In the case of the claim holding representing the part of the benefit of an established claim which was the subject of the relevant disposition, if it was not a claim holding to which sub-paragraph (5) of this paragraph applies—

(a) the area of that claim holding is to be taken to be the claim area of that established claim, less the area of any claim holding to which the said sub-paragraph (5) applies which represents part of the benefit of the same established claim ; and

(b) the value of the claim holding immediately after the relevant disposition is, subject to sub-paragraphs (2) and (3) of this paragraph, to be taken to have been that part of the amount of the established claim to which the holder purported to become entitled under the terms of the relevant disposition.

(5) Where any person who was entitled to a claim holding representing part only of the benefit of an established claim—

(a) at any time while so entitled was also entitled to the interest in land to which the established claim related in so far as that interest subsisted in part only of the claim area ; and (*b*) became entitled to both that holding and that interest in such circumstances that the authority making the apportionment in question or the Lands Tribunal, as the case may be, were or are satisfied that the holding and the interest were intended to relate to one another,

the area of that claim holding is to be taken to be that part of the claim area, and the value of the holding immediately after the relevant disposition (however that or any other disposition affecting the holding was expressed, but subject to sub-paragraphs (2) to (4) of this paragraph) is to be taken to have been an amount equal to so much of the amount of the established claim as might reasonably be expected to have been attributed to that part of the claim area if the authority determining the amount of that established claim had been required to apportion it, in accordance with the same principles as applied to its determination, between that part and the residue of the claim area.

16. Paragraph 1 of this Schedule shall apply for the purposes of this Part of this Schedule as it applies for the purposes of Part I thereof.

PART IV

ADJUSTMENT IN RESPECT OF PAYMENTS UNDER PART I OF ACT OF 1954

17. The provisions of this Part of this Schedule shall have effect where, by virtue of Part I of the Act of 1954, a payment became or becomes payable in respect of a claim holding.

18. Subject to the following provisions of this Part of this Schedule, if either—

(*a*) the principal amount of the payment was or is not less than the value of the claim holding ; or

(*b*) the payment (whatever its amount) became or becomes payable under Case D (that is to say, by virtue of section 8 of the Act of 1954, which related to cases where a claim holding had been disposed of for valuable consideration),

the claim holding shall be deemed to have been extinguished ; and if the principal amount of the payment (not being a payment under Case D) was or is less than the value of the claim holding, the value of that holding shall be deemed to have been reduced by the principal amount of the payment.

19. Paragraph 18 of this Schedule shall apply where two or more payments under Part I of the Act of 1954 were or are payable in respect of the same claim holding, with the substitution, for references to the principal amount of the payment, of references to the aggregate of the principal amounts of the payments.

20.—(1) Where one or more relevant acts or events have occurred in relation to a claim holding (in this paragraph referred to as " the parent holding ") and any such act or event did not extend to the whole of the area of the parent holding, then, for the purposes of the

Sch. 15   preceding provisions of this Part of this Schedule, and for the purposes of Part V of this Schedule and of Part VII of this Act—

(a) the parent holding shall be treated as having been divided immediately before the time of completion, into as many separate claim holdings, with such areas, as may be necessary to ensure that, in the case of each holding, either any relevant act or event extending to the area of that holding extended to the whole thereof or no relevant act or event extended to the area of that holding;

(b) the value of each of the separate holdings respectively shall be taken to have been that fraction of the value of the parent holding which then attached to the part of the area of the parent holding constituting the area of the separate holding; and

(c) the portion of the amount of any payment under Part I of the Act of 1954 which, by the authority determining that amount, was or is apportioned to the area of any of the separate claim holdings shall be taken to have been a payment payable under the said Part I in respect of that claim holding.

(2) In this paragraph "relevant act or event", in relation to a claim holding, means an act or event whereby, in accordance with the provisions of Part I of the Act of 1954, one or more payments became or become payable in respect of that claim holding.

21. For the purposes of this Part of this Schedule—

(a) a payment shall be treated as having become payable notwithstanding that the right to receive the payment was extinguished by section 14(2) of the Act of 1954 (which enabled the Central Land Board to set off payments against liabilities in respect of development charges);

(b) any reduction of the principal amount of a payment by virtue of that subsection shall be disregarded; and

(c) where in accordance with subsection (3) of section 14 or subsection (6) of section 58 of the Act of 1954 (which provided for cases of failure to apply for a payment within the appropriate period) an amount was determined as being the principal amount of a payment to which a person would have been entitled as mentioned in those subsections respectively, that payment shall be treated as if it had become due and as if the principal amount thereof had been the amount so determined.

22.—(1) Where in accordance with the preceding provisions of this Part of this Schedule a claim holding is deemed to have been extinguished or the value of a claim holding is deemed to to have been reduced, the extinguishment or reduction, as the case may be, shall be deemed to have had effect immediately before the time of completion.

(2) References in this Part of this Schedule to the value of a claim holding are references to the value thereof immediately before the time of completion.

PART V

ADJUSTMENT IN RESPECT OF COMPENSATION UNDER PART V OF ACT
OF 1954

23. Where compensation under Part V of the Act of 1954 became or becomes payable by reference to a claim holding, then (subject to the following provisions of this Part of this Schedule) for the purposes of Part VII of this Act—

(a) if the principal amount of the compensation was or is equal to the value of the claim holding at the time of completion (ascertained apart from this Part of this Schedule) the claim holding shall be deemed to have been extinguished immediately before that time ;

(b) if the principal amount of the compensation was or is less than the value of the claim holding at that time (ascertained apart from this Part of this Schedule) the value of the claim holding shall be deemed to have been reduced immediately before that time by the principal amount of the compensation.

24. Where compensation became or becomes payable as mentioned in paragraph 23 of this Schedule, and at any time an amount became or becomes recoverable in respect thereof under section 29 of the Act of 1954, as applied by section 46 of that Act, or under section 159 of this Act as applied by Schedule 24 to this Act to compensation under Part V of the Act of 1954, then, for the purposes of Part VII of this Act, paragraph 23 of this Schedule shall have effect as from that time as if the principal amount of that compensation had been reduced by a sum equal to seven-eighths of the amount which so became or becomes recoverable.

25. Where, in the case of a claim holding (in this paragraph referred to as " the parent holding "), compensation under Part V of the Act of 1954 became or becomes payable in respect of depreciation of the value of an interest in land by one or more planning decisions or orders, and any such decision or order did not extend to the whole of the area of the parent holding, then, both for the purposes of the preceding provisions of this Part of this Schedule and for the purposes of Part VII of this Act—

(a) the parent holding shall be treated as having been divided immediately before the time of completion into as many separate claim holdings, with such areas, as may be necessary to ensure that, in the case of each holding, either any such decision or order extending to the area of that holding extended to the whole thereof or no such decision or order extended to the area of that holding ;

(b) the value of each of the separate holdings respectively shall be taken to have been that fraction of the value of the parent holding which then attached to the part of the area of the parent holding constituting the area of the separate holding ; and

(c) the portion of the amount of any such compensation which, by the authority determining that amount, was or is apportioned to the area of any of the separate claim holdings shall be taken to have been compensation payable under Part V of the Act of 1954 in respect of that claim holding.

PART VI
SUPPLEMENTARY PROVISIONS

26. Where in accordance with any of the provisions of this Schedule a part of the benefit of an established claim constituted a separate claim holding, the interest in land to which that claim holding related—

    (a) if the established claim related to the fee simple of the claim area, shall be taken to have been the fee simple of the area of the claim holding ;

    (b) if the established claim related to a leasehold interest, shall be taken to have been that leasehold interest in so far as it subsisted in the area of the claim holding.

27. Where in accordance with any of the provisions of this Schedule a claim holding (in this paragraph referred to as "the parent holding ") is to be treated as divided into two or more claim holdings, a person who was the holder of one of those holdings shall be treated as having been the holder thereof at any time when he was the holder of the parent holding.

28. Expressions used in this Schedule and in Part VII of this Act have the same meanings in this Schedule as in that Part of this Act.

29. In this Schedule "the holder ", in relation to a claim holding, means the person for the time being entitled to the holding, or, in the case of a holding subject to a mortgage made otherwise than by way of assignment, means the person who would for the time being have been entitled to the holding if it had not been mortgaged, and " the time of completion " means the time when, in accordance with section 138 of this Act, the adjustment of claim holdings is deemed to have been completed.

SCHEDULE 16
CALCULATION OF VALUE OF PREVIOUS DEVELOPMENT OF LAND

1. Where for the purposes of section 141 of this Act the value of any development initiated before a time referred to in that section has to be ascertained with reference to that time, the value of the development shall be calculated in accordance with the provisions of this Schedule.

2. Subject to the following provisions of this Schedule, the value shall be calculated by reference to prices current at the time in question—

    (a) as if the development had not been initiated, but the land had remained in the state in which it was immediately before the development was initiated ; and (*b*) on the assumption that (apart from the provisions of Part III of this Act, the provisions of Part III of the Act of 1962 or the provisions of the Act of 1947, as the case may be) the development could at that time lawfully be carried out,

and shall be taken to be the difference between the value which in those circumstances the land would have had at that time if planning permission for that development had been granted unconditionally immediately before that time and the value which in those circumstances the land would have had at that time if planning permission for that development had been applied for and refused immediately before that time, and it could be assumed that planning permission for that development, and any other new development of that land, would be refused on any subsequent application.

3. If the development involved the clearing of any land, the reference in paragraph (2)(*a*) of this Schedule to the state of the land immediately before the development shall be construed as a reference to the state of the land immediately after the clearing thereof but before the carrying out of any other operations.

4.—(1) If the development was initiated in pursuance of planning permission granted subject to conditions, paragraph 2 of this Schedule shall apply as if the reference to the granting of permission unconditionally were a reference to the granting of permission subject to the like conditions.

(2) If the permission referred to in sub-paragraph (1) of this paragraph was granted subject to conditions which consisted of, or included, a requirement expressed by reference to a specified period, the reference in that sub-paragraph to the like conditions shall be construed, in relation to the condition imposing that requirement, as a reference to a condition imposing the like requirement in respect of a period of like duration beginning at the time in question.

5. In the application of the preceding provisions of this Schedule to development initiated, but not completed, before the time in question, references to permission for that development shall be construed as references to permission for so much of that development as had been carried out before that time.

SCHEDULE 17

APPORTIONMENT OF UNEXPENDED BALANCE OF ESTABLISHED DEVELOPMENT VALUE

Determination of relevant area

1.—(1) Where, in the case of a compulsory acquisition to which section 142 of this Act applies, any area of the relevant land which, immediately before the relevant date, has an unexpended balance of established development value does not satisfy the conditions set out in sub-paragraph (2) of this paragraph, that area shall be treated as divided into as many separate areas as may be requisite to ensure that each of those separate areas satisfies those conditions.

(2) The conditions referred to in sub-paragraph (1) of this paragraph are—

(*a*) that all the interests (other than excepted interests) subsisting in the area in question subsist in the whole of that area ; and

(*b*) that any rentcharge charged on that area is charged on the whole of it.

(3) Any area of the relevant land which has an unexpended balance of established development value and which complies with the conditions set out in sub-paragraph (2) of this paragraph is in this Schedule referred to, in relation to the interests subsisting therein, as " the relevant area ", and the subsequent provisions of this Schedule shall have effect separately in relation to each relevant area.

Preliminary calculations

2. There shall be calculated the amount referable to the relevant area of the rent which might reasonably be expected to be reserved if the relevant land were to be let on terms prohibiting the carrying out of any new development but permitting the carrying out of any other development ; and the amount so calculated is in this Schedule referred to as " the existing use rent ".

3.—(1) If, in the case of an interest in fee simple which is subject to a rentcharge, or in the case of a tenancy, so much of the rent reserved under the rentcharge or tenancy as is referable to the relevant area exceeds the existing use rent, there shall be calculated the capital value of the right to receive, for the period of the remainder of the term of the rentcharge or tenancy, an annual payment equal to the excess ; and any amount so calculated in the case of any interest is in this Schedule referred to as " the rental liability " of that interest.

(2) Where the interest in fee simple is subject to more than one rentcharge, then, for the purposes of sub-paragraph (1) of this paragraph, in relation to any period included in the term of two or more of those rentcharges, those two or more rentcharges shall be treated as a single rentcharge charged on the relevant area for the duration of that period, with a rent reserved thereunder of an amount equal to the aggregate of so much of their respective rents as is referable to the relevant area.

4. In the case of any interest in reversion—

(*a*) there shall be calculated the capital value, as at the time immediately before the relevant date, of the right to receive a sum equal to the unexpended balance of established development value of the relevant area at that time, but payable at the end of the tenancy upon the termination of which the interest in question is immediately expectant ; and the amount so calculated in the case of any interest is in this Schedule referred to as " the reversionary development value " of that interest ;

(*b*) if so much of the rent reserved under the said tenancy as is referable to the relevant area exceeds the existing use rent, there shall also be calculated the capital value as at the said time of the right to receive, for the period of the remainder of the term of that tenancy, an annual payment equal to the excess ; and any amount so determined in the case of any interest is in this Schedule referred to as " the rental increment " of that interest.

Apportionment of unexpended balance between interests

5. Where two or more interests (other than excepted interests) subsist in the relevant area, the portion of the unexpended balance of established development value of the relevant area attributable to each of those interests respectively shall be taken to be the following, that is to say—

(*a*) in the case of the interest in fee simple, an amount equal to the reversionary development value of that interest, less the amount (if any) by which any rental liability of that interest exceeds any rental increment thereof ;

(*b*) in the case of a tenancy in reversion, an amount equal to the reversionary development value of that tenancy, less the aggregate of—

(i) the reversionary development value of the interest in reversion immediately expectant upon the termination of that tenancy ; and

(ii) the amount (if any) by which any rental liability of that tenancy exceeds any rental increment thereof ;

(*c*) in the case of a tenancy other than a tenancy in reversion, the remainder (if any) of the said balance after the deduction of the aggregate of—

(i) the reversionary development value of the interest in reversion immediately expectant upon the termination of that tenancy ; and

(ii) any rental liability of that tenancy.

Application of Schedule to past acquisitions

6. In relation to any compulsory acquisition to which section 142 of this Act applies, where the relevant date was a date before the commencement of this Act, the preceding provisions of this Schedule shall have effect with the necessary modifications.

Interpretation

7. In this Schedule—

(*a*) " the relevant land ", in relation to a compulsory acquisition to which section 142 of this Act applies, means the land in which the interest acquired subsisted or subsists ;

(*b*) " tenancy " does not include an excepted interest ;

(*c*) any reference to an interest or tenancy in reversion does not include an interest or tenancy in reversion immediately expectant upon the termination of an excepted interest ;

(*d*) " the relevant date " and " excepted interest " have the same meanings as in section 142 of this Act ; and

(*e*) other expressions have the same meanings as in Part VII of this Act.

Sections 168,
169, 180 and 278.

SCHEDULE 18

Condition Treated as Applicable to Rebuilding and Alterations

1. Where the building to be rebuilt or altered is the original building, the amount of gross floor space in the building as rebuilt or altered which may be used for any purpose shall not exceed by more than ten per cent. the amount of gross floor space which was last used for that purpose in the original building.

2. Where the building to be rebuilt or altered is not the original building, the amount of gross floor space in the building as rebuilt or altered which may be used for any purpose shall not exceed the amount of gross floor space which was last used for that purpose in the building before the rebuilding or alteration.

3. In determining under this Schedule the purpose for which floor space was last used in any building, no account shall be taken of any use in respect of which an effective enforcement notice has been or could be served or, in the case of a use which has been discontinued, could have been served immediately before the discontinuance.

4. For the purposes of this Schedule gross floor space shall be ascertained by external measurement ; and where different parts of a building are used for different purposes, floor space common to those purposes shall be apportioned rateably.

5. In relation to a building erected after the appointed day, being a building resulting from the carrying out of any such works as are described in paragraph 1 of Schedule 8 to this Act, any reference in this Schedule to the original building is a reference to the building in relation to which those works were carried out and not to the building resulting from the carrying out of those works.

Section 190.

SCHEDULE 19

Proceedings on Listed Building Purchase Notice

Action by council on whom listed building purchase notice is served

1.—(1) The council on whom a listed building purchase notice is served, shall, before the end of the period of three months beginning with the date of service of that notice, serve on the owner by whom the purchase notice was served a notice stating either—

(*a*) that the council are willing to comply with the purchase notice ; or

(*b*) that another local authority or statutory undertakers specified
in the notice under this sub-paragraph have agreed to
comply with it in their place ; or

(*c*) that for reasons specified in the notice under this sub-paragraph, the council are not willing to comply with the
purchase notice and have not found any other local authority
or statutory undertakers who will agree to comply with it
in their place and that they have transmitted a copy of the
purchase notice to the Secretary of State, on a date specified
in the notice under this sub-paragraph, together with a
statement of the reasons so specified.

(2) Where the council on whom a listed building purchase notice
is served by an owner have served on him a notice in accordance with
sub-paragraph (1)(*a*) or (*b*) of this paragraph the council, or the other
local authority or statutory undertakers specified in the notice, as the
case may be, shall be deemed to be authorised to acquire the interest
of the owner compulsorily in accordance with the provisions of
section 114 of this Act, and to have served a notice to treat in respect
thereof on the date of service of the notice under sub-paragraph (1)
of this paragraph.

(3) Where the council on whom a listed building purchase notice is
served by an owner propose to serve on him a notice in accordance
with sub-paragraph (1)(*c*) of this paragraph they shall transmit a
copy of the purchase notice to the Secretary of State together with
a statement of their reasons ; and section 182 of this Act shall then
apply in relation to the purchase notice as it applies in relation to a
purchase notice under section 180 of this Act with the substitution
for references therein to the Secretary of State taking action under
section 183 of this Act of references to his taking action under
paragraph 2 of this Schedule.

*Action by Secretary of State in relation to listed building purchase
notice*

2.—(1) Subject to the following provisions of this paragraph, if
the Secretary of State is satisfied that the conditions specified in
section 190(1)(*a*) to (*c*) of this Act are fulfilled in relation to a listed
building purchase notice, he shall confirm the notice:

Provided that, if he is satisfied that the said conditions are fulfilled
only in respect of part of the land, he shall confirm the notice only
in respect of that part and the notice shall have effect accordingly.

(2) The Secretary of State shall not confirm the purchase notice
unless he is satisfied that the land comprises such land contiguous or
adjacent to the building as is in his opinion required for preserving
the building or its amenities, or for affording access to it, or for its
proper control or management.

(3) If it appears to the Secretary of State to be expedient to do so
in the case of a listed building purchase notice served on account of
listed building consent being refused or granted subject to conditions,

he may, in lieu of confirming the purchase notice, grant listed building consent for the works in respect of which the application was made or, where such consent for those works was granted subject to conditions, revoke or amend those conditions so far as it appears to him to be required in order to enable the land to be rendered capable of reasonably beneficial use by the carrying out of those works.

(4) If it appears to the Secretary of State to be expedient to do so, in the case of a listed building purchase notice served on account of listed building consent being revoked or modified by an order under Part II of Schedule 11 to this Act, he may, in lieu of confirming the notice, cancel the order revoking the consent or, where the order modified the consent by the imposition of conditions, revoke or amend those conditions so far as appears to him to be required in order to enable the land to be rendered capable of reasonably beneficial use by the carrying out of the works in respect of which the consent was granted.

(5) If it appears to the Secretary of State that the land, or any part of it, could be rendered capable of reasonably beneficial use within a reasonable time by the carrying out of any other works for which listed building consent ought to be granted, he may in lieu of confirming the listed building purchase notice or in lieu of confirming it so far as it relates to that part of the land, as the case may be, direct that listed building consent for those works shall be granted in the event of an application being made in that behalf.

(6) If it appears to the Secretary of State that the land, or any part of the land, could be rendered capable of reasonably beneficial use within a reasonable time by the carrying out of any development for which planning permission ought to be granted, he may, in lieu of confirming the listed building purchase notice, or in lieu of confirming it so far as it relates to that part of the land, as the case may be, direct that planning permission for that development shall be granted in the event of an application being made in that behalf.

(7) If it appears to the Secretary of State, having regard to the probable ultimate use of the building or the site thereof, that it is expedient to do so, he may, if he confirms the notice, modify it either in relation to the whole or in relation to any part of the land, by substituting another local authority or statutory undertakers for the council on whom the notice was served.

(8) In section 182 of this Act as applied by paragraph 1(3) of this Schedule, any reference to the taking of action by the Secretary of State under this paragraph is a reference to the taking by him of any such action as is mentioned in sub-paragraphs (1) or (3) to (7) of this paragraph, or to the taking by him of a decision not to confirm the purchase notice on the grounds that any of the conditions referred to in sub-paragraph (1) of this paragraph are not fulfilled.

Effect of Secretary of State's action in relation to listed building purchase notice

3.—(1) Where the Secretary of State confirms a listed building purchase notice, the council on whom the notice was served (or, if under paragraph 2(7) of this Schedule the Secretary of State modified

the notice by substituting another local authority or statutory undertakers for that council, that other local authority or those statutory
undertakers) shall be deemed to be authorised to acquire the relevant
interest compulsorily in accordance with the provisions of section 114
of this Act and to have served a notice to treat in respect thereof
on such date as the Secretary of State may direct.

(2) If, before the end of the relevant period, the Secretary of State
has neither confirmed the purchase notice nor taken any such action in
respect thereof as is mentioned in sub-paragraphs (3) to (6) of
paragraph 2 of this Schedule, and has not notified the owner by
whom the notice was served that he does not propose to confirm
the notice, the notice shall be deemed to be confirmed at the end of
that period and the council on whom the notice was served shall be
deemed to have been authorised to acquire the relevant interest
compulsorily in accordance with the provisions of section 114 of this
Act and to have served a notice to treat in respect thereof at the
end of that period.

(3) In this paragraph—

(*a*) " the relevant interest " means the owner's interest in the
land or, if the purchase notice is confirmed by the Secretary
of State in respect of only part of the land, the owner's
interest in that part ;

(*b*) " the relevant period " is whichever of the following periods
first expires, that is to say—

(i) the period of nine months beginning with the date
of the service of the purchase notice ; and

(ii) the period of six months beginning with the date
on which a copy of the purchase notice was transmitted
to the Secretary of State.

(4) Where the Secretary of State has notified the owner by whom
a listed building purchase notice has been served of a decision on his
part to confirm, or not to confirm, the notice (including any decision
to confirm the notice only in respect of part of the land, or to
give any direction as to the granting of listed building consent), and
that decision of the Secretary of State is quashed under the provisions
of Part XII of this Act, the purchase notice shall be treated
as cancelled, but the owner may serve a further listed building
purchase notice in its place.

(5) For the purposes of any regulations made under this Act as
to the time within which a listed building purchase notice may be
served, the service of a listed building purchase notice under sub-
paragraph (4) of this paragraph shall not be treated as out of time
if the notice is served within the period which would be applicable
in accordance with those regulations if the decision to refuse listed
building consent or to grant it subject to conditions (being the decision
in consequence of which the notice is served) had been made on
the date on which the decision of the Secretary of State was quashed
as mentioned in sub-paragraph (4) of this paragraph.

*Special provision as to compensation where listed building
purchase notice served*

4. Where in consequence of listed building consent being revoked
or modified by an order under Part II of Schedule 11 to this Act,
compensation is payable by virtue of section 172 of this Act in
respect of expenditure incurred in carrying out any works to the
building in respect of which the consent was granted, then if a listed
building purchase notice is served in respect of an interest in the
land, any compensation payable in respect of the acquisition of that
interest in pursuance of the notice shall be reduced by an amount
equal to the value of the works in respect of which compensation
is payable by virtue of that section.

Section 217.

SCHEDULE 20

PROCEDURE IN CONNECTION WITH
ORDERS RELATING TO FOOTPATHS AND BRIDLEWAYS

PART I

CONFIRMATION OF ORDERS

1.—(1) Before an order under section 210 or 214(1)(*b*) of this Act
is submitted to the Secretary of State for confirmation or confirmed
as an unopposed order, the authority by whom the order was made
shall give notice in the prescribed form—

> (*a*) stating the general effect of the order and that it has been
> made and is about to be submitted for confirmation or to
> be confirmed as an unopposed order ;

> (*b*) naming a place in the area in which the land to which the
> order relates is situated where a copy of the order may be
> inspected free of charge at all reasonable hours ; and

> (*c*) specifying the time (not being less than twenty-eight days
> from the date of the first publication of the notice) within
> which, and the manner in which, representations or
> objections with respect to the order may be made.

(2) Subject to sub-paragraph (4) of this paragraph, the notice to be
given under sub-paragraph (1) of this paragraph shall be given—

> (*a*) by publication in the London Gazette and in at least
> one local newspaper circulating in the area in which the
> land to which the order relates is situated ; and

> (*b*) by serving a like notice on—

>> (i) every owner, occupier and lessee (except tenants
>> for a month or a period less than a month and statutory
>> tenants within the meaning of the Rent Act 1968) of any
>> of that land ;

>> (ii) every council, the council of every rural parish and
>> the parish meeting of every rural parish not having a
>> separate parish council, being a council or parish whose
>> area includes any of that land ; and

1968 c. 23.

(iii) any statutory undertakers to whom there belongs, or by whom there is used, for the purposes of their undertaking, any apparatus under, in, on, over, along or across that land ; and

(c) by causing a copy of the notice to be displayed in a prominent position at the ends of so much of any footpath or bridleway as is to be stopped up, diverted or extinguished by virtue of the order.

(3) In sub-paragraph (2) of this paragraph "council" means a county council, a county borough council, a county district council, the Greater London Council or a London borough council.

(4) Except in the case of an owner, occupier or lessee being a local authority or statutory undertakers, the Secretary of State may in any particular case direct that it shall not be necessary to comply with sub-paragraph (2)(b)(i) of this paragraph ; but if he so directs in the case of any land, then in addition to publication the notice shall be addressed to "the owners and any occupiers" of the land (describing it) and a copy or copies of the notice shall be affixed to some conspicuous object or objects on the land.

2. If no representations or objections are duly made, or if any so made are withdrawn, the authority by whom the order was made may, instead of submitting the order to the Secretary of State, themselves confirm the order (but without any modification).

3.—(1) If any representation or objection duly made is not withdrawn, the Secretary of State shall, before confirming the order, if the objection is made by a local authority cause a local inquiry to be held, and in any other case either—

(a) cause a local inquiry to be held ; or

(b) afford to any person by whom any representation or objection has been duly made and not withdrawn an opportunity of being heard by a person appointed by the Secretary of State for the purpose,

and, after considering the report of the person appointed to hold the inquiry or to hear representations or objections, may confirm the order, with or without modifications:

Provided that in the case of an order under section 210 of this Act, if objection is made by statutory undertakers on the ground that the order provides for the creation of a public right of way over land covered by works used for the purpose of their undertaking, or over the curtilage of such land, and the objection is not withdrawn, the order shall be subject to special parliamentary procedure.

(2) Notwithstanding anything in the preceding provisions of this paragraph, the Secretary of State shall not confirm an order so as to affect land not affected by the order as submitted to him, except after—

(a) giving such notice as appears to him requisite of his proposal so to modify the order, specifying the time (not being less than twenty-eight days from the date of the first publication of the notice) within which, and the manner in which, representations or objections with respect to the proposal may be made ;

(b) holding a local inquiry or affording to any person by whom any representation or objection has been duly made and not withdrawn an opportunity of being heard by a person appointed by the Secretary of State for the purpose ; and

(c) considering the report of the person appointed to hold the inquiry or to hear representations or objections as the case may be ;

and, in the case of an order under section 210 of this Act, if objection is made by statutory undertakers on the ground that the order as modified would provide for the creation of a public right of way over land covered by works used for the purposes of their undertaking, or over the curtilage of such land, and the objection is not withdrawn, the order shall be subject to special parliamentary procedure.

4.—(1) The Secretary of State shall not confirm an order under section 210 of this Act which extinguishes a right of way over land under, in, on, over, along or across which there is any apparatus belonging to or used by statutory undertakers for the purposes of their undertaking, unless the undertakers have consented to the confirmation of the order ; and any such consent may be given subject to the condition that there are included in the order such provisions for the protection of the undertakers as they may reasonably require.

(2) The consent of statutory undertakers to any such order shall not be unreasonably withheld ; and any question arising under this paragraph whether the withholding of consent is unreasonable, or whether any requirement is reasonable, shall be determined by whichever Minister is the appropriate Minister in relation to the statutory undertakers concerned.

5. Regulations under this Act may, subject to this Part of this Schedule, make such provision as the Secretary of State thinks expedient as to the procedure on the making, submission and confirmation of orders under sections 210 and 214(1)(b) of this Act.

Part II

Publicity for Orders after Confirmation

6. As soon as may be after an order under section 210 or 214(1)(b) of this Act has been confirmed by the Secretary of State or confirmed as an unopposed order, the authority by whom the order was made shall publish, in the manner required by paragraph 1(2) of this Schedule, a notice in the prescribed form, describing the general effect of the order, stating that it has been confirmed, and naming a place where a copy thereof as confirmed may be inspected free of charge at all reasonable hours, and shall—

(a) serve a like notice and a copy of the order as confirmed on any persons on whom notices were required to be served under the said paragraph 1(2) or under paragraph 1(4) ; and

(*b*) cause a like notice to be displayed in the like manner as   S<small>CH</small>. 20
the notice required to be displayed under the said paragraph
1(2):

Provided that no such notice or copy need be served on a person
unless he has sent to the authority a request in that behalf, specifying
an address for service.

SCHEDULE 21

P<small>ROVISIONS OF THIS</small> A<small>CT REFERRED TO IN</small>
S<small>ECTIONS</small> 263, 264, 269, 270, 271, 273 <small>AND</small> 274
<small>AND</small> P<small>ARAGRAPHS</small> 83 <small>AND</small> 84 <small>OF</small> S<small>CHEDULE</small> 24

Sections 263,
264, 269, 270,
271, 273 and
274 and
paragraphs
83 and 84 of
Schedule 24.

P<small>ART</small> I

Sections 1 to 3.

Section 22.

Section 23 except subsection (7).

Section 24 except subsection (6).

Section 25.

Section 29(1).

Section 30.

Section 31(1).

Sections 32 and 33.

Section 34(1) and (3).

Section 35 with the omission in subsection (4) of the reference
to sections 26 and 27.

Section 36(1) to (6) with the omission in subsection (5) of the
reference to section 27.

Section 37.

Section 40.

Section 45.

Sections 50 to 53.

Section 54 except subsections (8), (10) and (11).

Section 60.

Sections 63 to 68.

Section 89.

Sections 91 to 93.

Section 102.

Sections 104 to 111.

Sections 118 to 125.

Sections 127 to 133.

Section 164.

Section 165 with the omission in subsection (2) of the references
to sections 166 to 168.

Section 169 except subsection (5).

Section 170.

Section 174.

Section 176.

Sections 178 and 179.

Section 180(1) to (4).

Sections 181 to 183.

Sections 186 to 189.

Section 191(1).

Section 209.

Section 214 except subsection (1)(*b*).

Section 215.

Sections 218 and 219.

Section 220.

Section 222.

Sections 224 to 231.

Sections 233 to 236.

Section 237 except subsection (3).

Section 238 except subsections (4) and (6)(*b*).

Sections 239 to 241.

Section 242(1) except paragraphs (*d*) and (*e*).

Section 243 except subsection (5).

Section 244.

Section 246.

Section 249 with the omission in subsection (2) of the references to section 245.

Section 250.

Section 251(1).

Section 252.

Sections 254 and 255.

Section 263(1).

Sections 264 and 265.

Section 266(1) (the reference, in paragraph (*b*), to Part III being construed as not referring to sections 26 and 27 and the reference, in that paragraph, to Part IV being construed as not referring to sections 73 to 86) and section 266(2) to (5) and (7).

Section 267.

Section 270.

Section 272.

Section 274 except subsections (2)(*a*) and (4).

Section 275(2).

Section 276.

Section 280 except subsections (4) and (5).

Section 281.

Section 284.

Section 288.

Schedules 1 and 2.

Schedule 8.

Schedule 22.

Schedule 24, paragraphs 33 to 39, 46, 48 and 87 to 92.

Any other provisions of this Act in so far as they apply, or have effect for the purposes of, any of the provisions specified above.

Part II

Section 4.
Sections 6 to 21.
Section 26(2) to (6) except subsection (2)(*a*) and the reference to it in subsection (6), and subsection (8).
Section 28(2)(*b*) and (3).
Section 29(4).
Section 31(2) and (3).
Section 34(2).
Section 36(7) and (8).
Sections 41 to 44.
Sections 46 to 49.
Section 54(10) and (11).
Sections 55 and 56.
Section 58.
Sections 79 to 81.
Sections 87 and 88.
Section 90.
Sections 94 to 100.
Section 103(4).
Sections 112 to 117.
Sections 171 to 173.
Section 177.
Section 180(5) and (6).
Section 184.
Section 190.
Section 197.
Sections 201 and 202.
Sections 210 to 213.
Section 214(1)(*b*).
Sections 216 and 217.
Section 221.
Section 223.
Section 232.
Section 237(3).
Section 238(4) and (6)(*b*).
Section 253.
Section 256.
Section 271.
Section 285.
Schedules 4, 7, 9, 10, 11, 14, 19 and 20 and paragraphs 18 to 21, 24, 31, 40, 41, 43, 57, 58 and 77 of Schedule 24.

Part III

Sections 38 and 39.
Section 72.
Sections 134 to 163.
Sections 166 to 168.

Section 169(5).
Section 191(2).
Section 251(2) to (5).
Sections 257 to 259.
Section 261(2) to (4).
Section 268.
Section 274(4).
Section 275(1).
Section 279.
Section 280(5).
Schedules 15 and 16.

Any other provisions of this Act in so far as they apply, or have effect for the purposes of, any of the provisions specified above

PART IV

Section 28.
Section 54(8).
Section 57.
Section 59.
Sections 61 and 62.
Section 101.
Section 102(1).
Section 103.
Section 126.
Section 277.
Section 280(4).

PART V

Sections 22 to 25.
Section 29(1), (5) and (6).
Section 30.
Section 31(1).
Sections 32 and 33.
Section 34 except subsection (2).
Sections 35 to 37.
Section 40.
Section 45.
Sections 50 to 53.
Section 54 except subsections (2) and (9) to (11)
Section 60.
Sections 63 to 68.
Section 72.
Sections 87 to 95.
Section 102.
Sections 104 to 111.
Section 177.

PART VI

Section 28(2)(*b*) and (3).
Section 29(4).
Section 31(2) and (3).
Section 54(2) and (9) to (11).
Section 55.
Section 56.
Section 58.
Sections 96 to 100.
Sections 114 to 117.
Sections 171 to 173.
Section 180(5) and (6).
Section 190.
Schedules 11 and 19.

PART VII

Section 24(6).
Section 26 except subsections (2)(*b*) and (3) to (9).
Section 27.
Section 29(2) and (3).
Section 142 except subsections (2)(*b*) and (6)(*b*).
Section 143 (construed as if in section 142 the said subsections were omitted).
Sections 192 to 196.
Sections 198 to 200.
Sections 203 to 207.
Section 242 except subsection (1)(*a*) to (*c*).
Section 243(5).
Section 245.
Sections 247 and 248
Section 249(2).
Section 266(1) (construed as if the reference to Part III were a reference only to sections 26 and 27) and (6).
Section 274(2) except paragraph (*b*).
Schedule 17.

Any other provisions of this Act in so far as they apply, or have effect for the purposes of, any of the provisions specified above.

SCHEDULE 22

ENACTMENTS EXEMPTED FROM SECTION 287(6) OF THIS ACT

1. Section 107 of the Public Health Act 1936.   1936 c. 49.

2. The following provisions of the Highways Act 1959, that is to say—   1959 c. 25.

section 72(1), (2), (5) and (8) to (10).
section 73 except subsection (5).
sections 159, 163 and 166.
section 170(2) and (4).

SCH. 22

section 217.

section 222(7).

section 266(5) and (7).

Schedule 9.

1959 c. 25.

3. The following further provisions of the Highways Act 1959, that is to say—

(a) sections 158 and 170(1) so far as applicable for the purposes of section 159 of that Act ;

(b) section 222(11) so far as applicable for the purposes of section 217 of that Act ;

(c) in section 266—

(i) subsections (1) to (3) so far as applicable for the purposes of section 72 of that Act ;

(ii) subsections (1), (3) and (6) so far as applicable for the purposes of section 73 of that Act ;

(iii) subsections (1) and (3) so far as applicable for the purposes of section 163 and 170(2) of that Act ;

(d) section 270 so far as applicable for the purposes of section 73 of that Act.

4. Section 243 of the Highways Act 1959 so far as the purposes in question are the purposes of the exercise—

(a) by a county council in relation to county roads maintained by that council ; or

(b) by the Greater London Council in relation to any road for the time being designated by or under section 17 of the
1963 c. 33 London Government Act 1963 as a metropolitan road,

of their powers under section 72(1), (2), (5) and (8) to (10) or section 217 of the said Act of 1959.

5. Any enactment making such provision as might by virtue of any Act of Parliament have been made in relation to the area to which the order applies by means of a byelaw, order or regulation not requiring confirmation by Parliament.

6. Any enactment which has been previously excluded or modified by a development order, and any enactment having substantially the same effect as any such enactment.

Section 291.

SCHEDULE 23

CONSEQUENTIAL AMENDMENTS

PART I

The Land Compensation Act 1961 (*c.* 33)

In the Land Compensation Act 1961 any reference to an area defined in the current development plan as an area of comprehensive development shall be construed as a reference to an action area for which a local plan is in force.

The London Government Act 1963 *(c. 33)*

In section 21 of the London Government Act 1963 the reference to an area of comprehensive development shall be construed as a reference to an action area for which a local plan is in force.

Part II
The Finance Act 1931 *(c. 28)*

In section 28(6) of the Finance Act 1931 (inserted by the Land 1967 c. 1. Commission Act 1967) for the words " the Town and Country Planning Act 1962 " there shall be substituted the words " the Town and Country Planning Act 1971 ".

In Schedule 2 to the said Act of 1931, in paragraph (viii) (inserted by the Land Commission Act 1967) for the words " section 19(4) of the Town and Country Planning Act 1962 " there shall be substituted the words " section 34(1) of the Town and Country Planning Act 1971 ".

The Building Restrictions (War-Time Contraventions) Act 1946 *(c. 35)*

In section 7(1) and (5) of the Building Restrictions (War-Time Contraventions) Act 1946 (as amended by the Act of 1962) for the words " paragraph 12 of the Thirteenth Schedule to the Town and Country Planning Act 1962 " there shall be substituted the words " paragraph 34 of Schedule 24 to the Town and Country Planning Act 1971 ".

The Civil Aviation Act 1949 *(c. 67)*

In section 30 of the Civil Aviation Act 1949 (as amended by the Act of 1962)—

(a) in subsection (1) for the words " subsections (2) to (5) of section one hundred and seventy-one of the Town and Country Planning Act 1962 " there shall be substituted the words " section 238(2), (3), (5) and (6) of the Town and Country Planning Act 1971 " ;

(b) in subsection (2) for the words " Subsections (2) to (5) of the said section one hundred and seventy-one ", " subsection (2) of the last preceding section " and " subsection (5) of that section " there shall be substituted respectively the words " Subsections (2), (3), (5) and (6) of the said section 238 ", " section 237(2) of this Act " and " subsection (6) of that section ".

In Schedule 4 to the said Act of 1949 (as amended by the Act of 1962)—

(a) in paragraph 4 for the words " section one hundred and sixty-nine of the Town and Country Planning Act 1962 " and " section one hundred and sixty-six of that Act " there shall be substituted respectively the words " section 236 of the Town and Country Planning Act 1971 " and " section 233 of that Act " ;

(*b*) in paragraph 8 for the words " section one hundred and sixty-nine of the Town and Country Planning Act 1962 " and " section one hundred and sixty-eight of that Act " there shall be substituted respectively the words " section 236 of the Town and Country Planning Act 1971 " and " section 235 of that Act ".

The Town Development Act 1952 (c. 54)

In section 6 of the Town Development Act 1952 (as amended by the Act of 1962)—

(*a*) in subsection (1) for the words " the Town and Country Planning Act 1962 " and " or that Act " there shall be substituted respectively the words " the Town and Country Planning Act 1971 " and " the Town and Country Planning Act 1962 or the Town and Country Planning Act 1971 " ;

(*b*) in subsection (5) for the words " Part V of the said Act of 1962 " there shall be substituted the words " Part VI of the said Act of 1971 " ;

(*c*) in subsection (6) for the words " section sixty-eight of the Town and Country Planning Act 1962 " there shall be substituted the words " section 112 of the Town and Country Planning Act 1971 ", for the words " section sixty-eight of the said Act of 1962 " there shall be substituted the words " section 112 of the said Act of 1971 ", for the words " subsection (1) of section seventy-one, subsection (1) of section seventy-four, subsection (2) of section eighty-six and subsection (1) of section eighty-seven of that Act " there shall be substituted the words " section 119(1), section 132(2) and section 133(1) of that Act ".

The Highways Act 1959 (c. 25)

In section 19(1) of the Highways Act 1959 (as amended by the Act of 1962) for the words " section eight of the Town and Country Planning Act 1962 " there shall be substituted the words " paragraph 5 of Schedule 5 to the Town and Country Planning Act 1971 ".

In section 38(2)(*e*) of the said Act of 1959 (as amended by the Act of 1968) for the words " section 153 of the Town and Country Planning Act 1962 " and " section 94 of the Town and Country Planning Act 1968 " there shall be substituted respectively the words " section 209 of the Town and Country Planning Act 1971 " and " section 210 of that Act ".

The Town and Country Planning Act 1959 (c. 53)

In section 26(5)(*c*) (as amended by the Act of 1962) for the words " section seventy-eight of the Town and Country Planning Act 1962 " there shall be substituted the words " section 123 of the Town and Country Planning Act 1971 ".

The Local Employment Act 1960 *(c.* 18*)*

For section 21 of the Local Employment Act 1960 in its application to England and Wales there shall be substituted:—

> " 21. In this Act ' industrial building ' has the meaning assigned to it by section 66 of the Town and Country Planning Act 1971."

The Public Health Act 1961 *(c.* 64*)*

In Schedule 4 to the Public Health Act 1961 (as amended by the Act of 1968) for the words " section 32 of the Town and Country Planning Act 1962 " there shall be substituted the words " section 54(1) of the Town and Country Planning Act 1971 ".

The London Government Act 1963 *(c.* 33*)*

In section 21(4)(*a*)(i) of the London Government Act 1963 for the words " the Town and Country Planning Act 1962 " there shall be substituted the words " the Town and Country Planning Act 1971 ".

In section 85 of the said Act of 1963—

(*a*) in subsection (3) for the words " section 24(7) of this Act " and " the said section 24(7) " there shall be substituted respectively the words " paragraph 6 of Schedule 3 to the Town and Country Planning Act 1971 " and " the said paragraph 6 " ;

(*b*) in subsection (4) the words " (including any agreement under section 24(7)) " shall be omitted, and after the words " made under this Act " there shall be inserted the words " or of any agreement under paragraph 6 of Schedule 3 to the Town and Country Planning Act 1971 ".

The Water Resources Act 1963 *(c.* 38*)*

In section 71(4) of the Water Resources Act 1963 for the words " section 41 of the Town and Country Planning Act 1962 " there shall be substituted the words " section 40 of the Town and Country Planning Act 1971 ".

In section 123(5) of the said Act of 1963 for the words " section 199 of the Town and Country Planning Act 1962 ; and the provisions of subsection (6) of that section " there shall be substituted the words " section 266 of the Town and Country Planning Act 1971 ; and the provisions of subsection (7) of that section ".

The Harbours Act 1964 *(c.* 40*)*

In section 52(2) of the Harbours Act 1964 for the words " section 199 of the Town and Country Planning Act 1962 ; and the provisions of subsection (6) of that section " there shall be substituted the words " section 266 of the Town and Country Planning Act 1971 ; and the provisions of subsection (7) of that section ".

M

The Airports Authority Act 1965 (c. 16)

In section 17(6) and (7)(*d*) of the Airports Authority Act 1965 for the words " section 82 of the Town and Country Planning Act 1962 " and " Part V of that Act " there shall be substituted respectively the words " section 128 of the Town and Country Planning Act 1971 " and " Part VI of that Act ".

In section 18 of the said Act of 1965 (as amended by the Civil Aviation Act 1971) for the words set out in the first column below there shall be substituted the words set out opposite to them in the second column below:—

" sections 118 and 119 of the Act of 1962 "	" sections 164 and 165 of the Act of 1971 "
" section 123 of the Act of 1962 "	" section 169 of the Act of 1971 "
" section 170(1) of the Act of 1962 "	" section 237(1) of the Act of 1971 "
" section 134(2) of the Act of 1962 "	" section 187(2) of the Act of 1971 "
" section 129 of the Act of 1962 "	" section 180 of the Act of 1971 "
" the said section 118 "	" the said section 164 ".
" section 27 of the Act of 1962 " (in both places)	" section 45 of the Act of 1971 "
" section 130(2) or 133(1) of the Act of 1962 "	" section 181(2) or 186(1) of the Act of 1971 "
" section 122 of the Act of 1962 "	" section 168 of the Act of 1971 "
" Part III of the Act of 1962 "	" Part III of the Act of 1971 "

and in section 18(5) of the said Act of 1965 for the words " ' the Act of 1962 ' means the Town and Country Planning Act 1962 " there shall be substituted the words " ' the Act of 1971 ' means the Town and Country Planning Act 1971 ".

In section 19(1) of the said Act of 1965 for the words " section 221(1) of the Town and Country Planning Act 1962 " there shall be substituted the words " section 290(1) of the Town and Country Planning Act 1971 ".

The Gas Act 1965 (c. 36)

In section 4(6) of the Gas Act 1965 for the words " the Town and Country Planning Act 1962 " and " section 41 of that Act " there shall be substituted respectively the words " the Town and Country Planning Act 1971 " and " section 40 of that Act ".

In section 28(1) of the said Act of 1965—

(*a*) in the definition of " local planning authority " for the words " section 2 of the Town and Country Planning Act 1962 " there shall be substituted the words " section 1 of the Town and Country Planning Act 1971 " ;

(*b*) in the definition of " planning permission " for the words " Part III of the Town and Country Planning Act 1962 " there shall be substituted the words " Part III of the Town and Country Planning Act 1971 ".

In Schedule 3 to the said Act of 1965—

(a) in paragraph 3 for the words " section 100 of the Town and Country Planning Act 1962 " and " Part VI of that Act, together with sections 25 and 26 of that Act " there shall be substituted respectively the words " section 146 of the Town and Country Planning Act 1971 " and " Part VII of that Act, together with sections 38 and 39 of that Act ".

(b) in paragraph 7(2) for the words " the Town and Country Planning Act 1962 " there shall be substituted the words " the Town and Country Planning Act 1971 ".

(c) in paragraph 9(a) for the words " section 100 of the Town and Country Planning Act 1962 ", " Part VI of the said Act of 1962 " and " sections 25 and 26 of the said Act of 1962 " there shall be substituted respectively the words " section 146 of the Town and Country Planning Act 1971 ", " Part VII of the said Act of 1971 " and " sections 38 and 39 of the said Act of 1971 ".

The Compulsory Purchase Act 1965 (*c.* 56)

In section 1(4) of the Compulsory Purchase Act 1965 for the words " Part V of the Town and Country Planning Act 1962 " and " section 86(6) of that Act " there shall be substituted respectively the words " Part VI of the Town and Country Planning Act 1971 " and " section 132(4) of that Act ".

In section 10(3) of the said Act of 1965 for the words " Part V of the Town and Country Planning Act 1962 " and " section 86(6)(b) of that Act " there shall be substituted respectively the words " Part VI of the Town and Country Planning Act 1971 " and " section 132(4)(b) of that Act ".

The New Towns Act 1965 (*c.* 59)

In subsection (2) of section 6 of the New Towns Act 1965 for the words " section 14 of the Town and Country Planning Act 1962 " there shall be substituted the words " section 24 of the Town and Country Planning Act 1971 " ; and in subsection (3) of that section for the words " section 32 of the Town and Country Planning Act 1962 " there shall be substituted the words " section 54(1) of the Town and Country Planning Act 1971 ".

In section 54(1) of the said Act of 1965—

(a) in the definition of " local planning authority ", for the words " the Town and Country Planning Act 1962 " there shall be substituted the words " the Town and Country Planning Act 1971 " ;

(b) in the definition of " planning permission " for the words " Part III of the Town and Country Planning Act 1962 " there shall be substituted the words " Part III of the Town and Country Planning Act 1971 ".

In paragraph 3(3)(a) of Schedule 10 to the said Act of 1965 for the words " section 14 of the Town and Country Planning Act 1962 " there shall be substituted the words " section 24 of the Town and Country Planning Act 1971 ".

The Building Control Act 1966 (c. 27)

In section 6(1)(*a*) of the Building Control Act 1966 after the words " Part I of the Control of Office and Industrial Development Act 1965 " there shall be inserted the words " or section 74 of the Town and Country Planning Act 1971 ".

The Local Government Act 1966 (*c.* 42)

In section 8(5) of the Local Government Act 1966 for the words " the Town and Country Planning Act 1962 " there shall be substituted the words " the Town and Country Planning Act 1971 ".

In section 9(4) of the said Act of 1966 for the words " the Town and Country Planning Act 1962 " there shall be substituted the words " the Town and Country Planning Act 1971 ".

In section 37 of the said Act of 1966 for the words " the Town and Country Planning Act 1962 " there shall be substituted the words " the Town and Country Planning Act 1971 ".

The Land Commission Act 1967 (*c.* 1)

In section 14 of the Land Commission Act 1967 for the words set out in the first column below (in each place where they occur in that section) there shall be substituted the words set out opposite to them in the second column below: —

" the Act of 1962 "	" the Act of 1971 "
" section 81 "	" section 127 "
" sections 164 and 165 "	" sections 230 and 231 "
" sections 170(2) and 171 "	" sections 237(2) and 238 "
" section 68 "	" section 112 "
" subsection (1) of section 164 "	" section 230(1) "
" section 164 or 165 "	" section 230 or 231 "
" section 204 "	" section 273 "

In section 58(3) of the said Act of 1967 for the words " section 221(1) of the Act of 1962 " there shall be substituted the words " section 290(1) of the Act of 1971 ".

In section 89(6)(*b*) of the said Act of 1967 for the words " section 221(1) of the Act of 1962 " there shall be substituted the words " section 290(1) of the Act of 1971 ".

In section 99 of the said Act of 1967—

(*a*) in subsection (1) after the words " ' the Act of 1962 ' means the Town and Country Planning Act 1962 " there shall be inserted the words " ' the Act of 1971 ' means the Town and Country Planning Act 1971 " ;

(*b*) in subsection (2)(*b*) for the words " paragraphs 1, 2, 3 and 5 to 8 of Schedule 3 to the Act of 1962, as read with Part III of that Schedule and with section 1(4) of the Town and Country Planning Act 1963 " there shall be substituted the words " paragraphs 1, 2, 3 and 5 to 8 of Schedule 8 to the Act of 1971, as read with Part III of that Schedule " and for the words " the said Act of 1963 " there shall be substituted the words " the Town and Country Planning Act 1963 " ;

(c) in subsection (8) for the words "subsection (1) of section 221 (interpretation) of the Act of 1962" there shall be substituted the words "section 290(1) (interpretation) of the Act of 1971"

In Schedule 15 to the said Act of 1967, in paragraph (viii) for the words "section 19(4) of the Town and Country Planning Act 1962" there shall be substituted the words "section 34 of the Town and Country Planning Act 1971".

In Schedule 16 to the said Act of 1967, in Part I, for the words "section 82 of the Act of 1962" (in both places where they occur) there shall be substituted the words "section 128 of the Act of 1971" and for the words "Section 87(3) of the Act of 1962" and "section 82 of that Act" there shall be substituted respectively the words "Section 133(3) of the Act of 1971" and "section 128 of that Act".

The General Rate Act 1967 (c. 9)

In section 32(8) of the General Rate Act 1967 for the words "the Town and Country Planning Act 1962" there shall be substituted the words "the Town and Country Planning Act 1971".

In Schedule 1 to the said Act of 1967, in paragraph 2(c) (as amended by the Act of 1968), for the words "a building preservation notice as defined by section 48 of the Town and Country Planning Act 1968 or is included in a list compiled or approved under section 32 of the Town and Country Planning Act 1962" there shall be substituted the words "a building preservation notice as defined by section 58 of the Town and Country Planning Act 1971 or is included in a list compiled or approved under section 54 of that Act".

The Forestry Act 1967 (c. 10)

In section 9(4)(d) of the Forestry Act 1967 for the words "the Town and Country Planning Act 1962" there shall be substituted the words "the Town and Country Planning Act 1971".

In section 35 of the said Act of 1967 for the words "section 29 of the Town and Country Planning Act 1962" there shall be substituted the words "section 60 of the Town and Country Planning Act 1971".

In Schedule 3 to the said Act of 1967, in paragraph 2, for the words "section 22 of the Town and Country Planning Act 1962" and "the said section 22" there shall be substituted respectively the words "section 35 of the Town and Country Planning Act 1971" and "the said section 35"; and in paragraph 3 for the words "the Town and Country Planning Act 1962" there shall be substituted the words "the Town and Country Planning Act 1971".

The Agriculture Act 1967 (c. 22)

In section 49(5)(a) of the Agriculture Act 1967 for the words "section 180 of the Town and Country Planning Act 1962" and "Part IV of that Act" there shall be substituted respectively the words "section 246 of the Town and Country Planning Act 1971" and "Part V of that Act".

In section 50(3)(*b*) of the said Act of 1967 for the words " section 221(1) of the Town and Country Planning Act 1962 " there shall be substituted the words " section 290(1) of the Town and Country Planning Act 1971 ".

In section 52(2)(*g*) for the words " the Town and Country Planning Act 1962 " there shall be substituted the words " the Town and Country Planning Act 1971 ".

The Civic Amenities Act 1967 (*c.* 69)
In section 28 of the Civic Amenities Act 1967—
  (*a*) in subsection (2) for the words " Subsections (1) to (5) of section 212 " and " section 211 " (in both places where they occur) there shall be substituted respectively the words " Section 281(1) to (5) " and " section 280 " ;
  (*b*) in subsection (3) for the words " Section 213 to 215 " and " section 213 " there shall be substituted respectively the words " Sections 282 to 284 " and " section 282 ".
In section 30(1) of the said Act of 1967 for the words "'the Planning Act' means the Town and Country Planning Act 1962 " there shall be substituted the words "' the Planning Act' means the Town and Country Planning Act 1971 "

The Leasehold Reform Act 1967 (*c.* 88)
In section 28(6)(*a*) of the Leasehold Reform Act 1967 (inserted by the Act of 1968) for the words " the Town and Country Planning Act 1962 " there shall be substituted the words " the Town and Country Planning Act 1971 ".

In Schedule 4 to the said Act of 1967, in paragraph 1(7), for the words " the Town and Country Planning Act 1962 " there shall be substituted the words " the Town and Country Planning Act 1971 "

The Public Expenditure and Receipts Act 1968 (*c.* 14)
In Schedule 3 to the Public Expenditure and Receipts Act 1968 for paragraph 7(*b*) there shall be substituted: —
  " (*b*) The Town and Country Planning Act 1971 (c. 78) section 145(9)."

The Agriculture (Miscellaneous Provisions) Act 1968 (*c.* 34)
In section 13(2) of the Agriculture (Miscellaneous Provisions) Act 1968 for the words " sections 67, 68 or 72 of the Town and Country Planning Act 1962 " there shall be substituted the words " section 112 or 120 of the Town and Country Planning Act 1971 ".

The Countryside Act 1968 (*c.* 41)
In section 33 of the Countryside Act 1968—
  (*a*) in subsections (1)(*e*) and (2) for the words " section 28 of the Town and Country Planning Act 1962 " there shall be substituted the words " section 51 of the Town and Country Planning Act 1971 " ;

(*b*) in subsection (2) for the words " section 136 of that Act ", " Part VIII of that Act ", " section 134(2) of that Act " and " the said section 28 " there shall be substituted respectively the words " section 189 of that Act ", " Part IX of that Act ", " section 187(2) of that Act " and " the said section 51."

In section 34(2) of the said Act of 1968 for the words " section 28 of the Town and Country Planning Act 1962 ", " section 136 of that Act ", " Part VIII of that Act ", " section 134(2) of that Act " and " the said section 28 " there shall be substituted respectively the words " section 51 of the Town and Country Planning Act 1971 ", " section 189 of that Act ", " Part IX of that Act ", " section 187(2) of that Act " and " the said section 51 ".

In section 40(1) of the said Act of 1968 for the words " section 2 of the Town and Country Planning Act 1962 " there shall be substituted the words " section 1 of the Town and Country Planning Act 1971 ".

In Schedule 4 to the said Act of 1968—

(*a*) in paragraph 1(1) for the words " Part I of Schedule 2 to the Town and Country Planning Act 1962 " there shall be substituted the words " Part I of Schedule 2 to the Town and Country Planning Act 1971 " ;

(*b*) in paragraph 1(2) for the words " the said Act of 1962 " there shall be substituted the words " the said Act of 1971 " ;

(*c*) in paragraph 1(5) for the words " the said Part I of Schedule 2 to the Act of 1962 " there shall be substituted the words " the said Part I of Schedule 2 to the Act of 1971 " ;

(*d*) in paragraph 2(1) for the words " Part II of Schedule 2 to the said Act of 1962 " there shall be substituted the words " Part II of Schedule 2 to the said Act of 1971 " ;

(*e*) in paragraph 3 for the words " section 2(2) of the said Act of 1962 " there shall be substituted the words " section 1(2) of the said Act of 1971 ".

The Caravan Sites Act 1968 (c. 52)

In section 8(3) of the Caravan Sites Act 1968 for the words " section 22 of the Town and Country Planning Act 1962 " there shall be substituted the words " section 35 of the Town and Country Planning Act 1971 ".

In section 16 of the said Act of 1968 for the words " Part III of the Town and Country Planning Act 1962 " there shall be substituted the words " Part III of the Town and Country Planning Act 1971 ".

The Town and Country Planning Act 1968 (c. 72)

In section 59 of the Town and Country Planning Act 1968 after the words " listed building " there shall be inserted the words " (as defined by section 54 of the Town and Country Planning Act 1971) "

M 2

The Transport Act 1968 (*c.* 73)

In section 108 of the Transport Act 1968—

(*a*) in subsection (1) for the words " section 36 of the Town and Country Planning Act 1962 ", " the said Act of 1962 " and " the said section 36 " there shall be substituted respectively the words " section 65 of the Town and Country Planning Act 1971 ", " the said Act of 1971 " and " the said section 65 " ;

(*b*) in subsection (3) for the words " the said Act of 1962 " there shall be substituted the words " the Town and Country Planning Act 1962.".

In section 112(3)(*d*) of the said Act of 1968 for the words " section 36 of the Town and Country Planning Act 1962 " there shall be substituted the words " section 65 of the Town and Country Planning Act 1971 ".

In section 139(1)(*b*) and (*c*) of the said Act of 1968 for the words " section 129, 135 or 136 of the Town and Country Planning Act 1962 ", " section 139 of the said Act of 1962 " and " section 142 of the said Act of 1962 " there shall be substituted respectively the words " section 180, 188 or 189 of the Town and Country Planning Act 1971 ", " section 193 of the said Act of 1971 " and " section 196 of the said Act of 1971 ".

In section 141(2) of the said Act of 1968 for the words " section 221(1) of the Town and Country Planning Act 1962 " there shall be substituted the words " section 290(1) of the Town and Country Planning Act 1971 ".

In section 142(2) of the said Act of 1962 for the words " the Town and Country Planning Act 1962 ", " Part III of that Act " and " Part VIII of that Act " there shall be substituted respectively the words " the Town and Country Planning Act 1971 ", " Part III or Part IV of that Act " and " Part IX of that Act ".

The Redundant Churches and other Religious
Buildings Act 1969 (1969 *c.* 22)

In section 2 of the Redundant Churches and other Religious Buildings Act 1969 for the words " Section 40 of the Town and Country Planning Act 1968 " and " section 32 of the Town and Country Planning Act 1962 " there shall be substituted respectively the words " Section 55 of the Town and Country Planning Act 1971 " and " section 54 of that Act ".

The Town and Country Planning (Scotland)
Act 1969 (*c.* 30)

In section 64(1) of the Town and Country Planning (Scotland) Act 1969 for the words " section 62 of the Town and Country Planning Act 1968 " there shall be substituted the words " section 48 of the Town and Country Planning Act 1971 ".

In Schedule 6 to the said Act of 1969 for the words set out in the first column below there shall be substituted the words set out opposite to them in the second column below :— Sch. 23

" the corresponding provision of the Act of 1968 " (in the Table in paragraph 1)	" the corresponding provision of the Act of 1971 ".
" section 41 of the Act of 1962 " (in paragraphs 1 and 8(3))	" section 40 of the Act of 1971 ".
the words in paragraph 2(a)	" (a) ' the Act of 1971 ' means the Town and Country Planning Act 1971 ".
" or in the Act of 1962 " (in paragraph 3)	" or in the Act of 1971 ".
" section 22 of the Act of 1962 " (in paragraph 8(2))	" section 35 of the Act of 1971 ".
" section 23 of the Act of 1962 " (in paragraph 8(2))	" section 36 of the Act of 1971 ".
" section 17(2) or (3) of the Act of 1962 " (in paragraphs 8(2)(b) and 10(c))	" section 29(2) or (3) of the Act of 1971 ".
" and the Act of 1962 " (in paragraph 8(4))	" and the Act of 1971 ".
" section 62(1)(a), (b) or (c) of the Act of 1968 " (in paragraph 10(b))	" section 48(1)(a), (b) or (c) of the Act of 1971 ".
" in either of the said sections 62(1)(a) or (b) " (in paragraph 10(c))	" in section 62(1)(a) or (b) of this Act or in section 48(1)(a) or (b) of the Act of 1971 ".
" Sections 22(5) and 23(5) of the Act of 1962 " (in paragraph 11(2))	" Sections 35(5) and 36(4) of the Act of 1971 ".
" sections 21(6) and 22(4) of the Act of 1968 " (in paragraph 11(2))	" paragraphs 2(2) and 3(4) of Schedule 9 to the Act of 1971 ".
" Part III of that Act " (in paragraph 11(2))	" that Schedule ".

The Housing Act 1969 (*c.* 33)

In section 33 of the Housing Act 1969—

(*a*) in subsection (1) for the words "section 92 of the Town and Country Planning Act 1968" there shall be substituted the words "section 212 of the Town and Country Planning Act 1971";

(*b*) in subsection (2) for the words "section 92 of that Act" and "section 93 of that Act" there shall be substituted respectively the words "section 212 of that Act" and "section 213 of that Act".

The Transport (London) Act 1969 (*c.* 35)

In section 2(2)(*b*) and (*c*) of the Transport (London) Act 1969 for the words "section 25(2) of the London Government Act 1963" there shall be substituted the words "paragraph 8(2) of Schedule 5 to the Town and Country Planning Act 1971", for the words "section 26(2) of that Act" there shall be substituted the words "section 26(2) of the London Government Act 1963 or the said Schedule 5", after the words "Part I of the Town and Country Planning Act 1968" there shall be inserted the words "or Part II of the Town and Country Planning Act 1971" and after the words "the said Part I" there shall be inserted the words "or the said Part II"

In section 30 of the said Act of 1969 for the words "section 24(6) of the London Government Act 1963" there shall be substituted the words "paragraph 7 of Schedule 3 to the Town and Country Planning Act 1971".

In Schedule 3 to the said Act of 1969, in paragraph 1(3), for the words "section 69 of the Town and Country Planning Act 1968" and "the Town and Country Planning Act 1962" there shall be substituted respectively the words "section 223 of the Town and Country Planning Act 1971" and "that Act".

In Schedule 5 to the said Act of 1969—

(*a*) in paragraph 12(2) (as amended by the Land Commission (Dissolution) Act 1971) for the words "section 67(1) of the Town and Country Planning Act 1968" there shall be substituted the words "section 43(1) of the . Town and Country Planning Act 1971";

(*b*) in paragraph 20(*a*)(ii) for the words "section 221(1) of the Town and Country Planning Act 1962" there shall be substituted the words "section 290(1) of the Town and Country Planning Act 1971";

(*c*) in paragraph 22(4) for the words "Section 127 of the Town and Country Planning Act 1962" there shall be substituted the words "Section 178 of the Town and Country Planning Act 1971";

(*d*) in paragraph 22(5) for the words " section 27 or section 28 of the said Act of 1962 " and " section 118 or, as the case may be, section 124 of that Act " there shall be substituted respectively the words " section 45 or 51 of the said Act of 1971 " and " section 164 or, as the case may be, section 170 of that Act ".

The Post Office Act 1969 (*c*. 48)

In section 57 of the Post Office Act 1969 for the words set out in the first column below there shall be substituted the words set out opposite to them in the second column below:—

" Sections 211(6) and 212(1) to (3) and (6) of the Town and Country Planning Act 1962 "	" Sections 280(9) and 281(1) to (3) and (6) of the Town and Country Planning Act 1971 "
" section 211(1) to (5) thereof "	" section 280(1) to (8) thereof "
" the said section 211 "	" the said section 280 "
" section 211(6) "	" section 280(9) "
" section 212(1) "	" section 281(1) "
" Section 128 of the Town and Country Planning Act 1962 "	" Section 179 of the Town and Country Planning Act 1971 "
" Part VII of that Act "	" Part VIII of that Act ".

In Schedule 4 to the said Act of 1969—

(*a*) in paragraph 89(1) for the words from " section 69(1) " to " undertakers) " and for the words " section 221(1) of the Town and Country Planning Act 1962 " there shall be substituted respectively the words " section 223(1) of the Town and Country Planning Act 1971 " and " section 222 of that Act " ; and in paragraph 89(2) for the words " The said section 69 " there shall be substituted the words " The said section 223 ".

(*b*) in paragraph 93(1) sub-paragraphs (xix) and (xxxi) shall be omitted and after sub-paragraph (xxxii) there shall be inserted—

" (xxxiii) sections 22, 40, 48, 49, 118(2), 127, 128, 129, 149, 165(3), 181, 182, 183, 186, 192, 206(6), 210(2), 213(3), 216, 223, 225 to 241, 245(7)(*b*), 225 and 281(6)(*b*) of, and Schedule 10, paragraphs 1 to 3 of Schedule 19, and Schedule 20 to, the Town and Country Planning Act 1971 " ;

and for the words " section 164 of the Town and Country Planning Act 1962 " there shall be substituted the words " section 230 of the Town and Country Planning Act 1971 ".

(c) in paragraph 93(2) sub-paragraphs (*i*) and (*q*) shall be omitted and after sub-paragraph (*r*) there shall be inserted—

" (*s*) sections 206(6), 225 to 241 and 281(6)(*b*) of, and Schedule 10 and paragraph 4 of Schedule 20 to, the Town and Country Planning Act 1971 ".

(d) in paragraph 93(4) sub-paragraphs (*c*) and (*h*) shall be omitted and after sub-paragraph (*i*) there shall be inserted—

" (*j*) sections 149(3), 165(3) and 225 to 241 of, and Schedule 10 to, the Town and Country Planning Act 1971 ".

In Schedule 9 to the said Act of 1969—

(a) in paragraph 27 for the words set out in the first column below (in each place where they occur in that paragraph) there shall be substituted the words set out opposite to them in the second column below : —

" Parts VI and XI of the Town and Country Planning Act 1962 "	" Parts VII and XII of the Town and Country Planning Act 1971 "
" Section 7 of the Control of Office and Industrial Development Act 1965 "	" Section 78 of the Town and Country Planning Act 1971 "
" section 19(4) of the Town and Country Planning Act 1962 "	" section 34 of the Town and Country Planning Act 1971 "
" Section 69 of the Town and Country Planning Act 1968 "	" Section 223 of the Town and Country Planning Act 1971 "
" for the purposes of the Town and Country Planning Act 1962 "	" for the purposes of the Town and Country Planning Act 1971 "
" Sections 65 and 66 of the Town and Country Planning Act 1968 "	" Sections 41 and 42 of the Town and (Country Planning Act 1971 "

" Subsections (3) and (5) of section 67 of the Town and Country Planning Act 1968 "	" Subsections (5) and (7) of section 43 of the Town and Country Planning Act 1971 "
" sections 65 and 66 of that Act "	" sections 41 and 42 of that Act "

(*b*) in paragraph 28 for the words set out in the first column below there shall be substituted the words set out opposite to them in the second column below: —

" section 199 of the Town and Country Planning Act 1962 "	" section 266 of the Town and Country Planning Act 1971 "
" section 16 of the said Act of 1962 "	" section 27 of the said Act of 1971 "
" the said Act of 1962 " (in paragraph 28(2))	" the said Act of 1971 "

(*c*) in paragraph 29 for the words " paragraph 12 of Schedule 13 to the Town and Country Planning Act 1962 " and " section 15 of the Town and Country Planning Act 1968 " there shall be substituted respectively the words " paragraph 34 of Schedule 24 to the Town and Country Planning Act 1971 " and " section 87 of the said Act of 1971 ".

The Courts Act 1971 (*c.* 23)

In section 89(6)(*b*) of the said Act of 1967 for the words " section 29(1) of the Town and Country Planning Act 1968 " there shall be substituted the words " section 113(1) of the Town and Country Planning Act 1971 ".

The Highways Act 1971 (*c.* 41)

In section 3 of the Highways Act 1971—

(*a*) in subsection (1) for the words " section 91 of the Town and Country Planning Act 1968 " and " the said section 91 " there shall be substituted respectively the words " section 211 of the Town and Country Planning Act 1971 " and " the said section 211 " ;

(*b*) in subsection (4) for the words " Section 154 of the Town and Country Planning Act 1962 ", " section 91 of the Town and Country Planning Act 1968 " and " subsections (2) and (6) of section 154 " there shall be substituted respectively the words " Section 215 of the Town and Country Planning Act 1971 ", " section 211 of that Act " and " subsections (2) and (7) of section 215 ".

In section 4(1) of the said Act of 1971 for the words " section 91 of the Town and Country Planning Act 1968 " there shall be substituted the words " section 211 of the Town and Country Planning Act 1971 ".

In section 8(1)(*a*) of the said Act of 1971 for the words " section 91 of the Town and Country Planning Act 1968 " there shall be substituted the words " section 211 of the Town and Country Planning Act 1971 "

In section 40(3) of the said Act of 1971 for the words " the Town and Country Planning Act 1962 " there shall be substituted the words " the Town and Country Planning Act 1971 "

In section 63 of the said Act of 1971—

(*a*) in subsection (1) for paragraphs (*a*) to (*d*) there shall be substituted—

" (*a*) sections 230 and 231 of the Town and Coun*ry Planning Act 1971 (power to extinguish rights of statutory undertakers over land acquired under certain enactments or appropriated by a local authority for planning purposes) ;

(*b*) section 232 of that Act (power of statutory undertakers to remove or re-site apparatus affected by development) ; and

(*c*) sections 237(2) and (3), 238 and 240 of that Act (compensation), so far as applicable for the purposes of the said se~tions 230, 231 and 232 ; "

and for the words " Part V of the said Act of 1962 " there shall be substituted the words " Part VI of the said Act of 1971 " ;

(*b*) in subsections (2) and (3) for the words " the said Acts of 1962 and 1968 " there shall be substituted the words " the said Act of 1971 ".

In Schedule 10 to the said Act of 1971—

(*a*) in paragraph 1 for the words " sections 164, 165, 170(2), 171 and 173 of the Town and Country Planning Act 1962 " there shall be substituted the words " sections 230, 231, 237(2), 238 and 240 of the Town and Country Planning Act 1971 " ;

(*b*) in paragraph 2 for the words " in subsection (4) of the said section 164 and in subsection (2) of the said section 165 " there shall be substituted the words " in subsection (4) of the said section 230 and in subsection (2) of the said section 231 " ;

(*c*) in paragraph 3 for the words from the beginning to " that section " there shall be substituted—

" 3. In subsection (1) of the said section 230 the words from ' if satisfied ' to ' appropriated ' shall be omitted and after that subsection there shall be inserted the following :—

' (1A) A notice under this section ' " ;

(*d*) in paragraph 4 for the words "subsections (1) and (2) of section 73 of the said Act of 1968" there shall be substituted the words "subsections (1) and (2) of section 232 of the said Act of 1971";

(*e*) in paragraph 5 for the words "subsections (3), (6) and (7) of the said section 73" there shall be substituted the words "subsections (3) and (6) of the said section 232, subsection (3) of the said section 237 and subsection (4) of the said section 238".

The Civil Aviation Act 1971 (*c.* 75)

In section 14 of the Civil Aviation Act 1971—

(*a*) in subsections (6) and (9) for the words "subsections (1) and (2) of section 158 of the Town and Country Planning Act 1962" and "section 153 of that Act" there shall be substituted respectively the words "subsections (1) and (2) of section 220 of the Town and Country Planning Act 1971" and "section 209 of that Act";

(*b*) in subsections (7) and (9)(*d*) for the words "section 82 of the Town and Country Planning Act 1962" and "Part V of that Act" there shall be substituted respectively the words "section 128 of the Town and Country Planning Act 1971" and "Part VI of that Act".

In section 17 of the Civil Aviation Act 1971 for the words set out in the first column below there shall be substituted the words set out opposite to them in the second column below:—

"section 118, 119, 123, 134(2) or 170(1) of the Town and Country Planning Act 1962"	"section 164, 165, 169, 187(2), or 237(1) of the Town and Country Planning Act 1971"
"the said section 118"	"the said section 164".
"section 27 of the said Act of 1962"	"section 45 of the said Act of 1971".
"section 122 of the said Act of 1962"	"section 168 of the said Act of 1971".
"section 129 of the said Act of 1962"	"section 180 of the said Act of 1971".
"section 130(2) or 133(1) of the said Act of 1962"	"section 181(2) or 186(1) of the said Act of 1971".
"the said section 27"	"the said section 45".
"Part III of the said Act of 1962"	"Part III of the said Act of 1971".

In Schedule 5 to the Civil Aviation Act 1971—

(*a*) in paragraph 5, sub-paragraphs (*q*) and (*bb*) shall be omitted and after paragraph (*ee*) there shall be inserted—

"(*ff*) sections 22, 40, 48, 49, 118(2), 127, 128, 129, 149, 165(3), 181, 182, 183, 186, 192, 206(6), 209(3)(*b*), 210(2), 213(3), 216, 223, 225 to 241 (except section 230 as applied by section 13 of the Opencast

SCH. 23

Coal Act 1958), 245(7)(*b*), 255, 281(6)(*b*) of, and Schedule 10, paragraphs 1 to 3 of Schedule 19, and Schedule 20 to, the Town and Country Planning Act 1971 ";

(*b*) in paragraph 6, sub-paragraphs (*f*) and (*l*) shall be omitted and after paragraph (*m*) there shall be inserted—

"(*n*) sections 206(6), 225 to 241 and 281(6)(*b*) of, and Schedule 10 and paragraph 4 of Schedule 20 to, the Town and Country Planning Act 1971 ";

(*c*) in paragraph 7, sub-paragraphs (*c*) and (*g*) shall be omitted and after paragraph (*h*) there shall be inserted—

"(*i*) sections 149(3), 165(3) and 225 to 241 of, and Schedule 10 to, the Town and Country Planning Act 1971 ";

(*d*) in paragraph 8 for the words " section 69 of the Town and Country Planning Act 1968 ", " the Town and Country Planning Act 1962 " and " Section 70(2) of the said Act of 1968 " there shall be substituted respectively the words " section 223 of the Town and Country Planning Act 1971 ", " that Act " and " Section 225(2)(*b*) of the said Act of 1971 ".

Section 292

SCHEDULE 24

TRANSITIONAL PROVISIONS AND SAVINGS

PART I

GENERAL PROVISIONS

1.—(1) In so far as anything done under an enactment repealed by this Act could have been done under a corresponding provision in this Act, it shall not be invalidated by the repeal but shall have effect as if done under that provision.

(2) Sub-paragraph (1) of this paragraph applies, in particular, to any order, regulation, rule, development plan or amendment or alteration of a development plan, application, objection, representation, determination, decision, reference, appeal, declaration, agreement, arrangement, claim or apportionment made, payment made or recovered, report or proposal submitted, list or amendment of a list compiled or made, permission granted, consent, approval or authorisation given, certificate, permit, information or direction issued or given, enforcement or other notice or copy served, published or registered, inquiry held, delegation effected, register kept and requirement imposed.

(3) In relation to any permission which (whether by virtue of an enactment repealed by this Act or otherwise) was deemed to be granted under an enactment repealed by this Act, sub-paragraph (1) of this paragraph shall apply as it applies to permission granted under such an enactment.

(4) Sub-paragraph (1) of this paragraph shall not apply to any regulations or order revoked as from the commencement of this Act in the exercise of the powers conferred by section 294.

2. Without prejudice to section 291 of, and Schedule 23 to, this Act, where any Act (whether passed before, or in the same Session as this Act) or any document refers, either expressly. or by implication, to an enactment repealed by this Act, the reference shall, except where the context otherwise requires, be construed as, or as including, a reference to the corresponding provision of this Act.

3. Where any period of time specified in an enactment repealed by this Act is current at the commencement of this Act, this Act shall have effect as if the corresponding provision thereof had been in force when that period began to run.

4. Without prejudice to paragraph 1 of this Schedule, any reference in this Act (whether express or implied) to a thing done or required or authorised to be done, or omitted to be done, or to an event which has occurred, under or for the purposes of or by reference to or in contravention of any provisions of this Act shall, except where the context otherwise requires, be construed as including a reference to the corresponding thing done or required or authorised to be done, or omitted, or to the corresponding event which occurred, as the case may be, under or for the purposes of or by reference to or in contravention of the corresponding provisions of the enactments repealed by this Act.

5.—(1) Nothing in this Act shall affect the enactments repealed thereby in their operation in relation to offences committed before the commencement of this Act.

(2) Where an offence, for the continuance of which a penalty was provided, has been committed under an enactment repealed by this Act, proceedings may be taken under this Act in respect of the continuance of the offence after the commencement of this Act, in the same manner as if the offence had been committed under the corresponding provision of this Act.

6.—(1) Any reference in this Act to an order or scheme made or confirmed under an enactment which is not repealed by, and re-enacted (with or without modifications) in, this Act, shall be construed as a reference to any order or scheme so made or confirmed whether before or after the commencement of this Act.

(2) Without prejudice to sub-paragraph (1) of this paragraph, any reference in this Act to an order or scheme made or confirmed under an enactment contained in the Highways Act 1959 or the New Towns Act 1965, or under any other such enactment as is mentioned in that sub-paragraph, shall be construed as including a reference to any order or scheme made or confirmed under any corresponding provisions of an enactment repealed by the said Act of 1959 or 1965, or repealed by the enactment in question, as the case may be. 1959 c. 25. 1965 c. 59.

7. In the preceding provisions of this Part of this Schedule, references (however expressed) to things done under enactments repealed by this Act shall be construed, in relation to the Act of 1962, as including references to things which, by virtue of paragraph 18 of Schedule 13 or Part I of Schedule 14 to the Act of 1962 fell to be treated as if done under that Act.

PART II
CENTRAL AND LOCAL ADMINISTRATION

Transfer of property and officers to local planning authorities

8. Nothing in this Act or the Act of 1962 shall affect, or be treated as having affected, the operation of any regulations made by virtue of section 101 of the Act of 1947 (provisions for transfer of property and officers to local planning authorities and for other matters consequential upon or supplementary to section 4 of that Act) in so far as any such regulations do not have effect in accordance with paragraph 1 of this Schedule.

Delegation of functions : compensation in respect of tree preservation orders

9. The terms of any delegation of functions by a local planning authority effected in pursuance of section 3 of the Act of 1962 before 4th August 1968 may be varied, so as to take account of any liability under section 175 of this Act of a local authority to whom functions have been so delegated, in such manner as the local planning authority and the other local authority may agree, or, if they fail to agree, as may be determined by the Secretary of State.

PART III
DEVELOPMENT PLANS

Designation of land as subject to compulsory acquisition

10. The repeal by the Act of 1968 of the provisions of Part II of the Act of 1962 relating to the designation of land as subject to compulsory acquisition and to land so designated (which are accordingly not reproduced in Schedule 5 to this Act) shall not affect proposals for alterations or additions to a development plan submitted under section 6 of that Act before 1st April 1969, and the powers of the Secretary of State in relation to such proposals shall continue to be exercisable as if those provisions had not been repealed and had been reproduced in that Schedule.

Effect of existing commencement orders

11.—(1) In relation to so much of any order made under section 105 of the Act of 1968 (commencement) as brings into operation any of the provisions of that Act specified in the Table below, paragraphs 1 and 2 of this Schedule shall have effect subject to this paragraph.

(2) So far as the order brings any of the said provisions into operation it shall have effect as if it were an order made under section 21(2) of this Act repealing the provisions of this Act set out opposite to the first-mentioned provisions in the said Table.

(3) Any transitional provision made by the order in connection with any of the said provisions of the Act of 1968 which it brings into operation shall be construed so as to produce a corresponding effect in connection with the provisions of this Act which by virtue of this paragraph it is treated as repealing.

Tᴀʙʟᴇ

Provision of Act of 1968 *brought into operation*	*Provision of this Act treated as repealed*
In Schedule 9, paragraph 5.	In Schedule 6, paragraphs 3, 4, 5 and 7.
In Schedule 9, paragraph 35(*a*).	In Schedule 6, paragraph 2.
In Schedule 9, paragraph 54.	In Schedule 6, paragraph 9.
In Schedule 9, paragraph 55(*a*) as respects sections 1 to 12 of the Act of 1962.	In Schedule 6, paragraph 11.
In Schedule 11, the repeal of any provision of Part II of the Act of 1962.	In Schedule 5, the corresponding provision of Part I.
In Schedule 11, the repeal of section 210 of the Act of 1962.	In Schedule 6, paragraph 6.
In Schedule 11, the repeal of the definition of " development plan " in section 221(1) of the Act of 1962.	In Schedule 6, paragraphs and 8.
In Schedule 11, the repeal in section 24(6) of the London Government Act 1963.	In Schedule 6, paragraph 10.
In Schedule 11, the repeal of any provision of sections 25 to 27 of the London Government Act 1963.	In Schedule 5, the corresponding provision of Part II.

Pᴀʀᴛ IV

Gᴇɴᴇʀᴀʟ Pʟᴀɴɴɪɴɢ Cᴏɴᴛʀᴏʟ

Planning permission : general

12. Subsection (1) of section 23 of this Act applies (subject to the provisions of that section) to the carrying out of development whether before or after the commencement of this Act, except that it does not apply to development carried out on or before the appointed day.

13. In sections 26 and 27 of this Act references to an application for planning permission do not include references to any application made before 16th August 1959.

14. Subsection (2)(*b*) of section 26, and the other provisions of that section relating to subsection (2)(*b*), do not apply to any application made before 1st April 1969.

15. Where by virtue of paragraph 12 of Schedule 14 to the Act of 1962 (works for making good war damage which were begun between the appointed day and 13th December 1950) any works were, immediately before the commencement of this Act, treated for the purposes of that Act as if planning permission had been granted unconditionally in respect thereof, those works shall be so treated for the purposes of this Act also.

16. For the purposes of paragraph 1 of this Schedule, any order made or having effect as if made by virtue of subsection (3) of section 19 of the Act of 1962, being an order which was saved on the repeal of that subsection by the Secretary of State for the Environment Order 1970, shall be treated as having been made under provisions of the Act of 1962 corresponding to those of section 31 of this Act notwithstanding the omission from the said section 31 of provisions corresponding to those of the said section 19 which were repealed as aforesaid.

Review of planning decisions and orders under Part V of Act of 1954

17. For the purposes of paragraph 1 of this Schedule, any direction given under section 45(3) or (4) of the Act of 1954, whether before or (by virtue of paragraph 79 of this Schedule) after the commencement of this Act, as well as any direction given under section 23 of that Act or section 25 of the Act of 1962, shall be treated as a direction which could have been given under provisions of the Act of 1962 corresponding to those of section 38 of this Act.

Duration of planning permission

18. Sections 41 and 42 of this Act do not apply to planning permissions granted or deemed to have been granted before 1st April 1969.

19.—(1) Subject to sub-paragraph (2) of this paragraph, every planning permission granted or deemed to have been granted before 1st April 1969 shall, if the development to which it relates had not been begun before the beginning of 1968, be deemed to have been granted subject to a condition that the development must be begun not later than the expiration of five years beginning with 1st April 1969.

(2) Sub-paragraph (1) of this paragraph does not apply—

(a) to any planning permission which was granted or deemed to be granted before 1st April 1969 subject to an express condition that the development to which it relates should be begun, or be completed, not later than a specified date or within a specified period ; or

(b) to any such planning permission as is mentioned in section 41(3) of this Act.

20.—(1) Subject to sub-paragraph (2) of this paragraph, where before 1st April 1969 outline planning permission (as defined by section 42 of this Act) has been granted for development consisting in or including the carrying out of building or other operations, and the development has not been begun before the beginning of 1968, that planning permission shall be deemed to have been granted subject to conditions to the following effect—

(a) that, in the case of any reserved matter (as defined in that section), application for approval must be made not later than the expiration of three years beginning with 1st April 1969 ; and

(b) that the development to which the permission relates must be begun not later than whichever is the later of the following dates—

(i) the expiration of five years from 1st April 1969 ; or

(ii) the expiration of two years from the final approval of the reserved matters or, in the case of approval on different dates, the final approval of the last such matter to be approved.

(2) Sub-paragraph (1) of this paragraph does not apply to any planning permission granted before 1st April 1969 subject to an express condition that the development to which it relates should be begun, or be completed, or that application for approval of any reserved matter should be made, not later than a specified date or within a specified period.

21.—(1) In sections 30(3), 43(1), (5), (6) and (7), 44 and 46(6) of this Act references to section 41 and 42 of this Act shall respectively include references to paragraphs 19 and 20 of this Schedule.

(2) In sections 147(3), 169(7), 180(4) and 237(5) of this Act references to the conditions referred to in sections 41 and 42 of this Act shall include references to the conditions referred to in paragraphs 19 and 20 of this Schedule.

22. Until the coming into operation of the first regulations to be made for the purposes of paragraph (c) of section 43(3) of this Act (or the corresponding enactment previously in force), regulations made for the purposes of section 99(2) of the Land Commission Act 1967 shall have effect as if made also for the purposes of that paragraph.

PART V

ADDITIONAL CONTROL IN SPECIAL CASES

Buildings of architectural or historic interest

23. Section 55(1) of this Act does not apply to any works executed or caused to be executed before 1st January 1969.

24.—(1) Where, before 1st January 1969, consent under a building preservation order was given, either by the local planning authority or by the Minister on appeal, for the execution of any works, the consent shall operate in respect of those works as listed building consent, subject to the same conditions (if any) as were attached to the consent under the building preservation order.

(2) In the case of demolition works for which consent was given under a building preservation order compliance with section 55(2)(b) of this Act shall not be required.

Replacement of trees

25. Section 59 of this Act does not apply in relation to planning permission granted before 28th August 1967.

Industrial development

26.—(1) So much of sections 66 to 72 of this Act as corresponds to provisions of the Industrial Development Act 1966 does not apply in relation to any application for planning permission made, or any industrial development certificate issued, before 19th August 1966; and so much of those sections as corresponds to provisions of the

Local Employment Act 1960 does not apply in relation to any application for planning permission made before 1st April 1960.

(2) Section 70(3)(*b*) of this Act does not apply to any industrial development certificate issued before 1st April 1969.

(3) In relation to an application for planning permission made before 1st April 1960, " industrial building " has the meaning assigned

to it in section 15 of the Distribution of Industry Act 1945.

(4) In relation to a relevant application (as defined in subsection (4) of section 68 of this Act) on which a planning decision was made before 5th August 1965, that section shall have effect as if it contained provisions corresponding to those of section 39 of the Act of 1962 without the amendments made by section 20 of the

Control of Office and Industrial Development Act 1965.

27. Without prejudice to Part I of this Schedule, any order in force at the commencement of this Act under section 19 of the Control of Office and Industrial Development Act 1965 shall have effect as an order under section 69 of this Act, and section 68 of this Act shall accordingly have effect subject to the provisions of that order.

Office development

28.—(1) Subject to paragraph 29 of this Schedule, sections 74 and 75 of this Act do not apply to any application for planning permission made before 5th August 1965.

(2) Section 78 of this Act does not apply to any planning permission granted before 5th August 1965 and, in relation to any planning permission granted on or after 5th August 1965 and before 1st April 1969, shall have effect as if it contained provisions corresponding to section 7 of the Control of Office and Industrial Development Act 1965 (so far as applicable to such a permission) without the amendments made by section 84 of the Act of 1968.

(3) Section 76(2) of this Act does not apply to any application for planning permission made before 1st April 1969 and sections 79 and 80 of this Act do not apply to any planning permission granted before 1st April 1969.

29.—(1) Sections 74 and 75 of this Act apply in relation to an application for planning permission to carry out development to which those sections apply on land within the metropolitan region (as defined in section 85 of this Act) which was made before 5th August 1965 but on which no planning decision had been made before that date.

(2) In its application, by virtue of sub-paragraph (1) of this paragraph, in relation to an application made before the said date, section 74(1) of this Act shall have effect as if for the words " together with the application " there were substituted the words " as soon as practicable after the permit is issued ".

30. Without prejudice to Part I of this Schedule, any order in force at the commencement of this Act under section 2(7) of the Control of Office and Industrial Development Act 1965 shall have effect as an order under subsection (8) of section 75 of this Act, and subsection (7) of that section shall accordingly have effect subject to the provisions of that order.

Part VI
Enforcement of Control
Enforcement notices under enactments in force before 1st April 1969

31.—(1) This paragraph applies to any enforcement notice which was served before 1st April 1969 on the owner and occupier of the land to which it related under section 45 of the Act of 1962 or which has effect by virtue of paragraph 1 of Schedule 14 to that Act or to which paragraph 32, 33 or 34 of this Schedule applies.

(2) In relation to any such notice—

 (*a*) the provisions of this Act (other than this Schedule) shall not apply ;

 (*b*) notwithstanding their repeal or amendment by the Act of 1968, the provisions of the Act of 1962 and of any other Act passed before the Act of 1968 shall, subject to the subsequent provisions of this Schedule, have effect as they would have had effect in relation to the notice if the Act of 1968 and this Act had not been passed.

(3) In relation to an enforcement notice served before 1st April 1969, paragraph 4 of Schedule 12 to this Act shall have effect as if the references to provisions of this Act were references to the corresponding provisions of the Act of 1962.

(4) Nothing in this paragraph shall prevent the withdrawal, on or after 1st April 1969, of an enforcement notice so served or the service thereafter of an enforcement notice under Part V of this Act.

Enforcement notices served before 29th August 1960

32.—(1) This paragraph applies to any enforcement notice served before 29th August 1960 on the owner and occupier of the land to which it related other than a notice to which paragraph 33 of this Schedule applies.

(2) In relation to any such notice—

 (*a*) sections 45 to 49 and section 177(1) of the Act of 1962 shall not apply ;

 (*b*) notwithstanding their repeal by the Act of 1962, sections 23 and 24 of the Act of 1947 shall have effect as they would have had effect in relation to the notice if the Act of 1962 had not been passed ;

(c) section 50 of the Act of 1962 shall not apply if the planning permission in question was granted before the said 29th August ;

(d) for the references in section 51(3) and (4) of the Act of 1962 to section 48 of that Act, there shall be substituted references to section 24(1) of the Act of 1947 and in section 51(5) of the Act of 1962 the words from " and no person " onwards shall be omitted.

Enforcement notices served by virtue of section 75 of Act of 1947

33.—(1) This paragraph applies to any enforcement notice served before the commencement of this Act by virtue of section 75 of the Act of 1947 (which related to development contravening planning control under the enactments repealed by that Act), being a notice which had not ceased for all purposes to have effect before the commencement of this Act.

(2) The repeal by the Act of 1962 of the said section 75 shall not invalidate any enforcement notice to which this paragraph applies.

(3) In relation to any such notice which was served before 29th August 1960 on the owner and occupier of the land to which it related—

(a) sections 45 to 49 of the Act of 1962 shall not apply ;

(b) sections 23 and 24 of the Act of 1947, as applied by section 75 of that Act, shall have effect as they would have had effect in relation to the notice if the Act of 1962 had not been passed ; and

(c) section 50 of that Act shall not apply if the planning permission in question was granted before the said 29th August.

(4) In relation to any enforcement notice to which this paragraph applies, not being a notice falling with sub-paragraph (3) of this paragraph, section 45(3) and (5) and (subject to paragraphs 35 to 38 of this Schedule) sections 46 to 51 of the Act of 1962 shall have effect as they have effect in relation to an enforcement notice served under section 45 of that Act.

34.—(1) In so far as an enforcement notice could, if the Act of 1962 and this Act had not been passed, have been served by virtue of section 75 of the Act of 1947 at a time on or after the date of the commencement of this Act, in respect of any works or use of land of a description to which that section applied, there shall subsist by virtue of this paragraph a corresponding power in the like circumstances to serve an enforcement notice (to the like effect as that which could have been so served) in respect of those works or that use of land.

(2) Section 45(3) and (5) and (subject to paragraphs 35 to 38 of this Schedule) sections 46 to 51 of the Act of 1962 shall have effect in relation to an enforcement notice served by virtue of this paragraph as they have effect in relation to an enforcement notice served under section 45 of that Act.

35.—(1) Where an enforcement notice falling within paragraph 33(4) of this Schedule, or an enforcement notice served by virtue of paragraph 34 of this Schedule, was or is served in respect of any works being government war works within the meaning of the Requisitioned Land and War Works Act 1945, then, subject to the following provisions of this paragraph—

> (*a*) if the steps required by the notice have been taken by the owner or occupier of the land, any expenses reasonably incurred in that behalf shall be recoverable from the authority by whom the notice was served ;

> (*b*) where the steps required by the notice have been taken by that authority, the authority shall not be entitled, under section 48 of the Act of 1962, to recover the expenses incurred by them in that behalf.

(2) Where under section 2(1)(*b*) of the Compensation (Defence) Act 1939 compensation has been paid equal to the full cost (as estimated for the purposes of that compensation) of taking the steps required by the enforcement notice, sub-paragraph (1) of this paragraph shall not apply.

(3) Where compensation has been paid in respect of the land, being either compensation under the said section 2(1)(*b*) but not equal to the full cost (as so estimated) of taking those steps, or being compensation under section 3(4) of that Act, the amount which by virtue of sub-paragraph (1) of this paragraph is recoverable from the authority by whom the enforcement notice was served, or, as the case may be, is not recoverable by that authority, shall be reduced so far as may be just having regard to the compensation so paid.

36. In the application of section 46 of the Act of 1962 to an enforcement notice by virtue of paragraph 33 or 34 of this Schedule, subsection (1) of that section shall have effect as if for paragraphs (*b*) and (*c*) there were substituted the following paragraph—

> " (*b*) that the works or use to which the enforcement notice relates are not works or a use to which section 75 of the Act of 1947 applies "

37.—(1) The power of a local planning authority under Part III of this Act to grant planning permission for the retention on land of buildings or works constructed or carried out before the date of application, or for the continuance of a use of land instituted before that date, shall include power to grant such permission in respect of any buildings or other works, or use of land, in respect of which that authority are empowered to serve an enforcement notice by virtue of paragraph 34 of this Schedule.

(2) Where permission is so granted, paragraphs 33 to 35 of this Schedule shall cease to apply to the works or use to which the permission relates, but without prejudice to the application thereto of any provisions of Part V of this Act with respect to the contravention of conditions subject to which planning permission has been granted.

38. Where in pursuance of paragraph 89(3) of this Schedule permission is granted for the retention on land of works, or the continuance of a use, authorised as mentioned in the said paragraph 89(3), such of the provisions of paragraphs 33 to 37 of this Schedule as (apart from this paragraph) would be applicable thereto shall cease to apply to those works or that use, but without prejudice to the application thereto of any provisions of Part V of this Act with respect to the contravention of conditions subject to which planning permission has been granted.

39. The repeal by the Act of 1962 of section 75 of the Act of 1947 shall not affect the operation of any regulations made under subsection (8) of that section (which enabled provision to be made by regulations for applying the provisions of that section to contraventions, committed before the appointed day, of restrictions under enactments other than those relating to town and country planning) or of the provisions of that section as applied by any such regulations.

Enforcement of building preservation orders

40. The repeal by the Act of 1968 of section 30 of the Act of 1962 shall not prevent a council from taking such proceedings as could have been taken but for the repeal to enforce any building preservation order made under that section and for securing the restoration of a building to its former state ; and in relation to any such proceedings the provisions of the order, and of any provisions of the Act of 1962 incorporated therein, shall continue to have the same effect as if the Act of 1968 had not been passed.

Enforcement of duties as to trees

41. Subsection (3) of section 103 of this Act shall have effect in relation to a notice served under that section before 1st April 1969 with the substitution for the words from " section 88(2) " to " directions " of the words " subsections (2) to (5) of section 46 of the Act of 1962 ".

PART VII

ACQUISITION OF LAND ETC.

Consent of Minister to acquisition, appropriation or disposal of land

42. Nothing in Part I of this Schedule shall be construed as validating any transaction whereby a local authority purported, in the exercise of a power conferred by an enactment repealed by the Act of 1962, but without the consent of the Minister then required by that enactment—

(a) to acquire land by agreement in pursuance of a contract made before 16th August 1959 ; or

(b) to appropriate or dispose of land before that date,

notwithstanding that the transaction could have been validly effected without that consent under the corresponding provisions of Part VI of this Act.

Existing compulsory purchase orders

43.—(1) Sections 112 and 113 of this Act shall not apply, and (notwithstanding their repeal by the Act of 1968) sections 67 and 68 of the Act of 1962 shall continue to apply to any land the acquisition of which was, immediately before 1st April 1969, authorised by a compulsory purchase order made by a local authority or statutory undertakers or by a Minister, or was then proposed to be authorised by such an order which had not been confirmed by a Minister or, as the case may be, had been prepared in draft by a Minister, but with respect to which a notice had then been published in accordance with paragraph 3(1)(*a*) of Schedule 1 to the Acquisition of Land (Authorisation Procedure) Act 1946.   1946 c. 49.

(2) The validity of a compulsory purchase order made under section 67, 68 or 69 of the Act of 1962 shall not be affected by the repeal by the Act of 1968 of the section under which the order was made ; and a compulsory purchase order made (but not confirmed), or made in draft, before the repeal of that section took effect may be confirmed or made thereunder as if the Act of 1968 had not been passed.

44. In relation to a compulsory purchase order confirmed under Part I of Schedule 1 to the Acquisition of Land (Authorisation Procedure) Act 1946, or made under Part II of that Schedule, before 1st January 1966, section 132(4) of this Act shall have effect—

(*a*) with the substitution for the words " the Compulsory Purchase Act 1965 in relation to " of the words " the Lands Clauses Acts as incorporated (by virtue of paragraph 1 of Schedule 2 to the Acquisition of Land (Authorisation Procedure) Act 1946) with " ; and

(*b*) with the substitution in paragraph (*b*) for the words " section 10 of the said Act of 1965 to the acquiring authority " of the words " section 68 of the Lands Clauses Consolidation Act 1845, to the promoters of the underaking ".

45. The repeals effected by the Act of 1962 shall not affect the validity of any order authorising the compulsory acquisition of any land—

(*a*) under section 37(2) of the Act of 1947 (which enabled the Minister of Works or the Postmaster-General, during the period before a development plan had become operative with respect to any area, to be authorised in certain circumstances to acquire land compulsorily) ;

(*b*) under section 38(2) of that Act (which enabled certain local authorities, during any such period, to be authorised in certain circumstances to acquire land compulsorily) ; or

(*c*) under subsection (3) of section 38 of that Act in a case where the power conferred by that subsection was exercisable in lieu of the exercise of the power conferred by subsection (2) thereof,

or of any notice served or other thing done in pursuance of any such order.

46. Any compulsory purchase order made or confirmed under Part I of the Act of 1944 (whether before or after the appointed day) shall, if in force immediately before the commencement of this Act,

continue in force and shall have effect as if it had been made under the Acquisition of Land (Authorisation Procedure) Act 1946 as applied by Part VI of this Act.

Application of Part VI to land acquired or authorised to be acquired under previous enactments

47. The provisions of Part VI of this Act shall have effect in relation to land acquired, or authorised to be acquired, in pursuance of any such order as is mentioned in paragraph 45 of this Schedule as if—

    (*a*) in the case of land acquired, or authorised to be acquired, by a local authority, the land had been acquired, or authorised to be acquired, by that local authority under section 112 of this Act ;

    (*b*) in the case of land acquired, or authorised to be acquired, by a Minister, the land had been acquired, or authorised to be acquired, by that Minister under section 113 of this Act.

48. For the purposes of Part VI of this Act—

    (*a*) any land acquired by a local authority in pursuance of a compulsory purchase order under Part I of the Act of 1944 shall be deemed to have been acquired under section 112 of this Act ;

    (*b*) any land acquired by a Minister in pursuance of any such order shall be deemed to have been acquired by him under section 113 of this Act ;

    (*c*) any land acquired by a local authority by agreement under the Act of 1944 shall be deemed to have been acquired under section 119 of this Act.

49. The reference in subsection (1) of section 133 of this Act to the acquisition of land under section 68 or 71 of the Act of 1962 shall include a reference to the acquisition of land under section 38 or 40 of the Act of 1947 ; and the reference in that subsection to the appropriation of land for purposes for which land can be or could have been acquired under the provisions there mentioned is a reference to the appropriation of land for those purposes whether before or after the commencement of this Act.

Provisions as to Central Land Board

50. Section 127 of this Act shall have effect in relation to land acquired by the Central Land Board under section 43 of the Act of 1947 as it has effect in relation to land acquired by a local authority for planning purposes (as defined by section 133(1) of this Act).

Application of Small Tenements Recovery Act 1838

51. Until such day as may be appointed under section 35(5) of the Rent Act 1965, section 130 of this Act shall have effect as if it contained a provision corresponding to section 84(4) of the Act of 1962, the reference to Part V of that Act being construed as a reference to Part VI of this Act.

PART VIII

COMPENSATION UNDER PART VII OF THIS ACT

Compensation under Part V of Act of 1954

52.—(1) Subject to the following provisions of this paragraph, for the purposes of the construction of sections 158 to 161 of this Act in accordance with Part I of this Schedule, any compensation (whether by way of principal or interest) under Part V of the Act of 1954, and any claim for, or notice registered in respect of, any such compensation, as well as any compensation under Part II of that Act, or any claim for, or notice registered in respect of, compensation under the said Part II, shall be treated as compensation or, as the case may be, a claim for, or a notice registered in respect of compensation, under provisions of that Act corresponding to those of Part VII of this Act.

(2) For the purposes of the construction of section 158 of this Act in accordance with sub-paragraph (1) of this paragraph in relation to Part V of the Act of 1954, any reference to a planning decision shall be construed as including a reference to an order under section 21 of the Act of 1947.

(3) Where compensation under Part V of the Act of 1954 became or becomes payable in respect of an order modifying planning permission, then (notwithstanding anything in the preceding provisions of this paragraph) the provisions of sections 159 and 161 of this Act shall not apply to development in accordance with that permission as modified by the order.

Provision excluding recovery of compensation

53. For the purposes of the construction, in accordance with Part I of this Schedule, of section 160(4) of this Act—

    (*a*) the provisions of section 52(6) of the Act of 1954 as originally enacted ; and

    (*b*) those provisions as applied by any regulations made under section 52(8) of that Act,

as well as the provisions of the said section 52(6) as amended by section 51 of the Act of 1959, shall be treated as provisions corresponding to those of section 257 of this Act.

PART IX

COMPENSATION UNDER PART VIII OF THIS ACT

Compensation to statutory undertakers

54. Subsection (3) of section 165 of this Act shall not apply where the refusal or grant of planning permission referred to in subsection (1)(*c*) of that section was before 6th December 1968.

Contribution by Secretary of State towards compensation

55. For the purposes of the construction of section 167(1) of this Act in accordance with Part I of this Schedule, any compensation which could have been claimed and would have been payable under Part V of the Act of 1954, as well as any compensation which could have been claimed and would have been payable under Part II of

that Act, shall be treated as compensation which could have been claimed and would have been payable under provisions of that Act corresponding to the provisions of Part VII of this Act.

Recovery of compensation

56. For the purposes of the construction of section 168(3) of this Act in accordance with Part I of this Schedule, any grant paid—

(a) under the provisions of the section substituted by section 50 of the Act of 1954 for section 93 of the Act of 1947, but without the amendments made by the Local Government Act 1958 ; or

(b) under the provisions of Part IX of the Act of 1947 as originally enacted,

as well as any grant paid under the provisions of the said section 93 as in force immediately before the commencement of the Act of 1962, shall be treated as a grant paid under provisions corresponding to those of Part XIII of this Act.

PART X
BLIGHT NOTICES
Notices served before 1st April 1969

57. In relation to a notice served under section 139 of the Act of 1962 before 1st April 1969, and to any hereditament or agricultural unit which is the subject of the notice, sections 194 to 207 of this Act shall, on and after that date, have effect as if they contained the provisions in sections 140 to 151 of the Act of 1962 without any of the amendments made by Part IV of the Act of 1968.

Temporary inclusion of additional description of blighted land

58.—(1) For the purposes of the application of sections 192 to 207 of this Act to a district to which this paragraph applies—

(a) the description of land contained in section 138(1)(b) of the Act of 1962 shall be included among the specified descriptions as defined in section 192(6) of this Act ; and

(b) in sections 193(3) and 206(2) of this Act references to paragraph (b) of section 192(1) of this Act shall include references to the said section 138(1)(b).

(2) This paragraph applies to any district for which no local plan is in force under Part II of this Act—

(a) allocating any land in the district for the purposes of such functions as are mentioned in section 192(1)(a) of this Act ; or

(b) defining any land in the district as the site of proposed development for the purposes of any such functions.

PART XI
HIGHWAYS
Provisions as to telegraphic lines

59.—(1) In relation to an order made under section 153 of the Act of 1962 before 1st October 1969 or, as the case may be, an order under section 155 of that Act in respect of which the notice required by section 154 of that Act was published before that date, section 220(1), (2) and (3) of this Act shall have effect as if references to a telegraphic line belonging to or used by the Post Office were references to a telegraphic line belonging to or used by the Postmaster-General.

(2) Where the period referred to in paragraph (*a*) of subsection (3) of section 220 of this Act began to run before, and was current on, the said date, that paragraph shall have effect as if the reference to notice having been given by the Post Office before the end of that period included a reference to notice having been so given by the Postmaster-General, and paragraph (*c*) of that subsection shall have effect as if the reference to the Post Office included a reference to the Postmaster-General.

PART XII

STATUTORY UNDERTAKERS

Application of ss. 225 to 231 to matters arising before 6th December 1968

60.—(1) This paragraph shall have effect as respects the application, by virtue of Part I of this Schedule, of the provisions of this Act hereinafter specified in relation to matters arising before 6th December 1968 (in this paragraph referred to as " the relevant date ").

(2) In relation to any application for planning permission made before the relevant date or any appeal from the decision on an application so made, section 225 of this Act shall have effect as if it contained provisions corresponding to section 159(2) and (5) of the Act of 1962 and as if subsection (2)(*b*) were omitted.

(3) In relation to any decision made before the relevant date, section 226 of this Act shall have effect as if it contained provisions corresponding to section 160(1) of the Act of 1962.

(4) In relation to any order of which notice has been given under section 161(2) of the Act of 1962 before the relevant date, section 227 of this Act shall have effect as if it contained provisions corresponding to the said section 161(2).

(5) In relation to any order of which notice has been given under section 162(2) of the Act of 1962 before the relevant date, section 228 of this Act shall have effect as if it contained provisions corresponding to the said section 162(2).

(6) In relation to a compulsory purchase order made or confirmed before the relevant date, section 229 of this Act shall have effect as if it contained provisions corresponding to section 163(3)(*b*) of the Act of 1962.

(7) In relation to any order made before the relevant date under section 164 of the Act of 1962, section 231 of this Act shall have effect as if it contained provisions corresponding to section 165(3) of the Act of 1962.

Extinguishment of rights : notices served before 6th December 1968

61. In relation to a notice served before 6th December 1968, section 230(1) of this Act shall have effect with the omission—

(*a*) of the words from " if satisfied " to " appropriated " ; and

(*b*) of the words from " of twenty-eight days " to " as may be ".

Application of section 230 *to land acquired by Central Land Board*

62. In section 230(1) of this Act, the reference to land acquired by a Minister, a local authority or statutory undertakers under Part VI of this Act shall be construed as including a reference to land acquired by the Central Land Board under Part IV of the Act of 1947, as well as to land acquired under the said Part IV by a Minister, a local authority or statutory undertakers.

Right to compensation for decisions made before 6th December 1968

63. In its application, by virtue of Part I of this Schedule, to a decision made before 6th December 1968, section 237 of this Act shall have effect as if for subsection (1)(*a*) there were substituted provisions corresponding to section 170(1)(*a*) and (*b*) of the Act of 1962 and as if subsection (5) contained a proviso corresponding to that in section 170(3) of the Act of 1962.

Enactments applying section 25 *of Act of* 1944

64.—(1) This paragraph shall have effect for the purposes of any enactment which applies the provisions of section 25 of the Act of 1944 with adaptations consisting of or including adaptations of the references in that section to a purchasing authority or to the purchasing or appropriating authority.

1889 c. 63.

(2) Any such enactment shall be construed (in accordance with Part I of this Schedule or section 38 of the Interpretation Act 1889) as applying the provisions of section 230· and section 237(2) of this Act with corresponding adaptations of the references in those provisions to a Minister, a local authority or statutory undertakers, or to the acquiring or appropriating authority, as the case may require.

PART XIII

VALIDITY OF PLANNING DECISIONS ETC.

Orders made and action taken before 16*th August* 1959

65.—(1) Notwithstanding anything in Part I of this Schedule, the provisions of section 242 of this Act shall not have effect in relation to—

(*a*) any order made before 16th August 1959 under any of the provisions of the Act of 1947 corresponding to the provisions of this Act under which the orders mentioned in subsection (2) of that section can be made ; or

(*b*) any action on the part of the Minister of Housing and Local Government taken before the said 16th August under any of the provisions of that Act or of the Act of 1954 corresponding to the provisions of this Act under which action of the descriptions mentioned in subsection (3) of that section can be taken,

and section 245 does not apply to any such order or action as is mentioned in this sub-paragraph.

(2) In relation to any action which, in accordance with any provisions of the Act of 1947 corresponding to provisions of Part XI of this Act, was required to be taken by the said Minister and the appropriate Minister, the reference in sub-paragraph (1) of this paragraph to the said Minister shall be construed as a reference to that Minister and the appropriate Minister.

66. Section 247 of this Act does not apply to any decision of the Minister of Housing and Local Government made before 16th August 1959 under any of the provisions of the Act of 1947 corresponding to the provisions of this Act mentioned in subsection (2) of that section.

Notices relating to waste land and listed buildings

67.—(1) Section 243(3) of this Act does not apply to any notice served before 29th August 1960 under section 33(1) of the Act of 1947.

(2) Notwithstanding anything in this Act or the Act of 1968, section 177(3) of the Act of 1962 shall continue to have effect as originally enacted in relation to a notice served (or treated as served) under section 52 of the Act of 1962 on or after 29th August 1960 and before 1st January 1969.

Directions under Part V of Act of 1954

68. For the purposes of the construction, in accordance with Part I of this Schedule, of section 242(3)(c) of this Act (but without prejudice to paragraph 65(1) of this Schedule) any directions given on or after 16th August 1959 by the Minister of Housing and Local Government under section 45(3) or (4) of the Act of 1954, as well as any direction given by the Minister on or after that day under section 23 of that Act, shall be treated as a direction given under provisions of that Act corresponding to the provisions of section 38 of this Act.

PART XIV

FINANCIAL PROVISIONS

Grants

69. Nothing in this Act shall affect the payment (whether before or after the commencement of this Act) of any grant in respect of any period before the commencement of this Act.

70. Section 250 of this Act does not apply to any year earlier than the year ending on 31st March 1968.

Recovery of sums from acquiring authorities

71.—(1) In relation to any acquisition or sale of an interest in land in pursuance of a notice to treat served, or contract made, before 30th October 1958—

(a) Section 257 of this Act shall not apply ;

(b) the repeals effected by the Act of 1962 shall not affect any right of recovering any sum in respect thereof under the provisions of section 52(6) of the Act of 1954 as originally enacted, or under those provisions as applied by regulations made under section 52(8) of that Act.

(2) Subject to sub-paragraph (1) of this paragraph, section 257 of this Act shall have effect in relation to interests in land acquired or sold as therein mentioned whether before or after the commencement of this Act ; and for the purposes of the construction of that section in accordance with Part I of this Schedule, any notice registered under the provisions of section 28 of the Act of 1954 as applied by Part V of that Act, as well as any notice registered under those provisions as applied by Part IV of that Act, shall be treated as a notice registered under provisions of that Act corresponding to the provisions of this Act referred to in section 257 of this Act, and references in that section to compensation specified in a notice shall be construed accordingly.

72. Section 258 of this Act shall have effect in relation to interests in land acquired or sold as therein mentioned whether before or after the commencement of this Act, except that it shall not have effect in relation to any acquisition or sale in pursuance of a notice to treat served, or contract made, before 6th August 1947.

Treatment of sums received under section 261(4) before
1st April 1968

73. Any sums received by the Minister of Housing and Local Government before 1st April 1968 by virtue of the provisions re-enacted in the provisions mentioned in section 261(4) of this Act shall be treated as paid in satisfaction, or part satisfaction, of such one or more of the instalments payable under subsections (2) and (3) of that section as the Treasury may determine.

Part XV

Special Cases

Minerals

S.I. 1948/1522.   74. The revocation by paragraph 43(1) of Schedule 14 to the Act of 1962 of Regulation 6 of the Town and Country Planning (Modification of Mines Act) Regulations 1948 (being regulations made under the provisions of the Act of 1947 corresponding to section 265 of this Act) does not affect the operation of any of the other provisions of those regulations in accordance with Part I of this Schedule.

S.I. 1954/1706.   75.—(1) Regulation 10 of the Town and Country Planning (Minerals) Regulations 1954, and section 79 of the Act of 1947 as applied by that regulation, shall (notwithstanding the repeals effected by the Act of 1962) have effect after the date of the commencement of this Act in any case where they would have had effect after that date if the Act of 1962 had not been passed.

(2) The said Regulation 10, in so far as it has effect in accordance with sub-paragraph (1) of this paragraph, may be revoked or varied by regulations made under section 264 of this Act as if it were a regulation made under that section.

(3) In this paragraph any reference to the said Regulation 10 is a reference to that regulation as varied by any subsequent regulations.

76. In relation to any time before 10th April 1966, section 265 of this Act shall have effect as if for references to the Mines (Working 1966 c. 4. Facilities and Support) Act 1966 there were substituted references to the Mines (Working Facilities and Support) Act 1923 ; and accord- 1923 c. 20. ingly regulations made before that date which are in force at the commencement of this Act under section 198 of the Act of 1962, shall have effect as if made under the said section 265 and as if, in relation to any time on or after the said 10th April, references in them to the said Act of 1923 were references to the corresponding provisions of the said Act of 1966.

National Coal Board

77. Until the coming into operation of the first regulations made under section 204 of the Act of 1962 or section 273 of this Act after 6th December 1968 the provisions of Part X of the Act of 1962 applied by regulations under section 204(1) of the Act of 1962 in relation to the National Coal Board and land of that Board shall have effect as so applied as if Part XI of this Act contained provisions corresponding to Part X of the Act of 1962 without the amendments made by sections 69 to 71 of the Act of 1968.

Ecclesiastical property, settled land and land of universities and colleges

78. For the purposes of the construction of sections 274 and 275 of this Act in accordance with Part I of this Schedule, the provisions of section 46 of the Act of 1954, as well as the provisions of section 41 of that Act, shall be treated as provisions corresponding to those of section 168 of this Act.

PART XVI
MISCELLANEOUS AND SUPPLEMENTARY
Rights and liabilities in respect of certain payments

79.—(1) The repeal effected by section 223 of the Act of 1962 shall not affect any right to, or claim for, or any liability in respect of, any payment under an enactment to which this paragraph applies ; and any such right, claim or liability shall have effect and may be enforced, and moneys in respect of any such payment shall be applicable or may be raised, in accordance with the provisions of the enactment in question (including the provisions of any other enactment which, immediately before the commencement of that

Act, had effect for the purposes of that enactment) as if the Act of 1962 and this Act had not been passed, and any direction or proceedings relating thereto may be given, brought or continued accordingly.

(2) This paragraph applies to the following enactments, that is to say—

    (*a*) Parts I and V of the Act of 1954 ;

    (*b*) section 52(1) to (5) of that Act ;

    (*c*) the scheme made under section 59 of the Act of 1947 ;

    (*d*) any other enactment which (if contained in an Act) was not repealed by, and re-enacted (with or without modifications) in the Act of 1962 or (if not contained in an Act) has effect otherwise than by virtue of an enactment so repealed and re-enacted.

(3) Without prejudice to the preceding provisions of this paragraph, any proceedings relating to any such claim as is mentioned in section 135(1) of this Act may be brought or continued, and shall be determined in accordance with the relevant provisions (that is to say, the provisions of the Act of 1947 and of Schedule 1 to the Act of 1954 and any other enactment having effect for the purposes thereof) as if the Act of 1962 and this Act had not been passed.

(4) Sub-paragraph (1) of this paragraph shall have effect in relation to any such right, claim or liability as is therein mentioned notwithstanding that, immediately before the commencement of this Act, the right, claim or liability had not yet accrued or been made or become enforceable, as the case may be :

Provided that, in relation to any such claim which had not been made before the commencement of this Act, so much of that sub-paragraph as provides that the claim shall have effect in accordance with the provisions therein mentioned shall be construed as providing that the claim may be made in accordance with those provisions, and, when made, shall have effect accordingly.

Registration of payments under s. 59 of Act of 1954

80.—(1) The repeals effected by the Act of 1962 shall not affect the operation of subsections (1) and (2) of section 57 of the Act of 1954, in so far as those subsections would have continued to have effect if the Act of 1962 had not been passed.

(2) In subsection (1) of the said section 57, the references to subsection (7) of section 52 of that Act and to paragraph (*b*) of the proviso to that subsection shall be construed as including references respectively to subsection (1) and to subsection (2) of section 258 of this Act.

Entitlement to, and amount of, compensation etc. in cases arising before 25th February 1963

81. Notwithstanding Part I of this Schedule, the following provisions of this Act, that is to say, sections 168(4), 169(3)(*c*) and (6), in section 180(2) the words " or which would contravene the con-

dition set out in Schedule 18 to this Act ", section 180(3), section 278(1) to (4), paragraph 13 of Schedule 8 and Schedule 18 do not affect—

(a) any determination arising out of a notice to treat served before 25th February 1963, or served at any time in respect of a purchase notice or notice under section 139 of the Act of 1962 (or any corresponding enactment previously in force) which was served before that date ;

(b) any other determination under the Act of 1962 in respect of or arising out of a purchase notice served before that date ;

(c) any claim for compensation under section 118 or 123 of the Act of 1962 (or any corresponding enactment previously in force) which arose before that date.

Definition of " local authority "

82.—(1) In relation to any time before 1st April 1965 the definition of " local authority " in section 290(1) of this Act shall have effect—

(a) as if it included a reference to a metropolitan borough ; and

(b) as if for the words " the Greater London Council, the council of a London borough and any other authority (except the Receiver for the Metropolitan Police District) who are " there were substituted the words " and any other authority being ".

(2) For the purposes of the construction, in accordance with Part I of this Schedule, of any enactment which incorporates the definition of " local authority " in the Act of 1947, section 215 and the reference to it in section 290(1) of this Act shall be disregarded.

Saving for powers of Post Office

83. Except as provided by section 220 of this Act, nothing in the provisions of this Act specified in Part I of Schedule 21 to this Act or in any order or regulations made thereunder shall affect any powers or duties of the Post Office under the provisions of the Telegraph Acts 1863 to 1916 or apply to any telegraphic lines (within the meaning of the Telegraph Act 1878) placed or maintained 1878 c. 76. by virtue of any of the provisions of those Acts.

Saving in respect of works below high-water mark

84. Nothing in the provisions of this Act specified in Part I of Schedule 21 to this Act shall authorise the execution of any works (whether of construction, demolition or alteration) on, over or under tidal lands below high-water of ordinary spring tides, except—

(a) with the consent of any persons whose consent would have been required if the Act of 1962 had not been passed ; and

(b) in accordance with such plans and sections, and subject to such restrictions and conditions, as may be approved by the Board of Trade or the Secretary of State before the works are begun.

Land Compensation Act 1961 *s.* 31

1961 c. 33.   85. Any reference in this Act to the power conferred by section 31 of the Land Compensation Act 1961 to withdraw a notice to treat shall, in relation to any notice to treat falling within section 41 of that Act, be construed as a reference to the corresponding power
1919 c. 57.   conferred by section 5(2) of the Acquisition of Land (Assessment of Compensation) Act 1919.

References to Ministers : previous Transfer of Functions Orders

86.—(1) Where the functions of a Minister under any enactment re-enacted or referred to in this Act have at any time been exercisable by another Minister or other Ministers, references in the relevant provision of this Act shall, as respects any such time, be construed as references to the other Minister or Ministers.

(2) In this paragraph " Minister " includes the Board of Trade and the Treasury.

Schemes and agreements under enactments repealed by Act of 1947

87.—(1) The repeal effected by the Act of 1962 shall not affect the operation of—

> (*a*) any such scheme as was mentioned in paragraph 7 of Schedule 10 to the Act of 1947 (which related to certain
1932 c. 48.   schemes made under the Town and Country Planning Act
1925 c. 16.   1932 and the Town Planning Act 1925) in so far as, by virtue of that paragraph, the scheme continued to have effect immediately before the commencement of this Act ; or

> (*b*) any order made under that paragraph (which empowered the Minister to make provision by order for winding up any such scheme) in so far as the order continued to have effect immediately before the commencement of this Act.

(2) Any power to make orders under paragraph 7 of that Schedule shall continue to be exercisable notwithstanding the said repeal.

88.—(1) The repeal effected by the Act of 1962 shall not affect the operation of any such agreement as was mentioned in paragraph 10 of Schedule 10 to the Act of 1947 (which related to certain agreements made before the appointed day for restricting the planning, development or use of land), or of any order discharging or modifying a restriction imposed by such an agreement, in so far as any such agreement or order was in force immediately before the commencement of this Act ; and any such agreement may be enforced as if the Act of 1962 and this Act had not been passed.

(2) Nothing in any such agreement shall be construed as restricting the exercise, in relation to land to which the agreement applies, of any powers exercisable by any Minister or authority under this Act, so long as those powers are exercised in accordance with the

provisions of the development plan, or in accordance with any directions which may have been given by the Secretary of State by virtue of paragraph 6 of Schedule 6 to this Act, or as requiring the exercise of any such powers otherwise than in accordance with such provisions or directions.

(3) If the Secretary of State is satisfied, on application made to him by any person being a party to any such agreement, or a person entitled to land affected thereby, or by the local planning authority, that any restriction on the development or use of the land imposed by the agreement is inconsistent with the proper planning or development of the area comprising the land, he may by order discharge or modify that restriction so far as appears to him to be expedient.

(4) Without prejudice to sub-paragraph (3) of this paragraph, if any person being a party to any such agreement (whether as originally made or as modified under that sub-paragraph), or a person entitled to land affected thereby, claims that the agreement ought to be modified or rescinded, having regard to the provisions of this Act or to anything done under this Act or under the Act of 1947 or the Act of 1962, he may refer to arbitration the question whether the agreement should be so modified or rescinded, and the arbitrator may make such award as appears to him to be just having regard to all the circumstances.

Development authorised under enactments repealed by Act of 1947

89.—(1) Where any works on land existing at the appointed day, or any use to which land was put on that day, had been authorised by a permission granted subject to conditions under a scheme under the Town and Country Planning Act 1932 (or under an enactment 1932 c. 48. repealed by that Act) or under an order made under section 10(1) of that Act (in the subsequent provisions of this Schedule referred to as " a planning scheme " and " an interim development order ") the provisions of Parts III and V of this Act, the provisions of Part IX of this Act relating to purchase notices, and the provisions of sections 225 to 228 of this Act, shall apply in relation to those works or that use as if the conditions had been imposed on the grant of planning permission.

(2) Without prejudice to the generality of sub-paragraph (1) of this paragraph, where any such permission was granted subject to conditions (in whatever form) restricting the period for which the works or use might be continued on the land, then, if that period had not expired at the appointed day and the works were or are not removed, or the use discontinued, at the end of that period, the provisions of Part V of this Act relating to enforcement notices shall apply in relation thereto as if the works had been carried out, or the use begun, as the case may be, at the end of that period and without the grant of planning permission in that behalf.

(3) The power of a local planning authority under Part III of this Act to grant permission for the retention on land of buildings or works constructed or carried out before the date of the application, or the continuance of any use of land instituted before that date,

shall include power to grant such permission in respect of any works or use authorised by a permission granted subject to any such conditions as are mentioned in sub-paragraph (2) of this paragraph.

1946 c. 35.

(4) Where at any time before the appointed day it was determined under the Building Restrictions (War-Time Contraventions) Act 1946 that any works on land or any use of land should be deemed to comply with planning control (within the meaning of that Act) subject to any conditions specified in the determination, the provisions of this paragraph shall apply in relation to those works or that use as if those conditions had been imposed on the grant of permission under a planning scheme or an interim development order.

(5) Provision may be made by regulations under this Act for applying the preceding provisions of this paragraph, subject to such adaptations and modifications as may be specified in the regulations, to works on land carried out, or uses of land begun, at any time before the appointed day, in accordance with permission granted subject to conditions under any enactment repealed by the Act of 1947, other than the enactments relating to town and country planning ; and for the purposes of this provision any works or use in respect of which a notice was served under subsection (1) of 1943 c. 34. section 1 of the Restriction of Ribbon Development (Temporary Development) Act 1943 or was deemed by virtue of subsection (4) of that section to have been so served, shall be treated as carried out or begun in accordance with permission granted subject to a condition restricting the period for which the works or use might be continued on the land.

90.—(1) Where permission for any development of land was granted, at any time after 21st July 1943 and before the appointed day, on an application in that behalf made under an interim development order, then, if and so far as that development was not carried out before the appointed day and the permission was in force immediately before that day, planning permission shall be deemed to have been granted in respect thereof subject to the like conditions (if any) as were imposed by the permission under the interim development order as it had effect immediately before the appointed day ;

Provided that this sub-paragraph shall not apply in relation to any development for which permission was required before the 1935 c. 47. appointed day under the Restriction of Ribbon Development Act 1935 unless that permission was also granted.

(2) The provisions of section 45 of this Act shall apply in relation to planning permission which is deemed to have been granted by virtue of this paragraph as if it had been granted on an application under Part III of this Act ; and, in relation to any order made under that section for the revocation or modification of any such permission, any reference in section 164(3) of this Act to the grant of permission shall be construed as a reference to the grant of the permission under the interim development order.

(3) Where permission for any development of land was granted as mentioned in sub-paragraph (1) of this paragraph, and permission for that development was also granted under the Restriction of Ribbon Development Act 1935 then, if the permission so granted under the said Act of 1935 was granted subject to conditions, those conditions shall be treated for the purposes of this paragraph as conditions imposed by the permission granted under the interim development order.

91.—(1) Where any works for the erection or alteration of a building had been begun but not completed before the appointed day, then if—

> (*a*) immediately before that day those works could have been completed in conformity with the provisions of a planning scheme or of permission granted thereunder, or in accordance with permission granted by or under an interim development order ; and
>
> (*b*) where any permission was required under the Restriction of Ribbon Development Act 1935 for the carrying out of those works, that permission was granted,

planning permission shall be deemed to have been granted in respect of the completion of those works.

(2) The planning permission deemed to have been granted by virtue of this paragraph shall be deemed to have been so granted subject to any conditions applicable thereto under the scheme or the permission granted by or under the interim development order, as the case may be, and to any conditions imposed by the permission (if any) granted under the Restriction of Ribbon Development Act 1935 and shall include permission to use the building, when erected or altered—

> (*a*) where the purpose for which it could be so used was prescribed by or under the planning scheme, or by the permission granted by or under the interim development order, as the case may be, for that purpose ;
>
> (*b*) in any other case, for the purpose for which the building, or the building as altered, was designed.

(3) In relation to any such works as are mentioned in sub-paragraph (1) of this paragraph, being works in respect of which permission was granted after 21st July 1943, on an application in that behalf made under an interim development order, the provisions of this paragraph shall have effect in substitution for the provisions of paragraph 90 of this Schedule.

92.—(1) Any reference in Part VII of this Act, or in Schedule 15 thereto, to a planning decision shall, where the context so admits, include a reference to any decision deemed to have been made by virtue of the provisions of paragraph 90 or paragraph 91 of this Schedule.

(2) Sub-paragraph (1) of this paragraph shall have effect without prejudice to the provisions of Part I of this Schedule.

Appeals to the Crown Court

93. As respects any time before the coming into force of section 3 of the Courts Act 1971, sections 106, 114(7) and 117(6) of this Act shall have effect as if for references to the Crown Court there were substituted references to a court of quarter sessions.

Supplementary

94.—(1) Where in this Act (including this Schedule except Part I thereof) express provision is made in respect of any matter, the provisions of Part I of this Schedule, in so far as they are applicable to that matter, shall have effect subject to that express provision.

(2) Except as provided by sub-paragraph (1) of this paragraph, the mention in any provisions of this Act (including this Schedule except Part I thereof) of any matter to which Part I of this Schedule is applicable shall not be construed as affecting the generality of the provisions of Part I of this Schedule.

Section 292.

SCHEDULE 25

Repeals

Chapter	Short Title	Extent of repeal
5 & 6 Eliz. 2. c. 20.	The House of Commons Disqualification Act 1957.	In Schedule 1, in Part II, the words " A Planning Inquiry Commission constituted under Part VI of the Town and Country Planning Act 1968. "
10 & 11 Eliz. 2. c. 38.	The Town and Country Planning Act 1962.	The whole Act except sections 222, 224 and 226 and Schedule 12.
1963 c. 17.	The Town and Country Planning Act 1963.	Section 1. Section 3. Section 4(1) to (3). The Schedule.
1963 c. 29.	The Local Authorities (Land) Act 1963.	Section 12(2).
1963 c. 33.	The London Government Act 1963.	Sections 24 to 29.
1963 c. 38.	The Water Resources Act 1963.	In section 71(5) the words " and in the Town and Country Planning Act 1962 ".

Chapter	Short Title	Extent of repeal
1964 c. 51.	The Universities and College Estates Act 1964.	In Schedule 3, in Part II, the entry relating to the Town and Country Planning Act 1962.
1965 c. 33.	The Control of Office and Industrial Development Act 1965.	Sections 1 to 16. Sections 18 to 20. Section 22(1). Sections 23 and 24. Section 25(1) to (4). In section 26(2), the words from the beginning to " 1962 to 1965; and ". Schedules 1 to 3.
1965 c. 56.	The Compulsory Purchase Act 1965.	In Schedule 6, the entry relating to the Town and Country Planning Act 1962. In Schedule 7, the entry relating to the Town and Country Planning Act 1962.
1966 c. 4.	The Mines (Working Facilities and Support) Act 1966.	In Schedule 2, paragraph 3.
1966 c. 34.	The Industrial Development Act 1966.	Part III. In section 31(3) the words from " together with the Town and Country Planning Acts 1962 to 1965 " to " 1962 to 1966 and ". In Schedule 3, in Part III, the entry relating to the Town and Country Planning Act 1962.
1966 c. 42.	The Local Government Act 1966.	Section 7.
1967 c. 69.	The Civic Amenities Act 1967.	Section 1. Section 3. Section 6. Section 8. Section 11. Part II except section 15(2). In section 28(1), paragraph (*a*) and, in paragraph (*c*), the words " section 6, section 14 ". In section 30(1) the definition of " the Planning Act of 1968 ".
1968 c. 13.	The National Loans Act 1968.	Section 11.
1968 c. 23.	The Rent Act 1968.	In Schedule 15, the entry relating to the Town and Country Planning Act 1962.
1968 c. 41.	The Countryside Act 1968.	Sections 25 and 26.

Chapter	Short Title	Extent of Repeal
1968 c. 72.	The Town and Country Planning Act 1968.	Sections 1 to 26. Section 27 except paragraph (*b*). Sections 28 and 29. Sections 32 to 38. Sections 40 to 57. Sections 60 to 87. Sections 90 to 98. Sections 100 to 102. Section 103(*a*). In section 104(1), the definition of "the Greater London development plan", and subsections (2) and (4). Section 108. Section 109(2). Schedules 1 and 2. Schedules 4 to 8. Schedule 9 except paragraphs 9, 10, 68 and 75. Schedule 10 except paragraphs 13 and 14. Schedule 11.
1969 c. 33.	The Housing Act 1969.	Section 34.
1969 c. 48.	The Post Office Act 1969.	In Schedule 4, paragraphs 71 and 89(3).
1970 c. 43.	The Trees Act 1970.	Section 1.
1970 c. 57.	The Town and Country Planning Regulations (London) (Indemnity) Act 1970.	Section 2.
1971 c. 18.	The Land Commission (Dissolution) Act 1971.	In Schedule 2, paragraph 1.
1971 c. 23.	The Courts Act 1971.	In Schedule 9, the entries relating to the Town and Country Planning Act 1962 and the Town and Country Planning Act 1968.
1971 c. 41.	The Highways Act 1971.	Section 50. Section 77. Section 78(2). Schedule 7.
1971 c. 62.	The Tribunals and Inquiries Act 1971.	In Schedule 3, the entries relating to the Town and Country Planning Act 1962 and the Town and Country Planning Act 1968.
1971 c. 75.	The Civil Aviation Act 1971.	In Schedule 5, paragraph 8(3).

PRODUCED IN ENGLAND BY PRODUCT SUPPORT (GRAPHICS) LTD., DERBY
FOR BERNARD M THIMONT
Controller of Her Majesty's Stationery Office and Queen's Printer of Acts of Parliament
Dd 0627262   K8   3/80   83174/3921